P.O. Box 57757
Oklahoma City, OK
73157-7757

www.blessedhopepublishing.com

Blessed Hope Publishing, Inc.
P.O. Box 57757
Oklahoma City, OK 73157-7757
© Gary Stearman

ISBN: 9780983621638
A CIP catalog record of this book is available from the Library of Congress.
Cover illustration and design by Danel M. Wright - www.createdwright.com

All Scripture references are taked from the Authorized King James Version.

(NOTE: This work was originally published as a Defender Book in 2011)

Dedication

This book is dedicated to Doris, my wife of forty years. She is the perfect biblical "helpmeet," or as we say in modern English, "helpmate." Brilliant in math and computer science, she has helped raise our two sons, and is the loving Grammy to our nine grandchildren. She has filled the gaps in my life as the perfect stabilizer and loving provider of intelligent companionship (and on occasion, debate). Her judgment rises when mine falls. Her editorial help on this manuscript has been invaluable.

I've often mentioned that she is perfectly described in Proverbs 31:

Who can find a virtuous woman? for her price is far above rubies.
The heart of her husband doth safely trust in her, so that he
    shall have no need of spoil.
She will do him good and not evil all the days of her life.
She seeketh wool, and flax, and worketh willingly with her hands.
She is like the merchants' ships; she bringeth her food from afar.
She riseth also while it is yet night, and giveth meat to her
    household, and a portion to her maidens.
She considereth a field, and buyeth it: with the fruit of her
    hands she planteth a vineyard.
She girdeth her loins with strength, and strengtheneth her arms.
She perceiveth that her merchandise is good: her candle goeth
    not out by night.
She layeth her hands to the spindle, and her hands hold the distaff.
She stretcheth out her hand to the poor; yea, she reacheth forth
    her hands to the needy.
She is not afraid of the snow for her household: for all her
    household are clothed with scarlet.
She maketh herself coverings of tapestry; her clothing is silk and
    purple.

Her husband is known in the gates, when he sitteth among the
elders of the land.

She maketh fine linen, and selleth it; and delivereth girdles unto
the merchant.

Strength and honour are her clothing; and she shall rejoice in
time to come.

She openeth her mouth with wisdom; and in her tongue is the
law of kindness.

She looketh well to the ways of her household, and eateth not
the bread of idleness.

Her children arise up, and call her blessed; her husband also,
and he praiseth her.

Many daughters have done virtuously, but thou excellest them all.

Favour is deceitful, and beauty is vain: but a woman that feareth
the LORD, she shall be praised.

Give her of the fruit of her hands; and let her own works praise
her in the gates.

PROVERBS 31:10–31

CONTENTS

Acknowledgments

My sincere thanks go to the late J. R. Church, with whom I worked for twenty-four years. His knowledge of Scripture and desire to expound biblical prophecy gave me both the opportunity and platform from which the truth of the Bible could be directed toward an audience in search of solid, rational, understandable … and groundbreaking … explication.

I've also worked closely with Bob Ulrich for the last twenty-one years. During that time, he has earned my deepest respect and appreciation. Especially in the last few years, we've become close friends who constantly and consistently rely upon each other.

Bob's attention to relationships in the world of books and other media resulted in our connection with Tom Horn and Defender Publishing. Ultimately, that's how this book was brought to print, along with the expert editorial skills of Angie Peters and the imaginative cover design by Daniel M. Wright.

Finally, I must express my highest esteem for Tom Horn, a man who came alongside in a time of need and proved himself to be a valued and helpful friend of unquestionable integrity. Thank you so much.

Gary Stearman

FOREWORD

Though for nearly twenty years I had read, quoted, and steadily grown in my appreciation of the consistently thorough research and proper application of theology by biblical scholar Gary Stearman, it was not until 2007, following an invitation to be on the syndicated television show *Prophecy in the News*, that I met him face to face. Since then, our friendship has grown and I have come to believe Stearman is one of, if not the, timeliest, most important writers in Christianity today.

This is not a bold statement, as you will learn in *Time Travelers of the Bible: How the Ancient Prophets Shattered the Time Barrier*. This work is simply unparalleled in modern times—a revolutionary and instant classic providing clear answers to age-old conundrums presented throughout history by prophets and sages, philosophers and physicists regarding "time" (the fourth dimension after length, width, and height) and "reality" *as we perceive it.*

At first, you may ask yourself what this subject and specifically "time travel" has to do with understanding theology or prophecy. Besides perhaps offering a framework for discussing certain theological issues like predestination or God's foreknowledge, what practical application would such edgy inquiries serve anyway? Traveling backward or forward in time is simply mental gymnastics for physicists, philosophers, and novelists, right? The stuff of science fiction better left to H. G. Wells' *The Time Machine* or modern films such as *Back to the Future*.

Truth is, by the time you reach the end of this book, you will wonder whether you ever thoroughly understood any of the most pertinent aspects of the Lord's gospel, or the timeline of biblical history, including our prophetic future, without exposés in the following pages.

Yet while the theological, philosophical, interdisciplinary, and cross-disciplinary investigation in *Time Travelers* is astonishing in scope, it is Stearman's ability to parse these complex issues regarding spatio-temporal existence (that which subsists in both space and time) down into common language that the average person will find easy to understand and seamless in narrative. Equal or perhaps superior in value, once the multifaceted implications in this book are grasped, a series of "wow" moments lead the reader through the labyrinths of life's most challenging questions to meaningfully significant answers. In fact, I venture to say that, after reading this book, you will never think of the death, burial, and resurrection of Jesus Christ quite the same way again. If you are a Christian, your faith and confidence in the Creator and His plan for your life will skyrocket to new heights. If you are a non-believer, you may find yourself wanting to become one.

Interestingly, the world's most respected professors in physics and mathematics are fascinated today as much or more than theologians with finding the very answers Stearman provides: What is the substance of reality? Do we live in a multidimensional universe? Is there a unified theory of everything? Is time travel possible? Stearman's extraordinarily lucid exploration of these and numerous other daring questions provides spiritual-empirical evidence, concluding in the fact that numerous dimensions exist wherein dynamic and invisible agencies operate. This is something Rod Serling may have cleverly imagined in the 1960s, when he so famously said in the introduction to the American television series *The Twilight Zone:* "There is a fifth dimension beyond that which is known to man. It is a dimension as vast as space and as timeless as infinity. It is the middle ground between light and shadow, between science and superstition, and it lies between the pit of man's fears and the summit of his knowledge. This is the dimension we call 'The Twilight Zone.'"

As you journey with Stearman through a cosmological window past general relativity and quantum mechanics to a world of membranes in subatomic space, eleven-dimensional superstrings, parallel universes, mathematical super-symmetry, and finally, time travel, you will learn that a place "as timeless as infinity between light and shadow" really does exist, and that certain travelers actually ventured into this great beyond only to return to offer glimpses of what they discovered about the past, present, and future, as well as relativity of these dimensions to what the Bible calls "hades," "heaven," and "eternity." These voyagers were willed to this other-dimensional plane by the Master of Time Himself, the God of biblical prophecy, for very important reasons germane to *your* existence. For within these hyper-realities there rages a millennia-old battle boiling toward a finish line. Time as we know it spans the ages of this spiritual war, which itself is counting down toward an epic end. At a near future date, the hands on this cosmic clock will simply stop ticking and our familiar time-space universe will come to a conclusion. Central to this relative moment, Stearman vividly evokes important aspects of not only this limited continuum perceived as "time" and its relationship to our three dimensions, but that of "angels and demons" and their connection with "time" as well as ultimately the Creator Himself, as God's association with so-called natural and supernatural laws unfold. With that, what we discover in this spectacular and groundbreaking new book is not just *a* key, but *the* key to understanding the elusive scientific and supernatural wisdom surrounding a Grand Universal Theory of Everything that just happens to be located at a pivotal "center of the symmetry of time" at the crucifixion of Jesus Christ. You will be astonished at what an understatement I just made.

Man's relationship to time has, since the introduction of Einstein's famous theory of relativity $(E = mc^2)$, often been compared to a leaf floating at a leisurely pace down a river from a beginning point to a final destination. It now seems clear to me that, included in the stream God devised for Gary Stearman's journey through time—from his family's famous connection to aircraft (the Stearman Aircraft Corp., now known as Boeing) and his formal education in classical literature to his media experience and decades of responsibility for communicating complex theological concerns in everyday language for *Prophecy in the News Magazine*—was the practical training this fabulous thinker would finally need to become so eminently qualified as the writer of this most ingenious, judicious, and important work. All I can say is: Hold on to your hats, folks. You are in for one amazing journey through *time*.

Thomas Horn

INTRODUCTION

We now begin an exploration of the common fascination with the properties of time.

The writers of books and screenplays have long been obsessed with the subject of time. Its inscrutable qualities are fraught with the sort of tantalizing incongruities that are most likely to fire the imagination. Unfulfilled dreams and trips into the world of the fantastic are the stock in trade of modern fiction. Imagination is based upon, "Long, long ago, in a land far into the future, there lived a Man who changed the past and present in ways yet unimagined."

Time travel opens the possibility of repairing the gaffes of the past, righting horrible wrongs, finding lost love, or investing in something you know will grow in value. In a world where you lost your only chance, it offers another. Where there is no hope, the time machine offers a way to regain it. Tales of time travel spin around themes of love, money, and justice…of changing a world that we instinctively regard as unalterable.

How often do we shake our heads in sadness as we realize that this world isn't really fair. Some are born rich and healthy, others poor and sickly; some into affection and devotion, some into rejection and despair.

Both philosophers and housewives grope for some sense of order… some indication that there is a Someone who has mastered time. This deep longing is universal. It may take different forms, but it is always there, a nagging unease.

By nature, we are meant to live in the eternal state, and will never be fully satisfied while trapped in time.

In a sea of books, only the Bible speaks authoritatively on the subject of time travel. Furthermore, its pages are not theory, but fact, based in history. Only the Bible sees the future and the past as one, thereby giving sense to the present.

———

Length, width, and height give form to our world. Time gives conscious reality. Most people wear or carry a timepiece of some sort—perhaps a watch or a phone. Everybody knows what time is, unless asked to explain it. Time gives sense to our world.

But through human eyes, time is an illusion and a paradox. It exists, yet it doesn't exist. Philosophers of ages past observed that the future has not yet come into being, and the past is gone forever. The fleeting present, in constant motion, cannot be captured or examined. Yet everyone knows by experience that our entire creation exists as a function of time.

A long-forgotten jester once observed, "Time is God's way of keeping everything from happening at once." This wisecrack tells a cogent truth.

Only the present exists as a series of tiny, indivisible moments that give the illusion of flowing events, much as a series of movie frames yields a picture. Yet, to look at an unwinding strip of film is to realize that the pictures there are dead, even if some of the people in the photos are still alive. That's not to say that their lives are not captured somewhere. Those lives—our lives—are real, and will be reviewed one day, if Scripture is to be believed. What we do here is real…has been real…always will be real.

Though time has the qualities of an illusion, we will forever be held responsible for the reality of it. Judgment is coming, based upon elapsed time and its encapsulated events. Time is real in the mind. Yet we must ask: *What* is the mind? Perhaps not that so much, but: *Where* is the mind? Consciousness is the storage bin of time—but not so much the consciousness of man as the consciousness of God.

In spite of its illusory nature, time is real. It has a living reality, beginning with the eternal God of time and space. "In the beginning, God created the heavens and the earth." And, "In the beginning was the Word." Only a timeline has a beginning. The Bible assigns the qualities of mind and matter—both literal and metaphysical—to those things yet to come and those that are long past.

As Christians, we believe that God created what we glibly refer to as "reality." The universe had a beginning, as testified in the first few words of the Bible. The earth and its living creatures also had a beginning. They will have an end, too. Some will come to ignominy; some to glory. God took upon Himself the flesh, blood, and bone of fallen man, and it became immortal once again. The temporal body of Jesus became eternal, yet somehow able to remain in our time-space reality. The flesh-and-bone body of the little Child who grew up to be a Man in Nazareth still exists today in glorified form. He lives in eternity, but is still able to experience time.

Only within the purview of God do we find answers to time's paradoxes. He is the Creator of a reality that is simply an extension of the Lord Himself.

God and Prophecy

Scripture is a hundred percent prophecy! For example, the words written by Moses are timeless. He is called Israel's greatest prophet. And we know with certainty that he wrote them. "And Moses wrote this law, and delivered it unto the priests the sons of Levi, which bare the ark of the covenant of the LORD, and unto all the elders of Israel" (Deuteronomy 31:9).

In the New Testament, Jesus acknowledged the same thing: "For had ye believed Moses, ye would have believed me: for he wrote of me" (John 5:46). Jesus is an eternal being. The words of Moses and the other contributors to Scripture are also eternal. We think of them as existing in our world of time. But their actual existence is in eternity, which is captured in the closing words of the Bible:

> For I testify unto every man that heareth the words of the
> prophecy of this book, If any man shall add unto these things,
> God shall add unto him the plagues that are written in this book:
> And if any man shall take away from the words of the book
> of this prophecy, God shall take away his part out of the book
> of life, and out of the holy city, and from the things which are
> written in this book. (Revelation 22:18, 19)

Thus, while time is consciously sensed, it is also inscribed in a Book, so that it can be referenced in the context of God's eternal world. This is what is meant by the word "prophecy." In a very real way, the Bible is a complete prophetic structure that cannot be broken into small, unrelated parts. It is an unbroken whole, a fundamental truth that unspiritual minds cannot comprehend. In their eyes, the Bible is a disjointed collection of folk narratives, fireside tales, and imaginative meanderings.

Scriptural reality lies in the fact that it must be spiritually discerned along a timeline of divine appointment. In the world, time may be an illusion. But in the mind of God, it is very, very real. Nothing illustrates this better than God's own words:

> Remember the former things of old: for I am God, and there is
> none else; I am God, and there is none like me,
> Declaring the end from the beginning, and from ancient
> times the things that are not yet done, saying, My counsel shall
> stand, and I will do all my pleasure. (Isaiah 46:9, 10)

Here the Lord God declares that there is both an "end" and a "beginning"—a linear layout we don't fully understand. He even declares the end before the beginning! Nevertheless, there is a flow of time. Our world lies within this channel; God's world is outside it.

Solomon Views Time

David's son, Solomon, prayed for wisdom and received it. Though his personal life ended in shambles, he was, nevertheless, a consummate observer of the natural world and the lives of those who dwelt in it. In his closing statement to the world, he made an observation about time. Its poetry is among the most powerful statements in history. At solemn gatherings, it has been voiced aloud many times.

To put the pain of grieving survivors in perspective, it has been incorporated into countless funeral services. It suspends the elements of life upon a scaffolding of time, illustrating that time is, at the very least, a framework.

But in the end, Solomon shows that time and the world are one, both separated from the true work of God, who can do something that we can't…view time objectively:

> To every thing there is a season, and a time to every purpose under the heaven:
> A time to be born, and a time to die; a time to plant, and a time to pluck up that which is planted;
> A time to kill, and a time to heal; a time to break down, and a time to build up;
> A time to weep, and a time to laugh; a time to mourn, and a time to dance;
> A time to cast away stones, and a time to gather stones together; a time to embrace, and a time to refrain from embracing;
> A time to get, and a time to lose; a time to keep, and a time to cast away;
> A time to rend, and a time to sew; a time to keep silence, and a time to speak;
> A time to love, and a time to hate; a time of war, and a time of peace.
> What profit hath he that worketh in that wherein he laboureth?
> I have seen the travail, which God hath given to the sons of men to be exercised in it.

He hath made every thing beautiful in his time: also he
hath set the world in their heart, so that no man can find out
the work that God maketh from the beginning to the end.
(Ecclesiastes 3:1–11)

Humans can sense the passage of time, but since we are embedded in
it, we cannot "see" time as God can. His spaceless and timeless perspective allows Him to observe everything—at once. To Him, the beginning
and the end are one. To us, they are two different things.

In his wisdom, Solomon concludes with the thought that God works
from a beginning to an end. He acknowledges that God is doing something in *time,* that only He can fully understand.

To Eastern mystics, Buddhists and Hindus, and secular scientists,
time is an illusion to be transcended. This thought goes back to the
Greek philosophers. To faithful Jews and Christians, time is a goal-
oriented creation that will result in a positive end.

THE CROSS AT THE CENTER OF TIME

More than anything, time has a purpose. The biblical timeline is not arbitrary. It speaks of an ancient past, a great fall, and the redemptive bloodline
of Christ. His First Coming and promise to come again are precisely ordered
to arrive in conjunction with the great change points of earth's history.

On a timeline that commences with the creation of the universe and
ends with the New Heavens and New Earth, the Bible tells us that its
midpoint would fall at the most significant event in all history. That, of
course, would be the moment when Christ paid for the sin of man with
the shedding of His own blood on the Cross:

And he is before all things, and by him all things consist.

And he is the head of the body, the church: who is the
beginning, the firstborn from the dead; that in all things he
might have the preeminence.

For it pleased the Father that in him should all fulness dwell;
And, having made peace through the blood of his cross, by
him to reconcile all things unto himself; by him, I say, whether
they be things in earth, or things in heaven. (Colossians 1:17–20)

Here, we find the ultimate paradox. Christ "is" before all things. He is outside our world. He is free from the strictures of our time and space. But He is also firmly planted in the center of our temporal universe.

His Cross *reconciled* all things, whether in heaven or on earth. Another way to say this is that His Crucifixion is the *crux* of all time-space. His sacrifice had the effect—only dimly understood by humankind—of reconciling every aspect of the distressed universe.

It is interesting that the word "reconcile" is a translation of the Greek *apokatalasso,* a term meaning "to change one thing into another." A creation split down the middle by sin and iniquity was healed in an instant.

But a question looms. It has been about two thousand years since His work was completed. Why, then, do we still see the evil fruit of sin? Perhaps the best answer is that time, from the divine point of view, is to be taken as a whole. We see a moving river of time; God sees the geography that directs the river's flow. From His perspective, the problems of rebellion and sin have already been fully resolved. From ours, resolution is yet to be realized. But by faith, we know that it is as good as completed. We must always remember that our view is limited by the fact that we are part of the ongoing timeline.

This explains why, when Moses asked God what name he should use to identify Him before Pharaoh, he received an unexpected answer:

And Moses said unto God, Behold, when I come unto the
children of Israel, and shall say unto them, The God of your
fathers hath sent me unto you; and they shall say to me, What
is his name? what shall I say unto them?
And God said unto Moses, I AM THAT I AM: and he said,
Thus shalt thou say unto the children of Israel, I AM hath sent
me unto you. (Exodus 3:13, 14)

Most probably, Moses expected some proper name, similar to those attached to other gods of Egypt, Canaan, or Babylon. Instead, he received a simple statement of eternal being: "I Am." In Hebrew, there is no literal verb form for "to be." Therefore, when God states His name to Moses, it is more than a mere statement of being; it is a proper noun. Not only that, it indicates God's transcendence over time and space. "I Am" is past, present, and future, an affirmation that God exists outside the timeline.

Similarly, in the New Testament, Jesus expressed His eternal nature in an answer to the Pharisees. When pressed about His true nature, He said:

> Your father Abraham rejoiced to see my day: and he saw it, and was glad.
>
> Then said the Jews unto him, Thou art not yet fifty years old, and hast thou seen Abraham?
>
> Jesus said unto them, Verily, verily, I say unto you, Before Abraham was, I am. (John 8:56–58)

Using the same words that His Father had used to inform Moses, Jesus declared to the leadership of Israel that He transcended time. He possessed something that no other human being had ever been able to claim: objectivity.

That is, He could relate to our world, not as someone *inside* time-space, but *outside* it. In this way, He could make statements about reality that others were simply incapable of making.

From that day to this, mankind has been seeking ways to understand reality. Where philosophy failed and mathematics fell short, the technology of the twentieth century gave new life to theory. Atomic physics sprang to life, stimulated by a global war that gave birth to nuclear weapons. The ideas of physicists and mathematicians suddenly took flight in machines and energy streams that beamed back their findings in ways hitherto undreamed of. Man began to see that time-space, matter, energy, and motion were all facets of the same thing. They began to fantasize about finding God in physics.

GOD POWER

In fact, this discussion would be incomplete without a look at the workings of modern physics and the advanced concepts of physicists. Daily, they are challenging our view of reality. Their mathematical theories are backed by research in laboratories all over the world. They now dream of time travel and interdimensional excursions.

They are able to smash atoms at increasing levels of energy. Doing this, they are able to see tiny particles spinning away from atomic collisions. Their patterns are clues to the building blocks and "mortar" that give matter its characteristic solidity. The deeper they look, the more they see that matter is really an arrangement of energy at different levels. It has long been known that in even the most dense of materials (lead or uranium, for example), there is more open space than solid matter. Energy is the central organizing factor of our universe. But time allows energy to be solidified and divided into succeeding numerical units that make it discernable in our physical world. (One second…two seconds… three seconds, and so on.)

Time, said Einstein, is variable, and changes with speed, particularly as one nears the speed of light. His famous "twin paradox" states that if one of a pair of twins boarded a spaceship and flew to a nearby star, then returned, he would be younger than his brother. This so-called "time dilation," he said, was a natural phenomenon within his theory of special relativity. Much of his thinking is now being tested in monstrous and complex research facilities designed to accelerate matter to near light speed.

The world's largest atom smasher is located near Geneva, on the Swiss-French border. It is the European Organization for Nuclear Research (CERN), a huge underground circular tunnel seventeen miles in circumference and three hundred feet below ground level. CERN consumes prodigious amounts of electrical power to produce collisions that range as high as 14 trillion electron volts.

Its building and maintenance has come at a cost of billions of dollars. Filled with an amazing array of complex generators, magnets, and super-refrigerated tubes, its latest design has a stated purpose: to find the "God Particle," referred to in scientific jargon as the *Higgs boson.*

This particle is believed by physicists to give mass to all other atomic particles. It is said to be the key to understanding the force that holds everything together. Theoreticians look to its discovery as the center of all contemporary research physics.

Atoms accelerated in CERN's giant circular tube almost reach the speed of light, orbiting until they are directed to collide with each other. Thus, time and matter are being manipulated, using the maximum focus of energy that man can produce.

The student of the Bible will quickly realize that this scientific quest is remarkably foreseen in the descriptions of events and material states that one finds in Scripture. For example, science teaches that the universe had a beginning. With their "big bang" theory, secular physicists agree with the Bible, which also speaks of an origination point: "In the beginning God created the heaven and the earth" (Genesis 1:1).

A theoretical explosion is the "scientific" explanation for God. Particle physics promises secular man a way to reach out and touch Him.

A beginning suggests a timeline, projected forward into the present, and onward into the future. Certainly, one can imagine a timeline, projected infinitely toward both past and future. But that is not what the Bible says. It depicts a definite starting point. In the New Testament, the idea is restated and embellished upon: "In the beginning was the Word, and the Word was with God, and the Word was God. The same was in the beginning with God. All things were made by him; and without him was not any thing made that was made" (John 1:1–3).

The mystical musings of ancient sages, philosophers, and mathematicians shape the perception of what we commonly call "reality." As though time were the enemy, they dream of some "nirvana" where they can blissfully merge with timelessness.

But the Bible, in its take-it-or-leave-it manner, simply defines the truth. God, who spoke all things into existence, also spoke time into existence. From His omniscient perspective, He introduces objective reason. He is the great "I Am"—that is, the One who *always is.*

Yet, at a certain point, He created time and a prophetic progression that moves toward a totally renewed creation. It seems that the current timeline will come to an appropriate close. Something new comes after that: "For, behold, I create new heavens and a new earth: and the former shall not be remembered, nor come into mind" (Isaiah 65:17).

Only the faithful truly understand that the nature of time-space is bound into the Person of the Lord, who is the God of prophecy: "And if any man shall take away from the words of the book of this prophecy, God shall take away his part out of the book of life, and out of the holy city, and from the things which are written in this book" (Revelation 22:19).

For the faithful, "this book" is eternal. It is the Bible, the only book ever created around a structure of prophecy. Certainly, Scripture is the exposition of God's plan of salvation. Virtually every syllable written within its pages adds to our understanding of His program, both collectively and individually. That is prophecy, the telling-forth of the truth.

But prophecy is also linked to the divine timeline. He created it for specific reasons, which, as we have seen, are linked to the center of that timeline: the Cross.

TIMES AND SEASONS

The Bible speaks of time in two different ways, using specific terms. They are "times and seasons," meant to express the action of God's will as it is impressed upon the world of man. The definitive use of these terms is found in the opening of Daniel's prophecy: "And he changeth the **times** and the **seasons**: he removeth kings, and setteth up kings: he giveth wisdom unto the wise, and knowledge to them that know understanding" (Daniel 2:21, emphasis added).

Here, "times" is translated from the Hebrew *iddan,* meaning "time, as duration." It indicates the flow of time as perennially observed by human beings. It speaks of what we all know by experience. Our lives are built around the numerical points along a perceived line of time.

On the other hand, "seasons" is a translation of the Hebrew *z'man,* which usually indicates a festival, season, or specified time. The first of these two terms speaks of generic time as a *quantity;* the second, a specified moment, as a *quality.*

Another Hebrew term for "seasons" is *mo'ed,* indicating an appointed location along a timeline. In the Hebrew calendar, the dates of certain festivals can shift from year to year, but even though the time may shift, the appointment is kept.

When we think about it, time in the natural world exhibits both quantity and quality. Quantity—the clicking of the second hand—is affirmation of what we all feel…the passing of time from one moment to the next.

Quality, on the other hand, depends upon a number of independent events all coming together, meeting with perfect synchronicity. In this way, a planned moment can be realized. Something anticipated—even greatly anticipated—will come. But its precise character and nature cannot be predicted in advance. Such a thing can only be hoped for. Seasons, then, occupy the medium of hope. In the days of the Old Testament prophets, the coming of Messiah to establish His Kingdom was the ultimate consummation of such a season.

In New Testament Greek, Paul makes a statement that also uses both of these terms: "But of the times and the seasons, brethren, ye have no need that I write unto you" (I Thessalonians 5:1).

Here, "times" is from the Greek *chronos.* Even those unfamiliar with biblical Greek will quickly make the connection to our modern English word "chronology." In modern terms, this word refers to the arrangement of events or dates along a line of time. It is quantitative, specifically measuring the progress of seconds, minutes, hours, and days.

Paul also refers to "seasons." It is taken from the Greek *kairos,* which refers to a period possessing definite characteristics, such as harvest or rain. But it also refers to proportion, when an object or environment under examination begins to exhibit certain necessary qualities at a certain moment, making its fulfillment imminent. It is therefore, qualitative in nature.

The Jewish festival calendar also models both forms of time: "These are the feasts of the LORD, even holy convocations, which ye shall proclaim in their seasons" (Leviticus 23:4).

These festivals are set at definite points in time, the first being Passover on the "fourteenth day of the first month" and Rosh HaShanah, "In the seventh month, in the first day of the month."

But they also place Israel's activities on a year-long timeline of seasons. These "seasons" may also shift from year to year, depending upon the relationship between the sun, moon, and maturation of crops. Two good examples of this kind of reckoning are seen in the Jewish feasts of Firstfruits and Pentecost.

At Firstfruits, the High Priest is instructed to wave the firstfruits of the harvest. This, of course, is ultimately based upon the availability of grain from the harvest. The sheaf, or *omer*, begins a fifty-day count toward Pentecost.

The Feast of Pentecost, called "the festival without a date," marks the end of the harvest. At that time, the high priest is required to hold aloft and wave two leavened loaves of bread, which symbolize the culmination of the harvest.

One of the best examples of this kind of reckoning is seen in Matthew's Gospel, where Jesus is seen explaining the parable of the harvest:

> Then Jesus sent the multitude away, and went into the house: and his disciples came unto him, saying, Declare unto us the parable of the tares of the field.
>
> He answered and said unto them, He that soweth the good seed is the Son of man;
>
> The field is the world; the good seed are the children of the kingdom; but the tares are the children of the wicked one;
>
> The enemy that sowed them is the devil; the harvest is the end of the world; and the reapers are the angels.
> (Matthew 13:36–39)

By experience, we all understand that the harvest season is set off by the maturity of the grain, which in turn depends upon the early and latter rains, as well as the changing weather patterns that produce the environmental requirements. Ironically, while the timeline is uniformly consistent, its seasons are variable.

THE PROBLEM WITH PROPHECY

Within the biblical matrix of times and seasons, major events have come and gone. The most important, Christ's virgin birth, death, and resurrection have already marked the high point of the timeline. He announced that He would come, depart, and return. Both the Old and New Testaments speak of the major, epoch-making events that would surround His first and second arrivals.

One of the major problems for those who take biblical prophecy seriously is that attempts to reconcile "times" and "seasons" can often lead to false conclusions. Still the "blessed hope" of the Rapture is so attractive to Christians that they are constantly motivated to search for ways to capture key points along the timeline. And who can be blamed for seeking that which the Lord encouraged us to observe? Did He not say, "Watch ye therefore, and pray always, that ye may be accounted worthy to escape all these things that shall come to pass, and to stand before the Son of man" (Luke 21:36)?

Who has not been drawn toward the beautiful words of Jesus in Matthew's Gospel, as he describes a phenomenon of the last days?

> Now learn a parable of the fig tree; When his branch is yet tender, and putteth forth leaves, ye know that summer is nigh:
>
> So likewise ye, when ye shall see all these things, know that it is near, even at the doors.
>
> Verily I say unto you, This generation shall not pass, till all these things be fulfilled.
>
> Heaven and earth shall pass away, but my words shall not pass away.
>
> But of that day and hour knoweth no man, no, not the

angels of heaven, but my Father only. But as the days of Noe were, so shall also the coming of the Son of man be. (Matthew 24:32–37)

Here, we have the classic passage of Israel's end-time emergence, as symbolized by the fig tree leafing out as summer approaches. This, of course, is a "season." Harvest and summer, as we have already seen, present images associated with Christ's coming. Naturally, when we see this sort of clustering of symbols, our curiosity is aroused, and doubtless, purposely so. Believers are *supposed* to be stimulated to watch.

Therefore, we watch Israel, born as a nation on May 14, 1948. We begin to calculate the length of a generation…forty years…sixty years… seventy years? Clearly, we live in proximity to a series of latter-day phenomena. Many have mistakenly inserted their numerical conclusions into the season of the fig tree. They have wrongly interpreted the timeline. Are they to be blamed for that? Certainly not! No one can tell in advance when the figs will ripen. Jesus instructed us to observe the times. This would include the length of a generation, and for that matter, the length of a day.

As the Lord instructed Hosea:

For I will be unto Ephraim as a lion, and as a young lion to the house of Judah: I, even I, will tear and go away; I will take away, and none shall rescue him.

I will go and return to my place, till they acknowledge their offence, and seek my face: in their affliction they will seek me early.

Come, and let us return unto the LORD: for he hath torn, and he will heal us; he hath smitten, and he will bind us up.

After two days will he revive us: in the third day he will raise us up, and we shall live in his sight.

Then shall we know, if we follow on to know the LORD: his going forth is prepared as the morning; and he shall come unto us as the rain, as the latter and former rain unto the earth. (Hosea 5:14–6:3)

In this classic prophecy, Jesus comes to Israel, departs, then returns. We understand this picture all too well. Israel, whom He has "torn," is now back in the Holy Land, but they are still in a spiritually unregenerate state. They remember something that has been a watchword among them for centuries, "that one day is with the Lord as a thousand years" (2 Peter 3:8). As they cry out for His salvation, they instinctively know that He will return after two thousand years have passed. This prophecy assumes that they have deduced that Jesus was their real Messiah.

Furthermore, the Jews know that He will come in the season of rain, ripening the crops so that the feasts of Firstfruits and Pentecost may be observed. We are at once encouraged and puzzled about the timing of His arrival.

This is the problem with "timed" prophecy, and probably the basic reason why Jesus said, "But of that day and hour knoweth no man." No calculation on earth is capable of capturing all the elements that must be brought together to fulfill a given season.

In Due Time

At His Ascension, Jesus addressed the assembled group, encouraging them. Moments before His departure, He made a significant remark that has as much meaning for us as it did for that gathering of saints: "And he said unto them, It is not for you to know the times or the seasons, which the Father hath put in his own power" (Acts 1:7).

In quite specific terms, He was informing them that they could not know the *exact* time of the Lord's return. Certainly, they hoped that He would return in their lifetimes. In the epistles of Paul, the teaching of the imminent return of Christ is firmly implanted.

To the Thessalonians, Paul taught that Christ might return at any moment...that they would be "caught up" in an instant, "to meet the Lord in the air" (1 Thessalonians 4:17). Surely, their anticipation must have been at fever pitch. No doubt, they wanted Him to come back immediately.

But in the next breath, Paul tempered their expectations with a statement about time: "But of the times and the seasons, brethren, ye have no need that I write unto you. For yourselves know perfectly that the day of the Lord so cometh as a thief in the night" (1 Thessalonians 5:1, 2).

In essence, he was saying, "Don't concern yourselves excessively with date-setting. The Lord's timing is perfect. He has already worked out all the details. Nevertheless, I have given you enough information to be aware of the times."

In contrast, those who don't believe in the Lord will be surprised.

For when they shall say, Peace and safety; then sudden destruction cometh upon them, as travail upon a woman with child; and they shall not escape.

But ye, brethren, are not in darkness, that that day should overtake you as a thief.

Ye are all the children of light, and the children of the day: we are not of the night, nor of darkness.

Therefore let us not sleep, as do others; but let us watch and be sober. (1 Thessalonians 5:3–6)

Here, Paul is saying that we believers have been given the means and methods that will allow us to be aware of the seasons. Unbelievers, whom he refers to as "they," have no such awareness. They will be taken by surprise.

As we think about time, let us remember that there is a precise, preordained moment when the Lord will reveal Himself by calling Christians into the atmospheric heavens above. This "Rapture" will set in motion a cataclysmic series of judgments inscribed in Scripture under the heading "Day of the Lord," which we also call "the Tribulation."

At all times, we are to remember that the Lord's exact plan is engraved on a timeline known only to Him. The seasons, however, are not only visible, but emphatic in their message. He's coming soon! Keep looking up!

I

THE LURE OF TIME TRAVEL

In the 2002 book and motion picture called *Time Changer,* a nine-teenth-century Christian travels to his future and our present. He is shocked to discover an insolent and ill-mannered society that has fallen away from its spiritual beliefs.

His journey causes us to wonder.

Who hasn't dreamed of traveling through time, either forward to the future or backward to view the world's great historical moments? For the Christian, the great epochs of the Bible would be at the top of the list. Seeing Noah's Ark, Moses standing before Pharaoh, or Joseph confronting his brothers would no doubt provide amazing revelations.

Perhaps the wish list would be topped by the great miracles, such as Egypt's ten plagues and the parting of the Red Sea. In New Testament history, the miracles of Christ and the events of His Crucifixion would greatly deepen the understanding of those who have trusted in His Name.

The sights, sounds, and smells of secular history would be equally alluring, not to mention educational. What was the real relationship between Alexander the Great and his father Philip? What did Nebuchadnezzar, Xerxes, Nero, and Pontius Pilate look like? How was the Great Pyramid built? Greece and Rome, at their heights, would provide astounding insights to the student of history. Has their greatness passed away, never to be seen again?

The past is one thing, but what of the future? This generation has just come through fifty years of amazing technological breakthroughs. The twentieth century witnessed the transition from the horse to the interplanetary rocket...from the quill pen to the supercomputer.

Thinking about these things, one is seized at times with the desire to see what's next. A fuel-cell powered car with the ability to levitate would neither pollute nor require the old-fashioned paved highways. Roads would not have to stand up to the constant pounding of tires. There would be no tires...or wheels...or gears and engines that need oil! What would that do to the oil industry?

Cars with computer-controlled collision avoidance and auto-navigation would complement computerized homes and communications systems. Food might be synthesized. One might wear a personal anti-gravity system! Robots might take over our menial work. The imagination soars.

Then fear strikes: Will technology replace God in the mind of the next generation? Will genetic engineering corrupt men, turning them into thralls who work at the behest of a few overlords? Will universal surveillance and real-time intelligence analysis completely eliminate privacy, allowing despots to reign unfettered?

Might those computers and robots, created as our servants, end up as our masters? Those who study Bible prophecy know that Scripture hints darkly at just such a scenario. The image of the Beast and the mark associated with the Antichrist must involve some form of high-tech intelligence work. Having seen the history of mankind, we cannot escape the simple fact that technology has always been abused.

Such thoughts knot our stomachs with fear. But relief comes when we remember that time travel is impossible. And, thank heaven for that! Traveling in the past might alter the present...and the future. Just think: Some rogue might visit the past to change things for his advantage. If he committed such a "time crime," he might catastrophically alter the future. For time crime, you need time police. They would not only know what you have done; they would know what you are doing, and what you *will* do.

Given the world of fallible and sinful human beings, time travel presents a multitude of horrors. To go back would be to court disaster. Merely being there would alter history.

To go forward would likely be a leap into a world of technocratic despotism and fiendish super-weapons. Or so the science fiction writers would tell us. This is the secular view of the future. Not that they really believe time travel possible. But their speculations are endless.

The Secular View

H. G. Wells' *The Time Machine* is the all-time model for such conjecture. The hero of this novel traveled into the future, only to find that man had destroyed himself in a series of wars, and he finally reemerged in the bleak future of primitive tribalism and genetic degeneration.

Such pessimism became the hallmark of the twentieth-century science fiction that followed Wells' original work. Fictional forays into the future invariably depict social breakdown coupled with mad science. Self-destruction and natural disaster are the twin themes of the visionary authors who imagine various methods of time travel.

Story-bound characters who travel backward are preoccupied with either accidental or purposeful alterations of the timeline. Their journeys are fraught with disasters, dilemmas, and finally, annihilation.

To the secular mind, time travel is always fantasy, comedy, or nihilistic chaos. Perhaps the oddest—and funniest—time traveler ever dreamed up was the brainchild of Polish author Stanislaw Lem. In *The Star Diaries,* his hero, Ijon Tichy, finds at one point that the rudder on his time spaceship is broken. The malfunction causes a new "him" to be created on each day thereafter. Somehow, he must fix the rudder. Here is his account:

> I sat down in the armchair to collect my thoughts and take
> stock of the situation. I'd lived through it twice now, first as
> that sleeper, on Monday, and then as the one trying to wake

him, unsuccessfully, on Tuesday. The Monday me hadn't believed in the reality of the duplication, while the Tuesday me already knew it to be a fact. Here was a perfectly ordinary time loop. What then should be done in order to get the rudder fixed? Since the Monday me slept on—I remembered that on that night I had slept through to the morning undisturbed—I saw the futility of any further efforts to rouse him. The map indicated a number of other large gravitational vortices up ahead, therefore I could count on the duplication of the present within the next few days. I decided to write myself a letter and pin it to the pillow, enabling the Monday me, when he awoke, to see for himself that the dream had been no dream.[1]

Poor Ijon's dilemma brings to mind the numerous paradoxes that face the time traveler. In *A Brief History of Time*, mathematician Stephen Hawking writes:

A possible way to explain the absence of visitors from the future would be to say that the past is fixed because we have observed it and seen that it does not have the kind of warping needed to allow travel back from the future. On the other hand, the future is unknown and open, so it might well have the curvature required. This would mean that any time travel would be confined to the future. There would be no chance of Captain Kirk and the Starship *Enterprise* turning up at the present time.

This might explain why we have not yet been overrun by tourists from the future, but it would not avoid the problems that would arise if one were able to go back and change history. Suppose, for example, you went back and killed your great-great-grandfather while he was still a child. There are many versions of this paradox but they are essentially equivalent: one would get contradictions if one were free to change the past.[2]

Hawking goes on to say that one explanation for this paradox is physical consistency: Physics will not allow you to go back in time unless history shows that you had already arrived in the past.

Alternatively, he postulates that visitors to the past might enter:

> ...alternative histories which differ from recorded history. Thus they can act freely, without the constraint of consistency with their previous history. Steven Spielberg had fun with this notion in the *Back to the Future* films: Marty McFly was able to go back and change his parents' courtship to a more satisfactory history.[3]

Hawking and other physicists who follow in the footsteps of Albert Einstein postulate layers of dimensions, time bridges, wormholes, and almost unimaginable energy strings and energetic particles.

The brilliant physicist Michio Kaku allows his theoretical mind to roam beyond the limits of most, but reigns in his theories with pragmatism. He reasons that advanced civilizations may have mastered time travel, but that they must have access to massive amounts of energy to do it. By that, he means the power of an entire galaxy!

In *Hyperspace,* he writes:

> To be masters of the tenth dimension, either we encounter intelligent life within the galaxy that has already harnessed these astronomical energy levels, or we struggle for several thousand years before we attain this ability ourselves. For example, our current atom smashers or particle accelerators can boost the energy of a particle to over 1 trillion electron volts (the energy created if an electron were accelerated by 1 trillion volts). The largest accelerator is currently located in Geneva, Switzerland, and operated by a consortium of fourteen European nations. But this energy pales before the energy necessary to probe hyperspace: 10^{19} billion electron volts, or a quadrillion times larger than the energy that might have been produced at the SSC [superconducting super-collider].[4]

Thus, time travel is limited in two ways—mind-boggling paradoxes and the inability to find sufficient power. But that doesn't keep the curious mind from probing the dark unknown to find ways out of the box. At the major universities around the world, many physicists continue to labor at solutions to what Einstein called a "unified field theory"—a mathematical way of explaining the universe. To the uninitiated, their world of electrons, anti-electrons, positrons, quarks, rings, strings, vortices, and a myriad of other descriptive terms verges on the supernatural.

THE BIBLICAL VIEW

In fact, that's the true nature of the work of these physicists; they want to touch the face of God. This brings us back to a very basic question: What is time travel?

As we have seen, the secular approach involves penetrating the wall between our dimension and other dimensions. Physicists see as many as ten of them...or perhaps even more.

The Bible actually depicts exactly the same structural idea. This should come as no surprise, given that it is the handbook offered to us by the Creator of the universe. Perhaps the most fundamental truth of our existence is that He stands outside the dimensional walls of our world. He is beyond length, width, height, time, and any other dimensions our mathematicians will finally discover. He made them all. He travels through them freely.

If time travel is the creation of a bridge or tunnel between parallel dimensions, then a time jump should be possible, given enough power. The Lord has that power.

But He also stands outside of what we would call a "timeline." We are on the line, or within it. He is outside it, and plainly states that He can view any part of it...or all of it, at His leisure:

Remember the former things of old: for I am God, and there is none else; I am God, and there is none like me, Declaring the end from the beginning, and from ancient times the things that are not yet done, saying, My counsel shall stand, and I will do all my pleasure. (Isaiah 46:9, 10)

In this famous exhortation, the Lord asks Israel to remember all that He has done for them. Not only that, He declares Himself to be the Lord of time itself.

Here, He graciously pleads with Israel to remember the "things of old." These are the things of *eternity,* represented by the Hebrew word *olam* (עוֹלָם). He asks Israel to remember eternal things, not the transitory idols of this earth. He declared the beginning (Genesis 1:1) and the end.

From our perspective, He is speaking of a timeline; from His viewpoint, the elements along that line are only aspects of His larger purpose. Because He is the Creator, He can appear at any point along the line we call "time." That is, *while remaining in His natural dimension,* He can insert Himself at any point in the one to which we are limited. He asserts that He is unique; He is the defining point of the universe. He is the One who originates.

Furthermore, He declares the redemptive events of our world, from the most ancient history to the far future. His purposes will be realized, and His desire will reign.

As the Lord of Time, He can "travel" to any point in history—past, present, or future. Actually, He is not traveling at all, since He is omnipresent—everywhere at the same time.

In a very real sense, the biblical view of time travel is simply another view of God. Put another way, to travel in time, one must be *allowed* to travel in time, and the Lord Himself is the gatekeeper.

THE REDEMPTIVE PLAN

While the secular man might speculate about interdimensional travel, he is actually omitting the most important part of the formula—namely, that God's timeline is *purposeful.* The history of our universe, insofar as we are permitted to see it, is dedicated to redemption and restoration.

Where did man even get the idea of time travel? The inspiration for it came from the Bible!

Moses and the other prophets of ancient Israel demonstrated over and over again that there was a discernable future. Through them, the Lord also declared Himself to be the God of eons past. As ancient priests held aloft their scrolls, they declared that the distant past and the far future were knit together for God's purpose. Even the ancients knew about "time travel."

Today, as we hold the Holy Bible, we realize that we have the world's only true link to that same timeline. It alone holds the correct philosophy of history. And it alone, as it tells of the new heavens and the new earth, shows the final outcome of this universe.

The prime principle of all creation is to rectify destruction that was initiated when the Old Dragon, Satan, overthrew the heavenly order. He caused waves of destruction that spread in every direction, including planet earth. In a very real way, the biblical timeline that begins with creation and ends with perfection exists only to fulfill God's purpose.

Secular man can never see this truth. His vision and purpose are not to follow the Lord; they are to assume the role of the Lord. Egotistical man desires to master the dimensions of time and space, without realizing that he is the possession of God. The Lord declares the realities of time-space, and He is inseparable from them:

> I have declared the former things from the beginning; and they went forth out of my mouth, and I showed them; I did them suddenly, and they came to pass.
>
> Because I knew that thou art obstinate, and thy neck is an iron sinew, and thy brow brass; I have even from the beginning declared it to thee; before it came to pass I showed it thee: lest thou shouldest say, Mine idol hath done them, and my graven image, and my molten image, hath commanded them.
>
> Thou hast heard, see all this; and will not ye declare it? I have

showed thee new things from this time, even hidden things, and thou didst not know them. They are created now, and not from the beginning; even before the day when thou heardest them not; lest thou shouldest say, Behold, I knew them. (Isaiah 48:3–7)

In this assertion, the Lord desires that Israel should know that He and He alone, not some false idol, is the God of history. From time immemorial, men have attempted to attribute the work of God to various false ideas. Sometimes these ideas are philosophies, sometimes they are religions, and sometimes they are "science." Whatever they are called, they are, in fact, ways of removing God from the causal center of the universe.

If the Bible tells us only one thing, it is that the Lord is both Creator and Finisher, Alpha and Omega—Aleph and Tahv.

ADAM AS A TIME TRAVELER

In the Bible, there is a great deal of time travel. But as we shall see, it is always with a purpose. It is never done lightly. And it is always accomplished with a view toward the future. There seems to be no instance in which the Lord takes men into the past.

Before we look at a few of the Bible's time travelers, we must reiterate that from humanity's point of view, the future hasn't happened yet. Attempting to look forward, man sees nothing but a dark void. Soothsayers, seers, and mediums often make great sums of money with claims that they can foretell the future. Their attempts present a notorious cavalcade of failures.

There is no doubt about why this is the case. To travel in His realm, one must know the Master of Eternity. False prophets follow either their own fleshly urges or the whisperings they hear from the dark side. They are not connected to the real Source of information.

The first man, Adam, is said by certain sages to have seen the future.

Jewish commentary upon the Torah (the first five books of the Bible) says that God gave Adam an opportunity for a forward view. In the moments following his sin, say the sages, Adam was allowed to examine the pages of future history to see whether anyone there would be adequate to act as leader, bringing the world back to the state of perfection that he knew God intended.

Adam was doomed to die in the day that he sinned. As it happened, he was 130 years old when Seth was born, and he lived another 800 years after that. He died at 930 years of age.

His age was just seventy years short of a full "day." (Second Peter 3:8 tells us, "But, beloved, be not ignorant of this one thing, that one day is with the Lord as a thousand years, and a thousand years as one day.")

The sages of Israel say that Adam was able to look into the future and see that David was the man destined to take over his own assigned purpose. But apparently, he also saw that David was destined to live for only a short time. At that point, he yielded up seventy years of his own life so David might fulfill his mission.

Now, this story is extrabiblical. But whether or not it is true, it illustrates the point that eternity doesn't lie outside mankind. Rather, it is found within the man of God. Thus, true prophetic vision is simply the God-given ability to peer across the dimensional wall. And whether one actually goes to the future bodily or simply travels there in the Spirit of God is immaterial. If the spirit of the man is joined by God's Spirit, he is there.

THE SONS OF SETH

There is much other evidence that Adam traveled into the future. Following the death of Abel, Seth was born. His genealogy led to the godly Noah, then to Shem, Abraham, Isaac, Jacob, and the twelve tribes of Israel. The sons of Seth, including Enoch and Methuselah, were also men in close communion with the Lord. Some of them were time travelers. When one looks back at the way they ordered their lives, this conclusion is inescapable.

Writing about the sons of Seth, the Jewish historian Flavius Josephus says, "They also were the inventors of that peculiar sort of wisdom which is concerned with the heavenly bodies, and their order."[5]

In other words, these early men were astronomers and mathematicians. We have contemporary evidence of this truth in the Great Pyramid, which theoretical mathematicians have declared to reflect the knowledge of our solar system and the physics of our planet. Did those ancient men build this pyramid? Josephus says so:

> And that their inventions might not be lost before they were
> sufficiently known, upon Adam's prediction that the world was
> to be destroyed at one time by the force of fire, and at another
> time by the violence and quantity of water, they made two
> pillars; the one of brick, the other of stone: they inscribed their
> discoveries on them both, that in case the pillar of brick should
> be destroyed by the flood, the pillar of stone might remain, and
> exhibit those discoveries to mankind; and also inform them
> that there was another pillar of brick erected by them. Now this
> remains in the land of Siriad [Egypt] to this day.[6]

Two things are seen in this statement. First, Adam had a view of the future; he was indeed a time traveler. He knew about the coming Flood. And second, he knew about the fiery Day of the Lord. Adam had seen it all. The weight of mankind's future was upon him. His sons also felt the burden, and wanted to preserve as much of their knowledge as possible. To this day, so-called "pyramidologists" study the Great Pyramid, hoping to discern man's prophetic future. Thus far, they have been unable to do so. But they are motivated by the knowledge that the sons of Seth were actually able to record future history. Time will tell.

ENOCH, INTERDIMENSIONAL MAN

Many have speculated about the biblical statement found in Genesis 5:24: "And Enoch walked with God: and he was not; for God took him." Enoch was in such close fellowship with God that he was able—literally—to step through the dimensional wall. As we have already seen, by definition, this means that he was a time traveler. From the other side of that dimensional barrier, he could travel in the Spirit of the Lord to any point along the timeline of redemption.

Furthermore, we have biblical proof of his future vision: "And Enoch also, the seventh from Adam, prophesied of these, saying, Behold, the Lord cometh with ten thousands of his saints" (Jude 14).

Enoch actually witnessed the Second Coming of Christ! Was he actually there? Yes...the Lord took him.

You may ask, "Was he there bodily, or only in his spirit?" We must answer that from our perspective; it doesn't really matter. He was there. And of course in Enoch's case, he was, in fact, taken bodily into the Lord's dimension, where time travel is a matter of simple fact.

THE TOWER OF BABEL

Following the Flood, the sons of Noah descended into the plains of Shinar, the foundation of what would become known as Mesopotamia. There, they set about the task of building a tower that would (in some way now unknown to us) enable them to "reach to heaven." Apparently, they retained enough of the pre-Flood knowledge that they believed themselves able to step across the forbidden dimensional barrier.

From the heavenly perspective, the reaction is quick and certain:

> And the LORD came down to see the city and the tower, which
> the children of men builded. And the LORD said, Behold, the
> people is one, and they have all one language; and this they

begin to do: and now nothing will be restrained from them, which they have imagined to do. (Genesis 11:5, 6)

These men of Shinar attempted to do nothing less than scale the dimensional wall. Once there, they reasoned that they would have control over time and space. In effect, they wanted access to heaven. Doubtless, they knew about Adam's prophecies, Enoch's translation, and the towers built by Seth's sons.

Now, they attempted in their own strength to assume that same, godlike position. They were endeavoring to do what today's theoreticians are still attempting through the principles of modern science.

But then, as now, such time travel is forbidden. If today's scientists even came close to realizing their goal, the Lord would somehow confuse their efforts, as He did at the Tower of Babel.

MOSES, THE DELIVERER

Moses wrote the Torah. Once, while condemning the leaders of Israel, Jesus affirmed this fact:

> Do not think that I will accuse you to the Father: there is one that accuseth you, even Moses, in whom ye trust. For had ye believed Moses, ye would have believed me: for he wrote of me. But if ye believe not his writings, how shall ye believe my words? (John 5:45–47)

Was Moses a time traveler? We must answer this question in the affirmative. If any man was ever privileged to cross the dimensional wall, it was Moses. His five books span the ages from before the creation of the earth to the establishment of the Kingdom.

His opening words in Genesis 1:1 speak of that day in the distant past when God commanded the Light of Creation to spring forth.

His concluding "Song of Moses" in Deuteronomy foretells the blessed day when the "Rock" of Israel—the Lord Jesus Christ—will finally avenge the blood of the prophets and of Israel.

But more than that, the words of the Torah are layered with internal meaning. The so-called "Bible Codes" of recent fame are but the current reflection of a truth known to the sages of Israel for countless generations since Moses: Timeless, universal, infinite truth is programmed into the very sequence of the Torah's letters. An eighteenth-century sage known as the Vilna Gaon wrote these words:

> The rule is that all that was, is and will be **unto the end of time** is included in the Torah, from the first word to the last word. And not merely in a general sense, but as to the details of every species and each one individually, and details of details of everything that happened to him from the day of his birth until his end. (emphasis added)

This rabbi is not a lone voice. In this quote, he is merely restating a general principle. And note his use of the phrase "unto the end of time." Here, he refers to the redemptive timeline. Dr. Eliyahu Rips, mathematician at Hebrew University, has led research into the Torah codes. He has strongly affirmed the beliefs of the ancient sages.

Only the Spirit of the Lord, in fellowship with Moses' spirit, could have produced such a transcendental document. It is, in fact, timeless in the sense that it surpasses the time and space of our dimension.

Moses communed directly with the Lord. He was shown things that break the bounds of our knowledge. Moses was infused with the light of God. His vitality remained intact, even when, at the age of 120 years, he was taken to his burial place in full health.

In the New Testament, he appears with Elijah before Jesus and the disciples. They are privileged to witness a preview of the Kingdom Age. If, as we believe, Moses is one of the two witnesses of the Revelation, he appears again at yet another future point. Thus, he is in a very real sense a time traveler.

But again, we must say that his travels are not arbitrary. They are specifically revealed to us as part of the redemptive timeline.

ELIJAH AGAINST AHAB AND ANTICHRIST

The prophet Elijah was given to Israel to offer hope during the reign of King Ahab, son of Omri. Ahab established a grove in Jerusalem dedicated to Ashtoreth, the goddess of fertility, and to Baal. Together, Ahab and his wife, Jezebel, were consummately evil. They attempted to turn Israel into their own Canaanite empire.

But Elijah came before the king as the Lord's spokesman. He told Ahab that because of his sin, the rain would be withheld...for three and a half years. Later, in a contest with the priests of Baal, Elijah demonstrated that the Lord was the one and only God of the universe.

Like Enoch, Elijah walked in such communion with the Lord that he was taken—alive—into heaven: "And it came to pass, as they still went on, and talked, that, behold, there appeared a chariot of fire, and horses of fire, and parted them both asunder; and Elijah went up by a whirlwind into heaven" (2 Kings 2:11).

Elijah was gone, but not forgotten. In the fifth century BC, Malachi prophesied that Elijah would return to his people:

Behold, I will send you Elijah the prophet before the coming
of the great and dreadful day of the LORD: And he shall turn
the heart of the fathers to the children, and the heart of the
children to their fathers, lest I come and smite the earth with a
curse. (Malachi 4:5, 6)

Here, in the closing words of the Old Testament, Elijah is seen as the forerunner of faith in the grim days of the Tribulation. As earlier mentioned, he is seen before that, with Moses at the Transfiguration.

Then, in the far future, Elijah appears as one of the two witnesses in Revelation. As he once did in the days of Ahab, he withholds the rain for three and a half years. Furthermore, just as he once stood against the priests of Baal, he will stand against the same evil spirits who are the power behind the throne of Antichrist.

But in the most vivid sense, Elijah became a time traveler the moment he stepped aboard that fiery chariot. Entering the dimension of the heavens, he had access to the entire timeline, available for God's service as his destiny called.

Malachi, as the last in the order of the twelve Minor Prophets, saw the future. Hosea prophesied of Israel's apostasy and final restoration.

Joel saw the horrific sights of the Day of the Lord. Amos foresaw the judgments that would befall Israel, as well as its final restoration. Obadiah was given a vision of Edom's final fate. Micah saw the birth of Messiah, His work, and His rejection. He also saw the establishment of the Kingdom.

Zephaniah saw the horrors of the Tribulation, the judgment of Israel's enemies, and the regathering of Israel. Haggai and Zechariah specifically prophesied that the Lord's Temple would be rebuilt in the days of the Kingdom. Zechariah, in fact, saw the final siege of Jerusalem and the deliverance of Israel.

All these prophets, each of whom has been the subject of many analytical treatises, saw the future. More than that, each of them experienced it.

THE MAJOR PROPHETS

Isaiah, Jeremiah, Ezekiel, and Daniel each saw the future in precisely the same way that all the other prophets did. To attempt to condense their writings into this chapter is impossible, except to say that each experienced a heavenly visitation that was followed by a series of revelations about the future timeline of Israel.

Isaiah was visited in the Temple by a fiery seraph:

In the year that king Uzziah died I saw also the Lord sitting upon a throne, high and lifted up, and his train filled the temple. Above it stood the seraphims: each one had six wings;

with twain he covered his face, and with twain he covered his feet, and with twain he did fly. (Isaiah 6:1, 2)

At this visitation, Isaiah was commissioned to go forth as a prophet. The *Shechina* glory (Hebrew for "spiritual presence") of God filled the Temple, as Isaiah was taken into the heavenly dimension, from which he would be able to glimpse future events.

Jeremiah's call illustrates the timeless nature of the prophet's office:

Then the word of the LORD came unto me, saying, Before I formed thee in the belly I knew thee; and before thou camest forth out of the womb I sanctified thee, and I ordained thee a prophet unto the nations. (Jeremiah 1:4, 5)

Here the Lord affirms to Jeremiah that He stands outside the vault of time. The prophet is ordained on the basis of the Lord's certainty that his ordination did not take place on the timeline, but in the realm of eternity.

Ezekiel, of course, was visited by the Lord's fiery chariot, whose wheels within wheels revealed four "living creatures," a crystalline firmament, and a sapphire throne—all surrounded by the glory of God. From that moment forward, he lived out the difficult life of a prophet.

His travels into the future included a view of Israel's regathering and the most detailed picture in all Scripture of a modern battle. We refer, of course, to the invasion of Israel by "Gog, the land of Magog." This prophecy is so complete in its vision that Ezekiel seems to be delivering an eyewitness account. He sees the invading force coming "like a storm," and "like a cloud." He sees Gog's defeat and offers us a view of his vast burial site at Hamon-gog. If he saw these things, he was there.

The "modern" mind might object to this statement. After all, we have television and can "see" something at a distance. Perhaps Ezekiel viewed the battle on some kind of celestial television screen. But in fact, Scripture clearly states that Ezekiel was taken into the spiritual realm where he actually saw the future. He was there.

In chapters 40 through 48, he says "the hand of the Lord" brought him to Jerusalem. There, he saw both the city and the future Third Temple. Chapter 41 begins, "Afterward he brought me to the temple." Chapter 42 brings another view: "Then he brought me forth into the utter court, the way toward the north." Chapter 43 says, "Afterward, he brought me to the gate, even the gate that looketh toward the east."

Finally, he was taken to a vantage point that allowed him to see a river of water flowing from the Temple. The spot upon which he stood was not merely a geographic location; it was, in fact, a time/space coordinate. Ezekiel's position was progressively shifted to allow him to see what the Lord wanted him to see. He was there as a time traveler. His purpose was to offer Israel the hope that comes with the certainty of the Third Temple's construction.

A Bridge to the New Testament

The close relationship between the book of Daniel and the Revelation of John is well known. The prophet Daniel was an interpreter of Nebuchadnezzar's dreams. He was also a visionary who was allowed to travel in the heavenly dimension.

In his "night visions," he was allowed to see the unfolding of future events. These included the geopolitical layout of the Gentile empires and two specific prophecies concerning the Antichrist. The first expounds the seventy-weeks prophecy and the "abomination of desolation." The second links him to the line of Alexander and the Seleucids.

Was he a "time traveler," in the real sense of the term? Only if one interprets visions as trips out of the body. In Daniel's case, he "saw" the future, but did not actually seem to visit it. An angelic messenger came to him, guiding his final vision of the future.

However, his visions are confirmed in the New Testament by Jesus, who has already been present at those future events. Jesus, locked for a brief time in human flesh, had once occupied a position of omnipresence. With authority, He spoke of the future: "When ye therefore shall see the abomination of desolation, spoken of by Daniel the prophet, stand in the holy place, (whoso readeth, let him understand:) Then let them which be in Judaea flee into the mountains" (Matthew 24:15, 16).

Here, Jesus confirmed the truth of Daniel's vision with His own sure knowledge of future events. Jesus *had been there.*

Once, He told His disciples: "Verily I say unto you, There be some standing here, which shall not taste of death, till they see the Son of man coming in his kingdom" (Matthew 16:28). Shortly afterward, with Peter, James, and John, He went to the mountaintop of the Transfiguration. There, they met the time-traveling Moses and Elijah. For a moment, past, present, and future were conjoined in a timeless, eternal present.

JESUS AND JOHN

Other than Jesus Himself, the ultimate time traveler of Scripture is John, who was taken bodily into the heavenly dimension and allowed to witness the Tribulation, the Kingdom, and the glories of the restored earth. His trip began when the risen Christ appeared to him and gave him a series of messages to seven specific churches.

Then, he was literally allowed to pass through a dimensional door. As this occurred, he was ushered into the timeless realms where the future may be viewed from a variety of perspectives:

> After this I looked, and, behold, a door was opened in heaven: and the first voice which I heard was as it were of a trumpet talking with me; which said, Come up hither, and I will show thee things which must be hereafter.
>
> And immediately I was in the spirit; and, behold, a throne was set in heaven, and one sat on the throne. (Revelation 4:1, 2)

John's spirit, in conjunction with the Lord's Spirit, now moves to the divine throne room for a formal procedure that will unfold a series of judgments upon the Gentile world. The Lamb takes a sealed book and begins to open it, unleashing the fury of heaven upon a sinful world.

John is an eyewitness to this event, which he reports as it unfolds. But from our perspective, it hasn't happened yet. John has quite literally traveled forward in time.

As the seals are opened one by one, John sees the Antichrist, war, famine, and pestilence. More importantly, he sees the twelve tribes as they struggle to overcome the trials inflicted upon them by Satan and the Antichrist.

He sees the Tribulation saints and the system of the Antichrist rise to power. Then, he witnesses the destruction of Mystery Babylon and the Second Coming of Christ.

The judgments come in three sets of seven: seals, trumpets, and vials. Over the centuries, various expositors have labored to make sense of their complex sequences. Earthquakes, astronomical catastrophes, demonic hordes, and disease wrack a world shaken by polar shifts and global rifts. The three sets of seven all contain elements of these judgments.

But try as one may, it seems impossible to overlay them in any way that makes sense from the confines of an earthly timeline. No doubt, from John's perspective, they mesh perfectly.

His situation as a time traveler (guided by the Spirit of the Lord) is established with a purpose. Like the prophets of the Old Testament, he is shown the events that will convey a particular message to those who will later study Scripture.

John is specifically led to return with the message of judgment, restoration, and eternal peace. But the precise *relative timing* of these events remains elusive.

Peter once asked Jesus about the destiny He had for John:

> Jesus saith unto him, If I will that he tarry till I come, what
> is that to thee? follow thou me. Then went this saying abroad
> among the brethren, that that disciple should not die: yet Jesus
> said not unto him, He shall not die; but, If I will that he tarry
> till I come, what is that to thee? (John 21:22, 23)

How could the disciples have known that Jesus would, in fact, come to John during his lifetime? How could they have known that John would visit the far future? They had only heard of it in part, when Jesus taught them upon the Mount of Olives. John was allowed to go there and see for himself.

The Third Heaven

Paul, the last apostle, was selected by the Lord specifically to deliver the message of the church to the Gentiles. He, too, was taken into the dimension of eternity:

> I knew a man in Christ above fourteen years ago, (whether in the body, I cannot tell; or whether out of the body, I cannot tell: God knoweth;) such an one caught up to the third heaven.
> And I knew such a man, (whether in the body, or out of the body, I cannot tell: God knoweth;) How that he was caught up into paradise, and heard unspeakable words, which it is not lawful for a man to utter. (2 Corinthians 12:2–4)

The term "third heaven" doubtless refers to the dimensional plane from which it is possible to visit various points in earth time. What did Paul see there? He says that he can't tell us. Probably, he saw parts of the future that the Lord did not want to be common knowledge.

But we know that he visited the future, because his epistles speak of future events. In his letters to the Corinthians, the Thessalonians, and Timothy, he speaks of future events with authority, describing the doctrinal dissipation of the latter days. He tells of the debased nature of the last generation. He encourages us with his descriptions of the Rapture of the church. He sees the "son of perdition" sitting in the Temple and calling himself a god.

Like the Bible's other time travelers, Paul is allowed to bring forth the Lord's message of redemption.

Without the Holy Scriptures, it is doubtful that mankind would have even dreamed of time travel. Scripture is the only example of it we have. From ancient days to the present, time travel is permitted only on a "need-to-know" basis. The Lord allows it only for the purpose of displaying His will to an unbelieving world.

2

REVERBERATIONS IN TIME AND SPACE

In chapter one, we ventured into the realm of time travel. As we saw, this subject is even more exciting from the biblical perspective than it is from the classic, secular point of view. For at least the last century, the subject of travel through time has been popularized in novels, plays, and motion pictures. Following World War II, the explosion of science fiction has produced an entire industry devoted to popularizing the idea that interdimensional forays will one day be routine.

The public imagination has been shaped in conjunction with developments in theoretical physics. Reviewing these scientific advancements, it is often hard to tell which came first, science fiction or science. In the mid-nineteenth century, Jules Verne wrote of advanced submarine travel and lunar excursions. A few decades later, submarines were common. A century after he wrote, man visited the moon.

At the turn of the twentieth century, Wells' *The Time Machine* popularized the thought that time travel might actually be possible. We have observed that without the biblical concept of a future world, it is doubtful that even he would have come up with the idea.

Nevertheless, in some strange way, the public imagination tends to precede actual scientific advancement. The concept of time travel is interwoven with quantum physics, which postulates various dimensions that may theoretically be reached by the application of dedicated technology and huge amounts of power. Even as fictional superheroes romp through time and space, today's scientists are assiduously working at cracking the dimensional barrier.

It is worth stating again that dimensional travel and time travel are one and the same. Piercing the dimensional wall brings one into the realm of eternity. Secular man deeply desires the acquisition of power that would follow the attainment of this ability. After all, the ability to "warp" time/space would theoretically result in the ability to travel inter-galactic distances in mere hours.

Or, as any fan of the *Star Trek* movies can testify, Captains Kirk and Picard often give the order to accelerate to "warp factor eight," or some such number. Actually, they are not really accelerating, but bending time/space to allow them to bypass normal time and arrive earlier than would be normal. Furthermore, if they run into a cloud of energy, vagrant nebula, or the blast from a supernova, their "warping" often results in an unwanted deviation into another time.

Seeking speed, they are bumped, instead, into another time. Their adventure, of course, involves finding a way to return to their own time. But to sci-fi devotees, the message is quite clear: When one crosses the dimensional barrier, navigation is expressed in both time and space coordinates. The Bible reflects exactly this same idea.

Proprietary Information

In real terms, however, time/space is the province of the Lord. We have already seen that His prophets and apostles were sometimes given the ability to transcend the dimensional barrier and travel forward (never backward) in time. In every case, the Lord ordained their travels for the specific purpose of expounding the redemptive history of mankind—past, present, and future.

Never were they allowed a whimsical side trip, nor were they permitted to report upon anything they saw, unless it applied specifically to the plan of God. For example, Elijah appears at different places along the biblical timeline to expound the glory of God and His Kingdom. But as we have seen, his appearances on planet earth reiterate a common theme.

First, he opposes Ahab, Jezebel, and the prophets of Baal. Then, at the Transfiguration, he foreshadows the Kingdom Age. Finally, as one of the witnesses of Revelation, he revisits his first role, standing in opposition to the Antichrist and the harlot called Mystery Babylon the Great. In both his first and final visits, he withholds the rain for three and a half years. Also, in both cases he fights a despotic monarch and a false religious system.

As a time traveler, Ezekiel is allowed to see Israel's regathering, war for survival, and the subsequent reestablishment of the Third Temple. These things he sees with his own eyes, describing them in tones of awe and reverence. The features of Temple rebuilding as he relates them in chapters 40–48 are almost photographic in their detail.

In the New Testament, John passes through a dimensional door into the vastness of heaven and is allowed to view the future. But he doesn't view the future in general. Rather, he is shown key events in the age of the church, the defeat of Satan, and the restoration of the Kingdom. He is even allowed to see the far future. The New Jerusalem and the new heavens and earth are still over a thousand years into *our* future, today.

It is the Bible, and no other book, that really expresses the truth about the state of our existence. Again and again, we are impressed with the fact that men probably would never have even dreamed of time travel if the Lord's emissaries had not already achieved it. This leads us back to a thought that we touched upon earlier.

We have already spent some time on the fact that Adam and the antediluvians possessed heavenly knowledge. Put another way, they were aware of certain information that reached them from beyond the dimensional barrier. According to Hebrew history, the first man was given an overview of humanity's future, which he passed on to his children.

In particular, the sons of Seth were told of two future destructions that would befall planet earth. One would be by fire, the other by flood. With this knowledge, they sought to preserve the wisdom they had acquired through Adam. Reasoning that it might be lost in a future conflagration, they built two monuments encoded with their knowledge of astronomy, mathematics, and the timing of future events. One was made of fired brick, the other of stone.

Josephus tells us that one survived the Flood—the Great Pyramid of stone, in Egypt.[7] Modern mathematicians have stated that the pyramid contains astronomical knowledge such as the distance from earth to the sun and from the earth's poles to its equator. It is built to optical tolerances. Its original surface was ground to the dimensional accuracy of an eyeglass lens. This was an absolute impossibility for the ancient Egyptians. To this day, its dimensional structure has not been completely decoded.

FORBIDDEN KNOWLEDGE OF TIME AND SPACE

The sons of Cain also received heavenly knowledge. It was illicitly gained when the earth was contaminated by the traffic between fallen angels and mankind.

> And it came to pass, when men began to multiply on the face of the earth, and daughters were born unto them, That the sons of God saw the daughters of men that they were fair; and they took them wives of all which they chose.
>
> And the LORD said, My spirit shall not always strive with man, for that he also is flesh: yet his days shall be an hundred and twenty years.
>
> There were giants in the earth in those days; and also after that, when the sons of God came in unto the daughters of men, and they bare children to them, the same became mighty men which were of old, men of renown.
>
> And God saw that the wickedness of man was great in the earth, and that every imagination of the thoughts of his heart was only evil continually. (Genesis 6:1–5)

So, the sons and daughters of Cain were corrupted by an illegitimate intrusion from beyond the dimensional barrier between heaven and earth. These "sons of God" brought with them forms of knowledge that were explicitly forbidden by the Lord. Their traffic was, indeed, the reason for the world's destruction in the Flood of Noah.

Josephus writes that even the sons of Seth finally became perverted by the fallen angels:

> But for what degree of zeal they had formerly shown for virtue, they now showed by their actions a double degree of wickedness, whereby they made God to be their enemy; for many angels of God accompanied with women, and begat sons that proved unjust, and despisers of all that was good, on account of the confidence they had in their own strength, for the tradition is that these men did what resembled the acts of those whom the Grecians call giants.[8]

The apocryphal Book of Enoch contains an extended narrative that recounts the story of the angels who lusted after the women of earth. Then, having established themselves among men, they dominated and devoured the Lord's blessed creation.

One of the fallen was called Azazel: "And Azazel taught men to make swords, and knives, and shields and breastplates, and made known to them the metals of the earth" (Enoch VIII, 1).

Continuing through the text of Enoch VIII, we find other fallen angels. One, called Semjaza, " taught enchantments, and root-cuttings." Armaros gave men the gift of "enchantments" (sorcery). Baraqijal taught them astrology. Kokabel taught the starry constellations, Ezeqeel, meteorology, Araqiel, the "signs of the earth," Shamsiel, "the signs of the sun," and Sariel, "the signs of the moon."

But as men received this illegitimate intelligence, they became spiritually, physically, and genetically corrupted. Of Azazel, Enoch writes:

Thou seest what Azazel hath done, who hath taught all
unrighteousness on earth and revealed the eternal secrets which
were (preserved) in heaven, which men were striving to learn:
And Semjaza to whom Thou hast given authority to bear rule
over his associates.

And they have gone to the daughters of men upon the
earth, and have slept with the women, and have defiled
themselves, and revealed to them all kinds of sins.

And the women have borne giants, and the whole earth has
thereby been filled with blood and unrighteousness.

And now behold the souls of these who have died are
crying and making their suit to the gates of heaven, and their
lamentations have ascended: and cannot cease because of the
lawless deeds which are wrought on the earth.
(Enoch IX, 6–10)[9]

These "giants" were the Greek Titans such as Zeus, Apollo, and the
dozens of other demigods who walked among men. Assuming these
accounts to be basically true, it goes without saying that their cohabita-
tion with earthly humans gave mankind access to dangerous knowledge
from beyond the dimensional barrier.

The timeless knowledge of the ages from another dimension brought
men to destruction. In their fallen and sinful state, they were simply
unequipped to handle the temptations handed to them by a superior
power from on high. Like children given matches and dynamite, it
was—ironically—only a matter of time until they destroyed themselves.
Knowing this, the Lord extinguished the fire with a flood.

ATLANTIS: A SECULAR VIEW OF THE FLOOD

Who has not heard of the fabled Atlantis? In the history of the Greeks, it
was the cultural jewel of an idyllic society where gods and men gamboled
together in perfect peace. It was a magnificent city-state that existed in

technological splendor before it was destroyed by a cataclysm that caused it to sink into the sea.

From our point of view, this would seem to be a secular reference to the Great Flood of Noah. More than that, it echoes the biblical theme set forth in Genesis 6, detailing the activities of the Titans.

In *Critias,* Plato describes ancient Atlantis, as it experienced a:

> …single night of torrential rain [that] stripped the acropolis of its soil and reduced it to bare limestone in a storm that was accompanied by earthquakes. Before the destructive flood of Deucalion, this was the third such cataclysmic storm.[10]

According to Plato, this was the beginning of the end for Atlantis, the city of wonders where gods cohabited with men. But as the story continues, we find that Atlantis was a huge "island" that was destroyed in a great flood.

Plato's narrative addresses the events surrounding Atlantis as historical phenomena. To him, they were real history, not myth or fable. The god of Atlantis was none other than Poseidon, the principal sea god of the ancient Greeks. He was said to be the son of Cronos and brother of Zeus, Hades, and other gods.

Plato writes:

> As I said before concerning the distribution of lands among the gods, in some regions they divided the entire earth into greater apportionments and in others into lesser apportionments, as they established sanctuaries and sacrifices for themselves. So it was that Poseidon received as one of his domains the island of Atlantis and he established dwelling places for the children he had fathered of a mortal woman in a certain place on the island that I shall describe.[11]

Thus, the histories of Enoch, Plato, Josephus, and the sixth chapter of Genesis agree that something amazing happened before the Flood of

Noah, when extraterrestrial forces encroached upon humanity. A door between the eternal state and the timeline of planet earth was opened and began to dominate the affairs of humanity.

Plato describes how Poseidon saw a beautiful woman named Clito, whom he married. They had five pairs of twins. Poseidon built the domain of Atlantis for his family, moving earth and water to create an acropolis surrounded by two rings of land and three of water. This was said to be easy for him, since he was a god. The palace ground was said to be three thousand feet in diameter; the island, itself, 227 miles wide and 341 miles long! Poseidon's temple was three hundred by six hundred feet!

Of the ten sons, he writes:

> And he gave each of his sons names. To the son who was oldest
> and king he gave the name from which the entire island and its
> surrounding sea derive their names, because he was the first of
> the kings of that time. His name was Atlas; the island is called
> Atlantis and the sea Atlantic after him.[12]

He writes much more, but this vignette is enough to demonstrate once again that secular history agrees with the Bible. Poseidon's ten sons remind us of the fallen angels described by Enoch, and their title, "chiefs of tens."

Spiritual beings, whose natural realm was beyond the time/space limitations of earthlings, came to live with them. Imagine what secrets they revealed to their human companions!

THE LUST FOR ETERNITY

And this is precisely the point. Following the Flood, Noah's sons descended to the plain of Shinar. There, they created a new culture in a ravaged world now characterized by labor and struggle. Once, according to both Plato and the Bible, the climate had been tranquil and men lived in leisure. On top of that, the "gods" handed man the wonders of technology to use as he desired. Certainly, the fallen angels were despotic, but their fickle and erratic deviancies seemed a small price to pay for such convenience.

One can only try to imagine the longing that post-Flood men must have had for their ancient paradise. The Greeks later referred to it in their myths as Arcadia, a place where the climate, soil, and atmosphere were so perfect that crops grew to perfection and little labor was required to accomplish any feat. This was particularly true when they had the gods to rearrange the landscape to perfection.

Genesis chapter 11 states that the men of Shinar were skilled builders, using baked brick and bitumen to create elaborate structures. This would be the method of choice at Babel. Scripture is quite specific about this fact: "And they said one to another, Go to, let us make brick, and burn them thoroughly. And they had brick for stone, and slime had they for mortar" (Genesis 11:3).

We recall again the history of Josephus, which says that antediluvian man built two memorials to heavenly knowledge—one of stone and one of brick.[13] Apparently, the one made of brick didn't survive the Flood.

It therefore seems logical to assume that these men tried to rebuild it:

And they said, Go to, let us build us a city and a tower, whose top may reach unto heaven; and let us make us a name, lest we be scattered abroad upon the face of the whole earth.

And the LORD came down to see the city and the tower, which the children of men builded. And the LORD said, Behold, the people is one, and they have all one language; and this they begin to do: and now nothing will be restrained from them, which they have imagined to do. (Genesis 11:4–6)

It is hard for modern man to understand their goal. But if we simply remember that they had been accustomed to daily communion with the gods, their actions become quite easy to understand. They were in a state of constant longing to reestablish the contact that had been lost. In other words, they were attempting to reopen the heavenly door that had been slammed shut by the Flood.

Was their effort sheer madness? Apparently not, since the Lord assessed their project design and stated that it would work. They were about to realize their goal. Therefore, He confounded their scheme by breaking them up into diverse language groups. To this day, linguists trace man's languages back to a common, "Indo-European," mother tongue, which they say originated in Mesopotamia.

> So the LORD scattered them abroad from thence upon the face
> of all the earth: and they left off to build the city. Therefore
> is the name of it called Babel; because the LORD did there
> confound the language of all the earth: and from thence did
> the LORD scatter them abroad upon the face of all the earth.
> (Genesis 11:8, 9)

Babel, the vaunted "gateway to the gods," was reduced to babble. The Lord, master of time/space, continued His plan to redeem mankind through the bloodline that would bring forth the prophesied Messiah. Man may digress, but the Lord sets the course.

CYCLES OF TIME AND SPACE

This being the case, it is more than appropriate that the next chapter of the biblical narrative turns to the genealogy of Abram. It tells of the Lord's command for him to leave Mesopotamia and move to a new land. And it details the covenant of promise.

That covenant is ratified through a series of transactions between God and the young Abram. Seven times He visits the patriarch, and seven times He certifies His Word.

Just after the third such contact, Abram and 318 of his hand-picked servants were forced to engage an enemy in war. It happened in the years following the separation of Lot and Abram, when Lot chose to dwell in the fair territory near Sodom and Gomorrah. At that time, this region was said to compare in beauty to the Garden of Eden. Unfortunately for Lot, its citizens were exceedingly wicked.

Genesis 14 describes a series of battles in which four kings began to wage war in the Sodom/Gomorrah area:

> And it came to pass in the days of Amraphel king of Shinar, Arioch king of Ellasar, Chedorlaomer king of Elam, and Tidal king of nations; That these made war with Bera king of Sodom, and with Birsha king of Gomorrah, Shinab king of Admah, and Shemeber king of Zeboiim, and the king of Bela, which is Zoar. All these were joined together in the vale of Siddim, which is the salt sea. (Genesis 14:1–3)

Their battles took the four northern Gentile kings southward into the region of Sodom, where Lot had chosen to reside. They took him captive, but one man escaped and brought the news to Abram, who took immediate action. He gathered 318 of his own trained men. He rescued Lot and regained the spoils of war.

Amazing about this account is that a bit of research reveals the true nature of the four aggressor kings in this account. They are, in fact, representatives of four prophetically important nations. Together, they outline future history!

The June 1997 issue of *Prophecy in the News* magazine included an article stating that Amraphel of Shinar is none other than Nimrod of Babylon.[14] In Genesis 10:9, this ancient potentate is said to be "a mighty hunter before the Lord" who hunted and enslaved the souls of men. He is believed to be the first man to stand before men and proclaim himself a monarch. He defines the original, sinful, Babylon, which, in the end of days would grow to be a mystery that engulfs the entire world.

The article stated that Arioch, king of Ellasar, is an ancient ruler associated with the area later known as Greece. The writing known as the Dead Sea Apocryphon locates his area of regency in southwestern Asia Minor (the region that later became known as Cappadocia), and westward into today's Greece. Jewish historians connect Ellasar etymologically with Greece, since the Greeks refer to themselves as the people of "Ellas."

The article also noted:

> If this is true, Arioch would represent the Mediterranean seafarers who later came to control the region of the Aegean and Northwestern Mediterranean Seas. This ties in well with ancient history, which says that the people we refer to as the ancient Greeks began arriving in their land during the centuries preceding 1900 BC...the time of Abraham.[15]

Concerning Chedorlaomer:

> The territory of his rule is well known. Elam encompassed the area between the Persian Gulf on the south and the Caspian Sea on the north. It is the land that later came to be ruled by the Medes and the Persians. Chedorlaomer, then, is the progenitor of the Medo-Persian empire.

The last of the four kings is Tidal, king of the nations or, as the Hebrew text has it, "Goyim." This monarch seems to possess a power that extends across several Gentile regions.

He may be the easiest of these kings to place in history. Several references connect him with Tudhalia I, ruler of the Hittite empire. His region of rule would cover most of present-day Turkey, from the Bosporus on the west, to the eastern end of the Black Sea.

Historically, it is now known that in this period, the Hittite kings originated the practice of mounting large mercenary armies. To do this, they would pay the best warriors of surrounding tribes. Then, they were regimented through systematic training. Because of this practice, they became a fierce warrior nation, feared for centuries across the ancient civilized world.

The title, "king of nations," suggests a large sphere of influence. In fact, Jews say that Tidal is the progenitor of the large, Western, Gentile empires that would follow. They flatly state that "Tidal is Rome."

In the *Artscroll* commentary on Genesis (*Bereishis*), Vol. 1(a), by Rabbi Meir Zlotowitz, we find the following:

"According to the *Midrash, Goyim* [גוים, nations] refers to Rome which levies troops from all nations. Rav Eleazar bar Abina said: When you see the powers fighting each other, look for the advent [lit., 'feet'] of the King Messiah."

Even though Tidal's empire precedes imperial Rome by two millennia, it is the metaphoric progenitor of the final empire that prophecy says will one day encompass the entire earth.[16]

It is remarkable that the four kings give us an advance view of Babylon, Greece, Medo-Persia, and Rome. Their historical order is only slightly altered as we see them in the rulerships that Daniel later reveals as representatives of the future history of Gentile sovereignty.

Thus, when Abram engages the four kings in battle, he is really acting out a theme, which will later be expanded in the four world empires of Daniel and in the book of Revelation.

THE GENTILE TIMELINE

Moving forward in time, we see Daniel taken captive by the Babylonian forces of Nebuchadnezzar. He is brought to the potentate's special attention when the old king is unable to remember a dream that seems important. Daniel explains the dream in a visual trip forward through Gentile history to come:

Thou, O king, sawest, and behold a great image. This great image, whose brightness was excellent, stood before thee; and the form thereof was terrible.

This image's head was of fine gold, his breast and his arms of silver, his belly and his thighs of brass, His legs of iron, his feet part of iron and part of clay.

Thou sawest till that a stone was cut out without hands, which smote the image upon his feet that were of iron and clay, and brake them to pieces.

Then was the iron, the clay, the brass, the silver, and the gold, broken to pieces together, and became like the chaff of the summer threshingfloors; and the wind carried them away, that no place was found for them: and the stone that smote the image became a great mountain, and filled the whole earth. (Daniel 2:31–35)

In this well-known account, Daniel's recitation of Nebuchadnezzar's dream indelibly implants a symbolic, forward view of world history, in which Nebuchadnezzar himself is the statue's head of gold.

As we now know, the great image outlines Babylon (the head of gold), Medo-Persia (the breast and arms of silver), Greece (the belly and thighs of brass), and Rome (the legs of iron). The "great mountain" of this prophecy is the Kingdom of God.

Daniel's prophecy was given at the end of the seventh century BC. This is approximately thirteen hundred years after Abram's battle with the four Gentile kings! Yet he elaborates upon the theme that was set in the tableau originated in the days of Abraham. Here, we have a colossal reverberation in the time/space continuum!

That is, early history displays an initial form, which is later borne out as a fully developed historical climax. The pattern suggests that in the plan of God, themes and variations are used to achieve His predestined order.

Classical Jewish teaching states that Abraham was born in the year 1948 AC (After Creation). It goes on to say that he was forty-eight years old in 1996 AC, the year the nations were dispersed at the Tower of Babel.

Their history also notes that in the year following—1997 AC—lesser cities were subjugated, including the kings of Canaan. In particular, they teach that Chedorlaomer subjugated the five kings of the Sodom and Gomorrah region for about twelve years, until 2009 AC.

From that point on, warring continued until Abram defeated the northern alliance and returned victorious to Salem in about 2023, when he was seventy-five years old.

The amazing symmetry of this dating system reminds Israel that God is in control of their destiny. They link the birth of Abraham in 1948 AC with the birth of modern Israel in AD 1948. As we view these familiar-sounding dates, they remind us that we are seeing the emergence of a pattern in future history.

Abram fought his battle in approximately the year 1977 BC. Yet his actions distinctly foreshadow events that took place thirteen hundred to two thousand years later in the successive rise and fall of Babylon, Medo-Persia, and Greece.

Of course, Rome was at its full power during the first advent of Jesus Christ. The Bible also tells us that Rome was the foundation and heart of the dreadful Beast that will eventually control the world. Like King Tidal of old, it will be called "king of nations."

From the Lord's perspective, time unfolds in a series of images or types that first appear in the lives of the faithful ancients. Later, they are "fleshed out," when the time of their fulfillment arrives: "For I would not, brethren, that ye should be ignorant of this mystery, lest ye should be wise in your own conceits; that blindness in part is happened to Israel, until the fulness of the Gentiles be come in" (Romans 11:25).

Concerning Israel, Paul writes that their destiny is dependent upon the outworking of the Gentile powers. As shown above, these nations are symbolically distilled into the four kingdoms defeated by Abram's army. Following his victory, he returned to Salem, the city that would later become known as Jerusalem, the "Zion" of prophetic Scripture.

And the king of Sodom went out to meet him after his return from the slaughter of Chedorlaomer, and of the kings that were with him, at the valley of Shaveh, which is the king's dale.

And Melchizedek king of Salem brought forth bread and wine: and he was the priest of the most high God.

And he blessed him, and said, Blessed be Abram of the most high God, possessor of heaven and earth: And blessed be the most high God, which hath delivered thine enemies into thy hand. And he gave him tithes of all. (Genesis 14:17–20)

Here, Abram's return to "the king's dale" brings him to the future site of Mt. Zion, where he partakes of the sacramental bread and wine with Melchizedek, which means "king of righteousness."

The cup and bread foreshadow the future Jewish festival of Passover, which would not be initiated for about another six centuries. Furthermore, Melchizedek is a type of Christ, whose sacrifice brought the New Covenant and the called-out body of believers known as the church. After the Church Age, His superior priesthood will bring the same covenant to the houses of Israel and Judah.

But Abram's actions foreshadow the simple truth that the four kingdoms must be defeated before the Kingdom is established. His contemporaries—the Gentile powers—sought allegiance with the old gods. Through any means available, their plan is to control the world. The fundamentals of this plan never change. Over and over again, it emerges. Again and again, it must be defeated.

God's people are part of a different and opposing plan, which depends upon the righteous bloodline of the Messiah. It is not only a bloodline, but a blood sacrifice.

THE PASSOVER PROPHECY

With Melchizedek officiating, Abram celebrated "Passover" before there even was a Passover. Once again, we see a future theme that reverberates through time until its final fulfillment. This one is seen in the life of Abram, then of Moses, Jesus, and finally, in the Great Tribulation.

Old Testament Egypt typifies the world system, or world order. In the

New Testament, the term is reduced simply to "the world." It is the system of idolatry, political power, and wealth woven into a tapestry of despotism that is the model for Israel's battle with the final Gentile kingdom.

The book of Exodus begins with the severe afflictions of an Israel in bondage to the despotic Pharaoh. Their slavery would have been bad enough, but Pharaoh feared that their population would grow to such an extent that it would become uncontrollable.

His response was to instigate a plan of genocide. It involved drowning the newborn Israelite sons. Through his parents' actions, Moses was saved and adopted by Pharaoh's daughter. As a young man, Moses identified with his people's plight. In anger, he slew an Egyptian slave master and was forced to flee to Midian.

There, at the Mountain of God, called Horeb, Moses was instructed to go back and liberate his people. In the court of Pharaoh, He presented the Lord's demand to the obstinate monarch, who refused him. The Lord was thus moved to judge Egypt in a series of ten plagues: blood…frogs… lice…flies…cattle disease…boils…fiery hail… locusts…darkness…and finally, death of the firstborn.

These plagues foreshadowed the dark time of the Great Tribulation, when Israel will finally emerge from the ultimate enslavement of the world system under the control of the Antichrist.

But the final plague—the death of the firstborn, in which the blood of the lamb was painted upon Israelite doorposts—forms a remarkable connection between past and future. It looks back to the historic moment when Abram drank of the cup with Melchizedek. But it also looks forward to its ultimate fulfillment in the Passover cup, which Jesus drank with His disciples before giving His own life's blood for all mankind.

That plague was one of the darkest moments of history, when the Lord sent death to the houses of Egypt:

> For I will pass through the land of Egypt this night, and will
> smite all the firstborn in the land of Egypt, both man and
> beast; and against all the gods of Egypt I will execute judgment:
> I am the LORD.

And the blood shall be to you for a token upon the houses where ye are: and when I see the blood, I will pass over you, and the plague shall not be upon you to destroy you, when I smite the land of Egypt.

And this day shall be unto you for a memorial; and ye shall keep it a feast to the LORD throughout your generations; ye shall keep it a feast by an ordinance for ever.

Seven days shall ye eat unleavened bread; even the first day ye shall put away leaven out of your houses: for whosoever eateth leavened bread from the first day until the seventh day, that soul shall be cut off from Israel. (Exodus 12:12–15)

The elements of this first Passover became eternally memorialized for Israel. The blood on the Israelites' doorways became a great symbol of deliverance from judgment and freedom from bondage. The lamb from which it came foreshadows the great "Lamb of God, which taketh away the sin of the world" (John 1:29).

The seven days of unleavened bread speak of freedom from the physical corruption of sin, represented by the leavening that would usually be present in ordinary bread. Jews refer to it both as the "bread of affliction" and the "bread of liberation."

By the time of Jesus in the first century, the lamb was still being slain, but Passover had become an ordered meal, including the recitation of Scripture and the taking of the four cups. As far back as Talmudic times, it was urged that even the poorest man in Israel should take all four. In fact, these cups are a prophecy. Each of them has a label, taken from Exodus 6:6 and 7:

Wherefore say unto the children of Israel, I am the LORD, and **I will bring you out** from under the burdens of the Egyptians, and **I will rid you out of their bondage**, and **I will redeem you** with a stretched out arm, and with great judgments:

And **I will take you to me for a people**, and I will be to you a God: and ye shall know that I am the LORD your God, which bringeth you out from under the burdens of the Egyptians. (emphasis added)

The first cup—of salvation—is so named because the Lord saved the people from Egypt's judgments.

The second—of deliverance—celebrates the actions of Moses, the deliverer.

The third—of redemption—recalls the miracles of the desert.

The fourth—of relationship—exalts the contract between the Lord and His people at the Mountain of God, and His promise to bring them into the Kingdom.

When Jesus took the fourth cup at the last supper, He activated an ages-long plan that would bring Him into full relationship with the redeemed. Of course, it centered on His perfect sacrifice on the Cross. He referred to this destiny as His "cup": "O my Father, if this cup may not pass away from me, except I drink it, thy will be done" (Matthew 26:42).

Then, at His arrest, he made the following statement: "Then said Jesus unto Peter, Put up thy sword into the sheath: the cup which my Father hath given me, shall I not drink it?" (John 18:11).

After Jesus finished His work upon the Cross, He instructed His disciples that He had taken to Himself all the intrinsic meanings of the cup. Paul succinctly states a simple truth that theologians have explained in thousands of pages during the millennia of the Church Age:

> The cup of blessing which we bless, is it not the communion
> of the blood of Christ? The bread which we break, is it not the
> communion of the body of Christ? For we being many are one
> bread, and one body: for we are all partakers of that one bread.
> (1 Corinthians 10:16, 17)

The Christian communion is the distilled essence of Passover. Jesus, the ultimate Passover Lamb, now personifies the cup and bread taken so long ago by Abram in the presence of Melchizedek.

Expanding Cycles

The four kings, Melchizedek's cup and the bread, and the cups of Passover offer us an example of the way our Lord—the Master of Time—views history. To Him, it is an ever-expanding series of waves, or cycles, that begins in small ways then expands across time to its full and final destiny. The saints, the prophets, and the apostles are woven into a tapestry of time whose themes and variations will complete a pattern of utmost perfection.

Spiritual types are simply early manifestations of completed time. God's plan is fulfilled from beyond the limits of time and space. What appear to be defeats are only stages of victory. The Assyrian and Babylonian captivities, the destruction of the Temples, the Crucifixion of Christ, the myriad wars, and man's continuing inhumanity to man are but waves in a completed design.

By contrast, Satan and his fallen angels seek to break the pattern in any way possible. They present themselves to man as gods, ancient and modern. Unregenerate men have an inner knowledge that leads them to break free from the timeline of history and follow the gods. They wish to crack the vault of eternity and mine its treasures.

They seek power, glory, and the control of their own destiny. In the future, one of them will rise to unprecedented power: "And he doeth great wonders, so that he maketh fire come down from heaven on the earth in the sight of men" (Revelation 13:13).

But the Antichrist's seemingly wondrous powers are simply a repetition of the ancient sin in the days of Noah. The dimensional barrier cannot be broken without consequence. That consequence is the Lord's final judgment.

3

THE DARK SIDE OF TIME TRAVEL

As we continue to probe the biblical mysteries of time and space, we become increasingly aware that Scripture presents us with a physical universe that is enclosed within other, invisible, spaces. In this chapter, we shall look first at the activity of the Lord's forces, then at the dark nature of certain evil powers that penetrate the barrier of time and space.

As we have seen, many of the Bible's main characters traveled in time. More importantly, they appear to have broken through some kind of barrier between our world and another dimensional existence.

When Paul traveled to the "third heaven," the experience was of such a nature that he couldn't tell whether he had made the journey bodily. This being the case, the question as to the reality of the experience is moot. He went to paradise—that is, another dimension—and returned. The text seems to suggest that he made the trip bodily.

In that dimension, time as we know it ceases to exist. As we have already said, from that perspective, it is possible to view any point along the earthly timeline. Paul's writings provide a great many revelations about the fate of the world and the church. Like the other prophets and apostles, he was given certain vital information about the future. This he has shared with the faithful of the church.

In such unique cases, human beings from this side of the dimensional wall are ushered into the presence of the Kingdom of Heaven for specific reasons. Sometimes, their journey brings needed information back into the world of the righteous. At other times (for example, in the case of Moses and Elijah at the Transfiguration), they may precisely fulfill a future role.

Beings from the other side also regularly come into our world. Usually, they are invisible to us. Sometimes, they are apparently indistinguishable from ordinary human beings. Remember the words of the writer to the Hebrews: "Be not forgetful to entertain strangers: for thereby some have entertained angels unawares" (Hebrews 13:2).

This suggests that angels frequently appear among men in human form. What are they doing? Perhaps they are watching over special events or superintending critical decision points in the lives of believers. They are sometimes referred to as "guardian angels." This role is suggested by the words of Jesus, who once said, "Take heed that ye despise not one of these little ones; for I say unto you, That in heaven their angels do always behold the face of my Father which is in heaven" (Matthew 18:10).

His words suggest that all of us, from childhood onward, have angels who are in some way attached to us as overseers or guardians. But angels apparently also interact with humans in this dimension as curious observers. As the work of redemption proceeds among human beings, these heavenly beings watch us with great interest. In a discourse about prophecy, Peter reveals this fact:

> Unto whom it was revealed, that not unto themselves, but unto us they did minister the things, which are now reported unto you by them that have preached the gospel unto you with the Holy Ghost sent down from heaven; which things the angels desire to look into. (1 Peter 1:12)

THE ONGOING BATTLE

In fact, these heavenly beings are observing the great spiritual battle that rages around the spreading of the gospel. Satan's forces are arrayed to block, confound, or muddle the good news of Jesus Christ in any way possible. The forces of the Lord are dedicated to stopping their efforts.

This brings us to one of the most prominently featured aspects of angelic behavior. They are the "hosts of heaven," God's powerful army. Often, they are seen in the act of destroying the enemies of Israel. At such times, they are capable of materializing in our universe with devastating effect upon human forces.

Two historical events perfectly illustrate this role. First, recall the historical moment in the life of Elisha the prophet, when Syria was at war with Israel.

The king of Syria was mightily frustrated by Elisha's ability to foretell where he would strike next. Naturally, his next move was to send troops against the prophet himself. When he learned that Elisha and his servant were at the city of Dothan, he moved quickly:

> Therefore sent he thither horses, and chariots, and a great host: and they came by night, and compassed the city about.
>
> And when the servant of the man of God was risen early, and gone forth, behold, an host compassed the city both with horses and chariots. And his servant said unto him, Alas, my master! how shall we do?
>
> And he answered, Fear not: for they that be with us are more than they that be with them.
>
> And Elisha prayed, and said, LORD, I pray thee, open his eyes, that he may see. And the LORD opened the eyes of the young man; and he saw: and, behold, the mountain was full of horses and chariots of fire round about Elisha.
> (2 Kings 6:14–17)

Elisha's servant panicked when he saw the Syrian forces rallied against them. However, Elisha knew that angelic forces had been summoned to protect them. He could see through the barrier that separated our dimension from the heavenly realm. His prayer enabled the servant to observe what he had been able to see from the beginning.

As we look at this region beyond our vision, we can gain many insights about the nature of time and space.

Another example of angelic power came in the days of King Hezekiah and the prophet Isaiah, when the Assyrian army was wiped out by a single angel: "And it came to pass that night, that the angel of the LORD went out, and smote in the camp of the Assyrians an hundred fourscore and five thousand: and when they arose early in the morning, behold, they were all dead corpses" (2 Kings 19:35).

The text of the Bible makes it more than clear that the holy forces of God can and do come to our aid when called. Conversely, many dark forces constantly attempt to frustrate the work of God.

THE DARK SIDE OF TIME TRAVEL

These forces from the dark side regularly penetrate the time/space continuum to do their evil work. In many ways and on many levels, they seek to defeat the redemptive work of God. Like the angels, their natural domain is the dimensional realm just beyond our vision. But they routinely depart from that domain and enter the natural physical world of human enterprise. Paul's famous declaration of this fact is more than a simple warning. It is, in fact, an explanation of the enemy's function: "For we wrestle not against flesh and blood, but against principalities, against powers, against the rulers of the darkness of this world, against spiritual wickedness in high places" (Ephesians 6:12).

How can we be said to struggle against something we cannot see? One answer is that evil forces have a direct—in some cases, visible—effect upon our physical world. We wrestle in the power of the Spirit. They seek to influence this world both spiritually and physically.

The "principalities" mentioned by Paul are "archons," from the Greek word, *arche*, meaning ancient, primal powers. They are the remnant of the fallen angels who remain free to battle the angelic forces of God. In Romans 8:38, they are mentioned in the same context as the holy angels:

For I am persuaded, that neither death, nor life, nor angels, nor principalities, nor powers, nor things present, nor things to come, Nor height, nor depth, nor any other creature, shall be able to separate us from the love of God, which is in Christ Jesus our Lord. (Romans 8:38)

Second in rank below the archons are the "powers," called in the Greek *exousia,* or "delegated authorities." Presumably, they are also angels, perhaps lower in capability than their superiors.

Paul then mentions "rulers of the darkness." These are *kosmokrators,* or "world rulers." That is, they dominate the intricate bureaucracies of this world system. They are the hordes of demon spirits whose tasks are to tilt the minds of human leaders toward the cause of Satan.

It is important to understand the distinction between these ranks. Later, in chapter four, we'll take a longer, more detailed look at this hierarchy.

A Dark History

Many of the fallen angels are now imprisoned, awaiting judgment for the evils they concocted prior to the Flood. The epistles of Jude and Peter inform us about this vital information. These are the angels who left their primary domain in time/space to take human women to themselves. Such illicit unions brought forth monstrous hybrids, which became known as the Titans of ancient Greek mythology.

"And the angels which kept not their first estate, but left their own habitation, he hath reserved in everlasting chains under darkness unto the judgment of the great day" (Jude 6). In this statement, Jude clearly refers to the events of Genesis. Peter makes reference to the same historical events, which he uses as an illustration of the Lord's certain judgment of false teachers: "For if God spared not the angels that sinned, but cast them down to hell, and delivered them into chains of darkness, to be reserved unto judgment" (2 Peter 2:4).

These dark angels followed their iniquitous leader, Lucifer, in his ancient rebellion. Virtually every ancient world culture records historical references to this sad chapter in the chronicles of humanity. Any attempt to reconcile secular and biblical history must sooner or later face the fact that there were indeed hybrid offspring from the union of angels and human women.

The first wave of the hybrids was destroyed in the Great Flood. When this took place, their unredeemable souls were from that moment forward doomed to wander the earth. In one sense, they are the pitiful damned. In another, they are the hapless and evil thralls of the satanic world system, bound to give allegiance to the devil's schemes. But they began as the children of the gods.

Ancient Greek histories virtually always support this view. Hellenistic writers saw demons as friendly spirit guides and the bearers of gifts and ideas to humanity. Writing about their origins, Plato, in *Timeaus,* speaks in a matter-of-fact manner about their presence:

> As for the other spiritual beings [*daimonia,* or demons], it is
> beyond our task to know and speak of how they came to be.
> We should accept on faith the assertions of those figures of the
> past who claimed to be the offspring of gods. They must surely
> have been well informed about their own ancestors.[17]

Plato clearly states the Greek belief that the race of demons originated as the children of the gods. Elsewhere, he states that the gods' children were borne by earthly, human women.

Hierocles, in his commentary on the *Golden Verses of Pythagoras,* writes, "Honor likewise the terrestrial demons by rendering them the worship lawfully due to them." He makes a strong distinction between the gods and those he refers to as the "terrestrial demons," whom he considers to be the souls of glorified heroes, now separated from their former bodies.[18]

Thus, for Greeks, the spirits of the offspring of the gods were messengers and helpers. But the Bible relegates them to the lowest echelon of sentient life. They are the unredeemable *rephaim* (רפאים), who are always mentioned in the context of judgment:

> O Lord our God, other lords beside thee have had dominion over us: but by thee only will we make mention of thy name. They are **dead**, they shall not live; they are deceased, they shall not rise: therefore hast thou visited and destroyed them, and made all their memory to perish. (Isaiah 26:13, 14 emphasis added)

Here, the word translated "dead" is *rephaim*, the human/alien monster variously known as a "giant," or as the spirit of a household idol. In the Old Testament, these idols are sometimes referred to as *teraphim*.

But for the lost souls of these hapless monsters, there is to be no resurrection. As spirit creatures, they roam in search of a body to inhabit, knowing that they have no future other than to scavenge some kind of life from the living.

Jesus' own words on the subject make this clear:

> When the unclean spirit is gone out of a man, he walketh through dry places, seeking rest; and finding none, he saith, I will return unto my house whence I came out.
>
> And when he cometh, he findeth it swept and garnished. Then goeth he, and taketh to him seven other spirits more wicked than himself; and they enter in, and dwell there: and the last state of that man is worse than the first. (Luke 11:24–26)

For the present study, it is also important to note that the *rephaim* are also seen in the Old Testament as giants. A good example is Og of Bashan:

> For only Og king of Bashan remained of the remnant of giants; behold, his bedstead was a bedstead of iron; is it not in Rabbath of the children of Ammon? nine cubits was the length thereof, and four cubits the breadth of it, after the cubit of a man. (Deuteronomy 3:11)

The word "giants" in the above passage is translated from the Hebrew *rephaim,* the same word used in Isaiah 26 to describe the lost souls of the dead. But Og was physically very real. He slept in a fifteen-foot-long bed! Thus, the spirits of the *rephaim* intrude into this dimension as hybrid monsters. From time to time, they are capable of incarnating as fleshly creatures.

Apparently, rebellious spirit creatures in the heavens accomplish this in the same way as their predecessors did prior to the Flood. They interbreed with earthly women to produce a hybrid race bent on short-circuiting God's plan for the righteous.

Once separated from their bodies, however, they are the damned of the timeless dimension just beyond our sight. Ever in search of a bodily home, they are the demons so well known in Scripture.

It is extremely significant that Jesus prophesied that in the days just prior to His return, the horrors of pre-Flood existence would again arise to plague mankind:

> But of that day and hour knoweth no man, no, not the angels
> of heaven, but my Father only. But as the days of Noe were,
> so shall also the coming of the Son of man be. For as in the
> days that were before the flood they were eating and drinking,
> marrying and giving in marriage, until the day that Noe
> entered into the ark, And knew not until the flood came, and
> took them all away; so shall also the coming of the Son of man
> be. (Matthew 24:26–39)

Jesus makes it plain that when He comes back, the world will resemble that described in Genesis chapter 6. In that culture, the fallen angels interbred with human women, producing so-called "giants." They were the heroes of Greek mythology and Greek history.

In the discourse of Jesus, "marrying and giving in marriage" includes more than just human matrimony. It apparently also describes the illicit unions between fallen angels and their human victims. This being the case, if we are living in the days just prior to Jesus' return, we must expect the same sort of intrusion into human affairs...on the same, massive scale.

From the Dark Side

According to many witnesses and documentary studies, this is exactly what is happening. Transdimensional interlopers are coming in waves. So-called alien abduction is becoming a common occurrence. Demons doing this evil work routinely tamper with time and space.

Before looking at the current state of affairs in this arena, let us make a general statement about the history of demon lore as it has been revealed in the last few centuries. It is commonly held that the term "flying saucer" was coined around 1947. And indeed, that was the date when the imagination of the world was caught. But in 1978, when a Texas farmer referred to an object he described as a "large saucer," he was ignored by the world.

Long before, in the year 1180, a flying luminous object was said by witnesses in Japan to resemble an "earthenware vessel." In Japan, in the tenth, eleventh, and twelfth centuries, many similar sightings were recorded. Objects were called "drums," "flaming stars," and "wheels."

In India, ancient records refer to "Siddhas" that could become heavy or light at will and could fly into space and vanish from view in an instant.

France, Spain, and Germany all have hundreds of similar references in their medieval histories. UFO researcher Jacques Vallee quotes the words of Abogard, archbishop of Lyons, France. In the ninth century, this man was celebrated as among the most learned men alive. He wrote:

> We have, however, seen and heard many men plunged in such
> great stupidity, sunk in such depths of folly, as to believe that
> there is a certain region, which they call Magonia, whence ships
> sail in the clouds, in order to carry back to that region those
> fruits of the earth which are destroyed by hail and tempests;
> the sailors paying rewards to the storm wizards and themselves
> receiving corn and other produce. Out of the number of those
> whose blind folly was deep enough to allow them to believe
> these things possible, I saw several exhibiting in a certain

concourse of people, four persons in bonds—three men and a woman who they said had fallen from these same ships; after keeping them for some days in captivity they had brought them before the assembled multitude, as we have said, in our presence to be stoned. But truth prevailed.[19]

In his book, *Passport to Magonia,* Vallee documents the common historical belief—leading up to the present day—in Magonia, a timeless land just beyond human view. In Europe, and particularly in the British Isles, this belief was codified in the lore of elves, fauns, fairies, leprechauns, trolls, and other such supernatural creatures.[20]

Fairyland is actually nothing more than a cultural view of demonic activity, interpreted in the language of the local culture. In the latter part of the seventeeth century, a Scottish scholar and pastor, Robert Kirk, wrote *The Secret Commonwealth of Elves, Fauns and Fairies.* In it, he attempted to systematically describe the mythical land beyond the veil.

He described these wee folk as having "fluid" bodies occupying a zone between men and angels. He said they could appear and disappear at will, and carry away anything they like. They live inside the earth in caves, where they have a hierarchy of leaders. They have no devotion to God, nor do they have any religion.[21]

Clearly, he described demons, the *daimonia* of Greek history. These elves and fairies are deceptive liars who work their schemes among superstitious men. Their work conforms exactly to the demonic activity of every age, including ours.

Thus, Elfland by any of its many names has been described as a sort of "parallel universe" that exists alongside our own. From time to time, with the opening of a dimensional door, it becomes visible to certain people. In Scotland, Ireland, and Wales, the elves from the "other side" are thought of as the "good people." Like the *daimonia* of ancient history, they are thought to bring good luck, help, and guidance to humans who curry their favor.

The points where the little people meet humanity are called "fairy rings." These are spinning vortices of energy, sometimes said to hover above the ground or to be supported upon pillars. Their resemblance to the modern UFO is too obvious to be overlooked. As is repeatedly the case, they are able to modify their appearance to suit the contemporary culture where they appear. The "wee folk" of the Celtic tribes perfectly conform to the behavior of "alien space invaders" known to modern Americans.

The rings are often seen in conjunction with a mound in the earth or a circle of stones. Particularly in north Scotland, the local folk used to leave offerings of bread, butter, milk, cheese, meat, or poultry for the elves. In this way, they were placated and would desist from their thievery.

Such rings are in perfect concordance with the biblical "high places," where the ancient Canaanites and apostate Israelites brought offerings to the fertility gods and goddesses, including Baal.

However, in spite of the efforts to placate them, the Celtic elves could also be quite fickle, evil, and larcenous. In fact, one of their main activities is said to be kidnapping. This, they do in different ways and for different reasons. But their abductions follow the recognizable pattern of demonology throughout the ages.

Numerous accounts of fairy kidnappings deal with the phenomenon of the *changeling*. Accounts tell of the capture of pregnant women, whose babies were kept by the fairies or exchanged with one of their own, whom they allowed to return to this world. Virtually every tribe shared its own version of the changeling phenomenon.

The belief in changelings was quite widespread in the Middle Ages, and even later. For example, in Martin Luther's *Table Talk*, there is a passage in which Luther declares to the Prince of Anhalt that he should sink a certain local man in the River Moldau. This man, he feels, is a changeling. That is, Luther didn't regard him as completely human!

The common belief in changelings was explained as the elves' and fairies' need to improve their race by interbreeding. This familiar theme is often invoked in modern abduction lore. Often it was said that the elves would return and take the mothers for a time, to obtain their milk and loving care in the initial process of child-rearing.

As we shall see, this identical phenomenon is a central part of the demonic intrusions into today's world. Only today, it is much more widespread.

The Relativity of Time

However, before moving to the modern appearance of the ancient phenomenon, there is another aspect of fairy lore that should be discussed. It is the effect of time relativity.

A famous story from Wales (recorded in about 1825) counted as fact in a number of different sources, is the tale of two men—Rhys and Llewellyn—who worked for a local farmer. One night, on their way home after a long day's work, Rhys thought he heard music. He told Llewellyn to stop and listen, but the man heard nothing. Rhys felt compelled to dance to the beautiful music he heard, and told Llewellyn to go on ahead with the horses.

Llewellyn arrived home, alone, with the horses, and Rhys' panicked family accused him of having murdered his companion along the way. He was jailed, and the men of the town took poor Llewellyn to search for Rhys' murdered corpse. Returning to the spot where Llewellyn swore he had left him, the men found nothing. After hours of looking, Llewellyn suddenly cried, "Hush! I hear music. I hear sweet harps."

The other members of the search party heard nothing. But Llewellyn had discovered the outer rim of a fairy ring. He asked others to place their foot on his. Then they, too, heard the music. What's more, they were able to peer into the world of the elves. There, they saw Rhys dancing in the circle with the wee folk. On his next circuit, they grabbed his clothing and pulled him from the circle.

Rhys was shocked by the absence of the horses and the presence of the search party. He pleaded with the men to let him finish the dance, *which he swore had not lasted more than five minutes.* Try as they might, the villagers could not convince Rhys that a whole day had elapsed. He became depressed, was taken ill, and soon died.

His story is only one of many similar tales from all over the world. In Europe, China, and the Americas, Rip Van Winkle-type stories abound. The common man once believed that when the wee folk took one into their world, time stopped. Meanwhile, back in his home world, time proceeded at its normal pace.

Invaders from the timeless dimension visit humanity for dark and evil purposes. As stated, they have spiritual motives—primarily, to thwart the plan of God and the good news of the gospel. But they also seem to have physical motives having to do with genetic manipulation aimed at increasing the vitality of their own species. An evil side effect of their experiments is the corruption of human genealogy. Or, perhaps that is their prime purpose.

This brings us once again to the UFO phenomenon. It continues to plague the world as a transient spectacle that defies analysis, yet has come to influence governments around the world. The deep secrecy that surrounds its continuing presence has changed the very nature of the United States government. UFO files are held to be "above top secret."

Actually, the modern phenomenon is simply a slight modification of the demonic lore that has stretched out across the millennia since the Great Flood of Noah.

MISSING TIME

Mysterious lights in the night, daylight disks, flying saucers, and huge ships that land to disgorge various "extraterrestrial" aliens have become as familiar as the corner grocery store. Are they men from other planets who are simply exploring or observing? Are they tourists on an extended sightseeing trip?

The modern record, now over fifty years long, answers these questions in the extreme negative. It is now quite clear that the mysterious kidnappings in the enchanted energy circles of the elves and fairies were but a foreshadowing of the full-scale "UFO abduction" experience. Investigators and documentarians around the world have now established a chain of evidence showing that an evil program is underway.

As humanity inexorably heads into the latter-day social disintegration prophesied by the apostles, the dimensional door is opening wider and wider. What began in 1947 as a series of top-secret stories about saucer crashes and tiny alien bodies has widened into a broad, self-defined culture with its own hierarchy of beings, history, and interactive pattern of behavior with humanity.

The armies of little gray aliens, bureaucratic insectoid commanders, reptilian captains, and striking blond overlords have produced the illusion that earth is about to join a confederation of planets. This view, of course, is heavily bolstered by popular fiction, which almost always adopts this view of the future.

As our technology brings us to the dawn of space travel, the aliens are supposedly here to shepherd us into the realm of interplanetary society. We crude earthlings are incapable of handling the transition all by ourselves. Therefore, assistants from other galaxies have come as our mentors.

Or so they say. Actually, thousands of witness reports tell of a much darker reality. It began in the sixties in the famous case of Barney and Betty Hill. While returning home, they were abducted, taken aboard a "ship," and subjected to a series of pseudo-medical "tests." Only they didn't remember this. Instead, they later noted with great curiosity that the trip had taken hours longer than it should have. In what became a pattern that would be repeated thousands of times in the future abductions of others, their memories had been blanked out, leaving them floundering with the classic "missing-time" experience.[22]

The "alien" ships pop into view, take their victims through walls or ceilings, and pop out again...for hours or days on our time scale. But within their zone, time seems hardly to matter at all. For example, look at the following account of an actual interview from a 1994 book named *Abduction*. Paul, the abductee, is being escorted by an alien being aboard a "ship" during one of his experiences. His captor informs him that this isn't the first time he's been aboard:

The figure that was escorting Paul showed him a bed that was rather like a human bed with sheets, but "it's floating." He told Paul, "They're your quarters. You're here. You're here when we go on these trips." In fact, the "quarters" felt familiar to Paul, for he estimated he had been there "seventy times." Paul felt confusion and disbelief then and now, but says "I feel like I'm here. I feel like this is the room that he's showing me that I'm in when I go to where he takes me."

At this point, I asked Paul about the timing and frequency of these many visits. Paul replied, "He's saying they're all connected, that it's the same."[23]

This example is typical of the bizarre scenarios and revelations given by the victims of the so-called Non-Human Entities. The case studies in this book were assembled by a man of impeccable credentials. He is John R. Mack, MD, professor of psychiatry at the Cambridge Hospital, Harvard Medical School. He has investigated well over a hundred cases of alien abduction. Patiently, he has addressed the psychological and spiritual transformations that are hallmarks of this strange and growing spectacle.

But note one thing about young Paul's report. He believes that he has been abducted many, many times. To him, they are all separate events. However, his "host" is quick to tell him that they are "all connected." That is, from the perspective of his alien dimension, they are undifferentiated in time.

This illustrates a point that is made again and again as demons intrude into our realm. Specifically, there are curious gaps, dilations, and contractions in time/space, causing hapless victims to lapse into confusion. Victims may unexplainably "black out" and later recall what they did during a time period. Or, they may spend long periods of "time" that later turn out to be quite short in this dimension.

The exact opposite has also taken place, in which victims estimate that a very short time has passed while, in fact, they were gone for hours or even days.

In a famous South American incident reported in many sources, an Argentinian couple, Mr. and Mrs. Vidal, lived through just such a horrifying experience. Their case was first reported on June, 5, 1968, and has been validated in many studies.

Residents of Buenos Aires, the Vidals were driving between the cities of Chascomus and Maipu. They recall being enveloped in a mist or fog, then falling asleep. Seemingly, a short time later, they woke up to discover that they were in an unfamiliar location. Instead of a highway, they were now on a dirt road, in a rural area.

After a frantic search for something familiar, they finally discovered that they were in Mexico—almost a thousand miles away from their point of origin! After initial contacts with local police authorities, they ended up in the Argentine consulate in Mexico, where they received help in contacting relatives for their return trip.

Their car, a Peugeot 403, was in good shape, except for the fact that it was now totally devoid of all paint. It was confiscated "for further study," some reports saying that it ended up in the United States for laboratory analysis. It has never been seen again.

To their astonishment, the Vidals were missing forty-eight hours from their lives. Yet, to them, *virtually no time at all* seemed to have passed.

In South America, the ancient clans have many tribal histories of similar events. In the May–June 1968 *Flying Saucer Review,* Brian Stross writes of certain stories told about otherworldly beings among the Tenejapa tribes: "They are believed to be beings from another world, and some have been seen flying with some kind of rocket-like thing attached to the back. With this rocket they are said occasionally to have carried off people."[24]

In the same periodical, Gordon Creighton writes:

This *ikal* of the Tzotzils flies through the air. Sometimes he
steals women, and the women so taken are remarkably prolific,
and may bear a child once a week, or once a month, or even

daily. The offspring are black, and they learn the art of flying inside their father's cave.[25]

In their details, these legends seem ridiculous. But in general, they conform to the pattern of such phenomena in their myriad appearances to every world culture. How can a woman bear a child in a day? This seems impossible...unless she is taken to a place where nine months can pass in what—to us—is only twenty-four hours.

These *ikals,* of course, are the demons—capable of manipulating time and space, and appearing in any guise suitable to their deceptive purpose at the moment. They are spirit guides, little people, leprechauns, elves, fairies, or space aliens. *But they are all the same, and have been for thousands of years.*

DIMENSION OF DARKNESS

From the human perspective, these beings "materialize and dematerialize." In actuality, they are not dematerializing at all. They are simply disappearing through the time/space boundary. Humans, trapped in this dimension, cannot follow.

In the last few decades, our military forces have attempted—on countless occasions with complete ineffectuality—to catch the beings, but they are hopelessly outmaneuvered in every case. Most often, the otherworldly visitors simply disappear, winking out as if someone turned off a light. We don't know exactly where they go, but it has to do with the nether regions of their dimension, which is apparently quite close to our own.

A well-known biblical narrative offers some help with this question:

Then the angel that talked with me went forth, and said unto me, Lift up now thine eyes, and see what is this that goeth forth. And I said, What is it? And he said, This is an ephah that goeth forth. He said moreover, This is their resemblance through all the earth.

And, behold, there was lifted up a talent of lead: and this is a woman that sitteth in the midst of the ephah. And he said, This is wickedness. And he cast it into the midst of the ephah; and he cast the weight of lead upon the mouth thereof.

Then lifted I up mine eyes, and looked, and, behold, there came out two women, and the wind was in their wings; for they had wings like the wings of a stork: and they lifted up the ephah between the earth and the heaven.

Then said I to the angel that talked with me, Whither do these bear the ephah? And he said unto me, To build it an house in the land of Shinar: and it shall be established, and set there upon her own base. (Zechariah 5:5–10)

This vision of the woman of Shinar (Babylon) is quite graphic, offering a dramatic image of a "flying ephah." We have long since concluded that this is the archetypal unidentified flying object. In Hebrew history, the ephah is a basket of a specific size used for carrying grain and produce. It would roughly compare with the modern bushel basket. Its importance to this study is not in its size, but in its shape.

The ephah in this story is a container with a heavy lid of lead. If the entire apparatus, as described, were lifted into the sky and hovered there, spinning, it would resemble the innumerable sightings of flying earthenware, cylinders, drums, spheres, and so on. The angel says exactly this to Zechariah, telling him that this is the way they look all over the earth.

Then, an odd thing happens. The angel apparently lifts the ephah's leaden top and shows Zechariah an evil woman. The context suggests that she tries to get out. But the angel shoves her back down into the ephah and slams the lid back again, telling Zechariah in the process that she is the personification of wickedness. Given her final destination, it is not stretching things to say that she is the enigmatic spirit of Mystery Babylon.

After this, two winged women come forth. The three of them and the flying ephah return to Babylon, where it will land on a designated place. It is absolutely clear that this picture describes the phenomenon of the sort that we have been describing.

But what we have never called to attention in the past is the actual path of the flight back to Babylon. The ephah is said to rise to a space "between the earth and the heaven." Or, as the text says in Hebrew, "between the earth and the heavens."

What is the region described here? In Genesis 1:20, birds were created to fly "above the earth in the open firmament of heaven [the heavens]." In Hebrew, the same word is used here as in Zechariah's vision.

So the ephah flies *between the visible earth and heavens*, neither in the earth nor in the sky. In other words, it is *between* the place where men walk and birds fly. Can we conclude that it is operating in a zone that puts it just beyond the vision of ordinary mortals? It seems that this is exactly the case.

And this becomes particularly obvious when we compare Zechariah's vision with a New Testament Scripture that describes Satan's zone of operation: "Wherein in time past ye walked according to the course of this world, according to the prince of the power of the air, the spirit that now worketh in the children of disobedience" (Ephesians 2:2).

Paul's purpose here is to illustrate that the path of sinful man is dictated in the world system by a prince, whose power is situated in the "air." This word is translated from the Greek *aer*, the word used to describe the region of the atmosphere. Certainly, Satan can and does access the entire earth. Moment by moment, he searches it to see what he can devour. He travels in the same region as that used by the women in the ephah.

Is he visible to mortals? Absolutely not. But there are times when he and his demonic underlings *do* become visible to accomplish certain evil purposes.

In their dimension, lying just beyond our earthly sight, they conspire in an expanse where time and space can be bent toward their wicked goals. It seems that they cannot travel into the far future or the distant past. Nor can they know the things that are reserved for God alone.

But they can apparently see just enough to convince gullible earthlings that they do, in fact, know the future. Seers, trance channelers, clairvoyants, and soothsayers of all stripes are taken in by their multidimensional legerdemain. They operate through stealth, lies, and fear, not daring to operate openly and in the light of day.

In actuality, their power pales in comparison to the One who is truly in control. He is both omniscient and omnipresent. His intelligence encompasses all time and space.

Satan is limited to a zone of darkness that gives him just enough latitude to be destructive.

4

SEASONS ROLLING
TOWARD REDEMPTION

W

hen God created the heavens and the earth, He created more than just a physical universe; He created time. Its initiation is seen in the days of Creation, beginning with the command, "Let there be light" (Genesis 1:3). On the seventh day, the Creation was finished. For mankind, the flow of time had begun.

God created time with a pattern and a plan. It is neither arbitrary nor pointless. Time was created around the central theme of redemption. Humanity was born in a cauldron of evil and subjected to the schemes of the Serpent. Little did Satan know that he had entered a timeline that would carry him to his own doom. Like a raging river, time is carrying him toward Judgment Day.

The Bible deals uniquely with the abstruse matters of fate, destiny, and eternity. Across the millennia, spiritual schemes and philosophical assertions have attempted to deal with the paradoxical problem of evil. The human tendency is to view man as intrinsically good. But the human race is pockmarked by a twisted history of evil. The march of the Gentile kingdoms has produced a litany of repulsive and demoralizing outrages. Holocausts, genocides, enslavements, tortures and torments, thefts, dictatorships, wars, and myriad individual crimes are the hallmarks of humanity.

If man is good, how do we account for his evil history? Philosophers have used every cogitative trick in the book to put evil in a box. Some have imagined utopian solutions, planning perfect societies that will remove what they imagine to be the reason for evil: social injustice. Others have actually stated that evil is "good." They declare it to be the mechanism of cultural revolution (or evolution), whereby man is progressively lifted to his final destiny.

Comparative religion sees man's invented systems of worship as constructive, no matter how idolatrous or even murderous they may be.

Both of these beliefs deny the existence of a reigning evil superpower—a devil, or the biblical Satan. They see victory over evil as the institution of a superior system of thought, whether political or religious. In that imagined future, they see a world in which man has tamed his baser impulses, bringing a glorious unification of society and nature.

This is humanism, which is always tinged with some sort of religious effort.

The Bible's History of Philosophy

In stark contrast to the humanist view, the Bible declares that there is a heavenly order. Moreover, it is the principal cause in the course of human history. It is the source of a directed timeline aimed at redemption. Ultimately, it will bring the faithful remnant to the place of complete restoration. This is based upon the Messianic plan, in which Christ rose into the heavens until the time of His return: "Whom the heaven must receive until the times of restitution of all things, which God hath spoken by the mouth of all his holy prophets since the world began" (Acts 3:21).

Scripture speaks eloquently and respectfully of God's throne, even mentioning the covering cherubs who are its guardians. It also tells us about Lucifer, the revolutionary who attempted to overthrow the Lord God. We discover that the serpent fell to earth, where he has a political domain, a lordship, and physical realm, over which he reigns as a "roaring lion...seeking whom he may devour" (1 Peter 5:8).

It is this clash—not evolution or astronomical accident—that has produced human history. The Bible asserts that evil rulers are nothing more than pawns in the hands of Satan. All the religions and philosophies in the world ignore this simple fact, substituting a variety of explanations for this planet's troubled history.

SLAVES OF THE TIMELINE

Over the centuries, there has been a great deal of speculation about man's one-way journey along the timeline. Is it a detailed engraving, prewritten in the vaults of eternity? Or is it subject to moment-by-moment variation, as decisions and interactions tick off the milliseconds?

Perhaps the best way to understand this conundrum is to revisit the history of sin. In a curious way, Satan may provide the answer to the complex question that evokes the deep subject of predestination. Biblically, he has one foot in heaven and the other on earth. Therefore, viewing him gives us an exceptional perspective on the subject of time and space.

As we attempt to understand sin, salvation, and the restored universe, the Serpent's chronicled activities give us much insight into the workings of destiny. It is quite clear that he made a choice. He was anointed to watch over God's throne, but he chose instead to usurp that throne.

His choice determined his destiny. Destiny implies a future, and a future implies a timeline. Satan is (and apparently always has been) attached to the destiny of planet earth. The world system is a battleground measured in time. Yet Satan is a creature of eternity.

Did his sin ground him in time? Indeed, this seems to be the case. Once, in the realm of God's throne room, he apparently believed that he could discern—and even control—the future. Now, it is obvious that he is bound by the timeline of redemption and judgment.

Solar Clock, Festival Calendar

Our home planet, earth, is set in a kind of celestial timepiece. The complex motions of the solar system mark out myriad interactions between planets and their moons. They also create the seasons on our planet, marked by the ebb and flow of solar energy. Spring, summer, fall, and winter mark the flow of years as the arrow of time surges inexorably forward.

But biblically, the seasons are not mere markers of time. They are the harbingers of things to come. From the biblical perspective, they are the seven festivals seen in the Jewish calendar: Passover, Unleavened Bread, Firstfruits, Pentecost, Rosh HaShanah, Yom Kippur, and Tabernacles. Year by year, as the earth revolves around the sun and rotates upon its axis, they repeat the drama of creation, fall, and redemption.

God has ordained the motions of His immense chronometer. It is no accident that the hour angles and declinations of the earth's orbit have produced a pattern of planting and harvest, of pruning and picking, that are the template of our Lord's redemptive activities.

The pattern of these festivals is a microcosm of the ages. They foreshadow the march of the millennia, from the Exodus to the Tribulation—from the Crucifixion to the Kingdom—ultimately from the Garden of Eden to the New Jerusalem. Looking again at the order of the seven basic feasts shows that they demonstrate the Lord's view of history—past, present, and future.

Today, the nation Israel observes its new year on Tishri 1, the festival of Rosh HaShanah. This has come to be called the "civil New Year." Beginning with that date, and taken in order, Israel's seven feasts tell the story of a redeemed future of joy in the presence of the Lord.

Rosh HaShanah commemorates the creation, and is called "the birthday of the world." But just as in the biblical history, it is immediately followed by Yom Kippur, the Day of Atonement, recalling man's sin and the need for blood redemption.

Next in order of the feasts is Tabernacles. In prospect, it looks forward to Israel in the Kingdom Age. But its origin is in the Exodus, when Israel began a march toward the future possession of the Land:

> Ye shall dwell in booths seven days; all that are Israelites born shall dwell in booths: That your generations may know that I made the children of Israel to dwell in booths, when I brought them out of the land of Egypt: I am the LORD your God. (Leviticus 23:42)

That march out of Egypt toward the Promised Land began about three and a half millennia ago. It has yet to see its completion, but it is foreshadowed in the feast of Tabernacles.

The next four feasts are devoted to Messianic redemption. They begin with Passover.

Through the long winter, the land rests, awaiting spring and the spring festivals, beginning with Passover. Like Tabernacles, it was instituted in the Exodus from Egypt. It is centered around the blood of the lamb, which was, of course shed on the Cross at the First Coming of the Messiah.

In the Passover, only unleavened bread is eaten. Its ceremonial breaking is the symbol of the body of the Messiah, broken for His people.

Firstfruits is the feast of His resurrection. He is the "firstfruits of them that slept" (1 Corinthians 15:20).

Finally comes Pentecost, which Gentile believers recognize as the birth date of the Church Age. To the Jews, it is associated with the giving of the Law, and the birth and death of King David.

These feasts mark *time,* and it is in *time* that God has chosen to work out the myriad details of redemption. Though Satan has access to heaven, his authority is tightly linked to the physical reality of humanity's timeline. Once a ruler at the throne of God, his destiny is now linked to sinful man, whom he first corrupted. He is no longer "the anointed cherub that covereth" (Ezekiel 28:14). Now, he is but a dark shadow of his former self...a cruel overlord, doomed to walk the earth until his final destruction.

HIS EVIL WORK

This plain fact is seen in the narrative that opens the book of Job:

> Now there was a day when the sons of God came to present
> themselves before the Lord, and Satan came also among them.
> And the LORD said unto Satan, Whence comest thou? Then
> Satan answered the LORD, and said, From going to and fro in
> the earth, and from walking up and down in it. (Job 1:6, 7)

Satan is a "son of God." This meeting at God's throne is truly mysterious. Who are the other sons of God? We don't know. Nor do we know
exactly why they are meeting. When the Lord asks Satan about his daily
activities, the old Serpent says that he has been surveying planet earth.

If the Lord is omniscient, why does He even have to ask? Apparently
it is part of some public record, in which the Lord asks Satan to make
an open accounting of himself. Note that he does not tell Satan that he
has no right to the earth. Rather, he offers a challenge concerning Job,
an upright man. In effect, Satan is challenged to corrupt Job, if possible.
This is, in fact, the devil's major work. A bit farther along, we shall look
at the nature of the Lord's challenge to him.

The once-anointed cherub, now known as the evil Satan, is extremely
active. As he regularly penetrates the dimension barrier to do business
in our world, he moves in the arena of larceny and murder. First and
foremost, his domain and his rule are dark and depressing. Having first
corrupted man, he must now harvest the evil fruit of his work.

As we have already observed, Satan sinned in eternity. His sentence is
being meted out in time. Once, he was a watcher, appointed to the throne
of God. From what we know, his area of responsibility encompassed the
earth and its general neighborhood. Through a divinely established system of protocols unknown to man, but inferred by his behavior, he still
retains his dominion over this realm...even after his fall!

His first appearance in the Bible demonstrates that he considers the
earth his rightful regime. As the Serpent in the garden, he eloquently

convinced the innocent Eve that he—not God—held the secrets of eternity. She chose to believe him. Even as he did his evil deed, his initial sin was already past history. Long before, he had attempted to usurp the throne of God.

God allowed him to corrupt humanity even at its innocent beginnings. The universe must have shuddered at the moment in time when Eve decided to follow the Serpent's lead. At the consummation of this momentous occasion, she and her partner were doomed to a life of struggle that set the tone for future humanity.

A Mark in Time

More importantly, Eve's transgression placed a marker in time. The celestial clock began to tick off the minutes, hours, days, years, and millennia toward the final redemption of the world. The real significance of Adam and Eve's sin lay in its ultimate result, not its immediate effect. That is, it initiated the most important prophecy in the Bible:

> And the LORD God said unto the serpent, Because thou hast done this, thou art cursed above all cattle, and above every beast of the field; upon thy belly shalt thou go, and dust shalt thou eat all the days of thy life:
> And I will put enmity between thee and the woman, and between thy seed and her seed; it shall bruise thy head, and thou shalt bruise his heel. (Genesis 3:15)

Once free to plot, plan, and scheme in his own domain, Satan was now entangled in the prophetic timeline. Divine planning had reduced him to a mere player instead of the supreme leader of his own dreams.

The Messiah was coming to bruise his head, or may we say *his headship*. God proclaimed that the offspring of the woman whom he had corrupted would be the device of his own devastation.

At this point, Satan must have realized that instead of capturing humanity as his own personal company of slaves, he had sown the seeds of his own demise. From this point on, his bid for significance and continued power resided in his ability to corrupt humanity, creating for himself a doomed and damned following.

Suspecting that his own downfall was a possibility, what better plan than to bring as many souls as possible into his own camp? Remember, to this day, he still functions as though he can pull off a personal victory.

It hardly needs to be said that the activities of the Kingdom of Heaven are far above human understanding. There must be innumerable traditions and conventions among the countless created beings over whom God reigns. Furthermore, the heavens exist in a state that the Bible refers to as "eternity." It is somehow different from being locked in time, yet there is a sense of time there.

The angels, whose battles rage in that dimension, are nevertheless somehow subject to delay, which implies time. Perhaps it does not operate in the same way as what we call "time," but it is sequential in nature. Some events occur before other events. If there is the concept of "before" and "after," something like a timeline is presented. There is a well-known example of this thought.

In Daniel chapter 10, the prophet had sequestered himself in fasting and prayer for three weeks. Apparently, he was deeply troubled about a matter that had come to his attention, and needed to understand what it meant. At the end of his twenty-one days of supplication, an angel arrived. The heavenly messenger is unidentified, but some have suggested that he might have been Gabriel, since that particular angel had appeared to Daniel twice before.

Given the circumstances of the case, however, this seems unlikely. In any case, the angel revealed a strange thing to Daniel:

Then said he unto me, Fear not, Daniel: for from the first day that thou didst set thine heart to understand, and to chasten thyself before thy God, thy words were heard, and I am come for thy words.

But the prince of the kingdom of Persia withstood me one
and twenty days: but, lo, Michael, one of the chief princes,
came to help me; and I remained there with the kings of Persia.
(Daniel 10:12, 13)

The restraining process that kept the angel from his mission had taken place in the spirit world, beyond the range of human vision. But somehow, it had also taken place in time, since the restraint was measured in earth days. It is difficult for mortal men to understand how two heavenly persons wrestling in space could also be wrestling in time. Nevertheless, this is exactly what they were doing, and this reveals a great deal about Satan and his servants.

This "prince of the kingdom of Persia" was no mortal. He was a representative of Satan, empowered to control Persian territory. Amazingly, the heavenly messenger's most likely identity is the preincarnate Christ! This seems to make the delay a matter of dimensional protocol, not of strength or authority.

THE HIERARCHY OF SIN

In chapter three, we quoted from Ephesians, where Paul shows that there are levels of rank in Satan's realm: "For we wrestle not against flesh and blood, but against principalities, against powers, against the rulers of the darkness of this world, against spiritual wickedness in high places" (Ephesians 6:12).

To expand on this idea, many scholars have suggested that here we find at least four gradations of Satan's dark forces. First are the "principalities," from the Greek *arche,* indicating those angels who are prime rulers. This term is used of both good and evil angels. For example, in Ephesians 3:10, the phrase, "principalities and powers in heavenly places," refers to the high angels who never rebelled.

But in terms of spiritual warfare, these are the ancient, high rulers who were once loyal to God, then later followed Satan. The "Prince of the kingdom of Persia" is likely one of this number.

Second in rank are the "powers," from the Greek *exousia*, meaning "delegated authorities." This term suggest one under a higher authority who has, nevertheless, freedom to act on his own and make personal decisions about how to execute an order.

Next in order beneath these "powers" are the "rulers of the darkness of this world." They are the *kosmokrators,* or "world rulers" of the darkness. That is, they are behind the evil world system, represented by Babylon, Medo-Persia, Greece, and Rome. They haunt the halls of power, planting their evil schemes in places where they will affect the greatest number of people.

Beneath these rulers, at the fourth level, we find the Greek term, *pneumatikos,* which connotes power in the invisible realm. Called "spiritual wickedness" in the King James Version, it probably refers to Satan's vassals of the domain that we call "demonic." These are the hordes of demons, unclean spirits whose task is to damage humanity in any way possible.

Paul portrays prayer as a spiritual battle. Indeed, by its very nature, prayer is always a kind of spiritual battle. The dark forces of the heavens are arrayed in such a way as to thwart the efforts of any human who lives in the arena of faith.

Believers are central to the ages-long drama of redemption. From the initial struggle in the Garden of Eden and throughout the development of the Gentile powers, there has always been an elect remnant of faithful humanity.

HEAVENLY DAYS

The tone of the opposition is clearly seen in the first chapter of Job, which we have already quoted by way of explaining Satan's area and style of operation. But there is more.

And the LORD said unto Satan, Hast thou considered my
servant Job, that there is none like him in the earth, a perfect
and an upright man, one that feareth God, and escheweth evil?

Then Satan answered the LORD, and said, Doth Job fear
God for nought? Hast not thou made an hedge about him,
and about his house, and about all that he hath on every side?
thou hast blessed the work of his hands, and his substance is
increased in the land. But put forth thine hand now, and touch
all that he hath, and he will curse thee to thy face.

And the LORD said unto Satan, Behold, all that he hath is
in thy power; only upon himself put not forth thine hand. So
Satan went forth from the presence of the LORD. (Job 1:8–12)

If there is any dialogue in the Bible that shows how Satan works,
this is the one. The Lord presented Job to him as a good and upright
man who avoided evil. He asked Satan whether, in his earthly peregrina-
tions, he had investigated Job. It is obvious that he had, since he retorted,
"Does Job fear God for nothing?"

One can almost hear his mocking tones as he accuses Job of fearing
the Lord only because it will profit him to do so. He is saying that Job is
following the Lord because of what he can get out of it. He accuses Job
of cheap faith.

It is the quality of Job's faith that is then put to the test. The Lord
allows Satan to remove the blessing, which Satan cynically views as profit.
Job's entire story is the outcome of the test, as the evil one systematically
removes his cattle, sheep, and farms…even his family.

It was upon "a day" that the sons of God first gathered together to be
heard at the Lord's throne. Satan's challenge was met. Job passed the test.
But in the second chapter of Job, another "day" is mentioned: "Again
there was a day when the sons of God came to present themselves before
the LORD, and Satan came also among them to present himself before
the LORD" (Job 2:1).

This time, the Lord and Satan converse about the fact that Job has retained his faith, even though he has lost everything. Now, however, the cynical Satan proposes that Job's faith will fail if his health is removed. The Lord allows a deeper test; Satan departs from the presence of the Lord and goes forth to afflict Job with boils from head to toe.

Most interesting, from the perspective of our study on time and space, is that it is a "day" upon which the second meeting is held. What sort of day must this be? On earth, a day is measured by a single rotation upon its axis—measuring approximately twenty-four hours.

This cannot be the case in heaven, where an eternal state exists, and where light is an emanation from the Godhead. Nevertheless, somehow a different "time" is being referenced for the second meeting between the Lord and the sons of God. It follows the first "day" by some interval, during which "time" Job has been considerably tested down upon the earth.

As we shall see, the "day" referenced here is not a reference to a specific date, as we would think of it. Rather, it is an occasion. The meeting marked some sort of important ceremony. The suggestion is that it happens with some frequency, perhaps being an established convention or tradition of some sort. The "day" in question might be better understood as an "occasion."

EARTHLY DAYS

As we have said, time is linked to redemption. The "days of creation" in Genesis are six in number, the seventh being a day of rest following the creation of Adam. They are more than mere "days." They constitute the model by which the Lord will work out the salvation of mankind. Man was created on the sixth day and placed in a beautiful garden planted by God Himself. Then He created Eve, a perfect mate for the first man.

As the story develops, we note two problems. First, there is a strange and ominous tree in the center of the garden. The couple is warned not to eat its fruit. It is a grave warning that carries a death sentence: "But of the tree of the knowledge of good and evil, thou shalt not eat of it: for in the day that thou eatest thereof thou shalt surely die" (Genesis 2:17).

Thus, the first seven days of Creation established a test for humanity's first couple. Time and redemption became linked to a seven-day cycle. But the grand cycle of the millennia was established at the beginning. The days of Creation became the millennial days of redemption. As Psalm 90:4 says so clearly, the Lord sees the millennia as days: "For a thousand years in thy sight are but as yesterday when it is past, and as a watch in the night."

In the New Testament, Peter picks up the same theme, linking it to the Day of Judgment and the end of the prophetic ages:

> But the heavens and the earth, which are now, by the same word are kept in store, reserved unto fire against the day of judgment and perdition of ungodly men. But, beloved, be not ignorant of this one thing, that one day is with the Lord as a thousand years, and a thousand years as one day. (2 Peter 3:7, 8)

Peter makes this observation in the context of the Flood of Noah. In the process, he declares that in the future, the prevailing view will be that the Flood never took place. This denial will be the distinctive mark of latter-day thought.

Then Peter points out that the next judgment will be a fiery one. Like Noah's Great Flood, the fires of judgment are being held in abeyance for a specific moment in future history. Ever since the waters receded, Gentile powers have attempted to dominate the religion, money and politics of the world system.

Babylon, Medo-Persia, Greece, and Rome successively constructed their versions of world rule. According to the prophecies of Daniel and Revelation, Gentile power is to rise to its final state of debauchery before the wrath of God unleashes a series of natural and supernatural catastrophes.

SIX DAYS, AND THE SEVENTH

The time between the rise of the human civilization and this final cataclysm is measured in millennia—each a "day" in the Lord's perspective.

So far, the elapsed time has totaled about six thousand years, or six millennial days. Classic Christian belief has stated that after these six days of man, the seventh will belong to the Lord. Creation and redemption are brought together in a familiar pattern of time.

This doctrine was so pervasive in the days of the apostles that even secular historians have noted it in their works. Edward Gibbon, in his *Decline and Fall of the Roman Empire*, writes:

> The ancient and popular doctrine of the Millennium was intimately connected with the second coming of Christ. As the works of the creation had been finished in six days, their duration in their present state, according to a tradition which was attributed to the prophet Elijah, was fixed to six thousand years.
>
> By the same analogy it was inferred, that this long period of labor and contention, which was now almost elapsed, would be succeeded by a joyful Sabbath of a thousand years; and that Christ, with the triumphant band of the saints and the elect who had escaped death, or who had been miraculously revived, would reign upon earth till the time appointed for the last and general resurrection. So pleasing was this hope to the mind of believers, that the New Jerusalem, the seat of this blissful kingdom, was quickly adorned with all the gayest colors of the imagination. A felicity consisting only of pure and spiritual pleasure would have appeared too refined for its inhabitants, who were still supposed to possess their human nature and senses. A garden of Eden, with the amusements of the pastoral life, was no longer suited to the advanced state of society which prevailed under the Roman empire. A city was therefore erected of gold and precious stones, and a supernatural plenty of corn and wine was bestowed on the adjacent territory; in the free enjoyment of whose spontaneous productions, the happy and benevolent people was never to be restrained by any jealous laws of exclusive property.[26]

Though Gibbon acknowledges the early Christian belief in six millennial days followed by a millennial Sabbath, he is quite cynical about the source of its revelations. He is adamant that the prophecy was the product of man's imagination rather than divine disclosure. Taking the philosophical position, he views the founders of the general church as silly idealists, preoccupied with giving their innocent followers a vision sufficient to tickle their fancy.

Note the tone of ridicule as Gibbon reviews the first three centuries of history of belief in the prophesied Millennium:

> The assurance of such a Millennium was carefully inculcated by
> a succession of fathers from Justin Martyr, and Irenaeus, who
> conversed with the immediate disciples of the apostles, down
> to Lactantius, who was receptor to the son of Constantine.
> Though it might not be universally received, it appears to have
> been the reigning sentiment of the orthodox believers; and
> it seems so well adapted to the desires and apprehensions of
> mankind, that it must have contributed in a very considerable
> degree to the progress of the Christian faith. But when the
> edifice of the church was almost completed, the temporary
> support was laid aside. The doctrine of Christ's reign upon
> earth was at first treated as a profound allegory, was considered
> by degrees as a doubtful and useless opinion, and was at length
> rejected as the absurd invention of heresy and fanaticism.

In this observation, his ridicule almost turns to glee at the thought that their concocted millennial scheme had lost favor. To Gibbon, this simply affirms his personal belief that prophecy is an invention of man. He concludes that once the church is fully established, it no longer requires such childish beliefs. They become quaint and outmoded idiosyncrasies.

Actually, many in the modern organized church would agree with Gibbon, since they regard Scripture as the product of human reason and imagination. This being the case, its interpretation can be quite flexible, bending with the requirements of time and culture. Actually, the days of the scriptural timeline are self-interpreting, if one simply observes the Bible as God-breathed.

Attributing the idea of the millennial-day theory to the prophet Elijah is simply hearsay. Elijah's work was specific to the dark reign of King Ahab and his sorceress queen Jezebel. In fact, he said little about the historical flow of the dispensations or the events of the latter days.

FUTURE HISTORY

However, the prophet Hosea did exactly that, but not for himself. Rather, he spoke, "Hear the word of the Lord," to the kings of Israel at the tumultuous time of the Assyrian captivity. He asserted that his knowledge of future history came directly from the Lord.

Using Hosea's lips, the Lord spoke one of the clearest statements of the millennial day in the entire Bible:

> For I will be unto Ephraim as a lion, and as a young lion to
> the house of Judah: I, even I, will tear and go away; I will take
> away, and none shall rescue him. I will go and return to my
> place, till they acknowledge their offence, and seek my face: in
> their affliction they will seek me early.
>
> Come, and let us return unto the LORD: for he hath torn,
> and he will heal us; he hath smitten, and he will bind us up.
> After two days will he revive us: in the third day he will raise us
> up, and we shall live in his sight.
>
> Then shall we know, if we follow on to know the LORD:
> his going forth is prepared as the morning; and he shall come
> unto us as the rain, as the latter and former rain unto the earth.
> (Hosea 5:14–6:3)

Speaking the words of Jehovah, Hosea speaks in the Lord's own voice as he boldly states what He will do in the future. The preincarnate Lion of Judah says that He will be as a mature lion to Ephraim (Israel, the ten northern tribes). Then He says that He will come to Judah (the two southern tribes) as a vigorous young lion.

The Lord did both of these things. In 722 BC, during the life of Hosea, He allowed the Assyrians to ravage Israel like a roaring lion. Later, incarnated in the vigor of youth, he came to Judah and Benjamin—the Jews and the Temple of Herod. His death, burial, and resurrection created a new branch of redemptive activity that tore Jewish society apart.

Not long after His departure, Roman reaction to the new Christianity became more and more direct. Just over three decades later, in AD 70, Romans destroyed the Herodian Temple. By the time a few more decades had passed, Jewish society had been dispersed throughout the Roman world.

Through Hosea, the Lord said that He would stay away until the Jews came to the point of desperately seeking Him. It is significant that today, more and more observant Jews are becoming "Messianic." That is, they acknowledge that Jesus was—and is—the Messiah.

The Lord says that after two days—two millennia—He would come to revive His people. The so-called teshuvah movement (or revival movement) is a growing reality in today's beleaguered Israel. There is a growing sense of the knowledge that only His return can save the tiny nation.

After their revival, the Lord says that He will lift them up—in the third day (the third millennium). In other words, national Israel will be spiritually resurrected for life in the kingdom.

We are now approaching the third millennial day since He returned to heaven to be seated at God's right hand. The Lord's words in Hosea liken His return to the dawning early in the morning of the third day.

Combining the idea of morning with the picture of fiery judgment used in 2 Peter, Malachi's prophecy of Christ's coming says:

> For, behold, the day cometh, that shall burn as an oven; and
> all the proud, yea, and all that do wickedly, shall be stubble:
> and the day that cometh shall burn them up, saith the LORD of

hosts, that it shall leave them neither root nor branch.
But unto you that fear my name shall the Sun of righteousness
arise with healing in his wings; and ye shall go forth, and grow
up as calves of the stall. (Malachi 4:1, 2)

Here is sunrise; the Son is the sun, and He arises to renew the spirit
of His people, even as He judges the nations that have attempted to wipe
Israel from the face of the earth.

Early in the dawning of the third millennium since His departure,
the Son will come. Virtually every prophecy that speaks of Israel's regathering says that it will occur in two stages. First, the people will return to
the land. Then, at a later date, they will be infused with new life through
the Spirit of the living God.

Many are familiar with Ezekiel's "dry bones" prophecy, in which the
body of Israel is brought back to the land, followed by their spiritual
resurrection:

And ye shall know that I am the LORD, when I have opened
your graves, O my people, and brought you up out of your
graves, And shall put my spirit in you, and ye shall live, and
I shall place you in your own land: then shall ye know that I
the LORD have spoken it, and performed it, saith the LORD.
(Ezekiel 37:13, 14)

THE SEVENTH DAY

The seventh and final prophetic day belongs to the Lord and Him only.
Immediately after Peter pointed out the millennium as being a day in the
Lord's sight, he spoke of the seventh day:

The Lord is not slack concerning his promise, as some men
count slackness; but is longsuffering to us-ward, not willing
that any should perish, but that all should come to repentance.

But the day of the Lord will come as a thief in the night; in the which the heavens shall pass away with a great noise, and the elements shall melt with fervent heat, the earth also and the works that are therein shall be burned up. (2 Peter 3:9, 10)

Speaking through Peter, the Spirit of the Lord wanted His followers to know that His plan was clearly discernable from the beginning of the Creation. Seven, the number of completion, is also the number of days in a week and the number of basic Jewish festivals. The Day of the Lord is the seventh millennium...the Sabbath of a long week.

Its fiery judgments will come in a seven-year period that we call the Tribulation. But taken as a whole, they are ultimately the pattern of Satan's demise. His fall from the halls of eternity brought him to the chain of time and the pit of fire, in which he is doomed to count the passing days...without end.

5

TIME AS AN EXPANDING
SET OF RINGS

Archetypes are impossible unless their ultimate fulfillment is already an accomplished fact.

Like no other book ever written, the Bible declares authority over time and space. It opens with a dramatic beginning, in which God creates the heavens and the earth. It closes with a renewed heavens and earth.

But far more important than either of these two historical data points is its open declaration of the events that lead from the first state of the universe to the last. Some of these events are given by direct prophecy.

The Spirit of the Lord moves Moses and the later prophets, as well as the New Testament apostles, to present future history as though it has already taken place. For the faithful, it is uncritically accepted with the assurance that it will come to pass as written. The very existence of prophecy tells us that the Lord has already seen what, for us, is invisible. But anyone who has attempted to study it knows that its various revelations are interwoven with a complexity that requires much study. To harmonize individual prophecies isn't always even possible. But the prophecies are there, and it is an article of faith that they will be fulfilled.

Other accounts of the future are given by inference. They are seen in historical archetypes. The old saying that "history repeats itself" is nowhere clearer than in the biblical types that manifest themselves in proclamations of later—and greater—demonstrations of the Lord's authority over the events of history.

Earlier in this book, we mentioned one prominent archetype. It took place in the life of Abraham when, in Genesis 14, we see the land of Canaan being invaded by four kings. Abraham's nephew, Lot, had chosen the favorable environment of Sodom as his residence. Now, a coalition of four Gentile kings had come to invade this lush land.

The first of these kings was Amraphel, king of Shinar. He represents Babylon. With him was Chedorlaomer, king of Elam. This king characterizes the land of Persia. After him, we find Arioch, king of Ellasar. He is the progenitor of the Grecian kings. Finally, we come to Tidal, king of nations. Jewish sages flatly state that Tidal is Rome.

Here, nineteen centuries before Christ and thirteen centuries before the prophecy of Daniel, we find the distinct foreshadowing of four Gentile world powers mentioned by Daniel: Babylon, Medo-Persia, Greece, and Rome.

The times of the Gentiles are well defined by Daniel, being mentioned as the primary driving force of world history. The four invading kings, therefore, become the archetype of future history. The fact that their typology is so apparent makes it quite plain that from God's point of view, history is not so much a line as an expanding set of rings that enlarge upon an originating idea.

Like waves that emanate from a central point, ideas that begin in the mind of God intersect our physical dimension, producing repetitive designs, prefigurations, interactions, causes, and effects. For Him, they are all happening at the same "time." For us, they are past and future manifestations of remarkably similar concepts. Yet, history is His idea, and it is developed around the concepts of redemption and restoration.

Think of history as a 3-D hologram whose parts all exist simultaneously as intersecting patterns. The hologram contains the entire picture, but only one aspect of it can be viewed at any given time. Bible themes and forms are given for the edification of humanity. They are deliberately limited to perspectives that emphasize qualities needed for human spiritual development. Only the Lord of time and space can simultaneously view every aspect of the picture.

ISAAC, A WINDOW INTO THE FUTURE

On the subject of "theme," the life of Abraham features a key word: "promise." The Lord promised him descendants beyond number—children, both physical and spiritual. Yet, even in his old age, He and Sarah had not conceived even the first heir. The promised child seemed an impossibility. Once, when the Lord appeared to him, Abraham asked whether the promise had been forgotten. At one point, he even suggested that his household steward Eliezer might become his heir. The Lord's answer was certain:

> And, behold, the word of the LORD came unto him, saying,
> This shall not be thine heir; but he that shall come forth out of
> thine own bowels shall be thine heir.
>   And he brought him forth abroad, and said, Look now
> toward heaven, and tell the stars, if thou be able to number
> them: and he said unto him, So shall thy seed be.
> (Genesis 15:4, 5)

A bit later, in Genesis 17:19, the promised heir is divinely named, far in advance of his birth: "And God said, Sarah thy wife shall bear thee a son indeed; and thou shalt call his name Isaac: and I will establish my covenant with him for an everlasting covenant, and with his seed after him."

Isaac, a superb type of Christ, is forever linked to the covenant of promise. At the same time, he is given the curious name, "Isaac," meaning "he will laugh." Scripture tells us that his name came in response to Sarah's ironic laughter at the suggestion that she—at her advanced age—could actually bear a child.

But actually, laughter is a great metaphor. Here, it reflects the joy at overcoming the seeming impossibility of this world's tribulations. Isaac represents the joyous victory that humanity will experience when the elements of promise are finally realized. As in Psalm 2:4, the Lord will laugh at His enemies: "He that sitteth in the heavens shall laugh: the Lord shall have them in derision."

Jesus Himself expressed this promise in one of his first messages: "Blessed are ye that hunger now: for ye shall be filled. Blessed are ye that weep now: for ye shall laugh" (Luke 6:21).

Jesus was also divinely named in advance of His birth, as the angel Gabriel told Mary, "And, behold, thou shalt conceive in thy womb, and bring forth a son, and shalt call his name JESUS" (Luke 1:31).

Like Isaac, Jesus—"salvation"—is a child of promise. Both are named before birth, and both are linked through the promise of redemption. Their births are similar in another way. Namely, they are both miraculous. Sarah was barren. More than that, her advanced age placed her well beyond the normal hope of motherhood. Yet she bore Abraham a son "in his old age, at the set time of which God had spoken to him" (Genesis 21:2). The time and place of his birth were foreordained.

This miracle foreshadowed the miraculous virgin birth of Jesus, which also came at a precise historical moment. The promise begun in Abraham and Isaac, was completed in Jesus, who in John 3:16, is called the only begotten son: "For God so loved the world, that he gave his **only begotten** Son, that whosoever believeth in him should not perish, but have everlasting life" (emphasis added).

Isaac, too, was called an only son. He foreshadowed even this aspect of Christ's life, when the Lord told his father to offer him as a sacrifice. "And he said, Take now thy son, **thine only son** Isaac, whom thou lovest, and get thee into the land of Moriah; and offer him there for a burnt offering upon one of the mountains which I will tell thee of" (Genesis 22:2, emphasis added).

Isaac points the way to the final fulfillment of the Lord's promise. His life is an expression of the Lord's plan. Like notes in a musical score, he brings depth and harmony to the reality of the life to be lived by Jesus.

Many have pointed out the similarities in their lives. Isaac was mocked by those of his own household. In a much more open way, Jesus was mocked by His brethren.

Both were considered an acceptable sacrifice. The Lord commanded Abraham to sacrifice Isaac, clearly making it known that He would be satisfied with this supreme act. Jesus, born without sin, and never having broken the Law of Moses, was deemed ultimately acceptable.

Isaac carried the wood of the burnt offering to the place of his own sacrifice. In this way, he pointed to Christ, who carried His own Cross. Both men went willingly to the place of their sacrifice.

On the third day, Christ arose from the dead. Similarly, "On the third day Abraham lifted up his eyes, and saw the place afar off" (Genesis 22:4). On that symbolic third day, Abraham and Isaac arrived at the place of sacrifice. In the ensuing events, Isaac was placed upon the altar, but was spared when the angel of the Lord stayed Abraham's hand.

Then, the Lord provided a ram for the sacrifice, and Isaac arose from the altar as one risen from the dead, saved by the substitutionary atonement provided by the Lord. He prefigured the resurrection of Jesus.

Both Isaac and Jesus were "forsaken" by their fathers. It is the natural thing for a father to give his own life for his son. However, it is quite contrary to the natural order for fathers to deliberately lead their sons to the place of death. Abraham obediently took Isaac to certain death. God the Father led his own Son along the same path. But both sons were brought back from certain death.

Isaac's heart must have jumped for joy. On his way back from the place of sacrifice, he and Abraham must have excitedly shared their mountaintop experience. No doubt, their conversation was spiced with the laughter of rejoicing. Isaac's laughter prefigured Jesus' great victory over the dark forces of this world.

The metaphoric relationship between Isaac and Jesus is truly marvelous. The laughter of victory precedes the victory, itself. In terms of the historical timeline, it may be said that Christ's victory was considered as having been fully realized—nineteen centuries before it was accomplished at the Cross.

Here, the pattern is laid out from the beginning, fully accomplished in the vaults of eternity, but laid out in successive stages in our world of time. Resonances and harmonies along the timeline produce the grand Messianic designs that we perceive only in part…only in time. But biblical typology is time travel in its purest sense. Archetypes are impossible unless their ultimate fulfillment is already an accomplished fact.

It is quite beyond human understanding that the Lord holds men responsible for lives whose details are worked out in accordance with a future plan. Yet that is exactly what He does. And when we think about it, men's daily lives are shaped minute by minute in the vibrations of a future that lies beyond their vision.

JOSEPH, DELIVERER FROM TRIBULATION

How is it possible that a human life can foreshadow another life that hasn't yet been lived? That is, the key events of the first life are expressly aimed at emphasizing an important future existence. Not only that, but the former is lived as a proof that God's will is displayed in the latter. At first, this question might be shrugged off as unworthy of consideration…plainly an impossibility.

How can two lives, perhaps separated by millennia, be somehow connected outside what we perceive as a timeline? But, in fact, this question is intimately connected with the entire biblical narrative.

As seen in the life of Abraham, times and seasons are laid out in advance of their actual fulfillment. This could not happen unless someone—the Lord—was acting as a directive force from outside this dimension. Without a doubt, He is sovereign in weaving the fabric of our existence. Its patterns express His thoughts, as He carefully applies the elements necessary to accomplish the redemption and restoration of our broken universe.

Like the designs on a quilt, the patterns are recognizably repetitive. Sometimes, the designs are recognizable at the human level. At other times, we suspect that there are underlying links, but we can only dimly perceive them.

The life of Joseph offers us a very good example of this kind of phenomenon. Over the years, many students of Scripture have pointed out the ways in which he is a type of Christ. Many of them are blatantly obvious. But the longer one looks, the more complex the connections become. At last, one must concede that there are probably many more connections than we can possibly grasp.

Greatly beloved of his father, Joseph was the favored son of Jacob, the man who came to be called "Israel." He demonstrated his special love for Joseph by presenting to him the famous coat of many colors. This garment – variously translated as a "fine woolen tunic," a "tunic with sleeves," or a "long tunic reaching to the feet" – set him apart as the family's favored one. Like Christ, he was placed above his brothers. Joseph watched their initial jealousy turn to seething hatred.

No doubt their fervent envy passed the boiling point when, later, he had a pair of prophetic dreams that pictured him as sovereign over them. First, in a dream of harvest time, their sheaves of grain bowed before his. But his second dream went far beyond the first:

> And he dreamed yet another dream, and told it his brethren, and said, Behold, I have dreamed a dream more; and, behold, the sun and the moon and the eleven stars made obeisance to me.
>
> And he told it to his father, and to his brethren: and his father rebuked him, and said unto him, What is this dream that thou hast dreamed? Shall I and thy mother and thy brethren indeed come to bow down ourselves to thee to the earth? And his brethren envied him; but his father observed the saying. (Genesis 37:9–11)

The implications of this dream reach all the way to Revelation 12. Here, we find a famous metaphoric description in which a woman, clothed with the sun and standing upon the moon, has a crown of twelve stars upon her head. She symbolizes Israel, and her crown of stars is the fulfillment of Joseph's dream.

In the lives of Joseph and his brothers, we see Israel at its earliest beginnings. In Revelation, we are allowed to observe Israel during its Kingdom-Age birth pangs. Joseph's prophecy sets the stage for his exemplary symbolic life.

First, the fact that he was hated by his tribal brethren is, in itself, greatly suggestive of Christ, who was despised by His intimate acquaintances in Galilee, then later, by religious authorities and the overlords of Rome. As the prophet Isaiah put it, the Messiah was thoroughly discarded: "He is despised and rejected of men; a man of sorrows, and acquainted with grief: and we hid as it were our faces from him; he was despised, and we esteemed him not" (Isaiah 53:3).

From the beginning, Joseph marked out the essential aspects of the life of Jesus. His mother, Rachel, was barren. Unable to bear children, she was desperate, even to the point of suggesting to Jacob that her handmaid might bear children for her.

But in a miraculous reversal, the Lord remembered her plight and made it possible for her to bear children, the first of whom was Joseph. Thus, like Christ, his life begins with a miraculous birth.

As we have seen, Joseph was inordinately and unconditionally loved by his father. Jesus was also beloved of His Father in heaven. In Matthew 3:17, we read the famous words that accompanied His baptism: "And lo a voice from heaven, saying, This is my beloved Son, in whom I am well pleased."

Joseph was set apart by a special garment. As we have seen, the physical details of his mysterious garment are unclear. What is clear is that the garment gave him special status. Like Christ, he was separated—set apart:

But this man, because he continueth ever, hath an
unchangeable priesthood. Wherefore he is able also to save
them to the uttermost that come unto God by him, seeing he
ever liveth to make intercession for them. For such an high

priest became us, who is holy, harmless, undefiled, **separate from sinners,** and made higher than the heavens.
(Hebrews 7: 24–26, emphasis added)

Joseph declared that he would rule over His brethren. In His public ministry, Jesus also announced that He would be King. Both men were met with envy, anger, and opposition. Both were hated and unjustly convicted of crimes they did not commit. Joseph was accused of seducing the wife of an Egyptian official. He was thrown into prison. Jesus was accused of blasphemy for claiming that He was God. Rome explicitly proclaimed His crime: "And Pilate wrote a title, and put it on the cross. And the writing was, JESUS OF NAZARETH THE KING OF THE JEWS" (John 19:19).

Joseph was sent to his brethren by his father, Jacob. When he found them, they cruelly sold him into slavery. Jesus was sent to the lost sheep of the house of Israel…and was rejected.

In the end, however, Joseph was freed from prison. His close relationship with the Spirit of the living God was recognized even by the idolatrous Egyptians. In a stunning reversal, he was elevated to a position of rulership second only to Pharaoh. From our perspective, we know that He was divinely placed in this position to save his brothers. Like Jesus, He was unrecognized for a time. But then, he revealed himself to them. In the end, he saved his people.

Like Jesus, whose salvation reached beyond the House of David, Joseph even took a Gentile bride. Amazingly, he did so in his thirtieth year:

And Pharaoh called Joseph's name Zaphnathpaaneah; and he gave him to wife Asenath the daughter of Potipherah priest of On. And Joseph went out over all the land of Egypt. And Joseph was thirty years old when he stood before Pharaoh king of Egypt. And Joseph went out from the presence of Pharaoh, and went throughout all the land of Egypt. (Genesis 41:45, 46)

Joseph's Gentile name, *Zaphnath-paaneah*, roughly translates to "revealer of secrets." His wife's name, *Asenath*, means, "she who is of Neith." That is, she was dedicated to the Egyptian goddess Neith, who corresponds to the Roman Minerva, goddess of wisdom and patroness of the arts and business. She is similar to the Greek Athene, wearing a helmet and displaying a staunch and militaristic pose. To this day, female statues in martial apparel often appear in prominent places among the capitals of the world.

Joseph's bride thus bears a remarkable similarity to Western Gentile civilization. She is a remarkable symbol of the Christianized West in the Age of Grace.

After Joseph had obtained his bride, his father, Jacob, and his brethren suffered under a great famine. They came to him for grain during their time of trouble. In the future, there will be another time of "Jacob's trouble," when Israel will turn to their true Messiah for deliverance. This event resonates with that final time of trouble.

Joseph's brethren came to him twice. On their first trip, they didn't recognize him, even though he stood directly before them. They returned home, but the famine persisted, forcing them to return. On their second trip, Joseph revealed himself to them. Likewise, in Jesus' first appearance to His brethren, He was not recognized. In His Second Coming, He will reveal Himself to them. Every eye shall see Him:

> And there shall be signs in the sun, and in the moon, and in the stars; and upon the earth distress of nations, with perplexity; the sea and the waves roaring; Men's hearts failing them for fear, and for looking after those things which are coming on the earth: for the powers of heaven shall be shaken. And then shall they see the Son of man coming in a cloud with power and great glory. (Luke 21:25–27)

In their time of Great Tribulation, Jesus will reveal Himself. At last, like Joseph's brethren, national Israel will know that they are not forsaken. Jesus' love for them will at last be revealed.

The remarkable foreshadowing of Christ's life by Joseph tells us that God is sovereign in history. His way of accomplishing the goals of passing time is exhibited in the halls of heaven. Joseph will be an everlasting display of His purity and power.

ANOTHER EGYPTIAN CRISIS

The lives of Isaac and Joseph represent personal archetypes. But there are also archetypes that spring from historical events. They resound through history, bringing familiar themes that cause men to remember the glory of the Lord. Perhaps the most sweeping example of this sort of historical archetype is the Exodus. Significantly, it also involves Egypt, which typifies the world system at large.

About two centuries after the life of Joseph, the Israelites found themselves in trouble once again, this time as slaves under a despotic Pharaoh. In Exodus 13:3, Moses commanded his people never to forget the great day of their liberation: "And Moses said unto the people, Remember this day, in which ye came out from Egypt, out of the house of bondage; for by strength of hand the LORD brought you out from this place: there shall no leavened bread be eaten."

This day, forever after commemorated on the fourteenth day of Nisan, is Passover, when the angel of death recognized the blood on the doorposts and lintels of the Israelites. He passed over their homes, sparing them the awful curse meted out upon the Egyptians. The firstborn of every Egyptian home would be slain.

This was the tenth—and worst—of ten plagues afflicted upon the Egyptians. The hardness of Pharaoh's heart had brought on every one of these torments, as he refused to allow the Israelites to leave Egypt. They had begun when Moses and Aaron had stood before him with a clear request: "And afterward Moses and Aaron went in, and told Pharaoh, Thus saith the LORD God of Israel, Let my people go, that they may hold a feast unto me in the wilderness" (Exodus 5:1).

What was that feast? It was to be Passover, the feast of freedom. But only after Pharaoh's repeated refusals did this feast become a living reality. First, the Egyptian waters were turned to blood. Then came successive plagues of frogs, lice, flies, cattle disease, boils, fiery hail, locusts, and supernatural darkness. These plagues had failed to soften the heart of Pharaoh. Moses warned him that one final plague would come: The angel of death would visit every Egyptian household.

Egypt's power was negated by the blood of the Passover lamb. Moses commanded the elders of Israel to slaughter lambs in the evening. Their blood was to be used like paint around their doors. Then, they were to roast the lambs and eat them quickly with unleavened bread. With the expectancy of their imminent departure from captivity, the Israelites set a precedent that has resounded through the ages.

Of course, the blood-soaked wooden doorposts and lintels were types of the Cross of Christ. He Himself is the "Lamb of God, which taketh away the sin of the world" (John 1:29).

He is also the unleavened bread of the festival. Quite simply, He is the Bread of Life. During His public ministry, He once delivered this message in such openly manifest terms that the people turned away in stunned unbelief:

> Then Jesus said unto them, Verily, verily, I say unto you, Except ye eat the flesh of the Son of man, and drink his blood, ye have no life in you.
> Whoso eateth my flesh, and drinketh my blood, hath eternal life; and I will raise him up at the last day. For my flesh is meat indeed, and my blood is drink indeed. He that eateth my flesh, and drinketh my blood, dwelleth in me, and I in him. As the living Father hath sent me, and I live by the Father: so he that eateth me, even he shall live by me. This is that bread which came down from heaven: not as your fathers did eat manna, and are dead: he that eateth of this bread shall live for ever. (John 6:53–58)

Such talk sounded cannibalistic. The people failed to understand the import of his words. "Manna" is a Hebrew term meaning, "What is it?" He told them what it was, but they were not given spiritual ears to hear and eyes to see that He was the Passover. The manna was itself a type of Christ. He pointed to Himself as the only way to the freedom for which they so desperately searched.

But what is Passover, really? It is the festival of the new birth, when death directly resulted in resurrection. Its cup and bread become the symbols of salvation:

> And as they were eating, Jesus took bread, and blessed it, and brake it, and gave it to the disciples, and said, Take, eat; this is my body. And he took the cup, and gave thanks, and gave it to them, saying, Drink ye all of it; For this is my blood of the new testament, which is shed for many for the remission of sins.
>
> But I say unto you, I will not drink henceforth of this fruit of the vine, until that day when I drink it new with you in my Father's kingdom. (Matthew 26:26)

But even this moment had been foreseen centuries earlier, when Abraham met with Melchizedek after his battle with the four Gentile kings: "And Melchizedek king of Salem brought forth bread and wine: and he was the priest of the most high God" (Genesis 14:18).

As we have seen, Abraham's victory and subsequent blessing by Melchizedek looked into the far future, when the Gentile powers will be crushed by the returning Son of God. He will come with the armies of heaven to put them down as prophesied.

To today's Jews, Passover is commemorated with four cups of wine, unleavened bread, and the Seder plate. All of these conclude in the anticipation of a future deliverance: "Next year in Jerusalem!"

The annual celebration of this festival ends with a plea for the Lord's return in judgment to establish the rightful and prophesied kingdom, dominated by the throne of David.

This brings us to the other side of Passover, namely, the Plagues of Egypt. Though the ten plagues seem to have originated out of the stubbornness of a truculent Pharaoh, they were much more than that. They were, in fact, an outline for something much greater.

For example, when Jesus expounded upon the end times, He spoke of "famines, and pestilences, and earthquakes, in divers places" (Matthew 24:7). He also mentioned "great tribulation, such as was not since the beginning of the world to this time" (v. 21). Then He said:

Immediately after the tribulation of those days shall the sun be darkened, and the moon shall not give her light, and the stars shall fall from heaven, and the powers of the heavens shall be shaken:

And then shall appear the sign of the Son of man in heaven: and then shall all the tribes of the earth mourn, and they shall see the Son of man coming in the clouds of heaven with power and great glory. (Matthew 24:29, 30)

Many have written entire treatises about the many ways that Egypt's ten plagues typify the Tribulation judgments. They are quite obvious, as in the first vial of wrath, which afflicts men with some sort of skin disease, reminding us of the fifth Egyptian plague of boils.

The second vial turns the sea to blood, like the first Egyptian plague. The third vial completes this action, turning the fresh water to blood. One remembers the Nile, as Moses struck it with his staff.

The great heat of the fourth vial reminds us of the hail mixed with fire. The fifth brings the curse of darkness, like the ninth plague of Egypt.

The sixth and seventh vials of God's wrath bring judgment directly against mystery Babylon itself. Armies march, and a final cataclysmic earthquake coupled with giant hailstones brings an unimaginable, pounding destruction.

Thus, the Passover experience intertwines the atoning blood of the lamb with the judgment of the evil world. It combines salvation and judgment, the Bible's two major themes. Christians are urged to purge their lives of sin, even as Jewish homes are cleansed of leaven in anticipation of Passover: "Purge out therefore the old leaven, that ye may be a new lump, as ye are unleavened. For even Christ our passover is sacrificed for us" (1 Corinthians 5:7).

JESUS, TYPE OF ISRAEL

Though we might not have thought about it, even Jesus is an archetype. His attributes manifest themselves in surprising ways.

Author Vendyl Jones mentions a riddle of seven lines. He says:

1. I am thinking about someone in history. He left his indelible imprint on mankind. Without a biological miracle on the womb of his mother, his birth would have been impossible.
2. As an infant, he was called the Son of God.
3. He was taken into Egypt to preserve his life.
4. He returned to the land of Israel, hated by all those about him, despised and rejected of men—a man of sorrow and acquainted with grief.
5. He was hated so greatly that he was executed by the Romans.
6. At the third day, he came out of the tomb.
7. He will never die again![27]

Everyone would agree that these seven points emphatically outline the life of Jesus. It is quite extraordinary that they also describe national Israel—past, present, and future.

On the first point, we have already dealt with the miraculous birth of Isaac to the aged Abraham and Sarah. They were beyond the years of childbearing, yet they conceived Isaac. Without him, there would have been no Jacob, and no twelve tribes of Israel.

"And God said unto Abraham, Let it not be grievous in thy sight because of the lad, and because of thy bondwoman; in all that Sarah hath said unto thee, hearken unto her voice; for in Isaac shall thy seed be called" (Genesis 21:12).

The second point—also mentioned earlier—recalls the fact that Jesus was the only begotten Son of God. But it should be remembered that Israel is also called the son of God. Moses was commanded to make this clear in one of his appearances before Pharaoh:

> And thou shalt say unto Pharaoh, Thus saith the Lord, Israel is my son, even my firstborn: And I say unto thee, Let my son go, that he may serve me: and if thou refuse to let him go, behold, I will slay thy son, even thy firstborn. (Exodus 4:22, 23)

Point three mentions the flight to Egypt. Of course, Mary, Joseph, and Jesus fled there to escape Herod. But centuries before, Israel went to Egypt to receive deliverance from famine by a Pharaoh who had taken their brother Joseph as his prime minister. Indeed, Israel's life was saved in the refuge they found in Egypt.

On the fourth point, Jesus and Israel both experienced hatred upon their return to Israel. The experience of Jesus is well known. But Israel, at the conclusion of the wilderness march, was opposed by Amalek, Edom, Moab, and Ammon, as well as the Agagites, to name but a few. And upon entrance into the Promised Land, Israel was still forced to fight hostile and aggressive tribes on every hand. In fact, in Israel's current return to their land, they are in the same embattled position. Truly, they are acquainted with sorrow and grief.

Point five involves being put to death by the Romans. Certainly, Christ was crucified upon a Roman cross. But Israel experienced the same fate. In AD 70, their Temple was destroyed. The Jews fled for their lives. Roman opposition grew even stronger in the decades that followed. Finally, in AD 135, the Jews under Simeon Bar Kochba suffered a final defeat. They were driven to the four corners of the earth in the great Diaspora.

The sixth point refers to resurrection on the third day. Of course, the Resurrection is the key feature in the life of Jesus. He rose from the grave on the third day. It is fascinating that Israel is also prophesied to rise again...on the third day.

In the well-known prophecy of Hosea, that is exactly what is predicted:

> I will go and return to my place, till they acknowledge their offence, and seek my face: in their affliction they will seek me early. Come, and let us return unto the LORD: for he hath torn, and he will heal us; he hath smitten, and he will bind us up. After two days will he revive us: in the third day he will raise us up, and we shall live in his sight. (Hosea 5:15–6:2)

The Lord promised to raise Israel on the third day, just as He Himself had risen from the grave.

Finally, the seventh point refers to the eternal nature of the resurrected life. Jesus typifies such everlasting life. Through His rule, eternal life is also promised to the kingdom of Israel. Daniel's prophecy outlines the defeat of the Gentile world powers. In the end, he prophesies that the Kingdom will last forever: "And in the days of these kings shall the God of heaven set up a kingdom, which shall never be destroyed: and the kingdom shall not be left to other people, but it shall break in pieces and consume all these kingdoms, and it shall stand for ever" (Daniel 2:44).

Jesus as a type of Israel means that Israel's final victory and everlasting existence are as certain as His.

So many of the Gentile powers have sought to destroy Israel. Each has said that if only Israel can be forever wiped out, a utopian world can be established. But like their Messiah, Israel shall rise to eternal life.

This is the Lord's idea, and nothing can oppose it. In the purest sense, His idea has already been brought to its conclusion. It has already been inscribed in the historical hologram. It's just that we haven't the depth of perception to see it. Nevertheless, God exhorts us to think upon these things:

Remember the former things of old: for I am God, and there is none else; I am God, and there is none like me, Declaring the end from the beginning, and from ancient times the things that are not yet done, saying, My counsel shall stand, and I will do all my pleasure. (Isaiah 46:9, 10)

6

MILLENNIAL MAN

In our continuing study on the system of time and space that we call home, we repeatedly discover that time has purpose. It becomes increasingly clear that God created our universe of time and space as a design matrix upon which He could build the structure of redemption. The Bible states that eternity is His standard. But outside eternity, He chose to create a timeline with its own discrete dimensional field. He chose time like an artist chooses the proper canvas to display his work.

At the creation of man, eternity had long since been wracked by the destruction of a renegade force. Lucifer and those who became his followers had attempted to overthrow the divine order. The loving God and Father of Eternity took action to restore the damage. We know little of what He did in heaven. But on earth, we know that He ordained mankind to participate in His redemptive plan. Adam became the progenitor of the Messiah.

Beginning with Adam, each thousand-year period—in other words, each millennial day—features the character and personality of a dominant man. So, in a way, the men who highlight the passing millennia are important to understanding why the Lord chose time as the vessel of His redemption. As the successive ages came and went, Noah, Abraham, and David pointed the way to Christ and the answer to the problem of sin.

We have suggested that the times and seasons of the Bible are specifically attuned to the redemption and restoration of a sin-wracked universe. Time is neither arbitrary nor neutral. Rather, it is like a framework upon which certain necessary events are arranged according to divine protocols. They are displayed as an exhibit to the inhabitants of the eternal heavens. They are a graphic display of the conflict between sin and salvation.

Ultimately, the faith of the righteous comes to an end, to be replaced by sight. At Pentecost, the church had a discrete beginning. At the Rapture, it will realize its end. At that moment, all the saints will receive a bodily resurrection. Relative to this subject, Peter writes:

> Receiving the end of your faith, even the salvation of your souls. Of which salvation the prophets have inquired and searched diligently, who prophesied of the grace that should come unto you:
> Searching what, or what manner of time the Spirit of Christ which was in them did signify, when it testified beforehand the sufferings of Christ, and the glory that should follow. Unto whom it was revealed, that not unto themselves, but unto us they did minister the things, which are now reported unto you by them that have preached the gospel unto you with the Holy Ghost sent down from heaven; which things the angels desire to look into. (1 Peter 1:9–12)

Here, the word "end" is from the Greek *telos,* which in this context means "fulfillment." This new and different thing called salvation was described through the discourses of prophets who didn't understand their own messages. As written in the Old Testament, they were shown various scenes and scenarios, some of which were (and are still) reserved for the far future. And just as we attempt to place them in some understandable order, so they sought to make sense of things they could not possibly understand.

Despite all the revelations given to him, Daniel the prophet was baffled about the end times:

And I heard, but I understood not: then said I, O my Lord, what shall be the end of these things? And he said, Go thy way, Daniel: for the words are closed up and sealed till the time of the end.

Many shall be purified, and made white, and tried; but the wicked shall do wickedly: and none of the wicked shall understand; but the wise shall understand. (Daniel 12:8–10)

Daniel knew that prophecy was given to him with an end in sight. But he didn't know when that would be or how specific prophecies would directly relate to his people. He was told that the words given to him were to be sealed until "the time of the end."

How very curious! The angel allowed Daniel to know one thing for sure: that there would be an "end." This is the meaning of time. Without time, there will not be an end. It had a beginning, and it will have an end.

Prophecies of the great time of trouble were given to Daniel in the middle to late sixth century BC. More than twenty-five hundred years have passed, and they are still sealed. Parts of them are understood, but most are not. The point is, why give these prophecies so far in advance if they were to remain sealed until the end times? In part, at least, they give us hints about types and symbols. Of far greater import, however, is the fact that there are literal, physical events being held in abeyance by the Lord, to await the precise moment of their unveiling.

In the Scripture from 1 Peter, the apostle concluded his thought by saying that even the angels have a deep curiosity about prophecy. As creatures of eternity, the restrictions of time/space must seem especially peculiar to them. The fact that prophecy would be arranged around the calendar of seasons and festivals, hours, days, weeks, and months would be strange, indeed.

To the angels, this thing called "time" must seem constricting and limiting. How, they must ask, can anything at all useful come out of a single line of time? But as they watch us, they must surely be learning the lessons that can only come out of a strictly controlled redemptive timeline. Humanity is a like a continuing manual of instruction, a demonstration of the fruitlessness of evil.

The restrictions of time place natural limits upon this universe of sin. On the other hand, they allow the problem of evil to be addressed sequentially, or serially. Prophetic announcements are made, then fulfilled to the letter. History is no accident; it is a design.

MILLENNIAL MEN

We have already introduced the "millennial day" theological interpretation of Scripture. Briefly, it states that the six days of Creation followed by the seventh are but a model of future history. It will be played out upon the six millennial days of history, to be followed by a seventh: the millennial reign of Jesus upon the Davidic throne.

But the seven thousand years of human history are marked out in many different ways. They are seen in dispensations, covenants, and specific events, like wars, Israel's dispersions, Temple periods, and Christ's Crucifixion.

But the timeline is also marked out by the lives of specific men, each of whom is important to future history.

The first, of course, was Adam. Created from the dust of the ground, he was the perfect human being. As far as we know, the universe never witnessed a human being until his creation. From the human perspective, he was designed in God's image to live eternally. He was created in innocence, but was quite obviously equipped with an innate knowledge of God and nature.

EVIL IN THE GARDEN

Adam's condition has been called "innocence." He was placed into an environment that was the most favorable man can imagine. The weather was perfect, with no horrifying tempests, tornados, hurricanes, flooding rains, or droughts. Vegetation, wildlife, and natural ecosystems were in perfect harmony.

But with Adam, God went a step further. He planted a "garden" called Eden. It featured a glorious river and ideal conditions of physical and esthetic perfection. There, Adam was given a suitable helper, taken from his very flesh. He was anesthetized and God performed an operation:

> And the LORD God caused a deep sleep to fall upon Adam, and he slept: and he took one of his ribs, and closed up the flesh instead thereof; And the rib, which the LORD God had taken from man, made he a woman, and brought her unto the man.
>
> And Adam said, This is now bone of my bones, and flesh of my flesh: she shall be called Woman, because she was taken out of Man. (Genesis 2:21—23)

Adam and his mate lived without the knowledge of the sin that had raged through God's heaven and their own universe. They knew nothing of Satan and his angels. But they did know one thing for sure: There was a forbidden tree in the middle of Eden. The consumption of its fruit carried the sentence of death: "But of the tree of the knowledge of good and evil, thou shalt not eat of it: for in the day that thou eatest thereof thou shalt surely die" (Genesis 2:17).

This warning was given to Adam before the creation of Eve. Later, the first couple ate the fruit...and died, but not before centuries had passed. Adam lived to be 930 years of age. But he did die on the *very day* he consumed the fruit, if we reckon a day as a thousand years.

This is the basis of the redemptive timeline. It must be viewed from the Lord's perspective. But there is another point to be made about the forbidden tree. Its name, "the knowledge of good and evil," clearly shows that evil was present, even in the midst of innocence. Evil existed prior to their "original sin."

In other words, even Eden wasn't perfectly holy. Standing at its center like a dark ensign of the approaching enemy, the tree was a kind of gate.

Its fruit would apparently allow one to obtain a vision of the universe beyond Eden's boundaries. And what would one see? Quite simply, one would gain awareness of the great battle that already raged throughout the heavens.

The tree was a focal point of good and evil, meaning that God had made it so. In a very real way, it reminds us of another tree that grew some four thousand years later. This tree provided the wood for the Cross of Christ. It, too, was a focal point for the battle of good versus evil.

But unlike the first tree, this one provided a remedy for the problem of evil and its attendant harvest of sin. The first Adam ingested the preexisting evil, making it a part of humanity. It manifested itself in sin. Adam's descendant, Christ, nailed the weight and penalty of sin to His Cross. He became a second Adam, who did what the first was unable to do: "And so it is written, The first man Adam was made a living soul; the last Adam was made a quickening spirit" (1 Corinthians 15:45).

The Cross of Heaven and Earth

Just beyond the dimensional veil, there rages a battle. It has been boiling along for millennia. When the Serpent inveigled Eve and Adam to partake of the forbidden fruit, Adam took an unbearable burden upon himself. As a mere human, he became engaged in something much larger than himself. Both he and his wife were now involved in the battle to restore the broken universe.

But their thoughtless action resulted in another—and greater—action. God cursed the tempting Serpent with a curse that contained a blessing for mankind: "And I will put enmity between thee and the woman, and between thy seed and her seed; it shall bruise thy head, and thou shalt bruise his heel" (Genesis 3:15).

The bruising of the Serpent's head took place at Christ's Cross, when He paid the penalty for sin. He became accursed for mankind. Moses codified this principle in the Torah, when he gave the law concerning a rebellious son:

And if a man have committed a sin worthy of death, and he be to be put to death, and thou hang him on a tree: His body shall not remain all night upon the tree, but thou shalt in any wise bury him that day; (for he that is hanged is accursed of God;) that thy land be not defiled, which the LORD thy God giveth thee for an inheritance. (Deuteronomy 21:22)

Thus, the tree becomes both an active principle and a symbol…both the cause and the cure for man's sin. More importantly, it becomes both cause and cure for the broken universe:

For it pleased the Father that in him should all fulness dwell; And, having made peace through the blood of his cross, by him to reconcile all things unto himself; by him, I say, whether they be things in earth, or things in heaven. And you, that were sometime alienated and enemies in your mind by wicked works, yet now hath he reconciled. (Colossians 1:19–21)

In the exegesis of the Lord's redemptive activity, this is a key passage. And twice, it uses a key word: "reconciled." This term is from the Greek verb *katallasso,* which denotes "change" or "exchange." In the language of the first century, it was used to describe money changing, in which one type of money was exchanged for another.

Its core meaning is "to change something completely, from one thing to another." Thus, Christ's propitiatory activity changes man from a condition of enmity with God to a position of friendship, from wrath to acceptance, from alienation to adoption.

But note that the reconciliation of the Cross extends beyond the earth and humanity. The reconciliation extends to "things in heaven."

Amazingly then, the actions of the first Adam at the first tree are cancelled by the actions of the second Adam at the second tree. In the first instance, the Serpent is present as tempter. In the second, he is gravely wounded, as the force of the Crucifixion inflicts upon him a mortal wound.

The Serpent started a fire in the garden that flared up across ages of sin, finally burning out of his control. It blew back upon him at the Cross, and will one day be the place of his eternal residence. He started the fire of his own immolation.

THE TREE OF LIFE

But there was another tree in the garden. It is first mentioned in Genesis 2:9: "And out of the ground made the LORD God to grow every tree that is pleasant to the sight, and good for food; the **tree of life** also in the midst of the garden, and the tree of knowledge of good and evil" (emphasis added).

The third chapter of Genesis plainly tells us that the "tree of life" is connected with immortality. Its appearance in the garden strengthens the assertion that Adam and Eve were first created to experience eternal life. Apparently, its fruit was accessible and permissible. Along with the other fruit trees in the garden, it provided food.

However, this condition didn't last long. After the first couple had fallen to temptation and sin, God reassessed their condition. The decision was made that they should not be allowed immortality. Man was banished from the garden, and the tree remained under guard.

> And the LORD God said, Behold, the man is become as one of us, to know good and evil: and now, lest he put forth his hand, and take also of the **tree of life**, and eat, and live for ever:
> Therefore the LORD God sent him forth from the garden of Eden, to till the ground from whence he was taken. So he drove out the man; and he placed at the east of the garden of Eden Cherubims, and a flaming sword which turned every way, to keep the way of the **tree of life**. (Genesis 3:24, emphasis added)

This is the last time that the "tree of life" is directly mentioned until we reach the book of Revelation. There, access to it is extended to the overcomer…the faithful saint who patiently awaits the promises of Scripture: "He that hath an ear, let him hear what the Spirit saith unto the churches; To him that overcometh will I give to eat of the **tree of life**, which is in the midst of the paradise of God" (Revelation 2:7, emphasis added).

At the end of Revelation, the glorious tree is seen in the New Jerusalem:

> In the midst of the street of it, and on either side of the river, was there the **tree of life**, which bare twelve manner of fruits, and yielded her fruit every month: and the leaves of the tree were for the healing of the nations.…
>
> Blessed are they that do his commandments, that they may have right to the tree of life, and may enter in through the gates into the city. (Revelation 22:2, 14, emphasis added)

THE TREE OF TIME

It is quite significant that Adam, the man whose life measured out the first millennium, is connected to the redeemed world of the future by a tree. Though it cannot be said for sure, the "tree of life" appears to be unique. It is mentioned in two biblical contexts—the Garden of Eden and the New Jerusalem.

Its two appearances are separated by seven thousand years. First, in Eden, it offered the promise of eternal life. At last, in the New Jerusalem, its ancient potential is fully realized.

Is the tree seven thousand years old? Perhaps so, but that is immaterial. In fact, at some point during the life of Adam, it was taken back to heaven, where it will find its place in the City of God, the New Jerusalem.

Imagine, for a moment, that we might join it in its travels. After Adam is banished from the garden, it is whisked back to heaven and planted in a beautiful place, where it awaits the conclusion of the necessary historical elements prophesied in the Bible.

On earth, it resided in time. Here, in heaven, time is measured differently, if at all. Perhaps time is plastic and flexible. Perhaps it is possible to move back and forth, watching earth from various vantage points.

At some point, the New Jerusalem was sufficiently complete to receive the tree. From our perspective, this probably happened after Christ's Resurrection, as He rose to heaven "to prepare a place" for us (John 14:3). Revelation 22 reveals that "place" as a fully completed structure of unutterable beauty.

In its final situation, the tree has multiplied, so that replications of it appear on both sides of New Jerusalem's river. Furthermore, it is a real tree, whose leaves apparently have pharmaceutical qualities, since they are mentioned for their healing properties. They will heal the nations.

NOAH AND THE SECOND MILLENNIUM

The first millennium was marked by Adam's great fall from grace. Sin raged in unimaginable ways, as the evil powers of heaven trafficked openly among men, bringing forbidden knowledge and genetic corruption.

The garden was gone, along with the Tree of Life and the land of paradise. In their place, a debased, sensual, and power-crazed population spread immorality to the four corners of the earth. A grieving God looked down upon them with dismay. His resolution to destroy mankind resulted in the Great Flood of Noah:

> And God saw that the wickedness of man was great in the earth, and that every imagination of the thoughts of his heart was only evil continually.
>
> And it repented the LORD that he had made man on the earth, and it grieved him at his heart. And the LORD said, I will destroy man whom I have created from the face of the earth; both man, and beast, and the creeping thing, and the fowls of the air; for it repenteth me that I have made them.
>
> But Noah found grace in the eyes of the LORD. These are

the generations of Noah: Noah was a just man and perfect in his generations, and Noah walked with God. (Genesis 6:5–9)

In the extended narrative, God instructed Noah to build a ship that would survive the deluge. He, his wife, his three sons, and their wives brought humanity into the wreckage of the post-Flood world.

Noah, being "perfect in his generations," could boast a genealogy that went directly back to Adam through his son Seth. It had not been corrupted by the illicit interaction between the fallen angels and the daughters of men. Therefore, the Messianic line was still intact.

The descendants of Noah's three sons—Ham, Shem, and Japheth—repopulated the world. The line of Shem brought forth Arphaxad, whose lineage culminated in Abraham.

The righteous Noah, born in the first century of humanity's second millennium, kept his family line pure, thus enabling the human race to continue. More than that, from his son, the godly line of Shem would eventually bring forth the tribe of Judah, out of which came the Messianic line.

Noah was born was born six hundred years before the Flood. He lived to be 950 years old, and died within a few months of Abraham's birth.

As the man of the second millennium, Noah's importance lay in his refusal to become part of the wickedness that characterized the old world. He carried the unsullied "seed of the woman" through an entire thousand years, to be handed down to the man of the next millennium, Abraham.

ABRAHAM AND THE THIRD MILLENNIUM

Abraham was born approximately 1996 BC. His birth is strategically placed halfway between the birth of Adam and the birth of Christ. He is the celebrated man of faith, born into the idolatry of post-Flood Mesopotamia, who followed the Lord in obedience.

His faith was tested in many ways, but two are recorded in the book of Hebrews:

> By faith Abraham, when he was called to go out into a place
> which he should after receive for an inheritance, obeyed; and he
> went out, not knowing whither he went.... By faith Abraham,
> when he was tried, offered up Isaac: and he that had received the
> promises offered up his only begotten son. (Hebrews 11:8, 17)

Through his belief in God's promise, the seed of the Messiah was safely carried through the third millennium. His pivotal placement in history made him the "man of promise."

Genealogically, Abraham was a direct descendant of Noah's son, Shem. He was of wealth and noble stature. But the Lord told him to leave his homeland and venture far to the west, to an unknown and hostile territory. He and his family took up residence in Canaan. There, he experienced the challenge of a war against four Gentile kings. And there, he paid tithes to Melchizedek.

The Lord recognized the faith of the great patriarch. To Abraham and his progeny, the Lord unconditionally awarded the land grant that is disputed territory to this day: "In the same day the LORD made a covenant with Abram, saying, Unto thy seed have I given this land, from the river of Egypt unto the great river, the river Euphrates" (Genesis 15:18).

From Egypt to the Euphrates, the Kingdom will one day bring fertility and prosperity to the deserts and fiefdoms of the Middle East. Disputes about the land grant center on the question of descent. Arabs believe that through Ishmael, they have an unquestioned right to the land. But the biblical view of the inheritance is utterly unambiguous. Isaac and his offspring are to be the heirs of the Promised Land.

An incident in Abraham's own household predicts the family argument that would grow to worldwide significance. Ishmael scoffed at Isaac, and God promptly assured Abraham not to worry:

And Sarah saw the son of Hagar the Egyptian, which she
had born unto Abraham, mocking. Wherefore she said unto
Abraham, Cast out this bondwoman and her son: for the son
of this bondwoman shall not be heir with my son, even with
Isaac.

And the thing was very grievous in Abraham's sight
because of his son. And God said unto Abraham, Let it not
be grievous in thy sight because of the lad, and because of thy
bondwoman; in all that Sarah hath said unto thee, hearken
unto her voice; for in Isaac shall thy seed be called.
(Genesis 21:9–12)

The miracle of Isaac's birth to a couple well past childbearing age
is also celebrated as a memorable act of faith. Through Isaac, a type of
Christ, came the fulfillment of Messiah's birth. Thus, Abraham and Sarah
are divinely ordained parents of the faithful:

Therefore sprang there even of one, and him as good as dead,
so many as the stars of the sky in multitude, and as the sand
which is by the sea shore innumerable.

These all died in faith, not having received the promises,
but having seen them afar off, and were persuaded of them,
and embraced them, and confessed that they were strangers
and pilgrims on the earth. For they that say such things
declare plainly that they seek a country.
(Hebrews 11:12–14)

Abraham is the great pioneer of faith, pointing the way toward
Christ. But as the progenitor of the third millennium, his real importance lies in the fact that he is the first Hebrew. On the basis of this new
and exciting start, Isaac and Jacob go forth to further the Messianic line.
Judah, one of Jacob's sons, is the patriarch of the tribe from which Jesus
would come.

David and the Fourth Millennium

David, the man of the fourth millennium, established the kingdom and the throne that will one day be headed by the Lord Himself. He began his reign in Hebron. Soon thereafter, his armies took the high ground that would become Jerusalem. That site was occupied by the threshing floor of Ornan the Jebusite. David purchased the entire area, which became known as Mount Zion, for fifty shekels of silver. And for the heart of the threshing floor, he paid the enormous sum of six hundred shekels of gold, by weight.

Having obtained the sacred territory, he built an altar to the Lord and offered sacrifices. His precedent established this place as the beloved Zion, home of the Temples, past and future. His son Solomon built the First Temple there. Patterned after the Mosaic and Davidic Tabernacles, it was the model for the great Millennial Temple of prophecy.

Preaching at Antioch of Pisidia, the apostle Paul summarized the importance of David's position:

> And afterward they desired a king: and God gave unto them Saul the son of Cis, a man of the tribe of Benjamin, by the space of forty years.
>
> And when he had removed him, he raised up unto them David to be their king; to whom also he gave testimony, and said, I have found David the son of Jesse, a man after mine own heart, which shall fulfil all my will.
>
> Of this man's seed hath God according to his promise raised unto Israel a Saviour, Jesus. (Acts 13:21–23)

David, the warrior king, pointed the way to Christ. But he was also the amazing singer, poet, and prophet whose psalms stand like guideposts to the latter days. Early in his life, as he came to the court of King Saul, his attributes were extolled by a servant of the court:

Then answered one of the servants, and said, Behold, I have seen a son of Jesse the Bethlehemite, that is cunning in playing, and a mighty valiant man, and a man of war, and prudent in matters, and a comely person, and the LORD is with him. (1 Samuel 16:18)

David was all of this, and more. His very personality is imprinted upon Judaism to this day. David's life, songs, and poetry are all typical of a multitalented but imperfect Israel. Like Israel, David made many mistakes. But he always hearkened to the Lord's Word, and by grace, his salvation was secure.

The throne of David, Solomon, and the monarchs who followed them dominated the fourth millennium—forming the kingdom of Israel. It is interesting that four is the number associated with the kingdom, in general.

JESUS CHRIST AND THE FIFTH MILLENNIUM

In the West, it is almost universally acknowledged that the appearance of the Lord Jesus Christ on earth is the pinnacle of human history. His teaching and self-sacrifice shaped Western civilization in many ways, both bold and subtle. Until the last few decades, the Bible (particularly the New Testament) was the guide to law, society, and politics.

Christ is the Man of the fifth millennium. It seems a strange "coincidence" that five is the number of grace, the very quality imprinted upon the millennium of His First Coming. The Cross of Christ changed everything. John plainly shows that grace is His chief characteristic: "And the Word was made flesh, and dwelt among us, (and we beheld his glory, the glory as of the only begotten of the Father,) full of **grace** and truth" (John 1:14, emphasis added).

Two thousand years earlier, Abraham and Isaac had pointed the way to His ultimate sacrifice. Then, within the sphere of Abraham's faith,

Moses came along and delivered the twelve tribes from Egyptian bondage. In the process, the Law was given at Mt. Sinai. To Israel, it was as though the 613 commandments had superseded the grace that radiated from the promise of Abraham.

Actually, the Law was simply a primer, given to teach man the elementary truth about his sin. Grace came before Moses, and for that matter, it preceded Abraham. Jesus once said, "Before Abraham was, I am" (John 8:58).

But at Christ's coming, salvation came to all men, Jew and Gentile alike. His grace began to shine forth into the entire world. John 1:17 makes the contrast clear: "For the law was given by Moses, but grace and truth came by Jesus Christ."

The salvation that came by Christ's grace began to go forth into the evil ruling systems that covered the world with wars and a host of atrocities too long to enumerate. He came as a light shining into the sinister crevices of malevolent power. Men of faith, huddled together in the darkness, found His salvation and carried it to others.

Thus, Christ offered His saving grace to individual men. The Jews of the first century had hoped that His coming would bring a revolution that would overthrow Rome and make the throne of David a living reality. But that was not His plan.

Rejected by His own nation, He miraculously transferred the promise of His Kingdom to the nations. This, He did without interposing Himself upon them as a political power. Rather, He created a spiritual body, invisible to the world but influential in the strength of His spirit.

To this day, the most powerful force on earth is the Spirit of the Lord, acting through the body of Christ: "Now ye are the body of Christ, and members in particular" (1 Corinthians 12:27). The "members," or specific parts of the body of Christ, are to be found in every conceivable walk of life, from the highest office of power to the most impoverished ghetto. Through this body, the Lord is accomplishing the great miracle of calling out a special body of believers who will glorify His name eternally.

The Mysterious Man of the Sixth Millennium

This brings us to the sixth millennium, also dominated by a very special man. He is the "redeemed man." Not necessarily known for his worldly stature or influence, he is the man led by the Spirit of the Lord.

He leads a life of loving sacrifice…the life of Christ. He may be a missionary or a businessman, farmer, or academic. She may be a housewife or merchant, an intellectual, or a waitress.

In the Middle Ages, members of Christ's body might have been members of the nobility or lowly serfs. More likely, they were the latter. Some died in ignominy; others were celebrated for their faith.

At the beginning of the sixth millennium, the world had sunk into the deepest squalor. Truly spiritual men were objects of great persecution. We now refer to this period as the Dark Ages.

At the dawn of this millennium, the world was dominated by a transitory host of minor monarchs, warlords, chieftans, sultans, and pretenders of all stripes. History hardly remembers men like Grimus the Saxon, Ethelred II of Brittania, Robert the Sage of France, Leopold I of Austria, Otho II of Germany, the Olafs of Norway and Sweden, Alfonso V of Spain, Pope Sylvester, Basil II of Greece, Sultan Al Mahmoud, and Ching-Song, emperor of China. And these are but a few of the greats and near-greats of AD 1000. No one in particular stands out.

As one traces the march of the millennia, it is at first a great mystery that no single person seems to characterize the sixth. Then, it becomes clear. The sixth millennium—the sixth millennial day—is the millennium of mankind. Having been created on day number six, he has been imprinted with this number since the beginning.

This, the millennium of the common man, typifies the life and work of mankind under the bondage of sin. It was the era of repression, evil tyranny, and ignorance. It was characterized by degradation, drudgery, and hopelessness.

But then, in the sixteenth century, the light began to break out, shining through a tiny crevice. In 1521, Martin Luther delivered his theses on the grace of the Lord. Other reformers followed his lead. Freed from the bondage of a political priesthood, science began to lead man into a new consciousness. Copernicus, Galileo, Newton, Francis Bacon, and a host of brilliant men began to extol God's creation in an unprecedented era of discovery.

The Bible began to be printed in the languages of the common man. In 1611, James I, king of England, brought the Bible to the masses. In Europe and the rest of the world, this trend caught on in a magnificent way until, at last, global missions spread the Word of God to every country of the world.

By the late nineteenth century, Bible-believing churches had been established in the four corners of the earth. At the time, some thought that the world would be conquered for Jesus Christ. But, just as in the millennium of Christ's First Coming, this was not God's plan. The twentieth century brought global warfare, communism, and an intellectual "God is dead" agnosticism.

Through it all, the body of Christ survived...and thrives to this day. Its goal is not to conquer the world. Rather, it is to send out the call to those who will hear and obey.

We are now at the end of this millennium. As it draws to a close, the body of Christ awaits the coming of their Lord. In an instant...in the twinkling of an eye, the Age of Grace will come to a close. The millennium of the redeemed man will give way to the long-awaited millennium of our Lord.

THE DAY OF THE LORD, THE SEVENTH MILLENNIUM

This millennium is the seventh day of human history. We and others have often noted that the apostles and church fathers of the second century believed in the millennial day. The Day of the Lord begins with the seven-year "time of Jacob's trouble" (Jeremiah 30:7), which prepares the world for a millennium of Messianic rule.

The dominant man of this millennium will be the glorified Christ:

> For as the lightning cometh out of the east, and shineth even unto the west; so shall also the coming of the Son of man be. For wheresoever the carcass is, there will the eagles be gathered together.
>
> Immediately after the tribulation of those days shall the sun be darkened, and the moon shall not give her light, and the stars shall fall from heaven, and the powers of the heavens shall be shaken:
>
> And then shall appear the sign of the Son of man in heaven: and then shall all the tribes of the earth mourn, and they shall see the Son of man coming in the clouds of heaven with power and great glory. (Matthew 24:27–30)

Christ's First Coming, at the dawn of the fifth millennium, brought salvation, grace, and truth. It began an era which hearkened all the way back to Abraham and salvation by grace through faith. In the two millennia that followed, the institutions of man rose and fell, but individuals continued to answer His call.

His Second Coming, at the dawn of the seventh millennium, will bring dynamic rule over a restored earth. Sin will be controlled by force and decree:

> His eyes were as a flame of fire, and on his head were many crowns; and he had a name written, that no man knew, but he himself. And he was clothed with a vesture dipped in blood: and his name is called The Word of God. And the armies which were in heaven followed him upon white horses, clothed in fine linen, white and clean.
>
> And out of his mouth goeth a sharp sword, that with it he

should smite the nations: and he shall rule them with a rod of iron: and he treadeth the winepress of the fierceness and wrath of Almighty God. (Revelation 19:12–15)

Christ, the Man of the sixth millennium, is God Himself, visible among His people. His day will be the day when faith shall have turned to sight. For the preceding six millennia, man was asked to have faith. In the seventh, faith will not even be a factor.

And he shall rule them with a rod of iron; as the vessels of a potter shall they be broken to shivers: even as I received of my Father. And I will give him the morning star. He that hath an ear, let him hear what the Spirit saith unto the churches. (Revelation 2:27–29)

Men will see Christ in person. They will know who He is and what He stands for. Though sin will be present in the remnant which inherits the Kingdom, it will not be tolerated. His rule will be absolute, perfect, and just.

The first Adam was created to rule the earth in perfection. Six millennial days later, his descendant, the second Adam, will bring his destiny to reality. Our journey through time has a destination.

7

MULTIDIMENSIONAL ENCOUNTERS
IN THE SPIRIT WORLD

Life on planet earth presents the secular intellect with a curious set of challenges. Though he denies spiritual truth, man's science has led him to suspect that reality is something more than common experience would suggest. Yet, he is barred from access to the worlds that he suspects lie just beyond his sight. Mathematical theory has come close to making sense of the ghostly nether world of phantasms and creatures that pop into and out of our sight.

Other dimensions are tantalizingly near, yet they cannot be seen or touched. According to physicist Michio Kaku, author of *Beyond Einstein,* current theoreticians have identified at least ten dimensions. To the non-mathematical mind, they are as inscrutable as the structure of an atom.

Of our visible universe, Kaku writes:

> We now believe that the original expansion of the universe
> had its origin in a much greater, much more explosive process:
> the breakdown of the ten-dimensional fabric of space-time.
> Like a dam bursting, the ten-dimensional fabric of space-time
> ruptured violently and rapidly re-formed into two separate
> universes of lower energy: a four-dimensional universe (our
> own) and a six-dimensional one.[28]

Today, mathematicians are working overtime to solve the riddle of time, space, matter, and energy in our universe. Their hypotheses sound strange. But they do agree on one thing: there are other universes (other dimensions) that lie just beyond our sight. Spatially, they are as close as one's fingertips, but as far away as tomorrow.

By way of contrast, the man of faith accepts the reality of other dimensions as simple, factual truth. They are personalized in many ways. They may be seen as "God's throne," heaven, or the heavens.

Or, they may be closer to earth, in the angelic realm that lies just beyond our vision. It is so close to our dimension that it may sometimes be visible, or audible. The Bible is quite open about the fact that angels and demons frequent the regions of the atmospheric heavens.

Then, there is the Old Testament *sheol*, known in the New Testament as *hades*. *Hades* and *sheol* are the Bible's way of talking about the underworld. Within the dimension of *hades* is "paradise," sometimes called "Abraham's bosom." As biblical expositors have written about these places, they have developed a compartmentalized view of the underworld. There are at least three compartments: the place of torment, paradise, and the abyss. A bit later, we will deal with them separately.

Finally, there is "the future," or "the prophetic future." Routinely, the Bible mentions it as a certainty. Furthermore, it predicts Messiah's first and second appearances. His first—already past for us—validates the proposition that the future is laid out in advance...or may be perceived as such. One can argue about whether it is predetermined or simply viewed at its end point by an omniscient God. But the appearance of Jesus forever settles the question about the certainty of a future world. Among many other things, He came as the Lord of Time.

Therefore, when we read Old and New Testament prophecies about events still future to us, we view them as certainties. Prophetically, they are brought to us as "the future." Had it not been for God's prophets and the apostles of the New Testament, the existence of this dimension would not even be suspected. Tomorrow would be anybody's guess. Without the Bible, one might even speculate that the future exists only on a moment-by-moment basis. With it, the future is hopeful and bright, extending for ages upon ages. It is seen as *already existing, but not yet brought into play in our dimension.* In other words, the future resides in another area of time/space, *right now.* It is in another dimension.

Where are these other dimensions? Abraham's bosom is said to be somewhere beneath the earth's crust. It is the New Testament *hades…*the underworld abode of the dead. It seems to be characterized by a pleasant area (paradise) and an unpleasant one (hell). The two are separated by the "bottomless pit," sometimes called "the abyss" or "the great gulf."

From a rationalistic point of view, all these places are located in the region below the earth's surface that modern science identifies as zones of molten rock and metal. How could paradise have been established in a subterranean cavern? Molten rock under heat and pressure provide no place for relaxation. From the scientific perspective, there is no possible way that this could be true.

THE HOLLOW EARTH

However, it should be pointed out that over the years, the so-called "hollow-earth theory" has been adopted by many cults and pseudo-scientific groups. One of these was the inner circle of Adolf Hitler's staff, including Hans Horbiger, his minister of science. Hitler believed Horbiger, and attempted to prove that his bizarre belief was scientifically valid. Louis Pauwels and Jacques Bergier, writing in *The Morning of the Magicians,* record the events of their "scientific" efforts.

In April, 1942, at the height of World War II, when Germany's entire strength was being directed toward its military effort, the occultists of the Golden Dawn and Thule Societies persuaded Hitler to divert a dirigible, a small ship, and ground forces to a strange task. They also commandeered one of Germany's two precious, long-range radar sets—at the time, badly needed to spot allied bombers.

Then, Pauwels and Bergier say:

An expedition organized with the approval of [Herrman] Goering, [Heinrich] Himmler and Hitler set out from the Reich surrounded by the greatest secrecy. The members of this expedition were some of the greatest experts on radar. Under the direction of Dr. Heinz Fisher, well known for his work on infra-red rays, they disembarked on the island of Rügen in the Baltic. The expedition was equipped with the most up-to-date radar apparatus, despite the fact that these instruments were still rare at that time, and distributed over the principal nerve-centers of the German defense system.

However, the observations to be carried out on the island of Rügen were considered by the Admiralty General Staff as of capital importance for the offensive which Hitler was preparing to launch on every front.

Immediately on arrival at their destination Dr. Fisher aimed his radar at the sky at an angle of 45 degrees. There appeared to be nothing to detect in that particular direction. The other members of the expedition thought that a test was being carried out. They did not know what was expected of them; the object of these experiments would be revealed to them later. To their amazement, the radar remained fixed in the same position for several days. It was then that they learned the reason: Hitler had formed the idea that the Earth is not convex but concave. We are not living on the outside of the globe, but inside it.[29]

Gerard Kuiper, professor of astronomy at Mt. Palomar observatory, later wrote:

High officials in the German Admiralty and Air Force believed in the theory of a hollow earth. They thought this would be useful for locating the whereabouts of the British Fleet, because the concave curvature of the earth would facilitate long-distance observation by means of infra-red rays, which are less curved than visible rays.

Pauwels and Bergier further state:

> The defenders of the hollow earth theory, who organized
> the famous para-scientific expedition to the island of Rügen,
> believed that we are living inside a globe fixed into a mass of
> rock extending to infinity, adhering to its concave sides. The
> sky is in the middle of this globe; it is a mass of bluish gas, with
> points of brilliant light which we mistake for stars. There are
> only the Sun and the Moon—both infinitely smaller than the
> orthodox astronomers think. This is the entire Universe. We are
> all alone, surrounded by rock.[30]

Where could so-called "scientists" have come up with such an idea?
The answer seems readily apparent if one remembers that the biblical
paradise is inside a hollowed-out compartment in the underworld. All
the ancient ideas about a mythical paradise are tied to its being inside,
rather than outside, a solid enclosure.

Hitler saw his "paradise" inside an enclosure, isolated from everything else. His vision was to control this place, becoming its god, and
creating a utopia.

Actually, there are two "hollow earth theories." We have just seen an
example of one type. The other pictures the earth itself as being hollow.
In the mid-nineteenth century, the British author Edward Bulwer-Lytton
wrote a novel called *The Coming Race*. In it, he condensed legendary, religious, and mythological history into a story about the "Vril." Occultic
history believes in the existence of these super-beings with paranormal
powers. He wrote that they would one day rise from their cavernous
inner-world lairs to dominate humanity.

The traditions of the hollow earth are found throughout the literature
of the ancient world. The earliest epics of the Sumerian and Babylonian
cultures told of the Annunaki, who lived inside the hollow earth. In the
epic of the heroic Gilgamesh, he visited an ancestor, Utnapishtim, who
lived deep within the earth.

The ancient Greeks believed that their gods resided there. Ulysses once offered up sacrifices, believing that the ancients would rise to the surface of the earth to give him advice and counsel. Pluto was believed to reign over the underworld and was lord over the spirits of the deceased.

In America, the first record of the hollow earth theory was publicly recorded on April 10, 1818. The following letter was sent to scientists, Congress, and university leaders:

To All the World:
I declare that the earth is hollow and habitable in the interior. It contains several solid, concentric spheres, placed one inside the other and is open to the pole at an angle of from 12 to 16 degrees. I undertake to prove the truth of what I am asserting, and am ready to explore the interior of the Earth if the world agrees to help me in my undertaking.[31]

The letter was signed by John Cleves Symmes, a captain in the Ohio infantry. For the rest of his life, this man lectured and wrote treatises in support of his strange belief. He even stated that the "ten lost tribes of Israel" would one day be discovered living comfortably inside the earth.

It is fascinating that this belief is also well known among the tribal medicine men of the Americas. When Europeans came to North and South America, they discovered that the indigenous peoples strongly believed in subterranean societies of supermen. They still do…to this day.

In 1926, the famous Arctic explorer Richard E. Byrd circumnavigated the North Pole by airplane. Then, in 1929, he did the same thing in Antarctica, flying around the South Pole. Shortly afterward, he recorded in his memoirs that during these flights, he had seen what he believed to be the entrances to the hollow earth. It appeared to him as a tropical paradise, with trees, animals, and flowing water! In personal appearances all over the world, he spoke openly of this belief.

Today, no one would subscribe to Byrd's strange claims. By now, our satellites would have photographed any such openings. They would have been quickly explored, if not exploited. Yet the Bible maintains that there are places beneath the earth. To those who believe in the divine and complete inspiration of Scripture, it is a matter of faith that they are there. Perhaps we should think of them as being displaced into a different dimension. Where miners and drillers would find only solid rock, an interdimensional explorer might actually encounter the habitable places mentioned in Scripture. Like angels and demons, the underworld occupies a dimension just beyond our sight.

THE "GREAT GULF"

Perhaps the best description of this condition is seen in Luke's Gospel, where Jesus gives us the account of the rich man who died and went to hell. In the narrative, he is contrasted with a poor beggar, who was received into paradise:

> There was a certain rich man, which was clothed in purple and fine linen, and fared sumptuously every day: And there was a certain beggar named Lazarus, which was laid at his gate, full of sores, And desiring to be fed with the crumbs which fell from the rich man's table: moreover the dogs came and licked his sores.
>
> And it came to pass, that the beggar died, and was carried by the angels into Abraham's bosom: the rich man also died, and was buried; And in hell he lifted up his eyes, being in torments, and seeth Abraham afar off, and Lazarus in his bosom.
>
> And he cried and said, Father Abraham, have mercy on me, and send Lazarus, that he may dip the tip of his finger in water, and cool my tongue; for I am tormented in this flame.
>
> But Abraham said, Son, remember that thou in thy lifetime receivedst thy good things, and likewise Lazarus evil things: but now he is comforted, and thou art tormented. And beside all this, between us and you there is a great gulf fixed: so that they

which would pass from hence to you cannot; neither can they pass to us, that would come from thence.

Then he said, I pray thee therefore, father, that thou wouldest send him to my father's house: For I have five brethren; that he may testify unto them, lest they also come into this place of torment.

Abraham saith unto him, They have Moses and the prophets; let them hear them. And he said, Nay, father Abraham: but if one went unto them from the dead, they will repent.

And he said unto him, If they hear not Moses and the prophets, neither will they be persuaded, though one rose from the dead. (Luke 16:19–31)

When Jesus gave this account to the Pharisees, He was teaching that the worldly things pursued by lustful men are viewed by God as detestable. What better way to teach this lesson than to give a glimpse of the afterlife, where the physical realities of this world are no longer important? So He relates an event that actually happened. It is the account of the rich man who dies and goes to "hell."

Actually, the rich man goes to a place called *hades* in New Testament Greek. Sometimes, it is called the underworld. In the Gospels, Jesus uses the term four different times. It corresponds to the Old Testament *sheol*. This is the region of the departed, whether righteous or wicked. Prior to Christ's Ascension, this also included the blessed dead.

In the entire Bible, this is the only first-person account of what life is like in the underworld. In other words, it is a virtual certainty that Jesus was relating an incident that had actually happened and that He had personally witnessed.

Reliable expositors agree that the picture presented here is not really a parable, as such. Rather, it is simply a statement of the natural order of things prior to Christ's Crucifixion. Blessed Jews went to reside with Abraham in paradise—hence, the expression "Abraham's bosom," which suggests a vital and intimate relationship between brothers.

The unfaithful went to *hades*. Both the rich man and Lazarus went to a location that shared some kind of common space. The destitute Lazarus was taken to Abraham's bosom by the angels. The rich man ended up in a place of torment. Still, he could *see* Abraham and Lazarus. There is a sense of proximity.

By the description given, the rich man ended up in a hot, dry, and thoroughly miserable place. He complains of being tortured by "flame." We are reminded of the description given by Christ when He describes the journey of a disembodied evil spirit: "When the unclean spirit is gone out of a man, he walketh through dry places, seeking rest, and findeth none" (Matthew 12:43).

Given the above, the rich man probably came to be confined in the desiccated and smoldering realm of evil spirits. It seems likely that he was tormented by demons in an agonizing environment. Traditionally, this place is called "the underworld." But as we have already said, it doesn't seem to be the *visible* underworld. Demons are normally invisible to humans, although they can become visible upon occasion. The "dry places" of their lonely travels must be in the underworld dimension known as *hades*.

Therefore, it does not defy logic to say that *hades* is actually under the earth, in some sort of huge, cavernous interior space that is dimensionally shifted so that it is invisible and inaccessible to humans. It is a world that parallels our own, lying alongside it in the closest possible proximity. It is an invisible inner world, inside our visible inner world.

Furthermore, this alternate space is compartmentalized in some interesting ways. Though separated by a great distance, the rich man could actually see Abraham in a beautiful and desirable setting. The former beggar, Lazarus, was now in close relationship with the great patriarch.

Amazingly, even though Abraham appeared to him "afar off," he was able to converse with the beloved father of the Hebrews, begging him for comfort and consolation. In a kind but firm manner, Abraham reminded him of the sensual pleasures of his past, earthly life. The rich man had accomplished his own paradise while still in his body. Now, in spirit, there could be no comfort. He had placed his faith in the physical world, ignoring the time-honored teaching that victory in the world to come could only be realized through faith.

Abraham reminded him of something else. He told the rich man that travel between the place of torment and paradise was blocked by some sort of "great gulf." Though tantalizingly close, he could not reach it. Again, we would note that the underworld—*hades* in the greater sense—contains the area known as paradise.

The Greek word used to describe the impassable abyss is *chasma*, the source of our English word "chasm." It doesn't take much imagination to visualize an enormous canyon or pit that cannot be crossed.

This "gulf" may, itself, describe a dimensional barrier of some kind. In fact, it may correspond to the deepest part of *hades,* the place called *tartaros,* the deepest and most secure region of the underworld prison. In today's language, we might refer to it as "maximum security."

Peter mentions this forbidding place as the destination of false teachers. In the following verse, the word "hell," is a translation of *tartaros*: "For if God spared not the angels that sinned, but cast them down to hell, and delivered them into chains of darkness, to be reserved unto judgment" (2 Peter 2:4).

Looking at the geography of the underworld, then, it appears to be both horizontally and vertically compartmentalized. Coexisting side by side are paradise and hell, exhibiting the same sort of contrast we see on earth, between, say, Hawaii and Death Valley.

Below, in a chasm of unspeakable isolation, are the fallen angels who participated in Satan's original rebellion. They are somehow locked in an impassable pit *(tartaros)* that occupies the lowest portions of hades.

From the human perspective, spirit beings seem able to penetrate barriers with ease. Our walls and doors are nothing to them. Their imprisonment, then, must involve some sort of dimensional barrier that is beyond our understanding. They are locked, or held in stasis, perhaps by some form of energy.

Not only that, but when the time comes, they may be unlocked by the proper authority. This may be done many times in many ways. But we have one good example in the ninth chapter of Revelation. One who holds the key to the bottomless pit opens a passageway to the surface of the earth:

> And the fifth angel sounded, and I saw a star fall from heaven unto the earth: and to him was given the key of the bottomless pit.
>
> And he opened the bottomless pit; and there arose a smoke out of the pit, as the smoke of a great furnace; and the sun and the air were darkened by reason of the smoke of the pit.
>
> And there came out of the smoke locusts upon the earth: and unto them was given power, as the scorpions of the earth have power. (Revelation 9:1–3)

In this passage, the phrase "bottomless pit" is a translation of two Greek words that mean, "well shaft of the abyss." From this description, it appears that there is a long passageway leading from the abyss to the earth's surface.

This would complete the case that hades is, indeed, in a location somewhere beneath our feet. And if we interpret Scripture literally, then the abyss, hades, and paradise are all in roughly the same place under the earth.

The "key" that unlocks the passage must be some sort of dimensional security device that removes the energy barrier now in place between the abyss and the surface of the earth. That being accomplished, hordes of demons storm the surface of the earth, led by their overlord, Apollyon. His name, by the way, is that of the ancient Greek demigod, Apollo, god of the sun. It makes perfect sense that he was one of the angels mentioned in Genesis chapter 6 as one of the "sons of God" who took human women as wives.

Like Peter, Jude used these heavenly defectors as an example of the fate of those who promote a false gospel: "And the angels which kept not their first estate, but left their own habitation, he hath reserved in everlasting chains under darkness unto the judgment of the great day" (Jude 6).

Today, these angels are locked in the abyss, chained in a prison where they await judgment. Their time will come at the Great White Throne mentioned in Revelation 20. Specifically, the contents of hades—no doubt, including these wretched ex-luminaries—will be emptied out into the "lake of fire."

> And the sea gave up the dead which were in it; and death and
> hell delivered up the dead which were in them: and they were
> judged every man according to their works. And death and hell
> were cast into the lake of fire. This is the second death. And
> whosoever was not found written in the book of life was cast
> into the lake of fire. (Revelation 20:13–15)

In these verses, the word "hell" is a rendering of the Greek *hades*. At the time of the final judgment, it will be emptied of the righteous, but will still be the holding place of the unrighteous of the ages. One day, the miserable creatures who linger there in gloomy anticipation of their coming judgment will be dumped into a final, fiery, eternal residence.

PARADISE TODAY

Does the underworld exist today? Certainly, it does, since Scripture is clear that the unredeemed of our age go there after death, to await judgment. Likewise, the abyss of *tartaros* still holds its dark angels tightly bound.

What, then, of paradise? Are Abraham and Lazarus still there, awaiting resurrection into the Kingdom Age? Certainly, they were still there at the great day of Passover, when Jesus died for the sin of mankind.

In the story of Christ's Crucifixion, Luke records the account of the penitent criminal on the Cross next to the Lord. This wretched man openly acknowledges his guilt before God. Jesus turns to him and says: "Today, shalt thou be with me in Paradise" (Luke 23:43).

We have already seen that paradise is a special place within the general subterranean dimensions of hades. When Jesus went there, He accomplished at least two things. First and foremost, He proclaimed victory to the ancient minions of evil and insurrection:

> For Christ also hath once suffered for sins, the just for the unjust, that he might bring us to God, being put to death in the flesh, but quickened by the Spirit:
> By which also he went and preached unto the spirits in prison; Which sometime were disobedient, when once the longsuffering of God waited in the days of Noah, while the ark was a preparing, wherein few, that is, eight souls were saved by water. (1 Peter 3:18)

Peter tells us in no uncertain terms that Christ proclaimed His finished work in the presence of those who had so grievously sinned in the days prior to the Great Flood of Noah. He did not dialogue with them...He preached to them! Precisely what He told them remains a mystery to us. But it seems likely that He informed them about all the Old Testament prophecies that He had fulfilled during His earthly, physical life.

He probably reminded them that He was the fulfillment of God's promise to Adam and Eve. He had bruised the head of their leader the old Serpent. In every conceivable way, He had established His Messianic credentials. It must have come as the most devastating possible revelation to these despicable creatures that they had chosen the wrong side. Now, the Messiah appeared in the place of their imprisonment to drive the point home to them. As they listened, the angels and demons must have been driven into their final agony.

Secondly, He led the righteous into the Kingdom of Heaven, taking the faithful into the presence of the Almighty God. At His homecoming, heaven's populations must have rejoiced in the most remarkable way.

Paul mentioned Christ's triumphal actions in association with this trip to the lower earth. At His Ascension, He escorted the righteous from their temporary place of residence to their heavenly rest.

Wherefore he saith, When he ascended up on high, he led captivity captive, and gave gifts unto men. (Now that he ascended, what is it but that he also descended first into the lower parts of the earth? He that descended is the same also that ascended up far above all heavens, that he might fill all things.) (Ephesians 4:8–10)

Here, we have the plain statement that Christ descended into the regions we have been discussing, in order to ascend with the righteous in paradise. While there, He destroyed the power of the evil kingdom of Satan, as given in Colossians 2:15: "And having spoiled principalities and powers, he made a show of them openly, triumphing over them in it."

In other words, Christ destroyed and looted the powers of darkness. Then He led a triumphal parade into the heavens, in which the righteous dead were openly displayed as a trophy that celebrated the Son's victory. The precise details and state of paradise are to this day partially veiled. Does paradise still exist? There is no reason to doubt that. Are righteous souls there today? To say that there are not is to make an unsupportable statement.

Many make the point that paradise was removed to heaven as described in Ephesians 4:8, where "he ascended up on high, he led captivity captive." But there is not enough information to be dogmatic about this.

THE RESURRECTION

In the Resurrection of Jesus Christ, something completely new and exciting had happened. A dead human body had risen to newness of life—not in the sense of mere resuscitation, but in a fullness and perfection that it never possessed before. Humankind still does not fully realize what happened upon that day. But some part of eternity had forever been deposited in this dimension.

Christ's action had placed in motion an inexorable advancement toward bringing this entire dimension to the same, glorified state. The Bible refers to this coming condition as "a new heaven and a new earth" (Revelation 21:1).

Something happened on that day that still challenges human intellect in the most rigorous way. Yet it happened among common people, with all their foibles, prejudices, and presuppositions. In John 20, verses 18 through 28, a simple but astonishing narrative illustrates the coming of that new thing:

> Mary Magdalene came and told the disciples that she had seen the Lord, and that he had spoken these things unto her. Then the same day at evening, being the first day of the week, when the doors were shut where the disciples were assembled for fear of the Jews, came Jesus and stood in the midst, and saith unto them, Peace be unto you.
>
> And when he had so said, he showed unto them his hands and his side. Then were the disciples glad, when they saw the Lord. Then said Jesus to them again, Peace be unto you: as my Father hath sent me, even so send I you. And when he had said this, he breathed on them, and saith unto them, Receive ye the Holy Ghost: Whose soever sins ye remit, they are remitted unto them; and whose soever sins ye retain, they are retained.
>
> But Thomas, one of the twelve, called Didymus, was not with them when Jesus came. The other disciples therefore said unto him, We have seen the Lord. But he said unto them, Except I shall see in his hands the print of the nails, and put my finger into the print of the nails, and thrust my hand into his side, I will not believe.
>
> And after eight days again his disciples were within, and Thomas with them: then came Jesus, the doors being shut, and stood in the midst, and said, Peace be unto you. Then saith he to Thomas, Reach hither thy finger, and behold my hands; and

reach hither thy hand, and thrust it into my side: and be not faithless, but believing.

And Thomas answered and said unto him, My Lord and my God.

This account of the days immediately following Christ's Resurrection raises a number of questions about time-space dimensionality. At His first appearance on the Sunday of His Resurrection, He appeared in a locked room. It was a secure room...the hiding place of the disciples.

Suddenly, in some way, Jesus was there, right in the middle of the room. Moreover, He appeared in His physical body, showing them the wounds of His Crucifixion. That they were overjoyed is probably an understatement.

He offered them physical proof; they touched Him. Then, with the breath of His mouth, He conferred the Holy Spirit upon them. They became His apostles...His "sent ones." They had the power of His Spirit in salvation.

Thomas, however, had not been there to witness all this. It's not that he didn't believe that the Lord had been there. That's not what the text says. Rather, it indicates that Thomas didn't believe the Lord had been present *in physical form.*

It would probably have been easy for him to believe in a phantasm. That is, if Jesus had appeared to them as a spirit, Thomas wouldn't have had a problem. It was the Lord's physical presence that he doubted.

Some time before, while the disciples were fishing, Jesus had come to them at night...walking on the water. They had thought they were seeing a spirit—a ghost.

And in the fourth watch of the night Jesus went unto them, walking on the sea. And when the disciples saw him walking on the sea, they were troubled, saying, It is a spirit; and they cried out for fear. But straightway Jesus spake unto them, saying, Be of good cheer; it is I; be not afraid. (Matthew 14:25–27)

Then Jesus came aboard and soothed them. All was well. If He had simply walked away, they would have sworn to the end of their days that they had only seen the spirit of Jesus…not Jesus Himself.

Everybody believed in spirits, and so did they. That had been their first guess when He came across the water toward their boat.

A resurrected body…well, that was something else, entirely. There was no precedent for such a thing. Thomas may well have admitted that Jesus could have come to them in their locked room as a spirit being. But to admit that Jesus was there in His physical body…that was impossible. Thomas said that he would only believe if he *touched* the physical body of Jesus.

Thomas could have objected on another ground, as well. The room had been locked. How in the world could a physical body have come through a tightly barred door? He would probably have admitted that a ghost could have transmogrified through the walls. After all, it was a specter…made up of some sort of airy substance that could penetrate solids.

A physical body could not have done that. But it did. To drive the point home, Jesus later returned while Thomas was there. And lo and behold, He was there in a *physical body*—the one they had all walked with for more than three years! Thomas touched Him and believed, but Jesus' response to him was interesting: "Jesus saith unto him, Thomas, because thou hast seen me, thou hast believed: blessed are they that have not seen, and yet have believed" (John 20:29).

The real blessing of Christianity comes with the acknowledgement that Jesus was the first of a new race of the redeemed. He was raised physical and immortal, and so will they be who follow Him.

Still, we can't really blame Thomas for his skepticism. After all, how can a physical body come through a wall into a locked room? Twice Jesus appeared to the disciples in this way.

But if we read the text carefully, we discover that He didn't walk through the walls. Rather, He came and stood in their midst. Nor does the text say that He walked to the center of the room. He simply appeared there…physically.

Did He don a cloak of invisibility and convert Himself to energy? Did He then walk to the center of the room before converting Himself back to physical form? All this is possible. But in the light of our study of the Bible's view of time and space—of past, present, and future—something else is much more likely.

We have already seen that Jesus is the Lord of space-time. He travels through it to any point He desires. On that first Sunday, then, all He had to do was walk to the designated spot in the disciples' room and stand there... *a few moments in the future.* That is, a few seconds prior to the time of His appearance, He was *already there.* Then, He simply *stood still in time,* allowing the present to "catch up" with Him. At a preordained moment, all He had to do was begin to move again in synchronism with the flow of time. To the disciples, it looked as though He had appeared from nowhere.

It is reasonable to say that He had appeared from their future. Now, in His glorified state, He functions as a physical being, imbued with the ability to move uninhibited through the time-space continuum.

The glorified Christ is able to walk through all the dimensions... from the lowest to the highest. From the depths of hades to the mountain of God in heaven, He moves freely. Yet He is flesh and bone. This is the promise of the Resurrection.

> Hereby know ye the Spirit of God: Every spirit that confesseth that Jesus Christ is come in the flesh is of God: And every spirit that confesseth not that Jesus Christ is come in the flesh is not of God: and this is that spirit of antichrist, whereof ye have heard that it should come; and even now already is it in the world. (1 John 4:2, 3)

This is the importance of affirming that He was resurrected *in the flesh.* Physically, He once again exercises complete mastery of time-space. As the first of a new race of physical beings, He has conquered this dimension for the glory of God. He is the first of an army of followers who will overthrow sin and participate in the restoration of all things.

In the flesh!

8

THE END FROM THE BEGINNING

As we continue to examine the concepts surrounding time and its relation to biblical prophecy, our thoughts strain to place the many imponderables and paradoxes in some kind of order. The apostle Paul described God as one "who quickeneth the dead, and calleth those things which be not as though they were" (Romans 4:17).

How can one declare something to exist if it does not yet exist? Yet the fulfilled prophecies of the past tell us that He does just that. Our limited human thought can't conceive such a thing, yet we know that God does see things as fully realized before the fact. Given His oft-described ability to see the future as we see the present, He was in attendance both at their conception and their fulfillment.

This, of course, would portray Him as being in two places at once. The human equivalent of this would be to throw a ball, then be at the other end of its flight to catch it. Perhaps it would be more accurate to say that He is in an infinite number of places at once. Thus, His *omnipresence* and *omniscience* are defined by His complete mastery of both space and time.

Biblically, the future is already a settled matter. Anyone who has even glanced at the Scriptures is aware that they begin with creation and end with eternity. More precisely, they begin in eternity and end in eternity, taking a brief side tour through the timeline of world history. "By the word of the LORD were the heavens made; and all the host of them by the breath of his mouth.... For he spake, and it was done; he commanded, and it stood fast" (Psalm 33:6, 9).

In these verses, "the heavens" would include everything that the senses of human beings can perceive as reality. Galaxies, stars, planets, our moon, and earth have one thing in common: they are all linked to the passage of time. As the Lord spoke this realm into existence, He stood outside it. In the process, He started a clock that continues to define our physical reality. If it were to stop, so would we.

From our perspective, it is as though time itself is an anomaly. It is a created entity, best described, perhaps, as a discrete unit, suspended within the larger reality of timelessness—the eternal. Seen from this perspective, time must have been constructed. Someone superior to and separate from time must have built it. And that is exactly what the Bible says when it describes the relationship between God and the created universe that defines our existence: "Through faith we understand that the worlds were framed by the word of God, so that things which are seen were not made of things which do appear" (Hebrews 11:3).

In the sense of the original language of this text, "framed" (*katartizo*) describes the action of fabricating, fitting, and finishing a structure. To build the universe with its four obvious dimensions of length, width, height, and time means that you must be positionally objective, or positionally external to these dimensions. The Lord of the eternal created the world of time.

Note also that what He built is called "the worlds." This is the plural of the Greek noun *aion,* best translated "ages." Traditionally, these "ages" are thought of as successive periods of time, in serial order. For example, we think of the biblical dispensations as ages: Innocence, Conscience, Human Government, Promise, Law, Grace, Kingdom, and so on.

Perhaps they are more than that. In addition to being consecutive, they may also be thought of as parallel. That is, ages may be layers of dimensionality that are adjacent to our physical world. This, of course, is exactly what today's theoretical mathematicians are postulating. It is also what the Bible says about the aerial battle that rages between the forces of good and evil. Just beyond our sight, they do battle in a dimension that occasionally becomes visible to physical beings.

When we think of God's long-term plan, we think of a dichotomy: "time" and "eternity." But it is probably quite safe to say that God rules over many levels of time and space. Our universe is certainly not the only one. But whatever one thinks, He built (and perhaps even continues to build) discrete physical constructions. Some of them are visible to human eyes. Some (like the heavenly Temple) are only known because they are revealed in His Word.

No doubt, many are completely unknown to us. But to construct an "age" implies that God views time as just another construction material. This is why He can say that He has completed even the things that haven't yet happened to us:

> Remember the former things of old: for I am God, and there is
> none else; I am God, and there is none like me, Declaring the
> end from the beginning, and from ancient times the things that
> are not yet done, saying, My counsel shall stand, and I will do
> all my pleasure. (Isaiah 46:9, 10)

From our point of view, the universe of time is everything. There is nothing else we can see, even though we are straining to look beyond the edges of reality. Mathematically, other universes can be imagined, and other time-space continuums are possible. Spiritually, however, they represent the final destination of the faithful. In 2 Corinthians, Paul describes what can only be called a dimensional shift, as the believer leaves the body behind to enter the Kingdom of Heaven:

> Therefore we are always confident, knowing that, whilst we
> are at home in the body, we are absent from the Lord: (For we
> walk by faith, not by sight:) We are confident, I say, and willing
> rather to be absent from the body, and to be present with the
> Lord. (2 Corinthians 5:6–8)

Though we Christians might not be accustomed to thinking of it this way, our faith has always rested upon the promise of the Kingdom of Heaven. In many ways, we take heaven for granted.

But it is a New Testament concept, perceived in an entirely different way than the Old Testament references to the heavens in general. There, they are the created, visible universe. Though God is seen as being "up there," His Kingdom is not well defined, and never seen as the destination of the faithful.

Instead, they expected to enter paradise, the place in *sheol* (the underworld), where Abraham rests, awaiting the fulfillment of the Lord's promise to him. And that promise is not heaven…it is earth. Specifically, it is the full realization of future Israel, including today's Israel, plus surrounding lands.

JESUS AND HEAVEN

When Jesus began to teach in His public ministry, the concept of heaven changed dramatically. His coming was heralded with a statement that foretold something entirely new: "In those days came John the Baptist, preaching in the wilderness of Judaea, And saying, Repent ye: for the kingdom of heaven is at hand" (Matthew 3:1, 2).

Very shortly thereafter, Jesus announced the central theme of His teaching: "From that time Jesus began to preach, and to say, Repent: for the kingdom of heaven is at hand" (Matthew 4:17).

In the Beatitudes, He repeatedly promised that the Kingdom of Heaven would be the reward of the faithful. But as His ministry progressed, even His closest followers failed to fully grasp what He was saying. In fact, His promise of the new birth and the indwelling Holy Spirit didn't become a reality to them until after His Ascension.

After that signal event, the dimension of heaven began to be a part of Christian belief. Incidents like the stoning of Stephen brought the direct experience of heaven to the church. Just before being stoned to death by the council of Israel's elders, Stephen's final words spoke volumes to the witnesses of the early church:

> When they heard these things, they were cut to the heart, and they gnashed on him with their teeth.
> But he, being full of the Holy Ghost, looked up steadfastly into heaven, and saw the glory of God, and Jesus standing on the right hand of God, And said, Behold, I see the heavens opened, and the Son of man standing on the right hand of God. (Acts 7:54–56)

Now, the dimension of heaven was opened. Stephen had the privilege of announcing that the ascended Christ—Jesus Himself—stood at the right hand of God. From that point forward, it became a matter of scriptural record that heaven was not a distant place, but a reality as close as the next room…or even this room.

In other words, Stephen's experience firmly implanted the reality of heaven's proximity to the believer. He testified that heaven is as close as the Holy Spirit. Stephen was witness to an idea that has grown to become the central article of faith to every believer. Closely observing this new and strange phenomenon was a certain rabbi: Saul, later to become the apostle to the Gentiles. The zealous Pharisee stood by to guard the garments of those who stoned the young martyr.

At this time, Saul still lived in the world of the old Jewish legalisms. He was brought up under the strictest conceivable religious regimen. A graduate of the University of Tarsus and a student of the Jewish master Gamaliel, he was a realist whose concept of the Kingdom was rooted in the coming of Messiah, the rebuilding of Jerusalem, and the establishment of the Temple. Saul once mentioned those "which knew me from the beginning, if they would testify, that after the most straitest sect of our religion I lived a Pharisee" (Acts 26:5).

He described himself as "circumcised the eighth day, of the stock of Israel, of the tribe of Benjamin, an Hebrew of the Hebrews; as touching the law, a Pharisee" (Philippians 3:5). Yet, the incident of Stephen's stoning must have remained in his mind, even if he thought that Stephen was an insane heretic. Saul made it his personal mission in life to stamp out the new sect of Messianic Jews that we retrospectively refer to as early Christianity. Nevertheless, a seed had been planted, preparing Saul for the greatest revelation of his life. Later, as he traveled to Damascus to obliterate the infant church there, he was struck down by a "light from heaven."

Once again, a dimensional door between heaven and earth had been opened. This time, it was the opening action in a long series of events that would create Paul, the Apostle to the Gentiles, and the body of Christ, the church. Over the next two millennia, this living institution would provide the vital connection between heaven and earth.

The Appeal of Heaven

Walking the thin line between time and eternity, each of the saints would experience the leading of the Holy Spirit. His presence would ensure that each of them would have the resources of eternal life, even though their physical lives were to be grounded in the restraints of earthly existence.

Later, in his letter to the Ephesians, Paul detailed each saint's position in the body of Christ. He was fully convinced that believers were to think of themselves as *already* walking in the halls of heaven. Even though they (and we) are walking on earth, they are to think of themselves as heavenly beings.

> Blessed be the God and Father of our Lord Jesus Christ, who
> hath blessed us with all spiritual blessings in heavenly places
> in Christ: According as he hath chosen us in him before the
> foundation of the world, that we should be holy and without
> blame before him in love: Having predestinated us unto the
> adoption of children by Jesus Christ to himself, according to
> the good pleasure of his will. (Ephesians 1:3–5)

This multidimensional existence has produced an infectious attraction to people everywhere. It is so attractive, in fact, that virtually every religion on earth—including Judaism—has adopted the idea of heaven. As Christian missionaries carried the gospel to the four corners of the earth, many received it. Others remained fused to their own gods, goddesses, and strange beliefs, such as reincarnation. But even as they retained their pagan beliefs, they embraced the Christian idea of heaven.

Today, there is an almost universal heresy. It says that all people, regardless of belief, are bound for heaven. It teaches that there are many pathways to the Kingdom of Heaven.

But Paul was emphatic that only through Christ could one be vitally connected with heaven. And he had the personal communication with the risen Christ to back up his belief. More than that, he traveled there:

> I knew a man in Christ above fourteen years ago, (whether in
> the body, I cannot tell; or whether out of the body, I cannot
> tell: God knoweth;) such an one caught up to the third heaven.
> And I knew such a man, (whether in the body, or out of the
> body, I cannot tell: God knoweth;) How that he was caught
> up into paradise, and heard unspeakable words, which it is not
> lawful for a man to utter. (1 Corinthians 12: 2–4)

Here is the paradise of the New Testament. It is no longer beneath the earth in the place called *sheol.* Now, it is in the "third heaven," the dimension that first came to Paul's attention when, as Rabbi Saul, he heard the dying testimony of Stephen, who had gazed into its expanse, and described the Father and the Son.

Now, Paul's own experience took him into the dimension of the eternal, where the events on the face of this planet are visible in ways simply not possible in this physical realm. Paul made it clear that one can see things there that should not be talked about from here. Not only was heaven made real to Paul. His description made it real to us, as well.

PATTERNS OF CREATION

The first words in the Bible, "In the beginning," are translated from the Hebrew word, *bereshit.* But this word is built around a Hebrew root, *bara,* "to create." It indicates an active cause or prime mover.

To the average English speaker, "the beginning" suggests a moment before which there was nothing. Actually, the Hebrew language suggests another meaning entirely. In the purest sense, this word suggests a first principle, or first cause. So Genesis 1:1 could be translated, "As a prime mover, God created the heavens and the earth."

In other words, "the beginning" is not the absolute start, as we ordinarily think of it, but the *directive action* of the Creator. His action caused the coalescence of a localized idea…namely, our universe. The beginning was not a mark in time, but a thought in the mind of the Creator.

The same idea is expressed in John 1:1, where we find the expression, "In the beginning was the Word." As we think about this statement, there is the tendency to conceptualize it as, "at the beginning," as though nothing existed before the beginning.

But the New Testament Greek word translated "beginning" is *arche,* which means "an origination or active cause." The idea is that the Word originated all things. This is quite different from saying, "Nothing existed before the Word originated all things."

Our dimension was created out of nothing. But before its creation, the Word had endlessly existed. When the "Word was made flesh, and dwelt among us," His every action was based upon this simple premise.

Once, when the Pharisees asked Him who He really was, He told them plainly that He was the prime cause. Of course, they didn't have the slightest clue as to what He was really saying: "Then said they unto him, Who art thou? And Jesus saith unto them, Even the same that I said unto you from the beginning" (John 8:25).

A surface reading of Jesus' answer might overlook His true statement. It appears that He is saying, "I am just who I have always told you I was." As we have seen, this is the biblical term for an active cause.

Thus, Jesus plainly declares that He is the embodiment of the Word...the Prime Mover who exists above and apart from this created universe. Furthermore, He declares His unchanging doctrine, which existed before the Creation. Unbeknownst to them, the Pharisees were having a face-to-face conversation with the Word of Creation, who spoke all things into existence. The ancient teaching of their venerated sages clearly spoke of Him in that role. But when He came to them, they didn't recognize Him!

The epistle to the Hebrews contains yet another statement that links the origination of the universe with the doctrine of Christ. One might take the following verse at its surface level, which seems to say that the gospel first began to be spoken during the Lord's public ministry: "How shall we escape, if we neglect so great salvation; which at the first began to be spoken by the Lord, and was confirmed unto us by them that heard him" (Hebrews 2:3).

Actually, it doesn't say that at all. The word, "first," is here translated from *arche,* the first principle. Thus, the above statement says "having received a beginning to be spoken by the Lord." The beginning referred to is the prime cause. In other words, Jesus was salvation before He was ever incarnated in human flesh.

As the Word, He originated the course of this world. It included all the elements of restoration, restitution, salvation, justification, and all the other attributes of his finished work on the Cross.

This is why the writer to the Hebrews calls the Lord's message "so great salvation." The work of the Lord transcends all time and space. Long before He came in human form, He spoke the plan of salvation into existence. He saw the end of it before the beginning, that is, before He spoke it into action.

As mere human beings, we struggle to put these advanced concepts into words. The apostle Paul has been called the most brilliant writer in the history of Western civilization. Personally taught by the risen Christ, his epistles all present aspects of the great conjunction between heaven and earth...the coming of Christ:

Who hath delivered us from the power of darkness, and hath translated us into the kingdom of his dear Son: In whom we have redemption through his blood, even the forgiveness of sins: Who is the image of the invisible God, the firstborn of every creature:

For by him were all things created, that are in heaven, and that are in earth, visible and invisible, whether they be thrones, or dominions, or principalities, or powers: all things were created by him, and for him: And he is before all things, and by him all things consist. (Colossians 1:13–17)

In our language, there is no really effective way of describing the timeless dimension of the Lord. But the above statement is perhaps the ultimate testimony in Scripture, when it comes to the link between the Prime Mover and our personal salvation. It is the mind of the Lord that has produced our very reality.

A NEW HEAVEN AND EARTH

To Christians, the ultimate restoration of this broken universe is a long-awaited hope. We look forward to the prophetic promises of Scripture. It is difficult for us to see the plan of God as already accomplished. Yet, the Bible openly states that it is. Through faith, we accept this statement as present truth.

The prophecy of Isaiah looks far into the future. The Lord placed a vision of the far future in the prophet's mind, in which a restored universe at last becomes a realized fact:

For, behold, I create new heavens and a new earth: and the former shall not be remembered, nor come into mind.... For as the new heavens and the new earth, which I will make, shall remain before me, saith the LORD, so shall your seed and your name remain. (Isaiah 65:17; 66:22)

Notice that these two statements come from the last two chapters of Isaiah. The conclusion of his prophecy deals with the restoration of all things in the world to come. And this is no coincidence: The sixty-six chapters of Isaiah outline the sixty-six books of the Bible.

ISAIAH OUTLINED THE BIBLE

How could this be, unless the Lord—who sees the end from the beginning—had spoken through Isaiah?

Isaiah wrote his prophecy around 650 BC. Malachi, the last book of the Old Testament, would not even be written for another two centuries (about 425 BC)! Furthermore, even after the Old Testament was complete, it was not laid out in the final thirty-nine-book form, and would not be for about another thousand years.

It was actually arranged in twenty-two books, with Judges and Ruth combined as a single book. The books of 1 and 2 Samuel, 1 and 2 Kings, and 1 and 2 Chronicles were combined. Ezra and Nehemiah were joined together, as were Jeremiah and Lamentations. Finally, the twelve Minor Prophets were combined as a single book, called "The Twelve."

By the time of Jesus, the Scriptures had solidified into their traditional twenty-two-book arrangement. Yet Isaiah's outline foresaw the Bible arranged as thirty-nine Old Testament books. After the Diaspora, the Jews struggled to establish a standardized set of scrolls that would travel to any location in the world, yet remain preserved unchanged until that future day when they returned to the land.

Their actions would change the very look of the Old Testament.

About AD 500, the Jewish Masoretes (traditionalists) began this serious work of preservation. They evolved the present system of vowel pointers, annotations, and a rigorous method of transmitting texts, so that not even a single *yod* or vowel point would be lost. In the process, they laid out the *Tanach* (Old Testament) in a prescribed order of thirty-nine books.

As adopted into the Christian canon of Scripture, these thirty-nine books were finalized in their finished form, exactly as foreseen by Isaiah over a thousand years earlier!

The second part of Isaiah (Chapters 40 through 66), is twenty-seven chapters in length, exactly corresponding to the number of books in the New Testament. Liberal scholarship has noted that the style and message of this section is markedly different from the first. They assumed that it must have been written by another "Isaiah" who lived much later, perhaps as late as the fourth century BC. This later writer, believed to be anonymous, wrote of God's grace, comfort, and prophetic completion. They called him "Second Isaiah," or "Deutero-Isaiah."

What nonsense! They deny that the seventh-century Isaiah could have foreseen the end of days, saying that only the anonymous "second Isaiah" could have done that. Yet they totally overlook the fact that the entire book of Isaiah outlines the Bible…the sixty-six books of both Old and New Testaments. As if that weren't enough, each of Isaiah's chapters lays out the basic theme of its corresponding book in the Bible. That is, Isaiah chapter 1 reflects Genesis; Isaiah 2, Exodus; and so on. Isaiah 40 foresees Matthew and Isaiah 41 corresponds to Mark, etc.

The structure of Isaiah's prophecy beautifully illustrates the Lord's transdimensional position. The Lord knew the final form and disposition of Scripture…our complete Bible, as it appears, today! And he gave to Isaiah the testimony that would prove it.

THE WORD IS THE ALPHABET

Four times in the book of Revelation, the ascended Christ states that He is "Alpha and Omega." As we have repeatedly stated, these two Greek letters are simply an abbreviated way of stating the truth about the Word. The ancient sages of Israel and those who maintain their traditions have often said that the Word is made up of letters that are imbued with God's absolute power.

Rabbi Michael Munk, author of *The Wisdom in the Hebrew Alphabet,* quotes the following illustration: "If the letters [with which heaven was created] were to remove themselves for an instant, God forbid, and return to their source, the entire heaven would become an absolute vacuum."[32]

This reminds us of the statement in Hebrews 1:3, in which the Son is said to be continually "upholding all things by the word of his power."

Munk writes elsewhere that:

> The heaven continues to exist because not an instant goes by without God continuing to say, in effect, "Let there be a firmament"—otherwise they would return to the status that prevailed before God's will was uttered. So it is with every aspect of Creation. God's original Ten Utterances are repeated constantly in the sense that the Divine will of the original six days remains in force. Otherwise, everything would revert to the nothingness of before Creation.[33]

The Jewish *Pirke Abot Ethics of the Fathers* (from the Babylonian Talmud), teaches that, "By ten divine sayings, the universe was created" (Abot 5:1).[34]

Munk reflects that Jewish mystics believe:

> The twenty-two sacred letters are profound, primal spiritual forces. They are in effect, the raw material of Creation. When God combined them into words, phrases, commands, they brought about Creation, translating His will into reality, as it were.[35]

Creation is more than space; it is time. And the Creator upholds time, as the seconds tick off the hours, days, months, years, and millennia. In the most real way, He upholds time, and therefore, sees its end as easily as He sees its beginning.

We have demonstrated that His will transcends time. For Him, the beginning and the ending are equally clear: "I am Alpha and Omega, the beginning and the ending, saith the Lord, which is, and which was, and which is to come, the Almighty" (Revelation 1:8).

As this study has also shown, His creation is not limited to the mere physical aspects of the creation. It is primarily concerned with the body of the redeemed, represented in Revelation by the seven churches:

Saying, I am Alpha and Omega, the first and the last: and, What thou seest, write in a book, and send it unto the seven churches which are in Asia; unto Ephesus, and unto Smyrna, and unto Pergamos, and unto Thyatira, and unto Sardis, and unto Philadelphia, and unto Laodicea. (Revelation 1:11)

More than that, He is the source of eternal spiritual nourishment: "And he said unto me, It is done. I am Alpha and Omega, the beginning and the end. I will give unto him that is athirst of the fountain of the water of life freely" (Revelation 21:6).

His final description of Himself is as brief as it is powerful: "I am Alpha and Omega, the beginning and the end, the first and the last" (Revelation 22:13).

From our perspective, this is no doubt an understatement. Our meager attempts to understand His methods and motivations are worthless. Nevertheless, He has promised us eternal life!

In this light, we are brought in a new way to the truth of the words spoken by the Lord to Isaiah:

For my thoughts are not your thoughts, neither are your ways my ways, saith the LORD. For as the heavens are higher than the earth, so are my ways higher than your ways, and my thoughts than your thoughts. (Isaiah 55:8, 9)

9

SATAN...IMPALED ON THE ARROW OF TIME

The Lord is *omnipresent*. He resides everywhere at the same time. We receive this amazing truth by faith in the fact that He created the heavens and the earth. His position—outside the creation—means that he superintended its origination and is present in its every detail.

More than that, because of His existence in a higher dimension, He existed before their beginning and will exist after their end. By definition, He exists beyond the borders of our sharply defined zone of existence. His objective oversight of our universe is a way of saying that He is *omniscient.*

And because His judgment prevails over all things, He is *omnipotent,* or all-powerful. These three qualities are impossible for us to imagine, let alone understand. But because we recognize that He has mastered (in truth, created) all the dimensions, we accept His absolute superiority as simple truth. Today, even the uneducated commonly accept the existence of dimensions beyond our sight and senses. Television and movies regularly feature fictional forays into the past or future...crossing the barriers of time-space.

But this was not always the case. For example, in the days of the ancient Greeks, the unknown and unknowable God was thought to exist in another region that lay forever outside man's ability to penetrate.

He neither touched us nor could be touched by us. The abode of God was said to be separated from man by several levels of spiritual emanation. Our creation, said the Greeks, was defined by geometry in three dimensions.

For two thousand years, the brilliant theorems of Euclid, Pythagoras, and others defined our world. Each generation of mathematicians refined the mechanical proofs that described a universe of geometric precision. Isaac Newton's *Principia* brought the first systematic descriptions of gravity and motion. Still, he visualized the mechanics of motion as systems corresponding to the mechanics of everyday life. Planetary orbits and falling apples were locked into a system that would be easily recognized by anyone familiar with springs, gears, levers, weights, flywheels, and the motions of the natural world.

Time was time, and space was space. The two were regarded as separate and independent. But all this began to change when, in the mid-nineteenth century, Georg Riemann, a German mathematician, began to theorize that geometry and force were inextricably linked. Though it would be years before men began to speak of "time-space," the connection had been made.

Scientists began to plumb the mysteries of energy fields and gravity. It became common to speak of mankind's zone of reality as a place of four dimensions: length, width, height, and time. All four are necessary for existence as we know it. The first three have always been ours to manipulate. After all, they are the elements of design and construction. The imagination of man can be formed into real objects.

ENTROPY

But once created, these objects exist in *time*. Unlike length, width, and height, time cannot be manipulated. Nevertheless, without a timeline, physical objects would not exist as we know them. In our world, nothing can exist unless it exists for a period of time, no matter how brief. From this perspective, time is the friend of creation.

Ironically, time is also its enemy. Time is a one-way trip to deterioration and dissolution. We watch helplessly as time, like a flying arrow, takes us along at a fixed rate toward death and decay. And like that flying arrow, time inexorably takes us toward eventual annihilation, as energy systems slowly wind down toward ultimate dissolution. We search in vain for a way to make the arrow run in the direction of restoration.

Ever since the judgment of mankind in the Great Flood of Noah's day, there has been the sense that things are running down at a remarkable rate. Simple observation confirms that corrosion and decomposition are the stuff of everyday life. By extension, we know that everything contemporary will return to dust.

This arrow of time has been called "entropy." Things run down and wear out. Creation, the result of the localized application of energy, is gradually dispersed into a neutral state. To put it another way, creation requires the application of local force. Wood is cut, shaped, and joined. Clay is spun into a pot and fired to hardness. Metal is forged and formed. But in spite of all man's creative efforts, those crafted products will one day dissipate and decline into cold dust and rust.

Scientists call entropy the Second Law of Thermodynamics. All it means is that the universe is running down. All man's efforts are for naught. Unless this frightful condition is somehow changed, there is nothing ahead but hopelessness. Astronomers grimly predict that the universe will one day grind to a cold, dark, dead halt.

It's All About Time

Even the Bible acknowledges entropy. We find it in the words of Solomon, son of David, who was a superbly wise man. The Bible makes this abundantly clear:

> And God gave Solomon wisdom and understanding exceeding
> much, and largeness of heart, even as the sand that is on the sea
> shore. And Solomon's wisdom excelled the wisdom of all the

children of the east country, and all the wisdom of Egypt. For he was wiser than all men. (1 Kings 4:29–31)

Solomon was unrivalled in sheer wealth and power. He built the great Temple that was filled by the Spirit of the Lord. He had it in his hands to forge the greatest kingdom on the face of the earth. Yet with all his gifts, he made many errors.

Toward the end of his life, he reflected upon his inadequacy, filled with the conviction that in this world, mankind was powerless to improve its sad lot. In Ecclesiastes, he lamented his own inability to improve the human condition. In essence, this rich wise man was saying that if he couldn't do it, no one could:

> I the Preacher was king over Israel in Jerusalem. And I gave my heart to seek and search out by wisdom concerning all things that are done under heaven: this sore travail hath God given to the sons of man to be exercised therewith.
>
> I have seen all the works that are done under the sun; and, behold, all is vanity and vexation of spirit. That which is crooked cannot be made straight: and that which is wanting cannot be numbered. I communed with mine own heart, saying, Lo, I am come to great estate, and have gotten more wisdom than all they that have been before me in Jerusalem: yea, my heart had great experience of wisdom and knowledge.
>
> And I gave my heart to know wisdom, and to know madness and folly: I perceived that this also is vexation of spirit. (Ecclesiastes 1:12–17)

The phrase "under the sun," which appears twenty-nine times in the book, is an expression for our dimension in the created universe. By repeating this phrase in the context of "vanity," Solomon links the physical universe with the concept that we now call "entropy." The word vanity is a translation from the Hebrew *hebel* (הבל), meaning "vapor" or "breath."

The implication is that things created in this dimension pass away like a breath; from the eternal perspective, they evaporate. The second verse of Ecclesiastes says it all: "Vanity of vanities, saith the Preacher, vanity of vanities; all is vanity."

For Solomon, it's all about time. Possessed of the ultimate resources of wealth, health, and the wisdom of God, Solomon was still unable to reverse the arrow of time. As a mere human, he was consumed by the vanity of this creation.

In Ecclesiastes, he laments that under the sun, even hard labor, great accomplishments, pleasure, wisdom, wealth, and abundant offspring are no remedy for the erosion of entropy. The sun's rising and setting marks the days, weeks, months, and years. In essence, the sun is the pivotal feature of our energy system. Without its constant flow of heat, life on earth would cease.

Yet, even it measures off the steady deterioration of living systems, rather than their ascent. Today, the number-one worry among secular thinkers is the consistent decline in earth's remaining energy reserves.

Solomon wrote one of the Bible's greatest poetic passages. In it, he gave voice to the human view of entropy. In an emphatic way, his poem mourns the obvious decline of the material creation. More than that, it provides an amazingly accurate human vision of the time line:

> To every thing there is a season, and a time to every purpose
> under the heaven:
> A time to be born, and a time to die; a time to plant, and a
> time to pluck up that which is planted;
> A time to kill, and a time to heal; a time to break down, and a
> time to build up;
> A time to weep, and a time to laugh; a time to mourn, and a
> time to dance;
> A time to cast away stones, and a time to gather stones together;
> a time to embrace, and a time to refrain from embracing;
> A time to get, and a time to lose; a time to keep, and a time to
> cast away;

A time to rend, and a time to sew; a time to keep silence, and a
    time to speak;
A time to love, and a time to hate; a time of war, and a time of
    peace.
What profit hath he that worketh in that wherein he laboureth?
    (Ecclesiastes 3:1–9)

In the realm of the solar system, time is measured in the relentless
march of morbid events. Living and dying, planting and harvesting—all
ends in death. From the secular point of view, life under the sun is fruit-
less and hopeless. As we say today, "You can't take it with you."

Solomon's worldly view helps us to understand the fervency of scientists who seek to reverse the corrupting flow of events in this universe. If
only the key to a higher dimension could be found, perhaps the arrow of
time might be reversed or redirected.

Secular scientists wish to manipulate time, or time-space, in the same
way that we now manage the geometry of length, width, and height.
They have much in common with the mystics, who seek occult ways to
create an environment over which they have some sense of control. They
wish to be masters of their own domain.

Meanwhile, here on earth, the common man wrestles with frus-
trating forces that are at odds with his success. His energies (which for
a moment, seem effective) quickly dissipate. His body ages. The elec-
tro-chemical vitality, which once seemed so strong, wanes into a final,
tottering prelude to oblivion.

Solomon paints a picture of disastrous descent, in which all is fleeting and transitory. It is a grim picture in which time is the enemy and
man in his labor is the victim.

Moses expresses the same thought in Psalm 90, when he describes
men as transitory—growing and withering, like grass:

In the morning it flourisheth, and groweth up; in the evening
it is cut down, and withereth. For we are consumed by thine
anger, and by thy wrath are we troubled.

Thou hast set our iniquities before thee, our secret sins in the light of thy countenance. For all our days are passed away in thy wrath: we spend our years as a tale that is told.

The days of our years are threescore years and ten; and if by reason of strength they be fourscore years, yet is their strength labour and sorrow; for it is soon cut off, and we fly away. (Psalm 90:6–10)

Here, too, man is viewed as being under a death sentence, subject to the judgment of God. More accurately, man is judged under the strict limitations of space-time. Nominally he is allotted seventy years.

In the celestial scheme, this is hardly the blink of an eye. In fact, this very thought is precisely expressed in a verse that precedes the passage above: "For a thousand years in thy sight are but as yesterday when it is past, and as a watch in the night" (Psalm 90:4).

No one who has taken an objective look at life on earth can deny that man's fate is struggle, followed by death and oblivion. Man has been convicted in a higher court; he awaits judgment.

But Moses and Solomon both conclude that the situation is not hopeless. In the end, Moses prays, "Let the beauty of the Lord our God be upon us" (Psalm 90:17). And after much soul searching, Solomon concludes, "Fear God, and keep his commandments" (Ecclesiastes 12:13).

TIME AND PUNISHMENT

Before the creation of the heavens and the earth, we must assume that there was only the realm of the eternal. Then Satan fell. His sin produced a monumental rift in the Kingdom of Heaven. We are told very little about the actual effect of his great act of iniquity. But we do know that he corrupted about a third of the angelic host that had formerly been dedicated to the service of God.

Satan deliberately broke one heavenly law and probably several that we don't know about. The precise wording of heaven's ordinance is unknown to us, but Lucifer's act of iniquity is well known. In the well-known "proverb against the king of Babylon," Isaiah speaks a divine denunciation against an earthly king, who becomes the model for Satan:

> How art thou fallen from heaven, O Lucifer, son of the
> morning! how art thou cut down to the ground, which didst
> weaken the nations!
>   For thou hast said in thine heart, I will ascend into heaven,
> I will exalt my throne above the stars of God: I will sit also
> upon the mount of the congregation, in the sides of the north:
> I will ascend above the heights of the clouds; I will be like the
> most High. Yet thou shalt be brought down to hell, to the sides
> of the pit. (Isaiah 14:12–15)

Isaiah's fourteenth chapter begins as a prophecy against the earthly Babylon, but it extends far beyond the physical earth. The real "king" is Lucifer, whose fall starts a ticking clock, measuring off the years that will lead to the final collapse of the evil world system.

In this narrative, the prince of darkness is said to have taken a great fall. His name, "Lucifer," is a translation of *heylehl* (κκηϖ), meaning "shining one," but it can mean either "to shine" or "to be boastful." Lucifer is described as a bright and shining star, the brightest object in the sky.

Five times, Lucifer pronounces the proud and willful "I will." He already possessed the highest position in the heavens. But being in second place wasn't enough. Clearly, he wanted to expand his domain to include everything.

He had been given rule over all the earth and its environs, including the solar system. Nor was the earth the broken and damaged place we see today. As we shall see, the earth over which he originally presided was graced with an indescribable order and beauty.

In Isaiah's condemnation of Lucifer, the "stars of God" are probably symbolic of the angels, whom Lucifer wished to rule. Thus, he would place himself above the archangels. The "mount of the congregation" refers to the convocation of heavenly rulers around God's throne. And finally, "the heights of the clouds" refers to God's spiritual magnificence, the *Shechina* glory.

In the lust of pride, Lucifer, the shining one, became Satan, the adversary against God's children. His fall from heaven will take him to the pit of *sheol*, and, finally, to the lake of fire.

Once privileged to traverse the vaults of eternity, he was sentenced to the time line of the solar system. In other words, time was his punishment. Once, without limitation, he was free to serve the Lord throughout the expanses of the heavens. But his sin enclosed him within the restrictions of the Lord's redemptive timeline.

Even today, the remnants of his personal glory are the substance of myth and legend. Entire cultures still exalt the great dragon. The Chinese teach that he has temporarily lost his power, but will one day return. The Mayans once similarly invested their spiritual hope in Quetzalcoatl, the flying feathered serpent. Mythological memory of the dragon covers the earth, and many believe him to be a source of blessing. Paganism hopes for his return to power.

The degree of Lucifer's sovereignty is unknown. But the implication of the verses in Isaiah 14 is that he held high responsibility. Certainly, his rule was subordinate to God's, because it is clear that he resented not being at the very top. But he did, in fact, have some sort of throne, which he wished to magnify to the ultimate extent.

He may have been part of a ruling council. Undoubtedly, he was sovereign over the solar system, since, to this day, he patrols the earth, regarding it as his own domain. In any case, the once high-flying dragon became the creeping Serpent.

His motive—to become like God, or to supplant God—is perhaps the ultimate sin. But in fact, the "original" sin of humankind is exactly the same...an echo of his own sin. When the Serpent insinuated himself into the garden where Adam and Eve resided, he appealed to the woman in precisely the same terms that led to his own fatal temptation.

He told her, "Your eyes shall be opened, and ye shall be as gods, knowing good and evil" (Genesis 3:5).

Eve was beguiled by the prospect of being godlike in perspective. But iniquity is iniquity, and sin is sin. The first couple fell, just as Lucifer had fallen. And they took humanity down with them, just as Lucifer had taken a group of rebellious angels.

His primary abode had been a glorious eternity whose beauty and peace is far beyond our imagination. In the well-known scriptural narrative, we get a brief look at that glory:

> Thou hast been in Eden the garden of God; every precious stone was thy covering, the sardius, topaz, and the diamond, the beryl, the onyx, and the jasper, the sapphire, the emerald, and the carbuncle, and gold: the workmanship of thy tabrets and of thy pipes was prepared in thee in the day that thou wast created.
>
> Thou art the anointed cherub that covereth; and I have set thee so: thou wast upon the holy mountain of God; thou hast walked up and down in the midst of the stones of fire.
>
> Thou wast perfect in thy ways from the day that thou wast created, till iniquity was found in thee.
>
> By the multitude of thy merchandise they have filled the midst of thee with violence, and thou hast sinned: therefore I will cast thee as profane out of the mountain of God: and I will destroy thee, O covering cherub, from the midst of the stones of fire. (Ezekiel 28:13–16)

This is the brief story of an "anointed cherub." As such, Lucifer is not the chubby baby of medieval art, but an unimaginably powerful guardian of God's throne. The word "cherub" comes from the Hebrew *keruv* (כרוב). This name indicates both guarding and blessing, the role played by these beings as they serve God.

Biblically, cherubs are life forms of immense power who both watch over and protect the throne of God. They rank above all the other created beings in heaven. Some idea of this can be witnessed in the words of 2 Samuel 22:11, where David describes the Lord in the following way: "And he rode upon a cherub, and did fly: and he was seen upon the wings of the wind."

In Lucifer's specific case, the term "anointed" is taken from the Hebrew source of our word "messiah." A messiah is one whom God entrusts with a mission of highest importance. Imagine this: Among the myriad creatures in heaven, Lucifer outshone them all. He represented absolute perfection and beauty. Having received God's special anointment, he came to be filled with pride. To be "God's messiah" is the highest possible title.

Lucifer was perfection personified. Furthermore, he was wholly dedicated to serve God with all the facility represented by his perfection. But his anointment brought him to a place of temptation, which he simply could not resist.

This leads to another important point. He was given the authority to act autonomously. That is, the level of his perfection placed him in a position to make independent choices...even the choice to contradict his own perfect nature. Otherwise, he could not have sinned as he did. Among created beings, he had a unique taste of power. The old saying that "power corrupts, and absolute power corrupts absolutely" had its beginnings with the anointed cherub.

In Ezekiel's text, Lucifer is symbolically represented in the persona of an earthly king, the king of Tyre. As is the case in the Isaiah passage above, this prophecy begins with the condemnation of an earthly king. Then the view shifts to heaven, where events in the life of Lucifer are recounted.

Lucifer had been in God's garden. It, too, is called "Eden." But ancient Jewish commentary differentiates it from the earthly garden of lush vegetation. Rather, the heavenly Eden is a perfect and indescribably beautiful mineral creation. The cherub himself was apparently clothed in beautiful, precious stones and metallic decorations. Outranking all the other created beings, he must have ruled over them with absolute power. This, in conjunction with his overweening pride, led to his demise.

Note that in "Eden the garden of God," he appears as a cherub, not a serpent. At this time, he still retains his great splendor. By his very nature, he could create music. He had complete access to God's "mountain." Scripturally speaking, a mountain is the symbol of a king's rule. Here, it denotes the location of God's throne…the seat of God's government.

No human can know what the "stones of fire" might be. But the language suggests that they blaze with a piercing brilliancy unknown to mere mortals. They may hold the keys to great power and appear to be symbolic of a ritual or convention associated with the glories of heavenly rule.

As an "anointed cherub," Lucifer was created for a special role. We can only guess at what it might have been. But certainly, as the ancient dragon, he was reptilian. In the past, we have conjectured that he was probably the overseer of the reptile kingdom. Once, it ruled the world. Now, its greatest representatives—the dinosaurs—are extinct. Only the lowly snakes, lizards, and the like remain.

This thought is confirmed by the fact that God's throne is still surrounded by four remaining cherubs. Their faces—of man, lion, calf, and eagle—are usually said to represent four categories of created animal life: human beings, animals of prey, domestic animals, and birds. It is virtually certain that this is a minimal description of the roles they are assigned. But however we look at them, the kingdom of the reptiles is now without representation. Lucifer, the "anointed cherub," is missing from their ranks.

All of the foregoing is to say that Lucifer's fall was great. He plummeted from his exalted position as God's anointed to being a lowly outcast, doomed to death and dishonor.

Above all, he was sentenced to *time*. Once, he imagined himself to be like God, able to traverse time-space with freedom. Now, he had begun the long fall that would lead him to sheol (the hades of the New Testament), and finally, to the lake of fire.

WHEN DID SATAN SIN?

From the human perspective, the question of "when" is always at the top of the list. This is particularly true in the context of biblical prophecy, since we attempt to understand the time line in terms of the fulfillment of certain key events.

In the Genesis account of the six days of creation, we find a foreshadowing of the "millennial-day" explanation of God's redemptive program (discussed in chapter six), in which the six days of creation symbolize the coming six millennia of man's struggle on earth. Scripture teaches us that a thousand human years are but one day in the sight of God.

At the beginning of the first millennium (day one), the Serpent tempted man, precipitating the great fall of humanity. Obviously, Lucifer sinned at some point prior to the creation of humanity, and now appeared as the mesmerizing Serpent.

When God judged Lucifer, His sentence fell upon everything under Lucifer's authority. Though there is much discussion about this point, certainly that judgment fell upon the original earth and the mineral creation over which the anointed cherub originally ruled.

At the turn of the twentieth century, early dispensational teaching boldly interpreted the Bible in a way that supports this assertion. At some point, the earth was in a condition of chaos, as described in Genesis 1:2: "And the earth was without form, and void; and darkness was upon the face of the deep. And the Spirit of God moved upon the face of the waters."

Concerning this verse, the old *Scofield Study Bible,* originally copyrighted in 1909, has this footnote. Paraphrased, it reads as follows:

> Jeremiah 4:23–26, Isaiah 24:1, and Isaiah 45:18 clearly indicate that the earth had undergone a cataclysmic change as a result of divine judgment. The face of the earth bears everywhere the marks of such a catastrophe. Many verses connect it with a previous testing and fall of angels.[36]

Scofield and others linked the fall of Lucifer with the destruction of the old world. This happened *prior to* the creation of the world into which Adam and Eve were placed as the first humans. In other words, the Garden of Eden existed in a *recreated earth* that had formerly been in a condition of chaos.

Scofield quotes Jeremiah 4:23–26, in which the same chaos described in Genesis 1:2 is mentioned:

> I beheld the earth, and, lo, it was without form, and void; and the heavens, and they had no light. I beheld the mountains, and, lo, they trembled, and all the hills moved lightly. I beheld, and, lo, there was no man, and all the birds of the heavens were fled. I beheld, and, lo, the fruitful place was a wilderness, and all the cities thereof were broken down at the presence of the LORD, and by his fierce anger.

The phrase "without form, and void" comes from two Hebrew terms that cannot be translated to mean anything but chaos. The term indicates a physical calamity of universal proportion or absolute disorder. As the thinking goes, God would not have created chaos. Therefore, it is attributable to Lucifer's fall.

Thus, Scofield and others before him interpreted the condition described here as the absolute destruction of a former civilization. This being the case, Adam and Eve were "replacements" for an utterly sinful, former creation.

More than that, they provided a new bloodline out of which would arise the Messiah, whose life would provide a remedy for sin. And so, between Genesis 1:1 (the orderly creation of the universe) and Genesis 1:2 (utter chaos), there must exist an interval of time.

This interval, or "gap," as it came to be called, led to the general term, "gap theory." Today, we live in the era of the great debate about creation versus evolution. Evolutionists require hundreds of millions of years for their theoretical processes to be fully realized. Particularly in the last two or three decades, biblical creationists have argued that the earth is young, therefore the long periods of time required for evolution are simply not available. Thus their argument states that evolution cannot have happened.

Actually, the age of the planet is a moot point. Even if there were a prior creation, its judgment would have exterminated all life prior to the restitution of the earth. Therefore, an entirely new creation would have begun during the period described as the six days of Creation. In either case, evolution is an impossibility.

A SHORT TIME

Along this line of investigation, the important point to remember is the factor of *time*. The six-day pattern laid out by God during the Creation prophesied millennial days. In effect, this placed a time limit upon redemption. Only so much time is allowed before Satan's (and the world's) final sentence is concluded.

Once, in his glory days, Satan must have imagined that he had all eternity to celebrate his own magnificence. But on day one of Creation, he became enmeshed in the seven thousand years of human history that were laid out in advance. The scheming Serpent accomplished his goal, and humanity was corrupted. He had wrongly reasoned that the only escape from his own sentence was the defeat of God's plan.

His action brought a devastating result that he had not foreseen: God placed a curse upon him, and the prophecy of the Messiah was given: "And I will put enmity between thee and the woman, and between thy seed and her seed; it shall bruise thy head, and thou shalt bruise his heel" (Genesis 3:15).

At this point, Satan must have realized that his own doom was assured, and he began to act in desperation. Once, as the anointed cherub, he probably thought that he had mastered eternity. Certainly, he could easily manipulate our lower dimension of time-space.

But suddenly, he found that he was trapped in it, facing the disastrous certainty that time was measuring out the completion of his sentence.

This explains much of his enigmatic behavior. Why, if he had already been sentenced to the lake of fire, would he attempt to corrupt the righteous Job? Of course, Job is only one example of Satan's millions of attempts to derail the redemption of the righteous.

And why would Satan attempt to destroy the covenant people...the twelve tribes of Israel? Every time he tries, he is foiled. Yet to this day, he continues in that lost cause.

After the Holocaust came the Arab wars and the ongoing diplomatic perfidy of the world system. Instead of being celebrated as a fulfillment of God's promise, Israel is condemned as the source of all the world's woes. On every front, Satan fans the flames of anti-Semitism. But if he is already defeated, why does he still attempt to destroy the Jews?

The answer to these questions is that he is in a race against *time.* If he can prove to God that humanity is unworthy of redemption, he might still be saved…even at the eleventh hour. He is beyond desperation in his race for restoration to his former glory.

During the present period, Satan is functioning as the "prince of the power of the air" (Ephesians 2:2). He ranges across the domain of the atmospheric heavens, seeking to corrupt and enslave those who find their fatal attraction in the world system. He masquerades as an "angel of light" (2 Corinthians 11:14) and functions as a "roaring lion" (1 Peter 5:8).

Once, in his godlike glory, he must have thought that he could see—even influence—the future. But, having lost his position in heaven, he no longer commands a view of the timeline. He cannot access the future.

Still, he must know that judgment lies just ahead. He is in a race against time. Doubtless, he is aware that defeat awaits him during the coming Tribulation period. (He can read Scripture.) Nevertheless, he is still engaged in a frantic struggle to evade it.

It is most interesting that, in the midst of the Tribulation, Satan is cast down to earth. Until this time, he could still walk upon this earth, cloaked in the obscuring dimensional mist that placed him just beyond human vision. At this time, during the tumult of the mid-Tribulational battles of the Antichrist, the forces of the archangel Michael will, at last, overthrow Satan:

And the great dragon was cast out, that old serpent, called the
Devil, and Satan, which deceiveth the whole world: he was cast

out into the earth, and his angels were cast out with him.

And I heard a loud voice saying in heaven, Now is come salvation, and strength, and the kingdom of our God, and the power of his Christ: for the accuser of our brethren is cast down, which accused them before our God day and night.

And they overcame him by the blood of the Lamb, and by the word of their testimony; and they loved not their lives unto the death.

Therefore rejoice, ye heavens, and ye that dwell in them. Woe to the inhabiters of the earth and of the sea! for the devil is come down unto you, having great wrath, because he knoweth that he hath but a **short time**.

And when the dragon saw that he was cast unto the earth, he persecuted the woman which brought forth the man child. (Revelation 12:9–13, emphasis added)

In this key passage, Satan is the "great dragon." This elicits a vision of his former glory. As "that old serpent," Lucifer was the agent of man's temptation in the garden. As "the Devil," he is the accuser and slanderer of God's elect. As "Satan," he is the adversary.

In this scene, he is completely ensnared in the earthly time line. He has been robbed of his power to flee into another dimension. The clock is ticking and he knows that his time is dreadfully short.

In fact, since the setting is mid-Tribulation, he knows that he has only three and a half years left!

Soon, the anointed one—the Christ—will step out of the heavens with His armies and bind Satan with chains. He will languish in the bottomless pit for another thousand years, awaiting the end of the Kingdom Age. Bear in mind that while in that pit, he must still count off the hours until his final doom in the lake of fire. What an ignominious end... trapped in a fatal countdown.

Impaled upon the arrow of time, he has been brought to a predetermined point in time-space. His hope is gone.

Once, he had been God's own anointed one...the "anointed cherub" destined for greatness, glory, and power. But during the six thousand years of human history, he has been systematically replaced in a lengthy but precise plan to elevate God's Messiah to preeminence.

Now, instead of the cherub, the Lamb of God is the Anointed One!

PARADISE IN FIVE DIMENSIONS

Legends and stories abound. They tell of a hidden land. It is a garden of delights, where all the people enjoy perfect health in a glorious climate. There are no wars there, or petty disagreements, for that matter. The King reigns there, and evil is shut out. Christians call it heaven. Others have their own ideas. Buddhists call it Agharta…a subterranean land of peace and glory. The Bible regards paradise as subterranean, too. In fact, sheol, the place of the unrighteous dead, and Abraham's bosom, the abode of the righteous, were once closely associated.

As we pursue the questions of time-space, we now ask, "Where is paradise?" We know that over the millennia, its location has been periodically shifted. As we shall see, this fact is quite important in the understanding of Christ's finished work.

As discussed earlier, time is carrying man on a descending trajectory. When the old Serpent fell, he became trapped in a downward spiral. His domineering obsession brought him to the earthly paradise known as the Garden of Eden, where he committed the evil act of corrupting mankind. Little did he know that this act would ensnare him in the human timeline. Yet it did, and he's been paying the price ever since.

Once, from his ancient eternal perspective, Satan felt that he was capable of godlike achievements. Yet, as stated in Ezekiel 28:15, he was a created being who embodied the elements of perfection: "Thou wast perfect in thy ways from the day that thou wast created, till iniquity was found in thee."

Satan must have known that he was a created being, yet he lusted for primacy. In fact, he must have been even more aware than we are that the Lord created the heavens and earth. Satan was not there at the beginning, as the Lord was:

> Hearken unto me, O Jacob and Israel, my called; I am he; I am the first, I also am the last. Mine hand also hath laid the foundation of the Earth, and my right hand hath spanned the heavens: when I call unto them, they stand up together.
>
> All ye, assemble yourselves, and hear; which among them hath declared these things? The LORD hath loved him: he will do his pleasure on Babylon, and his arm shall be on the Chaldeans. I, even I, have spoken; yea, I have called him: I have brought him, and he shall make his way prosperous.
>
> Come ye near unto me, hear ye this; **I have not spoken in secret from the beginning; from the time that it was, there am I:** and now the Lord GOD, and his Spirit, hath sent me. (Isaiah 48:12–16, emphasis added)

Satan could in no way be compared with the preexistent, eternal God. In the words of the prophet Isaiah, we are distinctly reminded that at the very beginning, He was there. Certainly, Satan's appearance as a created being was subsequent to the existence of God. No doubt, though, he came into being before the creation of humanity.

Nevertheless, as this Scripture shows, the creation of man is intimately connected with the beginning of all things. In the Isaiah passage above, the Lord makes two promises to Israel. First, He assures them that with the same authority as His creation of the heavens, He will deal with the Gentile empires, beginning with Babylon.

Second, He declares that he is the Lord of time; He was already present "from the beginning"—that is, before time. He openly states that world empires will surrender to His will. But note that His divine acts of redemption are tied to His status as Creator. The beauty of the original creation is even now being restored.

A Brief History of Paradise

The paradise of heaven was sullied by Satan's act. As seen in Ezekiel 29, "Eden the garden of God," with its "stones of fire" and "mountain of God" must have been supremely beautiful. Traditional Jewish exposition says that this garden was mineral in composition, and located in the eternal realm of the Lord. Through the actions of the rebellious cherub, its harmonies were broken and its citizens were shocked by a schism in which many followed Lucifer, the rebel.

Subsequently, the paradise of Adam and Eve was vilified in the same way. The perfection of the Garden of Eden was shattered by the Serpent's unlawful act.

As mere humans, we live in a world of sin—dominated by evil forces, yet preserved by the Holy Spirit of God. Graciously, the Lord reassures us that He initiated the time line to bring us redemption. Following the same pattern, it will bring destruction to Satan and his earthly representatives.

One day, the original paradise will be restored, but in a new way. It is safe to say that every human being longs for paradise. Some even try to duplicate it in their own strength. Acquiring wealth, power, and land, they build mansions and villas, grandly isolating themselves from society at large. Needless to say, their worlds are far from a genuine paradise.

Its mellifluous sound and glorious history render the word "paradise" almost poetic. In our language, the term is reserved as a special, lavish place of peace and providence. It is a place of delight and never-ending fascination. As we shall see, it is also a place of great import, close to the heart of the Lord.

For humanity, it started in Eden. In the creation narrative of Genesis 1, man is brought into existence on the sixth day. On the seventh, God blesses and sanctifies the Sabbath.

The details of man's creation are given in chapter 2:

And the LORD God formed man of the dust of the ground, and breathed into his nostrils the breath of life; and man became a living soul. And the LORD God planted a garden eastward in Eden; and there he put the man whom he had formed.

And out of the ground made the LORD God to grow every tree that is pleasant to the sight, and good for food; the tree of life also in the midst of the garden, and the tree of knowledge of good and evil. (Genesis 2:9)

As a matter of faith, we take these details as a simple declaration of what really happened. We add nothing to them and take nothing away from them. Adam was created from the soil of the earth. Dust is the mineral and organic detritus that comprises the ground upon which we walk. In the hands of God, its raw materials provided for His most amazing creation. Man is several orders of magnitude more complex than any star, galaxy, or planet.

When God formed the man, his astoundingly complex array of genetics, his integrated electrochemical systems, his thinking apparatus of a trillion parts...all was perfect. But the body was not yet Adam; it lacked life.

Then, as God filled it with the spirit of vitality, he became a man. This spirit is called *neshamat chaim* (נשמת חיים), meaning "vital spirit of life." His formerly lifeless body then became a living soul.

Adam became a single being of three parts: body, soul, and spirit... created in the image of God. Then he was given a perfect environment. A beautiful river watered his garden. Every kind of perfect plant grew there. Doubtless, the fruit was far superior to anything seen today. But before Adam, the vegetation was uncultivated. Among Adam's many appointed tasks was to till and systematically harvest the bounty.

In Isaac Mozeson's Hebrew source dictionary entitled *The Word*, we find that linguistically, the idea of paradise is tied to a garden of delights. Its derivation stems from the root words *porat* (פרת), meaning "fruitful," and *pherach* (פרח), the term for "blossom" or "flower." In fact, the Hebrew word, *payrote* (פרות), "fruit," is very close to *pardes* (פרדם), or "paradise."[37]

However, as the Bible relates it, fruit is not simply something tasty and nutritious. It is also a concept...the final outcome of cultivation, pruning, and harvest. As such, it is the perfect symbol of spiritual maturity and responsibility.

In humanity's first garden, fruit explicitly bore this designation. It was more than just a symbol of spirituality. It was, in fact, the very essence of spiritual devotion. Fruit was not simply good; it was good *and evil!* For Adam, paradise was conditional. It depended upon his choice to obey God and avoid the evil fruit:

> And the LORD God took the man, and put him into the
> garden of Eden to dress it and to keep it. And the LORD God
> commanded the man, saying, Of every tree of the garden thou
> mayest freely eat: But of the tree of the knowledge of good
> and evil, thou shalt not eat of it: for in the day that thou eatest
> thereof thou shalt surely die. (Genesis 2:15–17)

The sages of Israel referred to this garden as paradise. Thus, it is most significant that the fate of the first human being is directly tied to the concept of fruit and fruitfulness. Eve ate the infamous forbidden fruit. As a result, human access to paradise was blocked.

It is interesting that paradise was not broken up; it did not cease. Rather, Adam was driven out of it. (Note the verses that follow this paragraph.) This emphasizes the fact that the Lord's paradise is manifested in different places at different times. As we continue, this concept will be clarified.

> Therefore the LORD God sent him forth from the garden of
> Eden, to till the ground from whence he was taken.

So he drove out the man; and he placed at the east of the garden of Eden Cherubims, and a flaming sword which turned every way, to keep the way of the tree of life. (Genesis 3:23, 24)

When he ingested the prohibited fruit, Adam's basic nature had been changed. Now, as the federal head of a fallen human race, his only hope was the coming One who was prophesied to destroy the Serpent.

But why wasn't the garden of paradise simply allowed to fall into ruin? Eventually, it would have become infested with weeds and wild beasts. Instead, God deployed cherubs and a flaming sword. Paradise was protected. Perhaps it was concealed behind an interdimensional veil. Put another way, it was moved to another dimension.

AND THEN THERE WAS SHEOL

The implication is clear: The existence of paradise and the Tree of Life continued. Furthermore, its location seems to have shifted in the period following earth's destruction in the Great Flood of Noah. For the rest of the Old Testament, paradise is seen in a subterranean location, closely associated with sheol...the underworld detention area of the unrighteous dead.

To the modern scientific mind, it might seem ridiculous to think of a literal underworld domain. Though the Bible is specific about it, most twenty-first-century citizens would stoutly deny that there is any habitable place under the earth.

After all, wells are drilled thousands of feet deep. Mines and underground tunnels have been bored for centuries. Has anyone ever reported seeing sheol...the underworld? At first, we would answer this question in the negative. But before we totally reject the literal nature of sheol, we must consider that many men have stoutly avowed that they not only went there, they lived there for a while and returned to tell about it!

Remember that the Bible regards the underworld as absolutely real. Job, in describing his death to his friends, described sheol as a place of darkness: "Before I go whence I shall not return, even to the land of darkness and the shadow of death; A land of darkness, as darkness itself; and of the shadow of death, without any order, and where the light is as darkness" (Job 10:21, 22).

Isaiah describes the unredeemed "dead" residents of sheol as beyond salvation. They believed in other gods, and now reside in the underworld, waiting for their final judgment:

> O LORD our God, other lords beside thee have had dominion over us: but by thee only will we make mention of thy name.
> They are dead, they shall not live; they are deceased, they shall not rise: therefore hast thou visited and destroyed them, and made all their memory to perish. (Isaiah 26:13, 14)

The "dead" here are the *rephaim*...the damned souls of those destroyed in the Great Flood of Noah. While they lived, they were the "giants" of Genesis 6. They were the corrupt offspring of the fallen angels who visited earthly women, producing an alien race. Now they reside in sheol, the dark place of alienation from God.

THE TIMELINE OF PARADISE

The sages of ancient Israel viewed sheol in quite real and literal terms. But to them, it was not a place of uniform darkness and doom. Rather, it was comprised of two regions—one for the condemned souls of the underworld and the other for the righteous dead.

As odd as it may seem, paradise and sheol existed side by side in the same dimension: the underworld. In *The Christian Doctrine of Immortality*, Dr. Stewart Salmond summarizes the situation of paradise in the following way:

> In the Rabbinical literature the term [Paradise] has various senses, and much is made of it. Sometimes it is the general

abode of the righteous dead; sometimes the happy side of sheol; sometimes the home of the specially privileged few, the abode of those who have never seen death, the place where Messiah Himself waits for the time of His manifestation.[38]

He continues:

In later Judaism a complete topography of it was attempted; "Abraham's bosom" was defined to be the place of highest honor in it; and strongly colored descriptions were given of its gates of rubies, its sixty myriads of angels, the 800,000 kinds of trees which flourished in it, and the way in which everyone who entered it was renewed during the three night watches.

It is most interesting that Jesus spoke of paradise. It happened during His excruciating death upon the Cross, when He told the repentant thief: "Verily I say unto thee, To day shalt thou be with me in paradise" (Luke 23:43).

This is the first of three New Testament references to paradise. And this was not simply an oblique remark. It was Jesus' way of telling the faithful of the coming centuries that the risen Messiah would dwell in the fruitful garden of heaven. The garden of paradise, which had once been the abode of Adam and Eve, then moved to the dimension of the underworld, would now rise to the dimension of the heavens, and to heaven itself.

Today, standard Bible scholarship teaches that the New Testament expression of sheol is hades, and that paradise was intimately associated with it until Christ's Resurrection. At that time, it was removed from the underworld and taken into the presence of God in the dimension of heaven.

Thus, the Bible tells us that paradise is a kind of "moveable feast." In eternity past, it was the "garden of God." Then, it became the earthly Garden of Eden. After the Fall, it was temporarily placed in the dimension of the underworld. And finally, it was removed from there to heaven, where it resides today. Prophetic Scripture tells us that it is scheduled for at least one more move in the future.

The locations of paradise, in and of themselves, form a timeline. From eternity past to eternity future, the Lord's promise to the faithful is emblematic of His power and grace. Remember the narrative of the rich man and Lazarus, in which Jesus relates an actual event, designed to clarify the reality of paradise prior to His Resurrection.

In the dimension of the underworld, this man is able to see the beggar Lazarus in the distance. Somehow, in spite of the distance and compartmental separation, he is able to plead his case before Abraham. But the patriarch dashes his hope with a simple statement of fact: "And beside all this, between us and you there is a great gulf fixed: so that they which would pass from hence to you cannot; neither can they pass to us, that would come from thence" (Luke 16:26).

What sort of gap or chasm would separate two regions at a seeming great distance, yet be close enough to allow conversation? The only imaginable answer seems to be that there is some sort of dimensional barrier that cannot be scaled. And this would further explain how paradise could later be removed to heaven as a unit, leaving hades behind as a holding area awaiting Judgment Day.

LEFT BEHIND

Hades was indeed left behind. It is still down there today. But where? Its existence must be regarded as literal. A number of men have asserted their own personal discovery of and travels to this place of the dead. Unless one has studied the abundant literature on the subject, this may seem hard to believe. But consider the following accounts.

Many theosophical societies have stated their strong belief in an underground race. A prime case in point is found in the history of the Thule Society that backed Adolf Hitler's Third Reich. He was (and they were) convinced that a group of super-beings lived beneath the earth's surface. So persuaded were they that at the height of World War II,

Hitler sent one of two valuable radar units, a dirigible, and a ship with accompanying troops to the Arctic Circle. He hoped to find the opening to the inner world.

Many of his own top leaders thought he had lost his mind. Allied bombers were raining death on Germany, and the radar that could detect them was sent to the distant lands in the north. So strongly did Hitler believe in the inner earth that he sacrificed the war effort to it!

The Thule Society derives its name from a legendary land in the far north called "Ultima Thule." Scandinavians believe that this land "beyond the pole" is a place of eternal warmth and plenty. To them, it is a kind of heaven, yet it is much more. Some of them report having visited this place…later returning to their own societies! They say that as one approaches the North Pole, the climate suddenly turns warmer and descent is made into an aperture so huge that it appears to be only a gentle slope.

After that, there is a peaceful paradise of perfect weather and fruitfulness. The people who live there are far superior to ordinary humans. Their land is so productive that they never have need of anything.

In his 1964 book, *The Hollow Earth,* Dr. Raymond Bernard published a collection of historical reports in which men purportedly entered the beautiful land inside the earth. As strange as it sounds, many Scandinavians have related supposedly true accounts that tell how they discovered the astonishing land.

In the following account, Bernard relates the story told by one Nordic man:

> I lived near the Arctic Circle in Norway. One summer my
> friend and I made up our minds to take a boat trip together,
> and go as far as we could into the north country. So we put one
> month's food provision in a small fishing boat, and with sail
> and also a good engine in our boat, we set to sea.
>
> At the end of one month we had traveled far into the north,
> beyond the Pole and into a strange new country. We were
> much astonished at the weather there. Warm, and at times at

night it was almost too warm to sleep. Then we saw something so strange that we both were astonished. Ahead of the warm open sea we were on was what looked like a great mountain. Into that mountain at a certain point the ocean seemed to be emptying. Mystified, we continued in that direction and found ourselves sailing into a vast canyon leading into the interior of the Earth. We kept sailing, and then we saw what surprised us—a sun shining inside the Earth![39]

Stories similar to this one are told again and again by different men in different times. The circumstances vary, but the details are remarkably consistent. Travelers to this bizarre land describe a world in which everything is gigantic—trees, plants, animals, and...people! They, too, are gigantic, and are usually reported to be quite friendly and hospitable.

In the above account, the two men stayed with their giant hosts for more than a year before sailing back to their own land. They told anyone who would listen about their adventure, and about the technological marvels they saw in the beautiful land.

Europeans who hold these tales to be true usually conclude that the inner-earth giants are descendants of the Atlanteans, who moved to their land prior to the Great Flood of Noah, thus surviving the deluge.

A Norwegian named Olaf Hansen reported a similar story. It was recorded in a rather famous book—*The Smoky God*—by American author Willis George Emerson.

Dr. Bernard summarizes the account as follows:

The title, *The Smoky God*, refers to the central sun in the hollow interior of the Earth, which, being smaller and less brilliant than our sun, appears as "smoky." The book relates the true experience of a Norse father and son, who, with their small fishing boat and unbounded courage, attempted to find "the land beyond the north wind," as they had heard of its warmth and beauty. An extraordinary windstorm carried them most of the distance, through the polar opening into the hollow interior of the Earth. They spent two years there and returned through the south polar opening.[40]

Reportedly, the pair traveled all the way through the hollow earth and returned via the south polar opening! But their trip was marred when an iceberg fractured and crushed their boat. The father was killed, but the son was rescued. Unfortunately, he was incarcerated as insane, as he repeatedly tried to convince authorities that his bizarre journey was real. He was imprisoned for twenty-four years. After his release, he worked as a fisherman for twenty-six years, maintaining a stony silence about his experience, lest he again be declared insane. By that time, he had saved enough money to come to the United States. As a very old man, he finally broke down and told his story—complete with carefully drawn maps—to author Willis Emerson. It was published only after he had died.

Sound unbelievable? Of course it does. Then what must we say about Norwegian explorer Fridtjof Nansen, who on August 3, 1894, trekked to the North Pole and found that he was entering a warmer climate? Approaching the pole, he found fox and musk ox tracks. He noted rising temperatures and the complete failure of his compass, with its needle swinging wildly.

Or what about Admiral Richard E. Byrd, who organized two polar flying expeditions in 1947 and 1956 to the North and South Poles? He, too, told of a mysterious region "beyond the pole." He wrote, "I'd like to see that land beyond the (North) Pole. That area beyond the pole is the Center of the Great Unknown!"

In his 1947 flight, he flew seventeen hundred miles across the North Pole...or as he put it, "beyond the Pole." Bernard writes, "He reported by radio that he saw below him, not ice and snow, but land areas consisting of mountains, forest, green vegetation, lakes and rivers, and in the underbrush saw a strange animal resembling the mammoth found frozen in Arctic ice."

On his later expedition to the South Pole, a similar phenomenon was encountered:

In January, 1956, Admiral Byrd led another expedition to the Antarctic.… The radio announcement at this time (January 13, 1956) said: "On January 13, members of the United States expedition penetrated a land extent of 2,300 miles beyond the Pole. The flight was made by Rear Admiral George Dufek of the United States Navy Air Unit."[41]

This 1956 South Pole air journey covered a distance of twenty-three hundred miles. Byrd was on that flight, and he reported that he had personally witnessed an iceless land whose environment was warm and strangely illuminated. He spoke of "that enchanted continent in the sky, land of everlasting mystery." Reportedly, he told his friends that he had encountered many phenomena so strange that he hardly dared speak of them.

The next year, in 1957, he died in the belief that he had discovered the doorway to a land inside the earth!

Nor was Admiral Byrd alone in his belief. In the mid-twentieth century, author Theodore Fitch wrote a book entitled *Our Paradise Inside the Earth.* In it, referring to two other men who believed in the hollow earth, he wrote:

Both William Reed and Marshall Gardner declare that there must be a land of paradise on the other side of the mammoth ice barrier. Both men are of the opinion that a race of little brown people live in the interior of the Earth. It is possible that the Eskimos descended from these people.[42]

HADES—SUBTERRANEAN OR SUBDIMENSIONAL?

As we shake our heads in disbelief, we must ask, "What were these men thinking?" Is there a land inside the earth? Geophycists would say, "Absolutely not!" The Bible says, "Absolutely so!" It's called hades. The general term "underworld" is universally used to describe the place of the damned.

Now we live in the age of satellite surveillance and transpolar jet travel. Today, no one reports having visited the "land beyond the poles." We assure ourselves that accounts like the ones above are simple imagination…or confabulation.

Did these men associate their belief in a hollow earth and underworld civilization with the biblical sheol? Given their beliefs, it is unlikely. However, over the centuries, Satan has perverted many scriptural ideas, and this is no exception.

Occult Buddhist schools of thought speak of the subterranean world of Agharta, whose capital is Shamballah, a glorious place of surpassing peace and jaw-dropping technology. Its residents are usually said to be survivors of the lost world that was destroyed in an ancient cataclysm.

In our era, it has been immortalized in print and on film as Shangri-La, the mystical land of eternal youth and peace. It was featured in the 1933 novel, *Lost Horizon,* by James Hilton. Travelers in Tibet became lost and wandered through a doorway to an inner world. There, they found peace and light, as well as an enlightened citizenry whose eternal youth was coupled with a marvelous wisdom.

Legends about a "middle earth" abound in literature. J. R. R. Tolkein's *Lord of the Rings* takes place in this legendary land. Hidden in a dimension just beyond human sight, it is the story of a long battle between the forces of good and evil. Its citizenry is comprised of ancient fairies (the wise people), gnomes, trolls, ogres, and the tiny hobbits who carry the torch of truth in a long and heroic battle.

And of course, virtually everyone is familiar with *The Chronicles of Narnia,* begun in 1950 by Christian author C. S. Lewis and adapted into a series of successful films in recent years. Its seven volumes began with *The Lion, the Witch and the Wardrobe,* in which four children discover a giant wardrobe closet in an old house. Peter, Susan, Edmund, and Lucy push their way through the hanging garments inside the wardrobe, and when they reach the back, they simply keep on going…into a beautiful land where everything is somehow different.

In Narnia, they encounter a magnificent talking lion named Aslan, who leads them progressively along a series of spiritual adventures. Their escapades are nothing less than the recounting of the eternal battle between virtuous and wicked forces. But again, the important factor is that Lewis takes the biblical theme of the underworld and renders it as metaphor.

Narnia, in short, is another vision of the underworld. The wardrobe is a dimensional door that allows one to go there.[43]

Accounts of encounters with the underworld abound, assuring us of one thing: We can believe the Bible when it describes hades as being under the earth. But perhaps it is not "under" the earth, in the physical sense.

"UNDER" IS NOT NECESSARILY UNDER

In the dimension of time-space, the realm of beings just beyond our sight, Satan and his demons, have the ability to appear and then, in the blink of an eye, just "wink out." They seem to range into the atmosphere, where Satan is called "the prince of the power of the air." Demons and angels have the power to become visible at will, then to recede into their own time-space. Numerous historical records tell of humans being taken into their realm.

This brings to mind the current "alien abduction" phenomenon. Abductees report being taken into some sort of nether world, where time is curiously stretched or compressed.

In like manner, just as the name suggests, the underworld is under the surface of the earth. But while it is generally located there, it is both subterranean and *dimensionally shifted*. That is, its generally subterranean location is inaccessible to humans living in our physical dimension.

Thus, coal miners working in the physical underworld need not fear cutting into it and dropping into the enormous void. On the other hand, demonic apparitions from the underworld appear in many historical records. In the Americas, native shamans were said to be able to call up underworld personalities into caves. Apparently, then, the underworld may be accessed only by popping through a dimensional door in time-space.

To those who haven't studied the history of this strange subject, a dimensional underworld may sound ludicrously strange. But credible students of history have strongly stated their belief in a literal underworld. A good example is the nineteenth-century British historian and parliamentarian, Edward Bulwer-Lytton. In his book, *The Coming Race,* he tells of a highly advanced subterranean civilization. Their strangely illuminated world features high-tech machines, fields, and orchards that produce with astounding bounty, perfect health, and virtual immortality.

Invariably, these advanced subterranean societies are said to be intellectually and spiritually superior to those of human beings. Their tunnels emerge at the surface in remote places all over the world. The Tunnel of the Incas and the Matto Grosso in Brazil are well known to many as entrances to the underworld.

Underground societies are linked to the ancient Atlanteans, who went underground to escape the Deluge. Lytton, a member of the Rosicrucian society—a theosophical and alchemic society originated in the seventeenty century by Christian Rosenkreuz—spoke often of the Asian (especially the Tibetan) doorways to the underworld. He believed that occult powers came from the residents of the many underworld cities.

And therein lies the root of the matter. Both the Bible and the writers of occult literature believe in the underworld. Scripture calls it hades, the place of the damned who are awaiting judgment. It is dark and forbidding...a place of torment.

But occultists see the same place as occasionally accessible, and they interpret it as a kind of heaven under the earth. Generations of occultists have called this place Vitriol, from the initials of the Latin sentence, *Vista interiora terrae rectificando invenes omnia lapidem,* or, "In the interior of the earth is hidden the true mystery."

The Persians called it *Aryana.* To the Celts, it was *Dananda.* The Greeks named it *Kalki.* The northern Europeans called it *Valhalla.* It has dozens of other names, but it is invariably said to be peopled by those who escaped a great catastrophe on the earth's surface. We remember it as the Great Flood of Noah.

We conclude that its legendary glories are simply a lie of Satan, who has masked hell to appear as paradise. The Atlanteans are nothing more than the souls of the dead who were drowned in the Flood.

PARADISE MOVES AGAIN

In his *Study Bible*, C. I. Scofield notes the following:

Hades before the ascension of Christ: The passages in which the word occurs make it clear that hades was formerly in two divisions, the abodes respectively of the saved and of the lost. The former was called "paradise" and "Abraham's bosom." Both designations were Talmudic, but adopted by Christ.... At the judgment of the great white throne, hades will give them [the lost] up, they will be judged and will pass into the lake of fire.... But a change has taken place which affects paradise. Paul was "caught up to the third heaven…into paradise" (2 Corinthians 12:1–4). Paradise, therefore, is now in the immediate presence of God.[44]

With slight variations, Scofield's summary of paradise has been adopted by the majority of today's conservative theologians. At Christ's Resurrection, sheol, hades, or hell, as it is now widely known, was left unchanged. As we have shown, we believe that it is still there today. But paradise was lifted up to heaven, as described in Ephesians and Colossians:

Wherefore he saith, When he ascended up on high, he led captivity captive, and gave gifts unto men. (Now that he ascended, what is it but that he also descended first into the lower parts of the Earth? He that descended is the same also that ascended up far above all heavens, that he might fill all things.) (Ephesians 4:8–10)

Here, in plain language, Paul describes the descent of the Lord into the underworld. There, He proclaimed His victory to the unrighteous dead. At the same time, he transported the righteous from the underworld paradise, moving it to heaven, where it remains today, in the presence of the Lord.

At one time in his life, the apostle Paul was privileged to visit paradise in its present location:

I knew a man in Christ above fourteen years ago, (whether in the body, I cannot tell; or whether out of the body, I cannot tell: God knoweth;) such an one caught up to the third heaven.

And I knew such a man, (whether in the body, or out of the body, I cannot tell: God knoweth;) How that he was caught up into paradise, and heard unspeakable words, which it is not lawful for a man to utter. (2 Corinthians 12:2–4)

Today, paradise is in God's heaven. As Paul put it, when believers die today, they are "absent from the body, and...present with the Lord" (2 Corinthians 5:8). That is the current location of paradise. No longer does it wait in the dimension beneath the earth. The Lord has risen and brought the faithful to the Kingdom of Heaven.

Paradise is scheduled for one more move. At some point in the future (perhaps just after Christ's millennial reign), it appears in the midst of the Holy City, the New Jerusalem. As would be expected, it appears as the perfect Garden of God. It is fruitful beyond our ability to imagine...watered by life itself, and illuminated by the light of the Father and the Lamb:

And he showed me a pure river of water of life, clear as crystal, proceeding out of the throne of God and of the Lamb.

In the midst of the street of it, and on either side of the river, was there the tree of life, which bare twelve manner of fruits, and yielded her fruit every month: and the leaves of the tree were for the healing of the nations.

And there shall be no more curse: but the throne of God and of the Lamb shall be in it; and his servants shall serve him. (Revelation 22:1–3)

Throughout the Bible, paradise is presented as the pinnacle of God's presence. First, we see it as Eden, the mineral garden of Ezekiel 29. Next, it is on earth as Eden, the fruitful garden where the Serpent tempted Eve.

After the fall of man, paradise was taken to the dimension of the underworld, where for a time, it coexisted with sheol, the Old Testament hell. At the resurrection of Christ, paradise was lifted to the third heaven, in the very presence of the Lord. Finally, it will one day be the crown jewel of God's Holy City in the heavens. Its five locations tell the remarkable story of redemption. Its chronicle begins with Lucifer's fall and is concluded with his judgment in the lake of fire.

Its glories await the faithful, who will soon learn the many mysteries of its long history.

II

THE SYMMETRY OF TIME

As we continue to look at the concepts of time and their relationship to biblical truth, we must remember that the Creator of all things stands above the ages, unbound by the universe of time-space in which we are confined.

The human perspective of past, present, and future fails to adequately explain the reality of time as it is presented in the Bible. The present, for example, is a constantly moving instant, traveling along a straight line from past to future. Seen in this way, that which is perceived as present reality is an infinitesimally small point. If it stopped moving, it would cease to exist.

The Bible, however, views time as a complete panorama, with interlocking events that are woven together to produce a tapestry that illuminates the purpose of God. Though He speaks of "the beginning" and "the end," these are concessions to the limitations of human thought that reference cause and effect.

Having created the ongoing human drama, the Lord has unlimited access to it in all respects. Positionally, He stands outside it, though He can occupy it in any way that He desires. In seven points (up, down, left, right, front, back, and center), He defines and maintains the status of our dimension. These seven points, plus the march of time (from beginning to end), constitute the span of our reality.

And since we have mentioned the number seven, it should be stated again that there is virtual unanimity about its special place in Scripture. From the books of Moses to the book of Revelation, it speaks of God's perfection and completion. It is used of groups, symbols, statements, and narratives, where it denotes a complete set of ideas. As we shall see, it reflects the dimensional truth of our universe.

In his famous book, *Number in Scripture,* E. W. Bullinger wrote:

> In the Hebrew, *seven* is שבע *(shevah).* It is from the root שבע *(savah), to be full or satisfied, have enough of.* Hence the meaning of the word "seven" is dominated by this root, for on the seventh day God rested from the work of Creation. It was full and complete, and good and perfect. Nothing could be added to it or taken from it without marring it. Hence the word שבת *(shaveth), to cease, desist, rest,* and שבת *(Shabbath, Sabbath, or day of rest).*[45]

Bullinger also deals with the issue of time:

> It is *seven,* therefore, that stamps with perfection and completeness that in connection with which it is used. Of *time,* it tells of the Sabbath, and marks of the week of seven days, which, artificial as it may seem to be, is universal and immemorial in its observance amongst all nations and in all times. It tells of that eternal Sabbath-keeping which remains for the people of God in all its everlasting perfection.[46]

Seven, then, is the number of *human* completeness. The sabbatical rest of the Lord at the completion of Creation is the model for the rest of humanity, when the time arrives to receive its inheritance. Far from being arbitrary, seven is the number chosen by God as a demonstration of His thought about the world of man. Sinful man's ultimate destiny—to become part of God's plan—is expressed by this number.

Seven also denotes the fullness or completion of our universe. Particularly in a spiritual sense, it displays the perfection of God's plan for man. Thus, at the opening of His dealings with Abraham, the Lord lays out His covenant before the patriarch in seven clauses (noted in the following with superscript, bracketed numerals):

> Now the LORD had said unto Abram, Get thee out of thy
> country, and from thy kindred, and from thy father's house,
> unto a land that I will show thee:
>   And I will make of thee a great nation,[1] and I will bless
> thee,[2] and make thy name great;[3] and thou shalt be a blessing:[4]
>   And I will bless them that bless thee,[5] and curse him that
> curseth thee:[6] and in thee shall all families of the earth be
> blessed.[7] (Genesis 12:1–3)

These seven clauses are a statement of human history, laid out in advance. Needless to say, God's promise to Abraham was made on the basis of His definition of the end of the timeline.

Four hundred and thirty years after Abraham, the Lord instructed Moses concerning Israel. In a proclamation that the Jews annually celebrate to this day, in the Passover festival, the Lord revealed His plan to Moses. Significantly, it too, has seven clauses. The magnificent number seven is once again used to lay out the Lord's plan (again, noted with superscript, bracketed numerals):

> Wherefore say unto the children of Israel, I am the LORD, and
> I will bring you out from under the burdens of the Egyptians,[1]
> and I will rid you out of their bondage,[2] and I will redeem you
> with a stretched out arm, and with great judgments:[3]
>   And I will take you to me for a people,[4] and I will be
> to you a God:[5] and ye shall know that I am the LORD your
> God, which bringeth you out from under the burdens of the
> Egyptians.

And I will bring you in unto the land,[6] concerning the which
I did swear to give it to Abraham, to Isaac, and to Jacob; and I
will give it you for an heritage:[7] I am the LORD.
(Exodus 6:6–8)

In a way, all seven of these clauses can be said to have been already
accomplished, though it might be argued that the last three have not
been completely fulfilled, and won't be until the age of the Kingdom.
Also, it has often been taught that the events of the Exodus presented an
archetype of the Tribulation, which is described in Revelation in interlocking groups of seven.

It was during the Exodus that Passover was instituted. And to this
day, at each Passover, four cups are required to be consumed by those
present. Each of them is labeled by one of these first four scriptural elements. With much ceremony and symbolic recollection, each of these
four cups is lifted in remembrance of the Lord's promises.

Significantly, the first four points have been generally fulfilled; they
bring us to the time of Christ's First Coming. Israel has already been
freed from the Egyptians, freed from bondage, redeemed, and taken to
the Lord as a nation.

The last three points still lie in the prophetic future. As to the fifth
point: Israel has *not* yet come to worship God in fullness. The prophesied Third Temple has not yet been built and they still await the coming
of Messiah.

On the sixth point: Though Israel has been brought into the Land,
they have not yet attained the Abrahamic land grant, which extends all
the way to the Euphrates River.

Seventh: The Kingdom has not been restored. This is Israel's long-
awaited and exalted heritage.

But it is exceedingly interesting that through both Abraham and
Moses, Israel's destiny was laid out in a seven-clause fashion. This is, of
course, a direct reflection of the seven days of creation. Once again, seven
symbolizes the ongoing nature of God's creative intent.

The sevens of the Bible are too numerous to mention in depth at this time, but in general, the number seven is present when something new is being created or completed. Therefore, when properly perceived, they add a great deal of deep truth to the already-enormous truths at the surface level of Scripture.

For example, the Gospel of John presents Jesus performing seven miracles. During Jesus' life, angels appeared seven times. In Revelation, the glorified Christ stands in the middle of seven lamps; He makes seven promises to seven churches. The seven seals, trumpets, and vials are used to mete out judgment to mankind.

In the seventh verse of Revelation 10, we find an announcement of finality. It should come as no surprise that it is brought by angel number seven: "But in the days of the voice of the seventh angel, when he shall begin to sound, the mystery of God should be finished, as he hath declared to his servants the prophets."

And so, the prophetic destiny of the world is written in sevens, just as the Creation was laid out in sevens. As we have often stated, the seven-day pattern of Creation is the schematic layout of God's plan for humanity, foreordained in seven thousand years of human history…and as we shall see, beyond.

THE MENORAH OF TIME

This brings us to the structure of finite time from the human point of view. As detailed some years ago in *The Mystery of the Menorah and the Hebrew Alphabet,* the sevens of the Bible are best understood in the structural design of the ancient Temple menorah. Its design was given to Moses as an eternal symbol of the presence of God's Spirit.[47]

The very shape of the menorah provides a key to God's perfection, representing the work of God's Holy Spirit in creation. In fact, its perfection even appears in association with the throne of God, as given by John in Revelation: "And out of the throne proceeded lightnings and thunderings and voices: and there were seven lamps of fire burning before the throne, which are the seven Spirits of God" (Revelation 4:5).

In the Tabernacle, and later in both Temples, the menorah was placed before the south wall of the Holy Place. Its lights were a constant reminder of the fact that "God is light, and in him is no darkness at all" (1 John 1:5).

Standing as witness of His constant presence, the menorah even more importantly symbolized the Creation. The almond tree was an important part of its basic design, a reminder of the miracle of Aaron's rod that came to life overnight. The designer of the menorah, Bezaleel, was handpicked by the Lord and imbued with special knowledge that allowed him to incorporate special features into its design. It was crafted from a full talent of gold, indicating that it weighed 150 pounds!

And he made the candlestick of pure gold: of beaten work made he the candlestick; his shaft, and his branch, his bowls, his knops, and his flowers, were of the same:

And six branches going out of the sides thereof; three branches of the candlestick out of the one side thereof, and three branches of the candlestick out of the other side thereof:

Three bowls made after the fashion of almonds in one branch, a knop and a flower; and three bowls made like almonds in another branch, a knop and a flower: so throughout the six branches going out of the candlestick.

And in the candlestick were four bowls made like almonds, his knops, and his flowers: And a knop under two branches of the same, and a knop under two branches of the same, and a knop under two branches of the same, according to the six branches going out of it.

Their knops and their branches were of the same: all of it was one beaten work of pure gold. And he made his seven lamps, and his snuffers, and his snuffdishes, of pure gold. (Exodus 37:17–23)

This is the biblical description of the familiar Temple menorah. Its knobs, leaves, flowers, and almond-shaped lamps are symbols of the material universe and of the creation as a whole. Its middle lamp, which typifies Christ, is called *Ner Elohim,* or the "Lamp of God." It is also referred to as the *shamash,* or "servant lamp," since it is the lamp from which the others are rekindled after their oil supply is renewed.

That it represents our dimensional universe is easily seen in the description of the menorah given by the Jewish historian Josephus:

> Over against this table [opposite the table of shewbread], near the southern wall, was set a candlestick [menorah] of cast gold, hollow within, being of the weight of one hundred pounds, which the Hebrews call *Chinchares;* if it be turned into the Greek language, it denotes a *talent.* It was made with its knops, and lilies, and pomegranates, and bowls, (which ornaments amounted to seventy in all;) by which means the shaft elevated itself on high from a single base, and spread itself into as many branches as there are planets, including the sun among them. It terminated in seven heads, on one row, all standing parallel to one another; and these branches carried seven lamps, one by one, in imitation of the number of the planets.
> (*Antiquities,* III, vi, 7)[48]

Clearly, Josephus was relating what he knew to be common belief about the menorah. Its central lamp, called the *shamash* (שמש), is spelled identically with the Hebrew word for "sun," which, with different vowel pointers, is called *shemesh,* (שמש). Its six lamps represented the six planets then recognized by the Jews: Mercury, Venus, Earth's Moon, Mars, Jupiter, and Saturn.

And so, it symbolized the Creation, with its resulting time-space, and the Creator Himself. It presents Him as the Great Servant, elevated at the center of the menorah. When the servant became incarnated in human flesh, He stood at the center of human history, as the Servant-King over all humanity.

But as the Creator of the universe, He was also the Creator of time-space. When the Lord inserted Himself into the very middle of history,

He was making a statement about how He views time itself. In effect, He was saying that His plan was designed from ages past. Time, rather than being a line from beginning to end, is a statement of symmetry that works from the center to both ends.

THE MENORAH EXPANDED

The seven-lamp menorah obviously symbolizes the design of history, with the Lord at its center. As Moses was given the Law, this historical design represented God's view of history during the period of the Tabernacle and Temples.

But the Bible also makes it plain that the menorah given under Law would later be expanded as the menorah of grace. In about 520 BC, an angel came to the prophet Zechariah with a new vision of the menorah:

> And the angel that talked with me came again, and waked me, as a man that is wakened out of his sleep, And said unto me, What seest thou? And I said, I have looked, and behold a candlestick all of gold, with a bowl upon the top of it, and his seven lamps thereon, and seven pipes to the seven lamps, which are upon the top thereof:
> And two olive trees by it, one upon the right side of the bowl, and the other upon the left side thereof. So I answered and spake to the angel that talked with me, saying, What are these, my lord? (Zechariah 4:1–4)

In this scene, we see two additions being made to the original menorah, one on each side. The two olive trees are the source of oil and a symbol of the Holy Spirit. More than simply providing oil for the lamps, they themselves become lamps.

The sixth and seventh verses of this passage bring us the key to understanding these two additions. Adjoining the outer lamps of the menorah, they bring the twofold message of "grace":

Then he answered and spake unto me, saying, This is the word of the LORD unto Zerubbabel, saying, Not by might, nor by power, but by my spirit, saith the LORDof hosts.

Who art thou, O great mountain? before Zerubbabel thou shalt become a plain: and he shall bring forth the headstone thereof with shoutings, crying, **Grace, grace** unto it. (Zechariah 4:6, 7, emphasis added)

The twofold "grace, grace" quoted above is a deep mystery that manifested itself before Israel when the going was roughest. It provided oil for the lamps…a figure of the Lord sending help for Israel. It also expanded the definition and scope of the original menorah in the promise of the two witnesses, who themselves became lamps. But many years would pass before the meaning of the additional lamps became clear.

This prophecy brings us an amazing statement about the nature of the relationship between God and Israel. The ancient menorah signified the work of the Holy Spirit in creative activity. During the post-captivity rebuilding of the ravaged Temple, it was necessary to conquer many natural obstacles before the building could be completed. Through Zechariah, the Lord assured the governor, Zerubbabel, that God's grace would see them through. "Then said he, These are the two anointed ones, that stand by the Lord of the whole earth" (Zechariah 4:14).

Earlier, in Deuteronomy, Moses enunciated the meaning of two witnesses, whose testimony was necessary for conviction: "One witness shall not rise up against a man for any iniquity, or for any sin, in any sin that he sinneth: at the mouth of two witnesses, or at the mouth of three witnesses, shall the matter be established" (Deuteronomy 19:15).

The principle of the two witnesses is one that we find throughout the Bible, particularly at the end, in the book of Revelation. But were it not for a turning point in Israel's history, the prophecy of Zechariah made in 520 BC could not be fully known to us.

Three hundred and fifty-three years after Zechariah—in 167 BC— Israel faced another seemingly intimidating challenge, when Antiochus

IV Epiphanes ordered twenty-two thousand soldiers to attack Jerusalem on the Sabbath. He knew that the orthodox men would not fight. The Holy City was sacked once again. Women and children were kidnapped and taken into slavery. The city itself was burned nearly to the ground.

Antiochus professed that he would wipe out the Jewish religion by legally forbidding its practice. The ultimate defeat came on Kislev 24 (December 16, 167 BC), when the Temple was officially declared to be the house of the Olympian Zeus. On the altar of the demigod, swine's flesh was offered. The Temple, its utensils, and its furnishings—including the golden menorah—were profaned and rendered ceremonially unclean.

But in a miraculous reversal, the Israelite troops of Judas Maccabeus overthrew Grecian forces in several key battles. Finally, they regained virtually all of Israel. On Kislev 24 (December 14, 164 BC), the daily sacrifices at the Temple were restored. Exactly three years to the day had elapsed.

At the rededication of the Temple, there was only a single day's supply of consecrated olive oil for the menorah. In a miracle that has been celebrated annually every year since, that small supply lasted eight days. This was long enough for a new supply to be provided in accordance with Temple practices. Here, on Kislev 24, was born the festival of Hanukkah (Hebrew for "dedication").

The eight days were memorialized as the eight peripheral lamps of the Hanukkah menorah. Since that time, it has eloquently spoken of God's immense grace. This new menorah, with its eight lights surrounding the central *shamash,* became the symbol of a God who lifts up Israel in its darkest days. The prophecy of Zechariah now had both a symbol and a holy day.

Thus, the seven-lamp menorah of Moses became the nine-lamp menorah of grace. Of course, the *shamash* (central servant lamp) still presides in the central position.

Truly amazing is that the structure of these two menorahs gives us an overview of history from God's point of view.

THE CENTER POINT OF TIME

When we review the parade of human history, one thing is clear: Christ stands at its center. Time was forever marked at the moment the Lord was incarnated in human flesh. Everything before this event had looked forward to it. Everything that came after His lifetime looks back, in examination of its great significance.

If we look at His life in relation to spiritual development, we find that the three millennia preceding His birth were delineated by the grace shown to Noah, the promise to Abraham, the Law of Moses, and the kingdom of David. Following His Ascension are the present two millennia of the Church Age, followed by the millennial reign of Christ in the Kingdom Age...approximately our present position in time.

Thus, Christ presents human history in symmetrical form. If we count backward three thousand years from His birth, we come to approximately the time of Adam's death and Enoch's translation. This was a time of important transition from the original order of things under Adam to the collapse of culture in a riotous spree of debauchery and dissipation.

The millennium that follows Adam's death—from 3000–2000 BC— marks the descent of man into genetic and spiritual dissolution. This resulted in the severe judgment of God by the great Flood of Noah, and the post-Flood evils of the occult, Nimrod's idolatry, and the Tower of Babel. Blessedly, this millennium ended on a note of grace, when Abraham arrived on the scene.

Thus, the wickedness of that millennium was overcome in the Abrahamic Covenant that came at about 2000 BC. Abraham, Sarah, and their son Isaac brought humanity a new promise. This covenant is perhaps the ultimate statement about the value of faith, for it was by faith that Abraham received the promise, and "it was accounted to him for righteousness" (Galatians 3:6).

It was during this second millennium before Christ that the children of Israel were held in Egyptian bondage and later delivered by Moses, who received the Law from God.

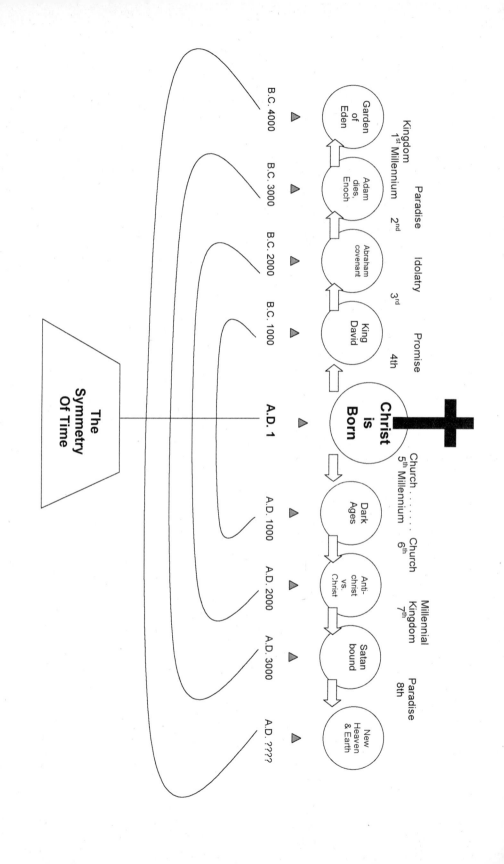

Then came 1000 BC, introduced by King David, the first monarch of the royal line that will one day be immortalized in the future Kingdom Age. This millennium was disfigured by the horrors of the Assyrian and Babylonian captivities. But it ended on the high note of Jesus' birth.

THE FULCRUM OF HISTORY

Christ was born and completed His work of grace, initiating the fifth millennium. He came as the central figure of the timeline. Everything in time—whether before or after—operated with a view toward His appearance. He is at the center of world history...the balance and symmetry of the timeline.

After His Resurrection and Ascension, the church was established. But in a remarkable and distressing turn of history, the faithful body of Christ was soon oppressed by an autocratic state church that would dominate the next thousand years, and more.

The fifth millennium ended in the year AD 1000, in the heart of the Dark Ages, in which there was no significant individual to stand up and mark the transition to the next time period. Sadly, it was a time of warlords, minor monarchs, tribal chieftains, and caliphs. Instead of a powerful figure to mark off the millennial change—an Abraham or Moses—we find the world ensnared in the clutches of an autocratic church. Perhaps its dark, collective leadership was as close as the world could come to a powerful human figure in that era.

The sixth millennium, moving toward AD 2000, oversaw the slow rise of mankind from darkness to the amazingly accelerated age of technology and the westernization of the world. It recently ended in a rising tide of world wars, the birth of modern Israel, and the increasing impact of Islam. An ominous tide of global destabilization darkly forebodes World War III...perhaps a series of Middle East campaigns that will lead to the battle of Armageddon.

More importantly, it witnessed a miraculous explosion of activity within the church. The Reformation, the rise of global missions, and the expanded prophetic understanding of the Bible offset the wars and atrocities that pockmarked the entire earth.

Since the appearance of Christ, time has been measured in years known as AD, or *anno domini:* "year of our Lord." Another two thousand years have now passed, and we are headed into the third millennium (sometimes called the "third day" in Scripture), during which many Christians believe we will witness the return of Christ to establish the Millennial Kingdom, where He is seated upon the throne of David.

Soon, the Lord will commence the judgments that will initiate the Tribulation period and the seventh millennium. A renewed earth and His Messianic spiritual rule will save an earth that would otherwise perish.

The man who will open the seventh millennium is the Antichrist, riding forth "conquering and to conquer" (Revelation 6:2). Thus, the pattern of the ages is reestablished. In other words, it is the appearance of an important personality that sets off the seventh millennium. In keeping with the traditional model, this period also ends with the emergence of another monumental figure from the annals of the past: Satan is cast into the lake of fire after a final rebellion.

Thus, history (from the death of Adam to the end of the Millennial Kingdom) is balanced, with three millennia on each side of the Cross. This pattern is familiar to anyone who has studied the structure of the sevens and the menorah.

PARADISE IS THE NORM

Now, we will deal with an interesting historical addition: The six millennia we have just discussed are bracketed by two additional time periods, as predicated in Zechariah. Preceding the millennium of the Flood, we find a thousand-year period that included Eden and paradise. It began with the perfection of the world God created for Adam.

Genealogically, it included the families of Cain, Seth, Enos, Cainan, Mahalaleel, Jared, Enoch, and Methuselah. Though this world was increasingly enveloped in sin and wickedness of the worst kind, it still retained the residual glories of its initial creation. Its climate and ecosystems were perfect and stable.

It was literally a paradise, but finally became so corrupt that it had to be utterly destroyed. Only Noah's righteous family was saved.

The other (and balancing) time period is found at the future end of the timeline. It follows the Millennial Kingdom, and is described as "new heavens and a new earth, wherein dwelleth righteousness" (2 Peter 3:13).

If this time period is added to the march of the millennia, we now have eight distinct ages. Including the Cross at the center, there are nine points, with the beginning and ending being expressions of paradise.

This pattern is remarkably foreshadowed by the two menorahs seen in Scripture. The first of them is the Tabernacle's menorah of seven arms, with six lamps (or millennia) surrounding the central lamp. The second is the menorah of dedication, with its nine lamps.

THE BALANCE OF TIME

The remarkable thing about this pattern is that it gives us a special look at the way God views time. For Him, time is a balanced pattern. The most important aspect of it is the Cross, which affects everything that came after it…and everything that came before it.

Even the invisible heavens are included in this pattern, as seen in Colossians 1:20, where the Cross is said to reconcile *all* things, whether heavenly, or earthly: "And, having made peace through the blood of his cross, by him to reconcile all things unto himself; by him, I say, whether they be things in earth, or things in heaven."

Here, the word "reconcile" is from the Greek *apokatallasso,* meaning "to effect change." Here, it is expressed in its intensive form, meaning "to completely change from one thing into another." Seen in this way, the Cross is a link between heaven and earth.

It is like an instrument of infinite length that reaches all the way from the throne of God to the finite world of man. And somehow, it changes everything…in both time and eternity.

For this reason, the diagram of the millennia reveals something to us that is otherwise invisible. The Cross reaches all the way back to the paradise of Adam, and all the way forward to the paradise of the new heavens and earth. Time, therefore, is bilateral and symmetrical. The Lord is the center of all things.

Time is far more than just the linear number seven…or nine, for that matter. It is no mere measure of distance, but a symmetrical structure that radiates in two directions from a dynamic center.

More importantly, paradise is seen as the norm. It begins the Creation, and it ends it. From this perspective, the ravages of the millennial time-line are but a temporary diversion in the long-term plan of God.

SHOCKWAVES IN TIME-SPACE

When did the Lord enter our timeline? The easy answer is "in the beginning." The reality is that He has probably entered our timeline in an infinite number of moments, from beginning to end. He is, after all, its Creator.

But the focus of His presence was the Cross and His physical incarnation in human flesh. That is when His power to affect the wicked world reached an amazing level. Far from defeat, His death and resurrection created victorious shockwaves in time-space.

Like the original menorah itself, time as we know it receives its illumination from the center. It is easy to see why God has foreknowledge of all that will ever happen. Furthermore, He can link the future with the past in a way that time-bound humans never can…at least, not as long as we dwell within corrupt bodies that are destined to move within physical parameters.

The Lord is the servant lamp for heaven as well as earth. We must remember that the original sin was committed in heaven. It spread darkness throughout the infinite realm that no man has ever seen. Satan, once called Lucifer, the "light bearer," became the chief exponent of darkness.

Whatever he touched receded in shadow and gloom. Though he masquerades as an "angel of light," he is the tyrannical ruler of the dark kingdom: "For we wrestle not against flesh and blood, but against principalities, against powers, against the rulers of the darkness of this world, against spiritual wickedness in high places" (Ephesians 6:12).

One fact seems obvious. Satan does not have access to time-space in the same way that the Lord does. Just like human beings, he can read Scripture. He has seen his demise written for all to understand, but he doesn't seem to believe it. His limited vision apparently gives him the hope that he can still succeed in subverting God's plan.

He walks throughout the earth, concealed by a dimensional veil that shields him from human eyes. But unlike the Lord of time and history, he cannot enter the timeline at any point he wishes. There is no scriptural instance of his having prophesied of the future. For example, it was not Satan, but Daniel, who foretold Nebuchadnezzar's role in history. Neither has the Old Serpent given any of his earthly lackeys an advantageous view of things to come.

Tyrants like Pharaoh, Haman, and Hitler, who have attempted to destroy the Jews, have always failed. Though Hitler communed with dark spirits—perhaps Satan himself—he was never given a view of the future whereby he might have saved his Third Reich. Satan cannot peer into the future.

Though he is doomed by divine edict, he presses on in the hope that he can "beat the system." He is apparently looking for some last-ditch escape.

He will not find it. Instead, he will discover that the Lord's plan, crafted in conformity with a large-scale, symmetrical pattern, has blocked his every ploy. The Lord of time has created a remedy for sin.

12

THE ADVENTURES OF EZEKIEL
AND THE TIME MACHINE

Our thinking is stretched to the breaking point when we try to reconcile time with eternity. The prophet Ezekiel uniquely illustrates the difficulty encountered when human reason attempts to understand the relationship between the heavenly and earthly dimensions.

It is the essence of understatement to say that Ezekiel had a special relationship with the Lord. Anyone who has had even the slightest contact with Scripture knows that Ezekiel encountered a true marvel. His exploits remind us of today's popular fiction...or the back-page reports of the bizarre and unusual. Today, flying disks are the stuff of modern mythology. But they are real. Celestial vehicles are real. A fiery, whirling flame flew toward Ezekiel at great speed, then landed right beside him!

Put in modern language, Ezekiel's adventure would certainly qualify as science fiction. A ship built with inconceivably advanced technology came to this man and presented him with a mission. During that contact, we see the vehicle described in a way that displays Ezekiel's utter awe. Though he observed the flying chariot, his mind could not completely grasp its workings. Nevertheless, he tried. His description connects the mystical with the mechanical. Heaven meets earth—time meets the eternal past and future—in a way that has never been duplicated, before or since.

Jewish writings speak of his mind-boggling encounter as *Ma'aseh Merkavah,* or the "Account of the Chariot." A closer look at the account reveals two things: One, that the "chariot" is a revelation of God's throne. Two, it was specially sent to lift Ezekiel up and convey him from Babylon to Jerusalem. There, he saw and reported upon the horrific idolatry that had insinuated itself into Temple worship. Later, the chariot even took him into the future! There, he saw the final disposition of that same Temple.

A whirling, fiery "something" whizzed across the Babylonian plain and stood before him. He instantly became what in the present parlance is called "a UFO percipient," an observer. In our era, his subsequent experience might become the subject of a lurid magazine article. The difference is that his UFO was not an unidentified flying object. It was positively identified as the throne of the Lord.

Then the Lord lifted Ezekiel up, taking him on the first known aerial tour, showing him sights from his own era. Finally, he was taken to the future, manipulating time as easily as we move from one place to another in our familiar dimension. His amazing journeys became the foundation of one of the Bible's most essential prophetic studies.

The events that led to the writing of Ezekiel's prophecy took place during the Babylonian captivity. Taken forcibly from Jerusalem in 597 BC, the prophet lived through one of the greatest calamities in the history of Israel. The opening scene takes place five years later, in 592 BC. Ezekiel is standing beside Nebuchadnezzar's great canal, the River Chebar:

> Now it came to pass in the thirtieth year, in the fourth month,
> in the fifth day of the month, as I was among the captives by
> the river of Chebar, that the heavens were opened, and I saw
> visions of God.
>
> In the fifth day of the month, which was the fifth year
> of king Jehoiachin's captivity, The word of the LORD came
> expressly unto Ezekiel the priest, the son of Buzi, in the land of
> the Chaldeans by the river Chebar; and the hand of the LORD
> was there upon him.

And I looked, and, behold, a whirlwind came out of the
north, a great cloud, and a fire infolding itself, and a brightness
was about it, and out of the midst thereof as the colour of
amber, out of the midst of the fire. (Ezekiel 1:1–4)

In the years since this amazing event, saints and sages have wondered
exactly what Ezekiel saw. Some have said that he experienced a dream or
vision, perceived in some sort of altered, half-waking state. Here, they
say, was the vision of a flaming chariot. It may have seemed to come close
to Ezekiel, but those who hold this view firmly cling to the idea that the
whole event was one of perception rather than physical reality.

In other words, this view asserts that Ezekiel had a spiritual experience in which his mind and soul were lifted up to the realms of heaven.

However, Ezekiel carefully notes that "the heavens were opened."
The word "heavens" is the Hebrew *shemayim* (שמים), which is the ordinary word for the sky. In other words, Ezekiel says that "the sky was
opened." As we shall see, this suggests that he experienced a visitation
from another dimension.

And then there is the conception of the vision itself, mentioned by
Ezekiel in the plural as "visions." Had this been a vision in an ecstatic,
dreamlike state, it would have been described by the Hebrew term *cha-
zon* (חזון). This is the common word for the phenomenon of prophetic
visions, sometimes coinciding with dreams or occurring at night.

On the contrary, the Hebrew word used by Ezekiel for "visions"
is *maroht* (מראות), plural for *mareh* (מראה), meaning an appearance,
sight, phenomenon, or spectacle. This would be something viewed
objectively—a "real" object. On the basis of simple grammar, Ezekiel's
experience is expressed as something substantial…physically viewed
with the eyes. So he saw a physical phenomenon rather than a mental or
spiritual perception.

The *Keil & Delitzsch Commentary on the Old Testament* puts it this way:

The phenomenon consisted in this, that the heavens were
opened, and Ezekiel saw visions of God. The heaven opens not

merely when to our eye a glimpse is disclosed of the heavenly glory of God, but also when God manifests His glory in a manner perceptible to human sight. The latter was the case here.[49]

Ezekiel actually witnessed a fiery whirlwind piercing through the sky and flying out of the north. This rift in the sky is, by definition, the best description we have of a dimensional portal being opened. Such a gateway gives access to the dimensions of eternity, enabling travel through both time and space.

Then, the wheel of fire drew closer to him. As it hovered, it became better defined. Ezekiel had time to examine it. He watched its multiplicity of "wheels." They remind us of another supernatural phenomenon mentioned in Scripture:

> I beheld till the thrones were cast down, and the Ancient of days did sit, whose garment was white as snow, and the hair of his head like the pure wool: his throne was like the fiery flame, and his wheels as burning fire.
>
> A fiery stream issued and came forth from before him: thousand thousands ministered unto him, and ten thousand times ten thousand stood before him: the judgment was set, and the books were opened. (Daniel 7:9, 10)

Here is Daniel's view of God's throne. The time is future. The event is the judgment of the nations. Note that His throne has a curious feature: "wheels as burning fire."

In the medieval era, artists actually painted Daniel's apocalyptic scene with the throne of God being carried along by oxen pulling a platform with spoked wagon wheels. These wheels were on fire! The impracticality of the matter didn't seem to matter to the primitive artists who had no idea that a burning wheel might actually be a flying disk, sent forth from God's throne.

As nearly as we can tell, Ezekiel sighted such a fiery wheel. Apparently, such "wheels" are common in the realm of heaven and the angels. Not only was it in flight; it drew close to the prophet and seemed to hover for a time. The prophet noted its many strange motions and physical features as he struggled to understand what he was seeing. Strangely, as it approached, Ezekiel noticed that it was borne along by four creatures. They seemed to him to be alive. Later in his writing, we discover that they are cherubs—the watchers over and bearers of God's throne:

> Also out of the midst thereof came the likeness of four living
> creatures. And this was their appearance; they had the likeness
> of a man.
>
> And every one had four faces, and every one had four
> wings. And their feet were straight feet; and the sole of their
> feet was like the sole of a calf's foot: and they sparkled like the
> colour of burnished brass. And they had the hands of a man
> under their wings on their four sides; and they four had their
> faces and their wings. (Ezekiel 1:5–8)

Ezekiel had probably read the psalms of David, so he would have been familiar with the words of Psalm 18:10, which describes a scene much like the one he was now seeing: "And he rode upon a cherub, and did fly: yea, he did fly upon the wings of the wind."

Cherubs are powerful creatures. They Lord rides upon them! They also act as guardians and representatives before His throne. We also see them in Revelation, as John relates the amazing view of God's throne:

> And before the throne there was a sea of glass like unto crystal:
> and in the midst of the throne, and round about the throne,
> were four beasts full of eyes before and behind.
>
> And the first beast was like a lion, and the second beast like
> a calf, and the third beast had a face as a man, and the fourth
> beast was like a flying eagle. (Revelation 4:6, 7)

Ezekiel saw virtually the same sight, the difference being that John was *taken to* the throne of the Lord, while the throne *came to* Ezekiel. As it came to rest before him, he noticed the faces of the cherubs: "As for the likeness of their faces, they four had the face of a man, and the face of a lion, on the right side: and they four had the face of an ox on the left side; they four also had the face of an eagle" (Ezekiel 1:10).

The rest of Ezekiel's first chapter is devoted to a detailed description of something that resembles a vehicle, except that it was light years beyond our twenty-first-century concept of high technology.

He wrote about how the "living creatures" were characterized by "coals of fire" and flashes of what resembled lightning. He struggled to express the way they touched the ground as wheels, one wheel beside each of the creatures.

The imagination boggles as Ezekiel tells us of the wheels, like polished metal and gemstones. Somehow, they incorporated "rings" with "eyes round about them four." The wheels and living creatures moved together in a symphony of motion that Ezekiel perfectly described. Yet, there is no way that we can rightly visualize what he saw.

Over the whole apparatus stretched a "firmament" that apparently went from one creature to another, touching each of their heads. He described it as a "terrible crystal," or awesome crystalline canopy. The creatures' wings touched as they moved. Their various motions were accompanied by the roar of moving water. One thinks of the sound of Niagara Falls...or of a jet engine.

Finally, above the crystal canopy was a throne made of sapphire. Upon that throne was a man who glowed like the "the color of amber." The whole thing was surrounded by a rainbow of radiance. It was, as Ezekiel put it, "the glory of the Lord."

Ezekiel was privileged to directly view the *Shechina* glory of the Lord. As would any of us, he fell upon his face before the throne of God. His experience demonstrates that in some way, the throne of God has the ability to project itself into an ordinary environment—in this case, Nebuchadnezzar's Babylon.

Christians often use the term "throne of grace," as in Hebrews 4:16:

"Let us therefore come boldly unto the throne of grace, that we may obtain mercy, and find grace to help in time of need." But in Ezekiel's case, the throne of grace came to him. At this time, the remnant of Israel had defiled itself and was in the process of being severely judged by the Lord. Many years before, in 722 BC, the ten northern tribes had been vanquished by the Assyrians. Now, Nebuchadnezzar had progressively destroyed the southern kingdom and finally, Jerusalem itself. Soon the Temple would be razed.

A Ride toward Destiny

At this dire historical moment, the Lord announced to Ezekiel that he was to be ordained as "watchman unto the house of Israel." At the beginning of this process, he was given a scroll to eat. It tasted to him like honey. This familiar motif reminds us of the apostle John in heaven. He, too, was given a small scroll, which he was commanded to eat.

Then Ezekiel was taken to his people in a most unusual way. His is perhaps the first recorded flying trip! And as we shall see, the "ship," if one can call it that, is able to travel through time as easily as it travels through space!

Apparently, he had been isolated—separated from his people—as he stood by the river Chebar. Upon being ordained, he was transported to another location and delivered to a place where a large group of his people was gathered:

> Then the spirit took me up, and I heard behind me a voice of a great rushing, saying, Blessed be the glory of the LORD from his place.
>
> I heard also the noise of the wings of the living creatures that touched one another, and the noise of the wheels over against them, and a noise of a great rushing.
>
> So the spirit lifted me up, and took me away, and I went in bitterness, in the heat of my spirit; but the hand of the LORD was strong upon me.

Then I came to them of the captivity at Telabib, that dwelt by the river of Chebar, and I sat where they sat, and remained there astonished among them seven days. (Ezekiel 3:12–14)

Was Ezekiel having what we call a vision, or was he riding in some sort of celestial transportation vehicle? The above description certainly suggests the latter, as the vehicle lifted him up with a roar, and took him (of all places!) to "Telabib." As it is written in Hebrew, the name of this place is Tel Aviv (תל אביב), just like the modern Israeli city, except this one is in Babylon. It means, "mound or hill or ripening ears of grain," such as barley. The ripening barley crop was once used as a sign that the Passover season would follow closely. Jews were required the visit the Temple at this time, since Passover was one of three annual pilgrimage festivals.

There is a pitiable sort of hope attached to the name of this place that was so far from the Jewish homeland. It seems that the exiles had given the place of their captivity a name that inspired hope, reminding them of home, and the Temple. The same thing happened in the last century—1909 to be exact—when with great hope, the modern city of Tel Aviv, was founded in modern Israel.

PULLING "G's"

As the vehicle lifts Ezekiel, there is another note that we in the twenty-first century can appreciate: We call it "g-force." It is the force of gravity, multiplied by acceleration. Ezekiel says that the Lord's hand pressed strongly upon him. If we were in a ship that accelerated rapidly, this is exactly what we would experience. To us, being pressed into our seat during acceleration is a common experience. To Ezekiel, it was something quite supernatural. What an adventure for an ancient prophet whose ride has features familiar to those of today's fighter pilots!

Ezekiel's flight (as we now assume it to be) was marked by sound and fury. He was overwhelmed by the rushing and roaring of its propulsion.

And he did not suffer the trip gladly; his mental state was bitterness and resentment. Who can blame him? He was now a hopeless exile.

His people had been vanquished, and he was probably angry with the Lord for allowing this to happen. Little did he know that he was about to be shown just why the calamity of the Babylonian captivity had been visited upon his people. He was to be given a first-person view of Israel's apostasy. But more than apostasy, Israel's leaders had fallen into utter immorality, corruption and wickedness. Their secret practices were an open shame before the Lord. Soon, thanks to His relationship with Ezekiel, the clandestine idolatry of the priesthood would be exposed to the entire world.

430 Days

After being transported to his people, Ezekiel sat with them for seven days. As captives, they were all in a state of shock. But he had been brought to them for a good reason. They badly needed encouragement. Then the Word of the Lord came to him, instructing him to demonstrate four prophetic signs that would outline His plan.

First, He told Ezekiel to take a tile labeled "Jerusalem" and set up a mock "siege" against it. Second, He told the prophet to lie on his left side for 390 days and on his right side for 40 days—a total of 430 days. Third, He told Ezekiel to bake and eat defiled bread. Finally, he was instructed to shave and weigh his hair and beard.

Collectively, these signs were a warning to Israel about the judgment that was being meted out. Taken together, they spell out a long period during which their power would be scattered among various Gentile dominions. They demonstrated the reasons for Israel's plight, as well as the nature and timing of Jerusalem's sieges and burnings.

Over the 430-day period, Ezekiel was ordered to act out God's judgment upon Judah and Jerusalem. Faithfully, he followed the Lord's order to perform a number of publicly humiliating and self-deprecating acts. Lying on his sides; eating bread defiled with dung, and shaving his head must have brought him deep shame. Moreover, he was a man who had always lived up to a standard of righteousness. Now, he was forced to receive the curses brought upon him by the sins of others…the corrupt priesthood of Israel.

An Interdimensional Descent to Abomination

But what had Israel's priests and leaders done that was so horrible? The Lord had spoken to Ezekiel in general terms about their spiritual adulteries and abominable practices. But he was ignorant of their daily wickedness. He and other righteous Jews were in the dark about the sins of their leaders. In fact, the prophet had already pleaded to the Lord that from his youth up, he had striven to keep the kosher diet and proper practices of worship. Before captivity, his habitual practices would have shielded him from the heinous practices of the cabal that had come into power over Jerusalem and Judah.

Now, Ezekiel was about to be shown what they did. The 430 days of his demonstration had come to an end. The chariot of the Lord was about to take him all the way to the Temple Mount! With his own eyes, he would witness their iniquity, hidden in places that no outsider to their abominable cult had ever entered.

Contemporary archaeology has unearthed many of the Jews' apostate practices. But the horrors revealed to Ezekiel have never been corroborated by modern research techniques. It is safe to say that, without the Lord's help in gaining access to these secret places, no one to this day would have completely understood the full extent of their evil practices.

Unlike his first trip to the Babylonian Tel Aviv, mentioned earlier, Ezekiel is taken from within his home. Through the ages since, opinion has been divided over whether he actually, physically, made the trip to Jerusalem. But in the third verse of the following passage, the word "visions" is translated by the same word (*maroht* [מראות]) that was used in the description of the Lord's chariot:

And it came to pass in the sixth year, in the sixth month, in the fifth day of the month, as I sat in mine house, and the elders of Judah sat before me, that the hand of the Lord God fell there upon me.

Then I beheld, and lo a likeness as the appearance of fire: from the appearance of his loins even downward, fire; and from his loins even upward, as the appearance of brightness, as the colour of amber.

And he put forth the form of an hand, and took me by a lock of mine head; and the spirit lifted me up between the earth and the heaven, and brought me in the visions of God to Jerusalem, to the door of the inner gate that looketh toward the north; where was the seat of the image of jealousy, which provoketh to jealousy. And, behold, the glory of the God of Israel was there, according to the vision that I saw in the plain. (Ezekiel 8:1–4)

Some might say that this Scripture describes a mental or spiritual visionary trip. But given the rest of his experiences, it seems that he actually made the trip bodily, witnessing both the hand of the Lord and the sights in Jerusalem with his own eyes. Being lifted by the hair is physical, indeed! Perhaps this is Ezekiel's way of describing being elevated in a supernatural way. But surely the weight of his body was not suspended by his hair.

This time, Ezekiel was taken from his room in a way that is quite familiar to those who have studied the literature of modern UFO abductions. This contemporary phenomenon sheds a great deal of light upon Ezekiel's adventure. Though current abductions are demonic in nature, they nevertheless demonstrate the ability of supernatural powers to remove a human being from a closed room.

What happened to Ezekiel was the work of the Lord. But today, it is regularly practiced by the "principalities...powers...and...rulers of the darkness of this world" spoken of by Paul in Ephesians 6:12.

The evil comings and goings of the dark powers have been chronicled by Dr. David Jacobs of Temple University and Dr. John Mack of Harvard University. Both men have written books that document the phenomenon of UFO abductions. Dr. Jacobs wrote *Secret Life* in 1992 and *The Threat* in 1998. Dr. Mack, a physician and psychiatrist, wrote *Abduction* in 1994.[50] All have studied the work of demonic forces, though they don't label them as such.

They are confused about the nature of the phenomenon they have chosen to investigate. In other words, they identify demons as "space aliens."

Still, the supernatural methods used by these "aliens" to penetrate the dimensional barrier seem to operate in somewhat the same way as the account in Ezekiel. That is, there are literally hundreds of contemporary accounts in which ordinary men and women are lifted through the ceilings of their locked rooms or floated through closed windows. Following their ghastly encounters with demonic entities, they are returned in the same manner. All of which is to say that it is perfectly conceivable that Ezekiel was physically transported to the Temple Mount.

Once there, the first of the abominations that met his eyes was "the seat of the image of jealousy." Jewish history says that this image was first erected by the wicked king Manasseh, son of Hezekiah. It was reputed to have had four faces, which looked in four directions. History says that it was constructed to incorporate the attributes of the true God of Israel, pretending to be His very image. That is, it was a graven image of Jehovah Himself! Thus, it was given the name "jealousy." This was horrible enough, but what followed was even more shocking.

The prophet was next brought to the door of the inner court. There, he was told to excavate an area of the wall. When he did, he found a secret door:

> Then said he unto me, Son of man, dig now in the wall: and when
> I had digged in the wall, behold a door. And he said unto me, Go
> in, and behold the wicked abominations that they do here.
> So I went in and saw; and behold every form of creeping

things, and abominable beasts, and all the idols of the house of
Israel, portrayed upon the wall round about.

And there stood before them seventy men of the ancients
of the house of Israel, and in the midst of them stood Jaazaniah
the son of Shaphan, with every man his censer in his hand; and
a thick cloud of incense went up. (Ezekiel 8:8–11)

In the secret room, Ezekiel saw every abomination known to man
painted on the walls that were concealed from the eyes of the people. In
his later years, Manasseh repented of his evil deeds. His successor, Josiah,
initiated a general repentance and reform, but was apparently unable to
prevent Israel's leaders from secretly clinging to the idolatry that they had
grown to love.

Perhaps the seventy men he saw were the actual Sanhedrin. They
stood before the pictures of cattle, vermin, reptiles, demonic gods and
goddesses...virtually every ancient idolatry...and they burned the Lord's
own Temple incense before them!

Did Ezekiel see a real secret room within the Temple? During the
initial phase of the captivity (in which Ezekiel was taken), the Temple
was still functioning. Presumably then, he was shown the actual events
of an ongoing idolatry.

Next, at the north gate of the Temple, Ezekiel was shown another
abomination:

Then he brought me to the door of the gate of the LORD'S
house which was toward the north; and, behold, there sat
women weeping for Tammuz.

Then said he unto me, Hast thou seen this, O son of man?
turn thee yet again, and thou shalt see greater abominations
than these. (Ezekiel 8:14, 15)

Tammuz, the Sumerian deity of flocks and spring crops, was the
legendary husband and brother of Ishtar. She, a fertility goddess, had

supposedly seduced, then betrayed him. Pagans annually invoked the saga of his death and trip to the underworld in June/July of each year. Their mourning rites were supposed to bring him back from the dead, resulting in a blessing of crops and herds.

As if this were not enough, Ezekiel was shown another sight: The priests worshiped the rising sun:

> And he brought me into the inner court of the LORD's house,
> and, behold, at the door of the temple of the LORD, between
> the porch and the altar, were about five and twenty men, with
> their backs toward the temple of the LORD, and their faces
> toward the east; and they worshipped the sun toward the east.
> (Ezekiel 8:16)

Worship of the solar disk was widespread among the peoples of the East, and well-known as the centerpiece of Egyptian idolatry. Ra, the god of the sun was regarded as the one who brings life to mankind.

In Deuteronomy 4:19, Israel was specifically warned against worshiping any heavenly object, and the sun in particular. However, sun worship had crept into the life of the Temple. For example, it is well known that Manasseh, son of Hezekiah, built altars there that were dedicated to worship and prayer toward all the host of heaven, including the sun.

Ezekiel's contemporary, Jeremiah, made the same observation about God's view of a priesthood that has abandoned its true calling to worship the sun. He prophesied that their ultimate end would be marked by dishonor and death:

> At that time, saith the LORD, they shall bring out the bones of
> the kings of Judah, and the bones of his princes, and the bones
> of the priests, and the bones of the prophets, and the bones of
> the inhabitants of Jerusalem, out of their graves:
> And they shall spread them before the sun, and the moon,
> and all the host of heaven, whom they have loved, and whom

they have served, and after whom they have walked, and whom they have sought, and whom they have worshipped: they shall not be gathered, nor be buried; they shall be for dung upon the face of the earth. (Jeremiah 8:1, 2)

Having been shown the defection of the priesthood, Ezekiel became the Lord's personal witness. Under the circumstances thus presented, His fury is now perfectly justified. No one reviewing the case against Israel's leaders can argue that the Lord acted rashly or arbitrarily.

THE GLORY DEPARTS

Now the judgment of Jerusalem and the Temple began in earnest, and Ezekiel was there to witness the chariot of the Lord as it carried out the work of removing the Lord's presence from the corrupted Temple. With its cherubim and wheels, it appeared exactly as it had when Ezekiel viewed it by the River Chebar in Babylon.

Ezekiel watched in sadness and disbelief as the Lord's chariot progressively moved the *Shechina* glory of the Lord, first from the Holy of Holies, then to the Temple threshold, and to the eastern gate. Finally, the glory departed into the heavens:

Then did the cherubims lift up their wings, and the wheels beside them; and the glory of the God of Israel was over them above. And the glory of the LORD went up from the midst of the city, and stood upon the mountain which is on the east side of the city.

Afterwards the spirit took me up, and brought me in a vision by the Spirit of God into Chaldea, to them of the captivity. So the vision that I had seen went up from me. Then I spake unto them of the captivity all the things that the LORD had showed me. (Ezekiel 11:22–25)

After his amazing tour of Jerusalem, Ezekiel was returned to Babylon (here referred to as *Chaldea*), where he delivered the news of his journey to the Jews he had left a short time before. The method of his return—via the Lord's chariot—is perfectly in keeping with the idea that he had been physically transported to Jerusalem in the first place.

After the Lord's departure, Ezekiel was dropped off among the captives back in Babylon. Imagine the stories that he told his people! Perhaps they had even caught a glimpse of the fiery wheel!

Their emotions were no doubt a mixture of despondency and elation. His report must have filled them with great sorrow. But at the same time, they had the reassurance that the Lord had not abandoned His faithful remnant.

FINAL JUDGMENT OF ISRAEL AND THE NATIONS

Ezekiel's remarkable journeys to Israel took him through space, probably much in the way that modern man experiences air travel: He heard the roar of propulsion and felt the weight of acceleration.

Upon his return to the captive Jews in Babylon, Ezekiel delivered a series of judgments, parables, and signs directed against the elders of Judah and Jerusalem. As always with the prophets, the Lord instructed him to give the people hope for the future.

He reviewed the gracious history of the Lord's past relationship with Israel. He reminds them of their wilderness journeys, their dealings with Egypt and the Caananites, and the many examples of His protection.

Then he tells them that Israel will be restored. He graphically explains that their traditional enemies—Ammon, Moab, Edom, Philistia, Tyre, Sidon, and finally, Egypt—are to be judged in the future.

Far and away his greatest prophecy is given in chapters 33 through 39 of his book. Once again, the Lord reminds Ezekiel that he has been appointed "watchman unto the house of Israel" (33:7), the Lord's personal witness.

In the following chapters, he begins to speak of the coming judgment of the nations, as Israel is regathered and returns to the true worship of the Lord. His visions of the dry bones and of the two sticks detail the ways in which Israel is to come back into the land originally promised to Abraham.

Of course, the highlight of this prophetic sequence comes in chapters 38 and 39, the prophecy that has stimulated much discussion about the great battles that will initiate the "Day of the Lord" judgments:

> Son of man, set thy face against Gog, the land of Magog, the
> chief prince of Meshech and Tubal, and prophesy against him,
> And say, Thus saith the Lord GOD; Behold, I am against thee, O
> Gog, the chief prince of Meshech and Tubal. (Ezekiel 38:2, 3)

Over the last century or so, many commentators have stated that this may be the only Scripture in the entire Bible that associates a military action with a contemporary nation. In it, the words "chief prince" may be rendered "Prince of Rosh," the modern Hebrew word for Russia. Many have mentioned that "Mechech and Tubal" represent the westernmost and easternmost extent of Russia.

Ezekiel 39:18 makes the prophecy plain: "And it shall come to pass at the same time when Gog shall come against the land of Israel, saith the Lord GOD, that my fury shall come up in my face."

Throughout the book of Ezekiel, the Lord has said that, because of Israel's apostasy, His fury will one day be released upon the nations of the world. Here, we have a plain and simple statement that links the Lord's promise with a future historical event.

FLIGHT TO THE FUTURE

Ezekiel had traveled through space, making an aerial journey that would give him the information necessary to make Israel understand the righteous judgments of the Lord. Then, he had lived in the midst of his people, delivering a series of messages essential to their spiritual growth and national redemption.

Finally, he told them how events would unfold in the battles of the Tribulation period. One day, this information will be vitally important to the leaders of modern Israel. As they observe the growing instabilities of the Middle East, they will be prepared for events still to come.

But the crowning glory of Ezekiel's prophecy is his view of the restored Temple to be built at the end of the Tribulation.

Now, Ezekiel is about to travel through time to the distant future:

> In the five and twentieth year of our captivity, in the beginning
> of the year, in the tenth day of the month, in the fourteenth
> year after that the city was smitten, in the selfsame day the
> hand of the LORD was upon me, and brought me thither.
>
> In the visions of God brought he me into the land of Israel,
> and set me upon a very high mountain, by which was as the
> frame of a city on the south. (Ezekiel 40:1, 2)

Ezekiel is brought once again to the land of Israel. The setting is post-Tribulational. The cataclysms of Revelation are past; the renewed Jerusalem and the new Temple are poised to initiate the long-promised Messianic reign of the Lord.

Did Ezekiel make this journey physically? Was this a vision, or was it a real trip? Once again, given the prophet's relationship with the Lord and previous experience, it is quite safe to say that he actually made the trip... in his body. In every sense of the term, Ezekiel was a true time traveler.

He is looking at a changed landscape. The great earthquakes that have reshaped the Promised Land have also remodeled the real estate in the vicinity of Jerusalem. He lands upon a great mountain. No doubt, that "very high mountain" is not there today. There, he witnesses the layout of a new city. The implication is that it has been laid out as a new and total design. Lying to the south, it may occupy roughly the same ground as the old City of David.

He watches as a man begins to measure out the ground of the new Temple:

> And he brought me thither, and, behold, there was a man, whose appearance was like the appearance of brass, with a line of flax in his hand, and a measuring reed; and he stood in the gate.
>
> And the man said unto me, Son of man, behold with thine eyes, and hear with thine ears, and set thine heart upon all that I shall show thee; for to the intent that I might show them unto thee art thou brought hither: declare all that thou seest to the house of Israel. (Ezekiel 40:3, 4)

Once again, at this time in the future, Ezekiel has been brought to the Temple Mount for a specific purpose. The measuring angel—whose appearance closely resembles that of the cherubim that he originally saw (1:7)—tells him to remember all that he sees. The hope of the new Temple is to be brought back to his people. They must be made to know that there is hope. The grace of God is far beyond human understanding!

Through the ages that were to follow the Babylonian captivity, Israel would experience many shocks and insults. The worst is yet to come. But all is not lost. The Lord's message to Ezekiel guarantees that.

The rest of Ezekiel's experience at the new Temple contains a myriad of astonishing details. One can hardly believe the glories that are promised in that coming era. The entire Temple complex is said to measure about nine million square cubits! In our measurement, that would make it at least a mile square! Or, if the following "measures" are cubits, it would measure over six miles in circumference: "It was round about eighteen thousand measures: and the name of the city from that day shall be, The LORD is there" (Ezekiel 48:35).

If you don't believe that time travel is possible, just remember that Ezekiel saw it with his own eyes. The Third Temple *will* be built. Through Ezekiel's eyes, we have already seen it.

13

THE CIRCLE OF TIME

The Bible presents time-space as linear, with the seven days of Creation providing the layout of seven thousand future years of human endeavor and divine redemption. As described previously, it also presents time as symmetrical, with Christ at its center. From that center, history is laid out in two directions—past and future. These two directions present mirror images of His redemptive work, with paradise dominating both past and future.

In this chapter, we'll see that the Bible also presents time-space as a circle. The circle—a line traced at a constant distance (radius) around a center point—has aspects of eternity. It is finite, yet continuous. A kinetically charged point can race around and around a statically balanced center. In a vacuum, absent the forces of atmospheric and electromagnetic drag, such circular motion is practically infinite.

As we shall see, the circle represents two metaphysical truths. First, it traces cycles in history, in which events tend to be repeated on a systematic basis. Second, the relationship between its circumference and its diameter is mathematically irreconcilable (irrational), transcending time-space and pointing toward the infinite. In fact, the circle has long been seen as a symbol of eternity.

In the preceding chapter, we examined the time-space travels of the prophet Ezekiel. As we saw, his encounters with the chariot of the Lord included phenomenal living creatures, precious materials, and wheels within wheels. The structure of his celestial transportation vehicle is not incidental. Its myriad rotational interactions are freighted with meaning.

We noted that Jewish writings speak of his mind-boggling encounter as *Ma'aseh Merkavah,* or the "Account of the Chariot." It is of great interest that this same term is used elsewhere by Jewish commentators, who use it to refer to "metaphysical secrets." In other words, the chariot's wheels and rings speak of deeper truths. Their very terminology allows us to see that Ezekiel's wheels reveal the deeper spiritual truths of Scripture. These wheels are described as having "eyes," and their complex interactions are truly inexplicable:

> The appearance of the wheels and their work was like unto
> the colour of a beryl: and they four had one likeness: and their
> appearance and their work was as it were a wheel in the middle
> of a wheel.
>
> When they went, they went upon their four sides: and they
> turned not when they went. As for their rings, they were so
> high that they were dreadful; and their rings were full of eyes
> round about them four. (Ezekiel 1:16–18)

The jewel-like wheels must have had the appearance of precious stones and metals. The vehicle rode upon a series of spinning devices. Its very emergence from another dimension links motion through space with rotating force.

Without going into great detail, it is very obvious that this description of a wonderful vehicle is based upon sets of circles. It apparently had sets of concentric wheels, rings and "eyes" (which are themselves circles).

Things that spin, revolve, and rotate remind us that the entirety of created nature is built upon myriads of spinning energy fields, ranging from the inner structure of atoms to massive rotating galaxies.

Ezekiel was visited by the Lord, who came visibly through a portal from another dimension. If there is any insight at all in this episode, it is that the interdimensional world must involve interactive circular fields.

What Is a Circle?

Throughout the ages, the geometry and mathematical structure of the circle has been viewed as a kind of Holy Grail. In the post-Flood era, when men began to build magnificent structures of all kinds, they designed circular enclosures, columns, posts, arcs, arches, and the wheel. All of these involved calculating measurements of length and area.

In all these endeavors, the engineers were faced with the problem of squaring the circle…calculating its area and describing the relationship between its circumference and its diameter.

It is quite easy to lay out a square, using a ninety-degree angle and simple ruler. Figuring its area by multiplying its length by its width is child's play. And finding the correlation between one of its sides and its total outside perimeter is a simple four-to-one ratio.

But the circle posed a special problem, since there was no obvious way to find the precise relationship between its circumference and its diameter. For the ancient Chinese, Indian, and Greek thinkers, the solution to this ratio became a quest pursued on many levels. But not until well into the eighteenth century would this ratio come to be represented by the Greek letter *pi* (π).

Petr Beckmann, author of *A History of* π *(pi)*, documents the continuing efforts of brilliant mathematicians to make sense of the simple circle. For very practical reasons, he says, they wanted to discover the relationship between a circle's circumference and its diameter.[51]

At first, he says, mathematicians used geometry, laying out various solutions on papyrus or vellum. Before that, their earliest efforts probably began when they drove a stake in the sand and scribed a circle with another stake at the end of a rope. Then another rope could be cut to measure the circle's diameter, which is simply double the radius. Having that, they could then lay the diameter-length rope in the groove of the circle's perimeter.

Using this technique, they would have quickly learned that just over three rope lengths (diameters) would go almost all the way around the circle. They could easily have discovered that the remainder required just over one-eighth of the rope's length to complete the circle.

By about 2000 BC, both the Babylonians and Egyptians had settled upon the figure of three and one-eighth, or 3.125. That is, they reasoned that it would take 3.125 diameters to reach all the way around the circumference of a given circle.

In about 1000 BC, King Solomon undertook the construction of the First Temple and its furnishings. One of the articles was a huge circular *mikvah*, or pool of water, for the ritual ablutions of the priesthood. It was cast from a single piece of brass, supported on the backs of twelve brazen oxen, and was nearly eighteen feet in diameter.

It is well known that the biblical account of its construction describes the relationship between its diameter and its circumference: "And he made a molten sea, ten cubits from the one brim to the other: it was round all about, and his height was five cubits: and a line of thirty cubits did compass it round about" (1 Kings 7:23).

This encompassing "line" supports the image of using a rope for scribing a circle and measuring the circumference.

It's easy to see that this picture gives a ratio of exactly three (thirty divided by ten)...far short of the value used by the Egyptians and Babylonians in the preceding millennium. It might seem that the Bible gives us an inaccurate rendering of the dimensions involved.

But then we read further: "And it was an hand breadth thick, and the brim thereof was wrought like the brim of a cup, with flowers of lilies: it contained two thousand baths" (1 Kings 7:26).

This "hand breadth" is usually about three and a half inches. Both rims would then make the inside diameter differ by about seven inches from the outside diameter. Since there is no precise description of the measurement points, a circumference-to-diameter ratio of well over three—nearing the modern value of π—is easily justified, depending upon how the measurements were actually made.

The Pursuit of Pi

It was not until years later that the pursuit of the elusive ratio began in earnest under Ptolemaic rule. Ptolemy I gained control over Egypt in 306 BC. Under the rulers of his dynasty, the academic community of Alexandria attracted scholars and mathematicians from Grecian, Egyptian, and Jewish sources.

Among them was Euclid, who is credited with establishing precise mathematical rigor in the solving of geometric proofs. Many men built upon his work.

But the most famous of them all was Archimedes of Syracuse. His life and work in the third century BC are legendary. In particular, he pursued the ancient problem of squaring the circle. With great tenacity and precision, he circumscribed circles with regular polygons, measuring them with increasingly greater precision. Finally, through this method, he arrived at a value of three and one-seventh, or 3.1428. By the time of Christ, this value was generally accepted.

The third and forth decimal places of that number are now known to be slightly high. And though it fails to go beyond two decimal places in accuracy, even today 3.14 is quite sufficient for ordinary reckoning in construction.

In the second century AD, the astronomer Ptolemy, using a value of 377 divided by 120, calculated π as 3.14166, a very accurate value.

In the seventeenth century, Sir Isaac Newton developed the mathematical method known as "the calculus." Using it, he arrived at a value of π that was correct to sixteen decimal places.

A Transcendental Obsession

In the eighteenth century, the Prussian mathematician Leonhard Euler derived the value of π to many more decimal places. After years of work, he pronounced this elusive ratio as "irrational." That is, by definition, it is a real number that cannot be expressed by the multiplication of any two integers.

Later, he pronounced π to be possessed of such peculiarities that it can't be compared with any other number. Its qualities, he called "transcendental." Mathematically, the definition of a transcendental number states that it is "incapable of being the root of an algebraic equation with rational integral coefficients." Unless you are a mathematician, let us simply say that π is unique.

Euler was the first to define π in this way. From that day to this, mathematicians have offered many proofs that the long-elusive ratio is "transcendental." In 1961, an IBM computer was used to calculate π to one hundred thousand decimal places.

In 1966, increasingly sophisticated programs computed π to 250,000 decimal places. And in 1967, this phenomenal number was extended to five hundred thousand decimal places. In all these calculations, π continues to be extended, *ad infinitum!* As far as anyone knows, it never repeats itself!

The culmination of thousands of years of calculation has gone far beyond the necessity of squaring the circle. In fact, π, as expressed to four decimal places (3.1416), is quite accurate enough for advanced engineering. Why then, has there been such an obsessive fixation on discovering the end of this "never-ending" number?

The answer is simple: Mankind is imbued with an inner impulse that drives him to the door of another dimension. In their own way, all men deeply desire to touch the Creator. Perhaps there is the thought that π will open that door, at least mathematically.

When we use the word "transcendental," we are usually thinking in philosophical terms. We envision ideal constructs that surpass mere visual and auditory perception. We imagine realities so far above our own that they barely intersect our world of "reality."

To the secular scientist, π summons up the Aristotelian idea of a quantity that lies beyond the boundaries of any category. In other words, the final determination of π is inexpressible, except as a representation of the metaphysical. Just as the full expression of π is unreachable, eternity is unreachable.

Spiritual men see the metaphysical as an expression of the Lord of Creation, who has created the heavens and earth for the purpose of bringing about a righteous Kingdom of the redeemed. When the Lord touches our finite world, transcendental truths emerge. Man is incapable of fully understanding them, but instinctively knows that his destiny is in the realm of the Lord...in eternity.

The circle—simple, yet complex—is the foremost symbol of that eternity.

THE CIRCLE AS A CYCLE

Perhaps the circle's main quality is its repetitive nature. It loops back upon itself endlessly, producing the idea of infinite action. In verbal expression, we speak of an imperfect thought that never resolves itself as "circular reasoning."

In human endeavor, we have the idea that "history repeats itself." That is, history is circular. Just like π, it is irrational, even transcendental. It never fully resolves itself. It awaits the resolution that can only come when a higher form of truth interposes itself upon our "real" world.

In short, the circle rolls on, in anticipation of the day when it will find its final resolution. For mortal beings, time is a circle...seen as a series of cycles that lead to a final and eternal determination.

In the scholarly methods of ancient Judaism, a link is made between the holiness of sanctified believers and cycles of growth. They teach that the nineteenth letter of the Hebrew alphabet— koph ק—expresses the circular development of any movement toward holiness.

The letter koph ק is said to stand for "holiness and cycles of growth." In Hebrew, holiness is kedusha (קדושה), indicating a degree of dedication and spirituality that exists on a higher level. The holiness of God is metaphysical; its full expression is inconceivable to man, even as is the case with the circle.

In The Wisdom in the Hebrew Alphabet, Rabbi Michael Munk writes about this letter as follows:

The most obvious manifestation of God's majesty is expressed in nature and its cycles. Therefore the Sages relate the name קוֹף [koph] to הקף [hakaph] *to go around,* and הקפה [hakafa], *cycle.*

The cycles of nature—the changing seasons, the monthly renewal of the moon, the twenty-eight year solar cycle—all teach man that there is a pattern and purpose to the universe. The daily rising and setting of the sun and moon led Abraham to the realization that the world has a Creator. The seven-day week climaxing in *Shabbos* [Sabbath], the seven-year cycle climaxing in *Shemitah* (the Sabbatical year), the seven-Shemittah cycle leading to *Yovel* (the Jubilee year), all remind the Jew that God created the world and continues to watch over it.[52]

Munk continues:

In this sense, הקפות, *hakafos,* the circular ritual processions on Hoshanah Rabbah and Simchas Torah, are likewise a manifestation of God's holiness. They have a tremendous mystical power—especially if the circling is sevenfold.[53]

No doubt, Rabbi Munk is referring to Israelite history. In Joshua's triumph over Jericho, the Israelites were instructed to march around the city seven times as a demonstration of faith and obedience. Obviously, the Lord could have toppled Jericho's walls even if the Israelites had not marched around them. But theirs was a march of faith, symbolically linking eternity with circles in time.

THE HISTORY OF THE SEVEN CHURCHES

The August through November 1998 editions of *Prophecy in the News* magazine featured a series of articles entitled "Twenty-Two Mysteries of the Bible" showing that the word "mystery" is found twenty-two times in the New Testament. An investigation of the mysteries reveals that, taken in order, each of the mysteries conformed perfectly with the meanings of the twenty-two Hebrew letters.

As it happens, the mystery of the seven churches falls upon the letter *koph* ק:

> The **mystery** of the seven stars which thou sawest in my right hand, and the seven golden candlesticks. The seven stars are the angels of the seven churches: and the seven candlesticks which thou sawest are the seven churches. (Revelation 1:20, emphasis added)

The letter *koph* ק, you'll recall, stands for "holiness and growth cycles," exactly conforming to the symbolism of the seven churches. Scholars have long associated each of these churches with a period of church history, saying that they represent the timeline of the church for the last twenty centuries. Beginning with the apostolic zeal of Ephesus, they culminate in the dissipation of Laodicea.

First, we'll review the way the seven churches reveal the generally accepted linear history, then we will address its circular nature:

Ephesus, the church of the apostles, is first on the list. It represents the years of the first century, from about AD 30 through AD 100. This church is commended for retaining the sound doctrine taught by the early founders of the church.

The second church is Smyrna, a church seen to be encountering tribulation and persecution. It is generally held to represent the time of Roman persecutions that ranged from about AD 100 through AD 313. The Lord praises this church for its faithful ability to endure suffering.

Third comes the church of Pergamos, the church that is seen to have intermarried with the world. It represents the period from AD 313 through AD 600, following Constantine's *Edict of Toleration* in AD 312. This church is judged for allowing idolatry and despotic authority to rule its members.

The next, and fourth, church is Thyatira, known as the church of the

Dark Ages, from about AD 600 to the time of the Reformation, around AD 1500. This church is symbolized by Jezebel, the idolatress of the Old Testament who brought pagan worship into Israel. It is counterfeit, and has introduced many false teachings. It also represents a system that will continue to exert its influence until the time of the Day of the Lord, since it is threatened with being cast into the "great tribulation" unless it repents. However, its doctrinal supremacy began to wane during the emergence of Martin Luther and the other reformers.

The fifth church is Sardis, representing the time from AD 1500 through AD 1700. This is the Reformation church, which restored the doctrines of salvation by grace and justification by faith. But it did little to correct the despotic authority of church-state liaisons. Its spiritual life was severely attenuated. Though it revived the ancient doctrines of the apostles, it was dead in spirit.

Next, comes the period of AD 1700 through about AD 1900. This is the living church that witnessed the birth and expansion of the great missionary movements. To this church was given an open door to carry the gospel to the four corners of the earth.

The last of the seven churches is Laodicea, the wealthy and self-important apostate church. It represents the church of AD 1900 to the present. This church is condemned for its lukewarm self-satisfaction. Spiritually, it is blind.

THE CYCLE OF THE SEVEN CHURCHES

The above timeline of church history is clear enough, but a linear history does not fully represent the idea of "growth cycles." In this view, we discover an entirely different way of seeing the seven churches.

Truly, these churches represent the natural cycle of church growth. It is circular, orbiting through the years in a remarkable succession of acquisition and loss. The churches can be viewed as a series of stages that are circular in nature. That is, they represent a continuing cycle that begins on a high plane, descends into dissolution, and collapses into self-absorption. At that point, only a revolutionary new beginning can bring life to the spiritually dead. A new cycle then begins, as the wheel rotates through a new cycle of downfall and rising again.

This circle is illustrated in the history of the seven churches. Each one presents a developmental stage.

Stage One: Zeal

The circle begins with the zeal of new birth, tinged with all the excitement and promise of dreams yet unrealized. This is represented by Ephesus. Its weakness is that it quickly loses its first love. In the case of the church, this refers to the love of Christ and His Word.

There is, however, a problem. For Ephesus, it manifested itself in the form of the Nicolaitans, who appeared as an authoritarian body that created a hierarchical separation between the clergy and the people.

At this point in the cycle, love begins to give way to formalism.

Stage Two: Persecution

The initial zeal of the church now rotates toward the next stage. Typified by Smyrna, it meets the world's persecution head-on. "Smyrna" means myrrh; since it is an embalming spice, it implies suffering. Separation from the support systems of the world means poverty and alienation. And so, tribulation, poverty, and hunger are the marks of the church at this stage. Zeal is confronted with the world's opposition. Stage two is now complete.

Stage Three: Yielding to the World

Opposition often batters the faithful into submission. And so it is with the third stage of the church. Pergamos exemplifies the church that has "saved" itself by compromising with the world...at last, marrying into the world while deceiving itself into believing that it has preserved its key doctrines.

This period was typified by the entry of paganism into the Christian world. Christ's deity was challenged; original sin was denied. Church hierarchy dominated the common believer. Yet there were many faithful martyrs.

Stage Four: Christianity Becomes a Religious System

Though this church has its good works and is known for service, faith, and patience, it has incorporated false teaching. Jezebel, the woman who introduced Baal worship into ancient Israel, represents debilitating religious authority. Here, she stands for the false doctrines that emanate from the concept of justification by works and the mysticism of Mariolatry...the deification of Mary.

This powerful religious system became intertwined with the state. Together, they became the rock-solid force known as the "Holy Roman Empire." But the New Testament never defines the church as a hierarchical system. Quite the opposite, it is characterized as the vital and dynamic "body of Christ."

Stage Five: Death, but Potential Revival

In this stage, the church experiences the natural death that follows institutionalization. Within it are the vital truths of Christianity, but they too, are "ready to die." Only the zeal of a few good men can revive this entombed edifice. If this church continues, it is only because of their clarion call.

Stage Six: Love Reborn

Assuming that in its preceding stage the church has listened to the stern voices of reform, it rises to new life, recalling the initial charge bequeathed to it by the apostles. It has revivified (brought to life again) the power and love of the Holy Spirit, who has come to reside in the believer. Individuals exercising the power of the Spirit in the love of Christ bring this church new hope. As a result, it is given renewed power to evangelize...an "open door." This stage is a weak reflection of the first stage's zeal and purity.

Stage Seven: The Weight of Wealth

Sadly, the last stage of the church is wealth and its ensuing self-centeredness. Though it grew in the power of the Lord's Spirit, this church has come to assume that its power is money, real estate, and politics. It is focused upon self-aggrandizement, collapsing under its own weight, but blind to its breakdown.

In a final observation about the cyclical nature of the seven churches, we bring to mind yet another of those historical (and in this case, geographical) "coincidences." Check a map of first-century Asia Minor. In so doing, you will discover that the seven churches—beginning with Ephesus and ending with Laodicea—are laid out in circular fashion! That is, they form a rough circle that runs clockwise on the map as you count the churches in order.

Surely this is not coincidence. All seven lie near Asia Minor's west coast. This was the "jumping-off place," where the gospel sprang from the Middle East into the Western world of the Roman Empire...and beyond. The grand cycle began there and continues today, encircling the entire world.

THE WHEEL OF LIFE AND DEATH

In the foregoing seven stages, we see the development of a remarkable picture. Taken together, they represent the pattern of the ages...the road toward completed faith that is marked by downfall and rising again.

The plain truth is that the seven churches depict a grand cycle. On a microcosmic level, every local church has the potential of going through these stages. From initial excitement through final, bloated collapse, the pattern is seen again and again. This cycle begins with life and ends with death, only to be born again to a new cycle of life.

Zeal (Ephesus), is opposed by evil (Smyrna), and is infiltrated by false doctrine (Pergamos). Finally, it is overwhelmed by a cabal of evil men who are on the verge of capturing it in totality. But the faint voices of the few (Sardis), in the power of the Spirit, breathe new life into the dead entity and it lives again (Philadelphia), only to grow fat, wither, and die (Laodicea). In the age of the church, this cycle has repeated itself thousands of times, and will do so again, and again…and again.

This is an ancient spiritual truth that was acknowledged in Jewish teaching long before the birth of the church. Rabbi Munk alludes to this in the following statement:

> The meal before the onset of the Tishah B'av [Fast of the 9th of Av] traditionally includes an egg dipped in ashes. The egg is used to symbolize mourning because its roundness signifies the turning of the "wheel of life" by Divine Providence, which can change a day of mourning into a day of festivity, and transform the destruction of the Temple into its reconstruction. For the same reason an egg is offered to the bereaved after a funeral to indicate *nechamah,* consolation, that after the sadness of the loss, joy will yet set in again.
>
> On *Simcha Torah* [rejoicing in the Torah], as soon as the annual cycle of the Torah-portions is concluded, a new cycle is begun. The new beginning signifies that the joy of Torah lies fundamentally not in its recitation as such, as in the constantly renewed acceptance of the Torah.[54]

In the entire panoply of spiritual endeavor, we see the repetitive movement of the grand cycle of faith. Faith begins with Adam, withers in the world of Cain, is reborn in Noah, and wanes in the idolatry of Nimrod. Then it rises again in Abraham, only to die in Egyptian bondage. It rises once again in Moses, only to die in the sinful world of the Judges. It rises in David and Solomon, then dies in the Assyrian and Babylonian captivities. It comes to a pinnacle in Christ, only to fall in the Dark Ages. It rises in the Reformation and missionary movements, only to die again in the apostasy of the latter-day world system.

In the larger view, the wheel turns from Adam to Christ to the Kingdom. Widening our view even farther, we see time-space represented as the cycle that begins with paradise, descends into the battle of this world, then rises again to paradise.

Thus, time-space can be viewed as a series of circles. Observation of this important fact was no doubt behind Solomon's classic observation:

> The thing that hath been, it is that which shall be; and that which is done is that which shall be done: and there is no new thing under the sun. Is there any thing whereof it may be said, See, this is new? it hath been already of old time, which was before us. (Ecclesiastes 1:9, 10)

THE CIRCLE IS TRANSCENDENTAL

We have observed that the Hebrew alphabet is reflective of the Bible's theme of creation and redemption. The Word spoke all creation into existence. Jewish teaching says that the Word is formed by the twenty-two letters of the Hebrew alphabet.

But the twenty-two letters are themselves a grand cycle not only for the church, but for each individual—and indeed, the entire cosmos! There is no better demonstration of this than the pattern found in Psalm 119. Its 176 verses are laid out in groups of eight verses, each beginning with a successive letter of the Hebrew alphabet. Together, they comprise a grand, acrostic circle.

Each of the eight-verse sections demonstrates the spiritual character and meaning of its respective letter. Thus *aleph* א—the letter of creation—begins the walk of the spiritual man: "א ALEPH. Blessed are the undefiled in the way, who walk in the law of the LORD" (Psalm 119:1).

As we move along the spiritual pathway with this blessed man, we quickly discover that his way is complex. It leads to completed righteousness in the world to come. But along the way, he suffers doubt, insult, tribulation and affliction, as in the following verse, found at the middle of the alphabet in the *nun* ‎נ section. This letter, of course, illustrates the difficulty of maintaining faith: "I am afflicted very much: quicken me, O LORD, according unto thy word" (Psalm 119:107).

The final verse of this Psalm shows without question that David's epochal work represents the grand cycle of faith. Instead of bringing the blessed man to eternal truth and perfection (seen in the final letter, *tahv*), it turns back to the beginning of the alphabet, where once again he moves step-by-step toward eternal righteousness: "I have gone astray like a lost sheep; seek thy servant; for I do not forget thy commandments" (Psalm 119:176).

Even at the end of his march, the spiritual man begs the help of the Lord in finding his way. Like all men of faith, he comes to the end of himself, beginning the cycle once again at creation, moving through the predictable circle of difficulty, but supported by the love of the Lord.

In short, the alphabetic pattern of redemption is a circle. Like all circles everywhere, it is unresolved; it is transcendental. Like the Greek letter π that stands for the ratio between the circumference and diameter of a circle, it is infinite.

It moves toward the dimension of the Lord. Only there will it find its final realization. Only in eternity will the circle finally be squared. It is interesting to observe that in Scripture, the Kingdom is represented by the number four, typical of the square. Rationality, in the person of the Lord, will finally bring the cycles of human endeavor to resolution.

For us, the Word of Creation—the Lord Jesus Christ—is the focus of eternity. He is, if you will, the center of the circle of time and the answer to the mathematical irrationality that has plagued theorists and philosophers since man began to build his pyramids and towers.

Man's view of the structure of history was merely an effort to solve the problem of separation from God. The tower of Babel could never have literally reached to heaven, as Scripture proclaims was the goal: "Go to, let us build us a city and a tower, whose top may reach unto heaven" (Genesis 11:4).

That is, earthly structures of brick and stone can only go so high. But it is the *design* of the tower (and of all the ancient pyramids), incorporating sacred geometry that would reach the *metaphysical* heavens. It is a fact, that the ancient pagan cultures all pursued forms of sacred mathematics, with which they hoped to discover the treasures of eternity.

More importantly, they sought (and still seek) the mathematical key to eternity and immortality. As we have seen, the pursuit of the transcendental number π has gone far beyond the refinement necessary to square the circle in practical endeavors. Yet man has still failed to resolve it.

A REVELATION IN REVELATION

Which brings us to a final point. The book of Revelation plainly answers all the philosophers' questions. And in so doing, it also squares the circle!

The metaphysical tower so desired by the ancients is completed in the structure built by the Lord Himself. It is the New Jerusalem, the eternal residence of the saints—a building that incorporates structural and metaphysical perfection: "And the city lieth foursquare, and the length is as large as the breadth: and he measured the city with the reed, twelve thousand furlongs. The length and the breadth and the height of it are equal" (Revelation 21:16).

It is based upon the square, but like the book of Revelation itself, must incorporate the mathematical truths that are exclusively available to the Creator. It is "foursquare," representing the eternal kingdom. Beyond that, little is said about its shape. Is it a cube, perhaps within a sphere? Is it a pyramid, or something more exotic? Whatever its true shape, it must perfectly resolve the circle as well as the square. Here, time-space intersects eternity.

As we have already mentioned, Revelation begins with the cyclical mystery of the seven churches. They illustrate both the linear and circular form of time-space.

Revelation Reveals π

Following these letters to the historical churches, the majority of the book of Revelation is devoted to the judgment of the world system. It is most interesting that the structure of the book is laid out in three sets of seven—seven seals, trumpets, and vials.

But Revelation is outlined by the number twenty-two. This is the total number of its chapters. It is a simple mathematical fact that this number (Can we call it the circumference?) when divided by seven (Does that represent the diameter?) results in an approximation of π!

$$22 \div 7 = 3.14$$

And incidentally, the twenty-two letters of the Hebrew alphabet reflect the same truth. They may be divided as three sets of seven, plus the final *tahv*, the letter of "truth and perfection." Even the alphabet... the Word of Creation...squares the circle and illustrates the truth of eternity.

Over two centuries ago, when Leonhard Euler declared that π is a transcendental number, he could scarcely have conceived the philosophical depth of his statement. Nor could he have imagined the supercomputers that today, reveal the magnificent truth of the circle. Indeed, it is transcendental.

Christ is the center of all things. Only He is capable of finally squaring the circle.

14

TIME IS THE ENEMY

I f there is a firm human belief, it is the conviction that all we see, hear, smell, feel, and taste is real. There is a solid appearance to our physical universe. Things don't change. The feel of wood, metal, or plastic is the same from day to day. The sky, wind, and earth are dependably predictable. In fact, scientists tend to formalize this observation in a belief system called "uniformitarianism." This is the belief that things change slowly, uniformly, and predictably.

Those who believe this operate on the assumption that physical qualities are so constant that change is mathematically predictable. Furthermore, they reckon the time scale of change in the billions of years! Their faith is in a long-term stability that bolsters the idea of perfect stability.

This almost religious belief in the superiority of science goes so far that it finally assumes that man actually *controls* physical reality. Particle accelerators and nuclear research labs around the world are dedicated to unlocking the secrets of the physical world.

Journalists hang upon every word spoken by the contemporary wise men. They are those arbiters of reality who call themselves "particle physicists" and who delve into the paradoxical realm of "quantum mechanics." Occasionally, news departments breathlessly report the latest proclamations of science about the nature of reality. Yes, their findings are exciting, even to the Christian mind. And yes, we all may benefit from the advances of high technology.

But we must never allow secular science to define ultimate reality. From their secular and scientific point of view, there descends an apparently plausible definition of reality, to be taken by the common man as true and dependable. All is well, they say. It is this sense of constancy and understandability that allows secular man to believe so profoundly in the things of this world.

They perceive our world of time and space as man's friend. As long as the clock ticks, they believe, man will continue to ascend. He will make discoveries about the mysteries of the universe. Finally, he will rise to the point that he will be able to control the processes of creation.

Biblically, however, time is the enemy. The household of faith is consistently urged to see this world as transient and afflicted by the blight and stain of sin. It will ultimately be judged by the myriad malfunctions of a flawed humanity. We are urged to see reality in the dimension of the spirit: "While we look not at the things which are seen, but at the things which are not seen: for the things which are seen are temporal; but the things which are not seen are eternal" (2 Corinthians 4:18).

Christians who read and understand the Bible see this world as temporary. However, insofar as it is touched by the metaphysical truths of the heavens, the physical world can and will be transformed. Entropy will be reversed, but not by science.

The Bible views all Creation as being spoken into existence by a God who had eternally existed in a higher dimension. Thus, at the foundational level, we are asked to regard this present world as inferior to the Kingdom of Heaven. It exists below the world of the angels.

Moreover, what we view as "Creation" had a beginning, something brought forth by God, the always-existing One. Though the truth of a beginning has been indirectly admitted by secular scientists who propose the "big bang" theory, they never take the next step. That is, they never declare the reality of a higher dimension having given birth to this—the lower creation.

"In the beginning God created the heaven and the earth" (Genesis

1:1). This, the first sentence in the Bible, is a matter-of-fact statement that our universe is positionally lower than another and former universe. How do we know this? We know it simply because, by definition, that which is created is inferior to the one who created it.

Of course, the recognition of our subordinate position is borne out in the myriad realities and spiritual truths of Bible history. Well over 150 times, the words "I am the Lord" ring through the Scriptures, always declaring His superior status.

In the New Testament, the truth of the Word of Creation is given with unimpeachable clarity: "In the beginning was the Word, and the Word was with God, and the Word was God. The same was in the beginning with God. All things were made by him; and without him was not any thing made that was made" (John 1:1–3).

The sages of ancient Israel profoundly believed that Creation was spoken into existence when God uttered a series of commands using the twenty-two letters of the Hebrew alphabet. While this is in no way an explanation of the actual creative principles used by God, it is a sound explanation of a scriptural truth. We know what God did; we do not know how He did it: "Through faith we understand that the worlds were framed by the word of God, so that things which are seen were not made of things which do appear" (Hebrews 11:3).

SOMETHING FROM NOTHING

The creation of something out of nothing represents a precept that is profoundly rejected by today's scientists. And here, they suffer an intellectual paradox. Though they find hope in the evolutionary progress of man, they foresee nothing but the death of the universe.

This brings us to another truth that physics has acknowledged for many years. As stated earlier, time impresses itself upon the physical world chiefly through entropy, defined in the *Webster's New Third International Dictionary* as "the ultimate state of the degradation of the matter and energy of the universe."[55]

In his book, *Hyperspace,* physicist Michio Kaku quotes a famous scientist on the subject of entropy:

> To understand how entropy death occurs, it is important to understand the three laws of thermodynamics, which govern all chemical and nuclear process on the earth and in the stars. The British scientist and author C. P. Snow had an elegant way of remembering the three laws:
> "1. You cannot win (that is, you cannot get something for nothing, because matter and energy are conserved).
> "2. You cannot break even (you cannot return to the same energy state, because there is always an increase in disorder; entropy always increases).
> "3. You cannot get out of the game (because absolute zero is unattainable)."[56]

Yet the writer to the Hebrews asserts that the Lord absolutely made something out of nothing. He got something for nothing.

The epistle to the Hebrews adds another dimension to this wonderful reality, even as it describes entropy. Referring to the Lord—the preincarnate Christ—it says that the heavens and the earth are but temporary places for the redeemed of all the ages. In other words, they were created with a purpose in mind. Once it is fulfilled, there will be no further need for them in their present state. Yet they will be renewed:

> And, Thou, Lord, in the beginning hast laid the foundation of the earth; and the heavens are the works of thine hands: They shall perish; but thou remainest; and they all shall wax old as doth a garment; And as a vesture shalt thou fold them up, and they shall be changed: but thou art the same, and thy years shall not fail. (Hebrews 1:10–12)

Furthermore, the opening words of Hebrews document another fact that contemporary physicists should always remember. Not only did He speak forth all creation, He continues—moment by moment—to hold it all together:

> God, who at sundry times and in divers manners spake in time past unto the fathers by the prophets, Hath in these last days spoken unto us by his Son, whom he hath appointed heir of all things, by whom also he made the worlds;
>
> Who being the brightness of his glory, and the express image of his person, and upholding all things by the word of his power, when he had by himself purged our sins, sat down on the right hand of the Majesty on high. (Hebrews 1:1–3)

Again, we see that the Word, here expressed as "the word of his power," is the mechanism of Creation. This time, there is the added meaning that present reality is also in His hands.

Physicists call this action the "strong nuclear force." As Kaku puts it, it is the force "holding the protons and neutrons together within the nucleus of the atom."[57]

If Jesus "upholds" everything, then at some moment, He could also let go, returning everything to the state of nonexistence that characterized it before it was brought to physical reality. For the moment, however, it continues. We see it as a timeline, always assuming that the next moment will be like the one before it.

THE ENEMY CALLED TIME

In other words, and in spite of the outward appearance of stability, things are running down. The robust energy of the beginning is slowly winding down. At some point, renewal will be necessary. Yes, the Lord is holding everything together; He is the foundation. But that which is built upon the substrate of Creation is in a state of deterioration. Our familiar time-space universe was made to be remade.

And one day, it will be rebuilt. In the book of Acts, the apostle Peter vigorously preaches to his kinsmen in the flesh that this universe is in desperate need of renewal…of restitution. He uses this very word, from the Greek *apokatastasis,* which means "to put back in order or restore." It is used in the following quote as the word "restitution":

> And he shall send Jesus Christ, which before was preached unto you: Whom the heaven must receive until the times of **restitution** of all things, which God hath spoken by the mouth of all his holy prophets since the world began. (Acts 3:20, 21, emphasis added)

Later, Peter expands upon this idea, invoking a dramatic image of future change, in which the present Creation is somehow recreated and restored:

> Seeing then that all these things shall be dissolved, what manner of persons ought ye to be in all holy conversation and godliness, Looking for and hasting unto the coming of the day of God, wherein the heavens being on fire shall be dissolved, and the elements shall melt with fervent heat? Nevertheless we, according to his promise, look for new heavens and a new earth, wherein dwelleth righteousness. (2 Peter 3:11–13)

All of the above makes the argument that our creation is to be regarded as temporary, on a rather abbreviated time scale. An intelligent Creator is quietly manipulating the universe which, from the human point of view, is seen as virtually eternal. It is not, nor should it be thought of in this way. It is temporary. Time is the enemy.

JESUS AND DIMENSIONALITY

As related in the first chapter of John, the Creator (called "the Word") became flesh, incarnated in the very temporal universe He had originated.

It is easy to forget that the man known as Jesus of Nazareth possessed a transcendent knowledge of the place we call home.

For us, the physical realities of time-space are physically limiting. We are restricted to a tiny portion of this solar system, which is a miniscule part of our local galaxy. We are also restricted to a very small segment of time…the "threescore years and ten" in Psalm 90:10.

We may live longer than seventy years, but our vitality quickly decreases in the eighth and ninth decades of life. We are time-limited.

Jesus deliberately limited Himself when He entered our universe as Messiah, but it is quite clear that He retained His knowledge of the basic fabric of time-space. There are many evidences of this. One of the most obvious is found in Luke chapter 4: "And all they in the synagogue, when they heard these things, were filled with wrath, And rose up, and thrust him out of the city, and led him unto the brow of the hill whereon their city was built, that they might cast him down headlong" (Luke 4:28, 29).

In this episode, Jesus had stood up in His hometown synagogue. As He read from the scroll of Isaiah, He announced that by His presence, He fulfilled the prophecy in the scroll of Isaiah. In other words, He claimed to be both prophet and prophecy.

Those in the synagogue were stunned and outraged at Jesus' implied claim, asking each other, "Is not this Joseph's son?" In their eyes, this was an ordinary man. Jesus did nothing to soothe their troubled thoughts. Instead, He warned them that the prophets Elijah and Elisha were both sent to the Gentiles after experiencing difficulty among their own people.

The topography of Nazareth is made up of steep, tree-lined hills and valleys. Several precipitous cliffs in the area plunge over a hundred feet. Jesus' long-time friends and neighbors found His claims so outrageous that they agreed to kill Him, as the Law requires: "But the prophet, which shall presume to speak a word in my name, which I have not commanded him to speak, or that shall speak in the name of other gods, even that prophet shall die" (Deuteronomy 18:20).

They escorted Him physically to the top of a cliff outside Nazareth, fully intent upon throwing Him to the rocks below. Then, something happened that has no full explanation to this day: "But he passing through the midst of them went his way" (Luke 4:30).

How did Jesus do this? An ordinary human being can't pass through the midst of a raging crowd that is bent upon executing him. But He did, "passing through" the middle of the mob, as described by the Greek verb, *dierchomai,* which is usually used to describe moving through a medium without changing it.

In other words, Jesus simply walked through the people as we might describe walking through the atmosphere—which we do every day, thinking nothing of it. This term is used in many places, where the meaning requires something to move through a locale. For example, Hebrews 4:14 uses the term to describe Jesus as "a great high priest that is passed into the heavens."

In other examples, the New Testament typically describes demons in the following way: "When the unclean spirit is gone out of a man, he walketh through dry places, seeking rest, and findeth none" (Luke 12:43).

The process of "walking" comes from the same above-mentioned Greek verb. Here, the demon freely passes through a dimensional medium in the spirit world, in this case illustrated as a "dry place." Taken as a whole, it implies an effortless freedom of movement that does not respond to any impediment.

Was Jesus able to alter the state of time-space so that He simply "walked through" a hostile crowd? Why not? For Him, it would be—to use the common expression—child's play.

In another well-known case, Jesus was in the Temple with Israel's religious authorities. There, He explained that He was the One whom Father Abraham had foreseen.

> Then said the Jews unto him, Thou art not yet fifty years old, and hast thou seen Abraham?
>
> Jesus said unto them, Verily, verily, I say unto you, Before Abraham was, I am.

Then took they up stones to cast at him: but Jesus hid himself, and went out of the temple, going through the midst of them, and so passed by. (John 8:57–59)

This incident graphically describes Christ's ability to warp time-space in such a way that He could literally walk through the middle of a crowd and depart at will. This was an angry horde of religious zealots intent upon doing what they perceived was the will of God. Any ordinary human being would have been trapped and stoned to death.

A HIGH MOUNTAIN

Jesus, though He was a physical human being, retained the capability to move at will through the dimensional barriers forbidden to ordinary man. When He was tempted by the devil, He was led into the wilderness by the Holy Spirit. There, for forty days, He was tested in the spirit world, and found acceptable.

The testing included travels in a world that is completely foreign to us. And again, the tests tell us something about the substance and reality of our daily existence. Beginning in the desert wilderness, Jesus allowed the devil to do his best. In effect, He placed Himself in the devil's hands. First, the devil attacked Him at the physical level, commanding Him to turn a common stone into bread. Though famished, Jesus refused.

Then, both of them somehow ascended to the holy city…Jerusalem. In his physical body, Jesus was placed in one of the most visible positions in the entire city. But He didn't create a spectacle; doubtless no one even saw Him there, even though He was present. How was this possible?

At best, we can only make a guess based upon our limited knowledge about the rules of our time-space world. Its set of natural laws states that when one stands in a particular place, others may see him there. But based upon the following narrative, there is a higher law that supersedes the one we know:

Then the devil taketh him up into the holy city, and setteth him on a pinnacle of the temple, And saith unto him, If thou be the Son of God, cast thyself down: for it is written, He shall give his angels charge concerning thee: and in their hands they shall bear thee up, lest at any time thou dash thy foot against a stone.

Jesus said unto him, It is written again, Thou shalt not tempt the Lord thy God. (Matthew 4:5–7)

In this setting, Jesus is obviously in His physical body. Otherwise, He could not be threatened by the consequences of falling from a high place. Yet both He and the devil are concealed from the eyes of Jewish worshipers below. Faced with amazing narratives such as this, one is inexorably forced to the conclusion that the temporal realities that produce our security are put in place as limitations.

But the story is taken—literally—to an even higher level: "Again, the devil taketh him up into an exceeding high mountain, and showeth him all the kingdoms of the world, and the glory of them; And saith unto him, All these things will I give thee, if thou wilt fall down and worship me" (Matthew 4:8, 9).

Technically, given the laws of optics and atmospheric diffusion, there isn't a mountain on earth (not even Mt. Everest) high enough to see all the world's kingdoms. But more than that, Jesus and the devil were even able to see the "glory" of these kingdoms. That is, it seems that the financial, political, and military power of these places was somehow made visible.

Remember, the devil's purpose was to tempt Jesus. He was being shown the totality of earthly power and glory…His for the taking. How was the devil able to make such an offer? Obviously, he could offer only something that he possessed. All Jesus had to do was worship the owner, then He could have it all.

But Jesus knew something that Satan didn't. There was a larger plan that included Messiah's death on the Cross, Resurrection, and Ascension into heaven. If He didn't weaken, there would be a future day in which

He—as the Lamb—would open the seven-sealed scroll that would legally return the earth to the possession of Christ. Jesus chose the way of personal suffering, in which He took upon Himself the sin of mankind.

And so they stood there with all the kingdoms of the world on display before them. Under the laws of visual imaging used to produce the huge astronomical telescopes, this kind of vision is impossible. Even a very powerful telescope can't see into the halls of power. But under the higher law that supersedes the natural law of this dimension, it is apparently possible to see beneath the landscape, into the very heart of a society.

Under such a set of operating principles, one can see into the very economics, politics, religions, and daily life of a civilization. For the sinful mind of man to have such vision would be the ultimate in voyeurism. It would also produce coveting and temptation of the highest order. Jesus remained unmoved.

He responded by telling Satan that only the Lord God is worthy of worship. The devil departed and Jesus returned to begin His public ministry. His own people never guessed that He had been to a mountaintop that lay far beyond their understanding.

And so it is today. We struggle to understand biblical truths that are far above us. There is a world just beyond our vision that is governed by a different set of natural laws than the physical world.

Angels in the Treetops

In a way, faith is measured by one's ability to accept the things not seen, yet validated by thousands of years and the rise and fall of many cultures. The statement in Hebrews 11:1 says it perfectly: "Now faith is the substance of things hoped for, the evidence of things not seen."

The world of the next dimension seems so distant, yet it is close enough to affect every human being on earth...believer or not. The world of darkness is close enough to control the power centers of the planet.

Fortunately, the forces for good are just as close, and they are fighting on the side of the faithful. There are many biblical proofs of this fact. They come in the form of historical accounts that tell of the exploits of faithful men.

When, for example, David was anointed as king of Israel, the Philistines sought to kill him. He prayed to the Lord, and was told that they would be delivered into his hand. But they invaded a second time:

> Therefore David inquired again of God; and God said unto him, Go not up after them; turn away from them, and come upon them over against the mulberry trees.
>
> And it shall be, when thou shalt hear a sound of going in the tops of the mulberry trees, that then thou shalt go out to battle: for God is gone forth before thee to smite the host of the Philistines.
>
> David therefore did as God commanded him: and they smote the host of the Philistines from Gibeon even to Gazer. (1 Chronicles 14:14–16)

The Lord answered David's prayer by telling him where to attack the enemy. More than that, He assured David that a force of angelic troops would assure his success. In the mulberry forest, their presence was revealed by a sound "of going."

Actually, the nature of this sound is made quite plain in the Hebrew language. It is *hatzadah* (הצעדה), literally, the sound of "marching." The image here is that of a well disciplined and ordered force, their rhythmic footsteps tramping across the tops of a local stand of mulberry trees! Were it not for our faith, such an image would be deemed nonsense… childish imagination.

But the faithful are urged to believe that our dimension is lower in scope than the higher one (or in the plural sense, many higher ones). Think of it, philosophers and scientists continually ask the question, "Are we alone?"

They scan the heavens with radio-telescopes, searching for some faint signal of intelligent life. They analyze the amazing Hubble Space Telescope photos, looking for planets orbiting around suns like our own. They believe that if they can only find a planetary grouping that resembles our own solar system, the likelihood is that intelligent life may be found there.

Of course, they believe that such life would have evolved from lower life forms. And it would have taken millions of years for that to happen. The bottom line is that science searches *this dimension* for signs of life. We know that the heavens literally teem with life…many forms of life.

Dark Heavenly Politics

Without a doubt, Satan is the king or commander-in-chief of the spirit world's dark forces. And we must remember that the fallen angels over whom he rules are powerful princes who govern their own earthly territories.

Their unswerving allegiance to him is based upon his apparent ownership of this planet and its environs. He is described as intimately connected with its past, its citizens, and even its future. His primary effort is to cast a pall of spiritual darkness over the mass of humanity. He functions as a literal demigod, whose proxies have had names like Zeus, Baal, Isis, Jupiter, and so forth. He is the real power behind the thrones of the world: "In whom the god of this world hath blinded the minds of them which believe not, lest the light of the glorious gospel of Christ, who is the image of God, should shine unto them" (2 Corinthians 4:4).

His regime is to be found in the "air." That is, he ranges through the atmospheric heavens close to the surface of the earth. And why not, given the fact that those whom he seeks to influence are confined to the surface of the planet? "Wherein in time past ye walked according to the course of this world, according to the prince of the **power of the air**, the spirit that now worketh in the children of disobedience" (Ephesians 2:2, emphasis added).

But he works through delegates, who are arranged into political zones for maximum effect. In Daniel 10, we note the "prince of Persia" and the "prince of Greece" who blocked the progress of the heavenly messenger who responded to Daniel's prayers. Doubtless, these are archons, who have the responsibility for large-scale territorial policies.

Their general area of responsibility is delegated from above, but they can make decisions. On the whole, they resemble upper-level bureaucrats who have carved out little empires that they have the right to rule. They were once obedient angels, before they decided to follow Satan.

As earlier mentioned, the third level of Satan's bureaucracy is indicated in the phrase, "rulers of the darkness of this world." These "rulers" are a translation of the Greek term *kosmokrator.* This word tells us that they are akin to human "lords." He would hold power and territory, but still be subordinate to the *archons* and *exousians.*

W. E. Vine has this explanation for *kosmokrator:*

In Greek literature, in Orphic hymns, etc., and in Rabbinic writings, it signifies a ruler of the whole world, a world-lord. The context…shows that not earthly potentates are indicated, but spirit powers, who under the permissive will of God, and in consequence of human sin, exercise Satanic and therefore antagonistic authority of the world in its present condition of spiritual darkness and alienation from God.[58]

These evil creatures order hordes of demons to do their daily demonic dirty work. They are the possessors of souls, the dealers in unclean thoughts and actions, and the directors of a whole catalog of the evils incumbent upon sinful man:

For men shall be lovers of their own selves, covetous, boasters, proud, blasphemers, disobedient to parents, unthankful, unholy, Without natural affection, trucebreakers, false accusers, incontinent, fierce, despisers of those that are good, Traitors, heady, highminded, lovers of pleasures more than lovers of God. (2 Timothy 3:1–4)

Yes, men are sinners, but their personal vices are subverted to be used by the dark side for the invisible bureaucracy that operates just beyond the dimensional veil.

The point is that this world is not the morally neutral place it seems to be. The higher reality of Satan and the fallen ones has already been judged by Jesus at His First Coming. This judgment will be prosecuted in the "day of the Lord." In the interim, grace has been extended to all mankind.

Those who see the earth and its cultures as simply physical and evolutionary are sadly blinded to the fact that our environment is but a thin image of the heavenly truths in the dimensions above us.

BOUND IN CORRUPTION

In fact, the Bible invariably refers to what we call reality as "corruption." The natural entropy of the universe means one thing: slow and steady degeneration. To exist without the hope of restoration, one must be in total denial.

To the secular man, our world system is a place of contrasts. Some are healthy and wealthy, others experience unfair suffering, terminated by death. For them, life has its moments of pleasure, and even of joy. But the true joy—the kind that comes with the hope of eternal life—is unknown outside the experience of redemption through Christ.

The evolutionary hypothesis teaches that physical life has progressed from the primordial slime to the level of human intelligence. Moreover, it is continuing to progress, presumably to the point that it will bring itself to higher levels of manifestation...finally reaching veritable glory. If this were the actual case, it would only be self-glorification, at best. And any true analysis of mankind reveals that man is irreparably flawed, just as the universe is flawed.

In short, both require renewal and restoration. The story of the Bible is the story of a God who gave of Himself so completely that through His suffering, glory might be brought into our universe.

For I reckon that the sufferings of this present time are not worthy to be compared with the glory which shall be revealed in us. For the earnest expectation of the creature waiteth for the manifestation of the sons of God. For the creature was made subject to vanity, not willingly, but by reason of him who hath subjected the same in hope, Because the creature itself also shall be delivered from the bondage of corruption into the glorious liberty of the children of God. (Romans 8:18–21)

MIRACLES ARE REAL

Our Lord is the One who walked upon the waters of the Sea of Galilee and appeared to the disciples in a closed room. He restored optical and neural systems that had been completely destroyed. He walked through dimensional barriers in ways that defy human explanation. He is the Lord of time-space, the term used by science to speak of Creation. He came to lead His children from time-limited corruption to eternal glory. This is the spectacular reality of the faithful.

15

KNOWING THE FUTURE, OR
BEING THE FUTURE?

There is a widespread notion that it is humanly possible to see the future. Untold multitudes of fortune tellers, trance channelers, prognosticators, and mediums have gotten rich selling the promise of a fortunate future. Through astrology and a variety of strange methods known in the Far East, it is common for individuals to make their daily living through the claim that they can know the future.

Occasionally, they even seem to seem to hit a target date by "predicting" an airplane crash, a volcanic eruption, or an earthquake. Chance usually accounts for such correct guesses. But there is no doubt that some consort with dark spirits. The Lord forbids this practice, but the demonic world seems to have the occasional ability to pick out a future event…enough, at least, to entice and ensnare the gullible. Scripture makes it clear that Satan cannot foretell the future.

Still, there is the persistent belief that a fixed future is out there, and that it will yield to analysis of some sort. It may take dice, candles, a Ouija board, or a trance, but it's there…somewhere. Where does this idea come from?

Without a doubt, it comes from the world's attempt to copy the feats and actions of God's prophets, from Moses on. The story of the Bible is constructed along its redemptive timeline, which is laid out in advance. When Jesus came to the House of David, He fulfilled dozens of specific Old Testament prophecies, validating His ability to foresee the future. He was to be the seed of the woman, who came through Abraham, Isaac, Jacob, and Judah. He would come at a set time, through the lineage of David, born of a virgin in Bethlehem. He would come to the Temple, preceded by a messenger. He would be meek, a miracle worker, rejected by His brethren, sold for thirty pieces of silver, smitten, spat upon, scourged, and nailed to a Cross. The facts of His Crucifixion were foretold, along with His Death, Resurrection, and Ascension. He would convert Gentiles and become the King of Zion and Israel. Even unbelievers must be impressed by this procession of fulfilled prophecies.

But the real motivating cause behind the drive to foresee the future is not spiritual. It is the desire to control it. Millions of starry-eyed devotees pursue the mutterings of crystal-ball gazers so that they won't miss the opportunity to latch onto the soulmate of their dreams when he (or she) comes along.

Others, seeking their fortune, try to discern the movements of money markets. Or, they try in some way to influence the winds of financial fortune.

Still others are driven by the desire to turn wealth into power. Their real motive is to rise to a position that will place them above other men, whether in the manipulation of natural resources, transportation, politics, or international diplomacy. It is well documented, for example, that throughout his adult life, Adolf Hitler was surrounded by his astrologers and occultist clairvoyants. All his decisions were made on the basis of their ability to foresee the future. Their track record and his colossal failure tell the whole story.

But he wanted to *control* the future. The very heart and core of the Nazi Party was based upon his vision of a thousand-year Reich, with the new Aryan superman at its head. His vision of the future was merely a perversion of the messianic Millennium and the full realization of the throne of David. His thinking was simple: If you can't create the future, steal it.

Hitler represents the thinking of secular man. Through the ages, hundreds of despots, large and small, have envisioned the future with the conviction that they could actually realize their visions. The highway of history is littered with the detritus of their desperate attempts to manipulate the future.

To See It, You Must Be It

Human beings live on a series of assumptions. First and foremost, we rely on our experience that the next second will be just like the one that came before it. This assumption has pretty much established itself as dependable.

In fact, it is so reliable that it is extended beyond the next second, into the next hour, the next day, the next week, the next month, and so on. The secular mind cherishes this "faith in the moment." It is lodged in the belief that the social and cultural environment will go on just as it always has, in a slow and steady progress toward some sort of utopia.

Here, we come to the Bible's way of demolishing that argument. It sees the future as a succession of revolutionary epochs, each initiated by some sort of crisis. Time after time, God's prophets received visionary glimpses of these crises. They were appointed to inform mankind that the Lord would shape the events of future history. That the prophets actually reported on the future is emphatically verified by subsequent events.

A leading example of this fact is seen in the words of Isaiah, probably written around 715 BC. They speak of Cyrus, king of Persia, who would not come to the throne until 559 BC, more than 150 years later! Yet Isaiah reports on the actions and words of this pagan Gentile king, mentioning him by name as the man who would allow the rebuilding of Jerusalem.

At the time of Isaiah's prophecy, Jerusalem had not yet been destroyed by the Babylonians! Thus, he prophesied not only of Jerusalem's destruction, but its restoration: "That saith of Cyrus, He is my shepherd, and shall perform all my pleasure: even saying to Jerusalem, Thou shalt be built; and to the temple, Thy foundation shall be laid" (Isaiah 44:28).

Liberal scholarship chokes on the idea that a prophet could predict the name and actions of a future king. To support that notion, these academicians have created the idea that from chapter 40 and onward, the book of Isaiah was written by a second scribe, who lived after the time of Cyrus, writing about him in the past tense.

Note, however, that he would be lying, since the prophecy is written in the future tense. This "second Isaiah" would have been pretending to be a prophet. Actually, the whole question is moot, since there is absolutely no proof that an anonymous writer finished Isaiah's work.

That prophecy continues in the book of Ezra the scribe. He tells the story of Jerusalem's spiritual restoration, opening with the awakening of the Persian king to the prophecies of the Lord:

> Now in the first year of Cyrus king of Persia, that the word of the LORD by the mouth of Jeremiah might be fulfilled, the LORD stirred up the spirit of Cyrus king of Persia, that he made a proclamation throughout all his kingdom, and put it also in writing, saying,
>
> Thus saith Cyrus king of Persia, The LORD God of heaven hath given me all the kingdoms of the earth; and he hath charged me to build him an house at Jerusalem, which is in Judah. (Ezra 1:1, 2)

Here, we discover that Cyrus knew about the prophecy of Jeremiah, which had been written about forty years before his time. Jeremiah had gone on record as saying that after seventy years of Babylonian captivity, Jerusalem would be restored:

> And this whole land shall be a desolation, and an astonishment; and these nations shall serve the king of Babylon seventy years. And it shall come to pass, when seventy years are accomplished, that I will punish the king of Babylon, and that nation, saith the LORD, for their iniquity, and the land of the Chaldeans, and will make it perpetual desolations. (Jeremiah 25:11, 12)

But how did Cyrus know about this prophecy? After all, he worshiped the false gods of Persia and Babylon. Certainly, he wouldn't have studied the Law and the Prophets of Israel.

But here, we discover that another "accident" of history brought this information to Cyrus. In all probability, he gained the information about Jeremiah from Daniel the prophet, who still lived at court, even after the seventy years of captivity. Daniel was a very, very old man at the time: "In the third year of Cyrus king of Persia a thing was revealed unto Daniel, whose name was called Belteshazzar; and the thing was true, but the time appointed was long: and he understood the thing, and had understanding of the vision" (Daniel 10:1).

Here, biblical narrative places the esteemed prophet Daniel in exactly the place (the third year of the Persian king's reign) that would explain how Cyrus decided to allow the rebuilding of Jerusalem. Because it was recognized that he was filled with the Spirit of the Lord, Daniel was held in high regard in the courts of Nebuchadnezzar and Belshazzar, and later, in the courts of Darius and Cyrus.

It seems very likely that he was the one who had informed Cyrus as to the meaning of Jeremiah's prophecy. Thus informed, the monarch must have acknowledged what today's liberal scholars deny...that he had been personally named by God. Thus enlightened, he followed God's will, and allowed the Israelites to restore Temple worship.

It had all begun with Isaiah's simple statement about a future king, preceded by the prophetic utterance, "Thus saith the Lord." Here, we must make a clear and critical distinction between the Lord and His prophet.

Isaiah "saw" the future, only in the sense that he believed what the Lord told him about the future. He simply repeated what the Lord told him. On the other hand, the Lord had actually *been there.*

As we have often stated, the Lord is Lord of time-space. He created it. Somehow, in ways beyond our perception, what we see as *future,* He sees as *now.* Perhaps it would be more accurate to say that what we see as past, present, and future, He sees as ALWAYS.

In other words, He hasn't simply *seen* the future, He has *been* there.

On the human level, we think of seeing the future as peering through a portal of some kind. The prophets had visions of the future...something we can understand.

However, the Lord lives in the eternal present. He exists on a non-temporal level. He is in the future...right now. Or, as He said to Moses: "And God said unto Moses, I AM THAT I AM: and he said, Thus shalt thou say unto the children of Israel, I AM hath sent me unto you" (Exodus 3:14).

The Lord's very name bespeaks His status. He is trans-universal... beyond our universe, dwelling in an unlimited condition that predates (and will post-date) time. When He became incarnated in human flesh, he told the elders of the Jewish Temple that father Abraham had seen His day...His coming:

> Your father Abraham rejoiced to see my day: and he saw it, and was glad. Then said the Jews unto him, Thou art not yet fifty years old, and hast thou seen Abraham? Jesus said unto them, Verily, verily, I say unto you, Before Abraham was, I am.
> (John 8:56–58)

The Lord used the same term that he had used long before, when He had spoken to Moses from the burning bush: "I am." Among the Jews, there was instant recognition that Jesus was claiming to be the Lord God. They picked up stones to kill Him.

It is likely that Jesus was speaking to them in Hebrew. This being the case, He would have used a term recognized by their sages as the Divine Name. As Munk writes in *The Wisdom in the Hebrew Alphabet*:

> To the Infinite Creator, there is neither past nor future; in the Divine conception, which is unfettered by place or time, everything is as accessible as the present. Therefore God is described as יהיה [*yiyeh*], הוה [*hoveh*], היה [*hayah*], *He was, He is, He will be.* These three Hebrew words are contained in the Divine Ineffable Name—[יהוה].[59]

The very construction of the Hebrew word יהוה (*Yahweh,* or *Jehovah*) is a reflection of the Lord's status. We tend to use the word "eternal" in a rather cavalier way, as though we really understand what it means. Actually, we don't. In fact, we don't understand eternity any more than we understand the Creator.

But one way to make sense of this incomprehensible truth is to say that the Lord doesn't just *see* the future; He *is* the future. In other words, to *see* the future, you must *be* the future.

SIN'S FUTURE CONSEQUENCES

The Bible systematically presents the Lord as having full knowledge of the future. More than that, He watches over His children from the perspective that He can see the hazards that are completely invisible to them. We find a perfect example of this in the story of Amalek. It begins in the Exodus from Egypt.

When Moses led the children of Israel out of Egypt, they were opposed by Amalek in a place called Rephidim. This location, while obscure, seems near Mount Horeb and the rock that Moses struck to produce water for the Israelites. Israel's history notes that the Amalekites were a particularly loathsome enemy, using guerilla-style raids to pick off the defenseless. Their targets were the elderly, children, strayed cattle, and those who were generally unable to defend themselves.

Genesis 36 tells us that the patriarch of the Amalekites was Amalek, the grandson of Esau, founder of Edom. The Edomites, of course, carried a historical grudge against the sons of Abraham through Isaac and Jacob. It had begun in the womb of Rebekah, where the battling twins, Jacob and Esau, were rivals before they were even born. Their conflict continued for the rest of their lives and continued to thrive in future generations, including the present. Jacob, father of the twelve tribes, became the target of Edomite forces.

The Amalekites were Israel's perennial enemy, dating all the way back to Esau. Now, Moses made war with them. The Israelite army, led by Joshua, battled in Rephidim.

As the prayer of Moses provided spiritual cover for Joshua's troops, the Israelites vanquished the Amalekites. After the battle, the Lord instructed Moses to remember the incident, for it would carry eternal significance:

> And the LORD said unto Moses, Write this for a memorial in a book, and rehearse it in the ears of Joshua: for I will utterly put out the remembrance of Amalek from under heaven.
>
> And Moses built an altar, and called the name of it Jehovahnissi: For he said, Because the LORD hath sworn that the LORD will have war with Amalek from generation to generation. (Exodus 14:14–16)

About four hundred years later, something happened that emphasizes the importance of God's instruction to Moses. At that time, the Lord sent the prophet Samuel to King Saul with a remarkable message. It dealt directly with the ancient battle at Rephidim:

> Thus saith the LORD of hosts, I remember that which Amalek did to Israel, how he laid wait for him in the way, when he came up from Egypt.
>
> Now go and smite Amalek, and utterly destroy all that they have, and spare them not; but slay both man and woman, infant and suckling, ox and sheep, camel and ass. (1 Samuel 15:2, 3)

The Lord had not forgotten Amalek. Nor had he forgotten the scurrilous way they had attacked a defenseless immigrant people in the desert. Samuel's message to Saul was specific. The Lord commanded the King to wipe out every trace of Amalek. His word was designed as a test for Saul. Had he passed it, he would have been anointed by Samuel. But he failed:

And he took Agag the king of the Amalekites alive, and utterly destroyed all the people with the edge of the sword.

But Saul and the people spared Agag, and the best of the sheep, and of the oxen, and of the fatlings, and the lambs, and all that was good, and would not utterly destroy them: but every thing that was vile and refuse, that they destroyed utterly. (1 Samuel 15:9)

Saul, fearing the public reaction to the total eradication of Amalek, chose to allow the king—Agag—to live. Furthermore, in direct disobedience to God's command, he took the best livestock and the spoils of victory. Had Saul precisely followed the Lord's instruction, he would have remained king. But his prideful choice affected the Lord's confirmation of his leadership: "And Samuel came no more to see Saul until the day of his death: nevertheless Samuel mourned for Saul: and the LORD repented that he had made Saul king over Israel" (1 Samuel 15:35).

At this juncture, David was made king of Israel. But what had caused the Lord to demand the total destruction of an entire tribe? To find the answer to this question, we must turn to the book of Esther, where we find the story of an evil man who tried to destroy the Jews.

A SHORT SIX HUNDRED YEARS

We jump forward in time over six hundred years to the days of the Persian king Xerxes, called "Ahasuerus" in the Bible. Here, we find that a powerful schemer in his court is enraged to discover among the king's servants a man named Mordechai.

The plotter is Haman. When Mordechai the Jew refuses to bow down before him, he is enraged and secretly arrives at a method of exterminating all the Jews in the Persian kingdom. After Haman's wicked plan is approved through subterfuge, a series of events plays out, in the midst of which the king learns that his queen—Esther—is a Jew. In a dramatic reversal, he has Haman hanged and Mordechai honored.

This episode had unfolded when the king promoted Haman to high office: "After these things did king Ahasuerus promote Haman the son of Hammedatha the Agagite, and advanced him, and set his seat above all the princes that were with him" (Esther 3:1).

In this verse, we find a historical fact that takes us all the way back to King Saul and even to Moses. We discover just why the Lord instructed Saul to wipe out the Amalekites, and especially King Agag. Had Saul been obedient, Haman, the Agagite (descendent of Agag), would never have been born!

Saul's reign rose and fell upon this test and its historical consequences. Haman was an Amalakite.

The future implications of Saul's disobedience were drastic, indeed! Had Haman's plan never come into existence, the threat to the Jews of Persia could conceivably have been totally avoided.

Of course, the Lord had seen all this six hundred years before. He had given Saul the opportunity to cut it off at the root...and he failed. Note that the Lord hadn't told Saul what would happen if he failed. Rather, he simply asked him to perform a task without knowing the consequences...a classic test of faith.

CHANGING THE FUTURE

But there was another man in the Bible who *was* told what would happen in the future. He was one of Jesus' disciples. He was told that he would fail his Lord, something that he thought he would never do, for he loved the Lord. Furthermore, the Lord told him that he would perform the evil action *that same night.*

For the Lord, the future is a living reality. As His midnight trial drew near, He informed the disciples that they would soon experience chaos and disillusionment:

> Then saith Jesus unto them, All ye shall be offended because of me this night: for it is written, I will smite the shepherd, and the sheep of the flock shall be scattered abroad.

But after I am risen again, I will go before you into Galilee.
Peter answered and said unto him, Though all men shall be
offended because of thee, yet will I never be offended.

Jesus said unto him, Verily I say unto thee, That this night,
before the cock crow, thou shalt deny me thrice.
(Matthew 26:31–34)

Among the Bible's many stories, Peter's threefold denial of Christ is
one of the most often recounted biblical episodes, for it demonstrates
both the Lord's absolute sovereignty and His loving grace. Peter vocif-
erously affirms his steadfastness, even saying that he would be the last
among men to deny his Lord. Mark's account of his statement includes
an even stronger statement: "But he spake the more vehemently, If I
should die with thee, I will not deny thee in any wise. Likewise also said
they all" (Mark 14:31).

Here, Peter says that he would die before turning from the Lord.
And note that the other disciples joined him in this affirmation. But the
Lord had said that on *this very night* Peter would deny any and all con-
nection with Him. What happened to Peter is history. In the wake of
Jesus' dramatic warning, and just a few hours later, he proceeded to do
the thing that he had sworn not to do!

It's one thing to be like Saul and disobey the Lord's direct command.
After all Saul, couldn't possibly have known what Haman would do in
the future. It's quite another to be directly told that you will do something wrong at a future date, and then to go right ahead and do that
thing, just as predicted.

Such was the case with the apostle Peter, who was told that he would
perform a wrong action. In fact, his future action was presented in a particularly dramatic way…a way that was so forceful that Peter couldn't
possibly have forgotten it. But he did, as an overwhelming series of
events robbed him of all rationality. High stress can do this to a man.
And Jesus had seen it happen…in advance. Let's look at what happened
after Jesus was taken into the quarters of the high priest, leaving Peter
behind:

And when they had kindled a fire in the midst of the hall, and were set down together, Peter sat down among them.

But a certain maid beheld him as he sat by the fire, and earnestly looked upon him, and said, This man was also with him. And he denied him, saying, Woman, I know him not.

And after a little while another saw him, and said, Thou art also of them. And Peter said, Man, I am not. And about the space of one hour after another confidently affirmed, saying, Of a truth this fellow also was with him: for he is a Galilaean. And Peter said, Man, I know not what thou sayest. And immediately, while he yet spake, the cock crew.

And the Lord turned, and looked upon Peter. And Peter remembered the word of the Lord, how he had said unto him, Before the cock crow, thou shalt deny me thrice. And Peter went out, and wept bitterly. (Luke 22:55–62)

Sitting and waiting in the dark of night, a million black thoughts must have coursed through Peter's mind. In a dozen different ways, Jesus had told His disciples that He would be betrayed, tried, and even killed. Though they heard Him, they hadn't really accepted what He said.

He also informed them that they would be similarly persecuted. Now, Peter sat by himself on a chilly night, pondering the nightmare spawned in his own broken dreams. No doubt, he hoped against all reason that Jesus would somehow extricate Himself and emerge triumphant, as the political and spiritual Messiah of their imaginations.

But the context of this scene, given in the foregoing verses, tells us that Peter had begun to believe that all was lost. To see the Messiah manhandled and taken to court meant that He was not the powerful figure that they had hoped for. Peter had seen the fierceness of the opposition. His thoughts were filled with defeat.

A young woman, then a man, studied Peter's general demeanor. They concluded that he was a follower of Jesus. In a tumult of emotion, he twice blurted out that he was not one of the followers. Silence ensued. An entire hour passed…an hour in which Peter had ample time to remember Jesus' prediction of his failure.

Shouldn't Peter have recognized that only a few hours before, Jesus had predicted that he would do this? And having tumbled to the fact of his failure, shouldn't he at that point have retracted his denial and stood up for Jesus?

But Peter was in such a state of anxiety and frustration that, apparently, his mind totally wiped out any reference to the experience of the Upper Room, where Jesus had directly told him about what he was now doing.

At the end of that hour, other accusers approached Peter once again, this time with certainty. They told him that his Galilean accent gave him away. Matthew's account says that he began to curse and swear, as he vehemently denied knowing Jesus.

Only then did Peter remember. Luke says that Jesus somehow recognized that Peter had fulfilled His dark prophecy. Even though he was in the house of the High Priest, He somehow looked at Peter. ("And the Lord turned, and looked upon Peter. And Peter remembered the word of the Lord" [Luke 22:61].) It had taken well over an hour for Peter's final denial to fully realize itself. In the interim, Peter had many opportunities to recognize his two previous denials and correct them. But he didn't.

WHAT IS THE FUTURE?

This raises a number of questions about our perception of the future. First and foremost: Is our future written in stone? Or, do our daily decisions affect it in some way?

Did the Lord cause Peter to deny Him, or did He simply know that Peter would do what he did? The latter seems far more likely, because Peter is held responsible for the denial. All four Gospels feature Christ saying to Peter, "You…shall deny me." There is no indication that He is compelling Peter to perform the wicked action. Rather, the Lord is simply reporting in advance upon what Peter will do.

If the Lord had dictated Peter's action, Peter could not have been blamed. But he did blame himself. He knew that the Lord demanded the right choices from his followers. In fact, all of Scripture commands that the household of faith be held to the simple standard of making the proper choices.

Certainly, it was Peter's distraught mental condition that had blurred his judgment, and he simply acted out of fear. He made a colossal mistake and was filled with remorse—and, doubtless, self-loathing as well. But the Lord's action certainly illustrates His absolute awareness of the future in general and its details in particular.

Jesus later tacitly acknowledges Peter's responsibility for his denial. In John 21, which features the incident by the Sea of Tiberias, Jesus asks Peter three times, "Do you love me?" And three times, Peter affirms that he does. He is thus released from the weight of his threefold denial. The Lord knew that Peter rightly held himself responsible, even though his actions had been named in advance.

A CHOICE AND A CHANGE

This view is borne out by the earlier example of King Saul. The Lord simply asked him to perform a task, and he refused. Certainly the task was gruesome and repulsive. No one would enjoy wiping out a tribal bloodline, including all that remained to remind anyone that they ever existed.

But this was no excuse. For the Lord, Saul's action was a testimony of his faith. He was given the opportunity to choose obedience or noncompliance, and his choice resulted in the Lord's reversal of Saul's anointing. First Samuel 15:35 says, "And the LORD repented that he had made Saul king over Israel" (1 Samuel 15:35).

Here, the word "repented" is translated from the Hebrew word, *nicham* (נחם), which means "to be sorry."

It is clear that the Lord's decision was made dependent upon Saul's decision. God's final decision was made clear when Saul demonstrated himself to be a man who would yield to temptation. He was neither solid nor stable in his faith. Certainly God knew in advance what Saul would do. But the Lord waited for his act before making His decision "official." In the following verse, He informs Samuel of His decision. It demonstrates that the Lord had now changed His course: "And the LORD said unto Samuel, How long wilt thou mourn for Saul, seeing I have rejected him from reigning over Israel? fill thine horn with oil, and go, I will send thee to Jesse the Bethlehemite: for I have provided me a king among his sons" (1 Samuel 16:1).

And thus did David become king. The Lord can see the future, but He graciously allows the plans of man to mature, and He allows man to reap the consequences of his actions, even when the result is evil and counter to God's desires.

HEZEKIAH, GOOD AND EVIL

In another incident from biblical history, we see a clear illustration of this same phenomenon. King Hezekiah of Judah experienced God's amazing view of the future. He was unequivocally informed that he was about to die: "In those days was Hezekiah sick unto death. And the prophet Isaiah the son of Amoz came to him, and said unto him, Thus saith the LORD, Set thine house in order; for thou shalt die, and not live" (2 Kings 20:1).

These words, coming from a respected prophet like Isaiah, struck fear into the heart of the monarch. But he didn't accept God's word. Rather, he faced the Lord directly, pleading his case:

Then he turned his face to the wall, and prayed unto the LORD, saying, I beseech thee, O LORD, remember now how I have walked before thee in truth and with a perfect heart, and have done that which is good in thy sight. And Hezekiah wept sore. (2 Kings 20:2, 3)

Hezekiah believed in the power of prayer to influence the mind of the Lord. In desperation, he cried out that his life might be saved. Isaiah had left the room, and Hezekiah passionately poured out his dire condition before the Lord. And he was healed:

> And it came to pass, afore Isaiah was gone out into the middle court, that the word of the Lord came to him, saying,
> Turn again, and tell Hezekiah the captain of my people, Thus saith the Lord, the God of David thy father, I have heard thy prayer, I have seen thy tears: behold, I will heal thee: on the third day thou shalt go up unto the house of the Lord.
> And I will add unto thy days fifteen years; and I will deliver thee and this city out of the hand of the king of Assyria; and I will defend this city for mine own sake, and for my servant David's sake. (2 Kings 20:4–6)

The Lord then apparently showed Isaiah how to cure the king. Taking a lump of figs, he applied it to the king's diseased skin. Not only was he cured; he was assured of fifteen additional years in which to expand his reign.

Ostensibly, this was all to the good. But though the Lord had listened to the king's plea, it can be argued that it might have been better if the king had expired at the time originally ordained by the Lord. Two evil things came from the extension of his life.

First, Hezekiah, flattered by gifts from Babylon, was pacified into allowing a Babylonian delegation to tour Jerusalem. In reality, they were spies. After seeing the palaces and Temple treasures, they viewed the city as a sitting duck. Upon their return, they began a long-term plan to overthrow the kingdom of Judah.

Second, three years after Hezekiah's cure, his son Manasseh was born. It can be argued that he was the worst king in the history of the twelve tribes. His long reign was so riddled with idolatry that it eventually led to the destruction of the southern kingdom in the Babylonian captivity.

Since Hezekiah did, indeed, die in fifteen years, Manasseh was a mere child of twelve when he came to the throne. He was obsessed by the false religions that surrounded his kingdom. Before long, he had built groves, altars, and idols, and even had his own son pass through the fire as a burnt offering! He filled his court with astrologers, seers, and soothsayers. It was a veritable exhibit of the occult.

As the Bible repeatedly demonstrates, the Lord can live in the future as easily as we live in the "now." He told Hezekiah not merely that he would die, but that he would die, "and not live." That is, his death was a certainty. How then, are we to understand the Lord's change of decree in response to Hezekiah's prayer?

First, we must say that the king is described as being terminally ill, so death was near. Isaiah's initial statement to him only confirmed something he already knew. The king received the word of his death as a curse. Perhaps the Lord, knowing about the Babylonian conspiracy and the evils that would be perpetrated by the yet-unborn Manasseh, saw it as a blessing.

Here, we have yet another example of the Lord's perfect future view contrasted with the short-sightedness of man. Hezekiah wanted the gift of longevity, and the Lord graciously granted it to him, but at the cost of a horrible defeat.

When Isaiah discovered Hezekiah's sin with the emissaries of Babylon, he prophesied again, telling Hezekiah that Jerusalem would be destroyed as a result of his action. Furthermore, he told the king that his own sons would become household slaves to the Babylonian king.

The king's response is chilling: "Then said Hezekiah to Isaiah, Good is the word of the LORD which thou hast spoken. He said moreover, For there shall be peace and truth in my days" (Isaiah 39:8).

In effect, he said, "I don't care what happens after I die. All that matters is that there will be good times as long as I live."

What we have here is perhaps the best illustration of human will in the entire Bible. Hezekiah washed his hands of the future, thinking that he was immune to it. Now, we know that as long as God's Word exists, he will always be blamed for one of the greatest calamities in history.

God's grace is so great that it even allows man to alter the timeline.

We can hardly imagine such a thing. Any of us might have been tempted to stop Saul, Peter, or King Hezekiah before their bad decisions unfolded as future disasters. But He allows men to make choices, although fully aware of their future consequences.

This makes His complete knowledge of the future even more amazing to contemplate.

16

THE SOFTWARE OF TIME

In our observations about the biblical view of time-space, we have seen that the world's timeline is devoted to redemption, both of fallen man and of the fallen universe in which he lives. When the Lord spoke time-space into existence, He set a system in motion.

This system is specifically designed to bring about a result. As we shall see, the human profession of systems design in the world of computer programming is an excellent analogy to the Lord's design of our present reality. But as a result of sin and rebellion, his perfect system has been corrupted; it is running down. One day, it will be gloriously restored.

At present, the creation is plagued by a myriad of conflicting motives and quests for power. According to the Bible, it is characterized by a vast struggle for power that has raged on for ages. The entire conflict is staged upon a time line that is systematically marked off in ages and dispensations that will ultimately seal the fate of Satan and his followers. For the evil one, *time* is the enemy, both of his rule and of the collective sin of humanity.

This point is first made in Genesis, when the Serpent is cursed for having brought downfall to Adam and Eve. God's condemnation of the evil one is a clear-cut prophecy: "And I will put enmity between thee and the woman, and between thy seed and her seed; it shall bruise thy head, and thou shalt bruise his heel" (Genesis 3:15).

This curse didn't bring immediate destruction to the Serpent. Rather, it initiated a timeline. It makes specific reference to the Cross of Christ, where Jesus would complete the act that would bring reconciliation between God and man. At that future moment, the Serpent's (Satan's) head would be bruised. That is, he would be wounded but not killed. This is exactly what the Church Age has witnessed...a wounded Serpent doing everything he can to stave off his final doom. In the end, he will be totally destroyed. Put in another way, he will run out of time.

This is precisely how the book of Revelation states his position:

> And I heard a loud voice saying in heaven, Now is come salvation, and strength, and the kingdom of our God, and the power of his Christ: for the accuser of our brethren is cast down, which accused them before our God day and night.
>
> And they overcame him by the blood of the Lamb, and by the word of their testimony; and they loved not their lives unto the death.
>
> Therefore rejoice, ye heavens, and ye that dwell in them. Woe to the inhabiters of the earth and of the sea! for the devil is come down unto you, having great wrath, because he knoweth that he hath but a **short time**. (Revelation 12:10–12, emphasis added)

Once a creature of eternity, Satan has been brought down into the world of time, where he will be judged. What a horror it must be for him, that he has been bound to a ticking clock that inexorably marks off the hours, minutes, and seconds that will lead to his ultimate demise.

Time is also the enemy of the sinful man whom he enslaves. As a result of sin, every man's life is a ticking time bomb. It is only a matter of time until he dies. Without a redeemer, he has no hope.

In an earlier chapter of Revelation, we are given a scene that clearly links the concept of God's judgment with time...more specifically, our time-space existence. Here, an angel announces that time is running out, and when it does, the redemptive plan of God (here called a "mystery") will be finished:

> And the angel which I saw stand upon the sea and upon the earth lifted up his hand to heaven, And sware by him that liveth for ever and ever, who created heaven, and the things that therein are, and the earth, and the things that therein are, and the sea, and the things which are therein, that there should be **time no longer:**
> But in the days of the voice of the seventh angel, when he shall begin to sound, the mystery of God should be **finished,** as he hath declared to his servants the prophets. (Revelation 10:5–7, emphasis added)

Here, time itself is on display. We see that it was created as the medium upon which sin will ultimately be judged. Put another way, it is the matrix upon which a specific plan was overlaid at the beginning. At its very initiation, its end was already in sight.

The Lord spoke creation into existence over a period of *time:* It was measured in six days…and He rested upon the seventh. Note that "days" are measures of time for weeks, months, and years. They also comprise the model for the grand time scale—the millennial "days" of man, from his creation to the establishment of the Messianic Kingdom.

The seven days were not arbitrary. Rather, they were structured as an exhibit that would forever stand as a demonstration of God's victory over sin. The Bible was laid out upon the basis of these days. As seen in chapter eleven, the pattern of the seven days is best witnessed in the menorah of the ancient Tabernacle of Moses. Its seven lights constitute a symmetrical design.

The central (fourth) light is dominant, just as the fourth millennium of human history is dominated by Christ and the Cross. Called the "Servant Lamp," it displays the design of God's redemptive plan. More to the point, it graphically presents a picture of the timeline. Viewed in this way, time has a grand design—beginning at the center, and radiating to both ends!

THE WORD OF CREATION

The Designer of this system (and it is a system) is called the Word. This is more than another name for Jesus. It is actually a title that describes the creative process.

The sages of ancient Israel speak of the Word in a special way. To them, He is the "Word of Creation," the One who spoke this universe into existence. They believe and teach that He did this, using the twenty-two letters of the Hebrew alphabet.

They teach that He uttered letters and words in a specific way, as recorded in the books of Moses. Those letters emanated from His mind to form a reality, and were the building blocks not just of language, but of our physical reality.

As Rabbi Munk describes the process:

> The letters of the [Hebrew alphabet] are the array of individual spiritual forces through which God articulates His will in Creation. When God's will is carried out, the phenomenon is described as His "utterance." One blend of spiritual forces produces light, another produces heaven and its fullness, yet another produces animal life of myriad species, and so on *ad infinitum.*
>
> The twenty-two sacred letters are profound, primal spiritual forces. They are, in effect, the raw material of Creation. When God combined them into words, phrases, commands, they brought about Creation, translating His will into reality, as it were.[60]

That is, Jesus, the Word, laid out the encoded ideas of all Creation in a specific language. It was then entered into a timeline and given impetus. It had a launch point, a planned form, and a sequential schedule that triggered key events.

The closest that contemporary man can come to imitating God's coding process might be a crude comparison to the writing and execution of a computer program. Upon the "nothingness" of electron strings, the programmer overlays a series of binary digits, using zeros and ones in a variety of combinations to form ideograms. The coding system used is referred to as a "computer language," and may manifest itself in a variety of forms.

MAN'S QUEST FOR KNOWLEDGE

We have now fully entered the age of the computer. Virtually everybody uses one, for everything from communication and recordkeeping to theoretical design. Four decades ago, computers were clumsy, room-filling boxes full of wires, transistors, and even vacuum tubes. A common IBM 1401 of that day could hold only between four and sixteen kilobytes (thousands of bytes or characters) of information. Its inputs and outputs came from punch-card machines or lumbering tape decks the size of refrigerators. Early disk drives were stacked platters that looked like a cabinet full of oversized dinner plates. Though bulky, they were capable of storing only twenty kilobytes (not megabytes!) of information.

Today, computers are everywhere. We take them for granted. Their storage capacities are measured in gigabytes (billions of bytes)...on tiny drives that can be about the size of a stick of gum. Digital electronic computational devices are now available any time and any place.

What makes them tick? Hardware is fine, and it is getting better all the time. Microcircuits are shrinking to the point of invisibility. Their speed is incredible...and getting faster. But even the best electronics would lie quietly useless without the resident software that commands their actions. Software is simply the name given to the coding systems that bring intelligent action to the electronic pathways provided by computers and their links.

Word processors, communications, business operations, graphic and design programs, and language and news analysis systems are just a few of the thousands of applications that come to life in software. Without the software that provides the operational matrix, the most efficient computer in the world would be worthless.

Software is simply coded commands, a digital string of zeros and ones arranged into some form of reality. Its systems are written in languages that allow the transformation and storage of intelligence. Probably the most common software allows the ABCs of language to be arranged and stored as electronic documents. But pictures, sound, and formulas can be just as easily handled.

Perhaps it is best to view software systems as the life of the electronic medium. It creates the worlds that populate the solid-state cosmos. Keyboards, microphones, cameras, and other assorted inputs connect our world of flesh and blood with the virtual world, flowing with its rivers of electrons. Though they have no palpable reality, as we think of it, they nevertheless create a form of reality that we can use.

Of late, entire worlds are digitally generated. What were once hand-drawn cartoons are now complex scenarios generated by digits through complex software. Feature-length epics like *Avatar* and other movies are stored in vast electronic repositories as coded records that are animated by software.

Software creates worlds that are daily becoming faster and more complex. Contemporary computers, providing the medium through which the software moves, are so speedy that human imagination simply can't keep up with them. Only a little over a decade ago, they were many orders of magnitude slower...and they operated as single, isolated units. Now, they are interconnected.

The Worldwide Web

The Internet is a global interconnection of computers and other devices. Imagine a spider web, then multiply it by a million—ten million, or even more. It is alive with words and pictures…packets of conversation, business, history, philosophy, and mathematic theory. (These packets number in the trillions.) The web buzzes with a multitude of facts, factoids, truths, untruths, lies, exaggerations, and science. It breathes with a life of its own, a ubiquitous tracery of information that can carry a computer and its operator along linked pathways of virtual reality.

Millions of computers join in a time-space universe of their own creation. Today, for the first time, man is actually capable of creating his own reality. True, it is only electronic, and wholly dependent upon a moment-by-moment infusion of data and electrical power. Technically, however, it exists along its own timeline. Though its world seems to fall far short of what we call "reality," it is nevertheless "real." Being connected to it is characterized by the term "real time."

To be immersed in this world is to be bathed in a whirlpool of infinite and infinitesimal synergies. Designs that once took years to complete can now be realized and tested in days, then converted to plastic, glass, and metal by robot "workers" whose capacity for precision far exceeds human potential.

Science fiction writers have imagined that, one day, given enough technical advancement and internal power, this digital world could acquire its own intelligence, perhaps even acquiring consciousness—self-awareness—in a world of its own design. Dark speculations have been written upon themes of computers taking over the world. More likely, human beings with a lust for power would use such systems to realize their own hubristic dreams.

Of course, the Bible mentions just such a scenario in which a powerful man creates a virtual god: "And he had power to give life unto the image of the beast, that the image of the beast should both speak, and cause that as many as would not worship the image of the beast should be killed" (Revelation 13:15).

Given recent advances in computer animation, we're now very close to creating an image that appears to be alive. If something like this were ever to happen, the one who creates a "living" digital "microworld" would think of himself as a god. In fact, that is exactly what the Bible predicts.

Today, some designers are probably already beginning to see themselves in the role of minor demigods. Think of it. In the world of computer gaming, it is now common for enthusiasts to become so obsessed with their game worlds that they come to regard them as real. Online gamesters are so fanatical about their own creations that they vicariously live in the realm of avatars, battles, quests, lusts, and philosophically mind-bending conjectures.

Through the Internet, they are connected with other devotees of the same mind. They have created their own timelines in which wars are fought over and over again. Millions die hideous deaths. Cities are destroyed, then rebuilt. Horrendous, unspeakable crimes are committed. Monstrous creatures thrive and multiply. Doom reigns.

For these zealots, knowledge has transcended objectivity, becoming its own reality. Their digital lives exist in a twenty-four hour, seven-day saga that is played out around the world. Hackers, nerds, and geniuses daily move in a united quest to produce worlds of ever greater reality.

Digital strings of zeros and ones become designs, and designs become complex themes based upon a new kind of knowledge that feeds upon itself. In the end, it becomes far greater than any of its components, growing in all directions, but lacking any unifying design. Unchecked by morals, ethics, and the mind of a superior Designer, it rages onward toward the global nightmare depicted in the pages of Scripture.

KNOWLEDGE BEGETS KNOWLEDGE

We have yet to see the full realization of this bizarre world. But the prophet Daniel spoke of it in a well-known prophecy that is given in the context of what he calls "a time of trouble, such as never was since there was a nation even to that same time" (Daniel 12:1).

This prophecy connects burgeoning knowledge with the Day of the Lord. It clearly says that when this time of trouble erupts, men's lives will be characterized by an accelerating knowledge base: "But thou, O Daniel, shut up the words, and seal the book, even to the time of the end: many shall run to and fro, and knowledge shall be increased" (Daniel 12:4).

From our present perspective, Daniel was given a vision of the digital world. It has been well said that his prophecy makes reference to the mobility of modern man. Planes, trains, and automobiles carry unprecedented numbers of people to the four corners of the earth. In itself, this activity enhances man's knowledge base by bringing acumen from the most remote places.

But mere travel is only the beginning. The twentieth century witnessed the phenomenal advance from horse-drawn carriages to hypersonic jets. The twenty-first promises a continuation of this exponential growth, but with a new twist: digital reality.

Now, on a daily basis, knowledge is literally exploding. The angel who spoke to Daniel matter-of-factly informed him that the end times would be marked by the growth of knowledge. To those who lived in former generations, our current methods of gathering and processing knowledge are so esoteric that they would have appeared supernatural. A magic screen with its colorful motion pictures, words, and juxtapositions of imagery would have boggled the mind of an ancient man.

But even modern man is on the verge of "supernatural" activity. We have almost reached that point. But there is still another facet of virtual reality. Consider the following: Through the neural implantation of microprocessors, it is now theorized that man's mind can directly access the digital world. The first experiments in producing a computer-man cybernetic union have already begun. Think of a mind with the speed and range of a computer. Will this produce a superman, or a super-monster? Might the Antichrist have such a connection? Global, real-time intelligence in the mind of a fanatical despot is a nightmare that now has the potential of bursting into reality.

It must be remembered that the worldwide digital web teems with the unchecked filth of a world gone mad in a rush for lust, power, and pleasure. It has been estimated that over half of its capacity is mired in pornographic traffic. And that doesn't even mention gambling and criminal machinations of all sorts. Like our real world, the digital world is a mix of idealistic dreams and the refuse of a billion perverted thoughts.

In James' epistle, he speaks of the world's false wisdom as a mixture of the worldly and the demonic. We should never forget that joining in the digital flow of the world's knowledge network directly exposes us to an unending flow of debasement: "This wisdom descendeth not from above, but is earthly, sensual, devilish" (James 3:15).

While it must be quickly added that the gospel is going forth on many of the web's information channels, it is included in only a tiny fraction of the total traffic. Like the real world, the vast majority of thought is devoted to lust and pride: "For all that is in the world, the lust of the flesh, and the lust of the eyes, and the pride of life, is not of the Father, but is of the world" (1 John 2:16).

At present, the Internet lacks only one thing...a central, unifying principle, or controlling mind. When that central evil comes to power, the digital world will vie with God's creation...the false, digital world versus the true creation.

ONCE UPON A TIME

What existed before "God created the heaven and the earth" (Genesis 1:1)? Of course, no human being really knows. But it is safe to say that before our time-space universe existed, there was simply "eternity," the timeless state that is God's natural domain.

Even secular scientists say that the universe had a beginning. They call it the "big bang," declaring that everything we see was once a tiny point of energy. Mathematically, this point is termed "a singularity." They conjecture that in one gigantic explosion, the universe was formed. Today, their observations tell us that it is still expanding.

Given the biblical explanation, it is much more likely that the "big bang" was really a "big inauguration." That is, an explosion implies the uncontrolled release of chaotic energy that produces a cloud of debris. Far from that, our universe has countless traits that exhibit an orderly pattern that has emanated from the initial moment of creation. As often stated, when God spoke the universe into existence, He did so in an exquisite display of design, not an uncontrolled detonation.

Encoded upon the substrate of time, the verbal utterances of God spun into motion. Galaxies, stars, planets, and moons began to make their appointed celestial rounds. Scripture tells us that from the beginning, their orbits marked the passage of the years: "And God said, Let there be lights in the firmament of the heaven to divide the day from the night; and let them be for signs, and for seasons, and for days, and years" (Genesis 1:14).

The Word had commanded that His creation begin to run. His "software" had been initiated, written in the programming language of the Hebrew alphabet's twenty-two letters. Imagine for a moment that humans were able to encode their software upon a base of twenty-two, instead of a binary string of zeros and ones! If you could do so, you could literally "write" the real world in which we live. Creation must have come about in much this way.

Then, the program began to "run" at the rate we call "time." We who live within the system can only guess at the realities that lie outside its constraints. We are bound within its restrictions, while remaining free to make key choices regarding our faith in the living God.

CREATION FROM NOTHINGNESS

John 1:1 speaks graphically about the Word of Creation. Before His incarnation as Jesus Christ, the Word initiated the Creation of our world. As we have seen, the Word is specifically an ancient Jewish idea. It is the intelligence of God translated into the verities of this universe in which we live.

In his opening passage, John invokes the Word, mentioning three key points: "In the beginning was the Word, and the Word was with God, and the Word was God. The same was in the beginning with God. All things were made by him; and without him was not any thing made that was made" (John 1:1–3).

First, John emphasizes that the Word was both "with God" and "was God." That is, the Word was both God and somehow separate from God, having His own identity. As best we can understand it, the Word is one aspect of God, devoted to creation and redemption. As we have already observed, the purpose of the Creation was the redemption of man and this fallen universe.

Second, the Word dwelt with God "in the beginning." The idea expressed here is that of an origin. The Greek word *arche,* translated "beginning," can mean "first place," "headship," "from the first," or "in the beginning of things." All these meanings (and probably more) are implied by John's statement. But the main idea is that our world descended from the eternal world of the Godhead.

Furthermore, it highlights the fact that our time-space continuum had a point of origin. The Word was there at that point…and therefore, prior to it. He is beyond our analysis.

Third, if He brought "all things" into existence, including absolutely everything, then He created our universe from nothing that formerly existed…absolutely nothing. This is the biblical way of saying that He literally originated *existence, itself!* As we have seen, only an encoded Word could do such a thing. God's will became reality. In our present world, the only way we can understand this is to appeal to the analogy of systems design…software. For literally thousands of years, Jewish thought has held this idea as a primary article of faith.

THE PROGRAM KEEPS RUNNING

In Psalm 119, the great acrostic psalm, we find that the section devoted to the Hebrew letter *lamed* ל is devoted to the truth of the Creation. It adds a particular dimension to the thought of creation from nothing:

ל For ever, O LORD, thy word is settled in heaven. Thy
faithfulness is unto all generations: thou hast established the

earth, and it abideth. They continue this day according to thine ordinances: for all are thy servants. (Psalm 119:89–91)

Lamed ל is the letter devoted to the concept of teaching. Its very name is almost identical with another Hebrew word, *lamad* (למד), which can be used in context to define either teaching or learning.

As the magnificent teacher, this letter points to the great King of kings and Lord of lords. It states, in effect, that learning is man's greatest promise. As the twelfth letter, it stands at the center of the alphabet. It is taller than the other letters, and is said to indicate the supremacy of God's rule.

But look at the teaching it emphasizes in Psalm 119. It begins by exalting the Word. This is the very Word of Creation that set our world in motion. In verse one, the Word is forever settled. The Hebrew word *natsav* (נצב) means "to take a stand, or be fixed in position...firm." The Word is immovable.

He is also faithful. His purpose and character are firm and dependable. He "established" (founded) the earth. Here, the idea is that the earth is built upon the Word. This idea is wholly in agreement with the opening words of John's Gospel, where we learn that He did, indeed, build everything...without exception.

But then, there is this added thought: the earth "abideth." In other words, it stands...it continues its existence. Not only did the Word create the earth, He maintains it. The Word implies far more than mere creation; it holds that creation firmly in place.

Michael Munk writes:

The word of God that brought the heavens into being remains within them. The heaven continues to exist because not an instant goes by without God continuing to say, in effect "Let there be a firmament"—otherwise they would return to the status that prevailed before God's will was uttered. So it is with every aspect of Creation. God's original Ten Utterances are repeated constantly in the sense that the divine will of the original six days remains in force. Otherwise, everything would revert to the nothingness of before Creation.[61]

Classic Jewish teaching states that in ten utterances ("Let there be..."), God created the heavens, earth, and man. But it also teaches that creation is a continuing process, in which the cosmos is supported, moment by moment, upon the steadfastness of His grace and faithfulness. This is the great teaching found in the *lamed* ל of Psalm 119.

This idea is also found in the New Testament. Here, the writer to the Hebrews expounds his great teaching upon Christ's function as High Priest. The opening words of the epistle echo the thoughts and ideas we have just seen in Psalm 119:

> God, who at sundry times and in divers manners spake in time past unto the fathers by the prophets, hath in these last days spoken unto us by his Son, whom he hath appointed heir of all things, by whom also he made the worlds;
> Who being the brightness of his glory, and the express image of his person, and **upholding all things** by the word of his power, when he had by himself purged our sins, sat down on the right hand of the Majesty on high. (Hebrews 1:1–3, emphasis added)

Here, we see the Son, elsewhere called the Word, identified as the essence of God, distinct from, yet in equality with Him. And the Son is shown as the One who continually "upholds all things." The Greek verb *phero* is used here. It means "to carry a burden or a load." The idea is that something is being held up or held together. Even a momentary release would allow creation to return to nothingness.

Note, too, that creation is being carried along "by the word of his power." Here, we see another view of the Word. Here it is a translation of *rhema,* indicating "that which is spoken, or uttered." As we have already seen, the term "utterance" implies an executive action. It speaks not of the Divine Person Himself, but of His command in Creation, which is both initiation and continuance.

In our attempt to characterize God's creative acts, we have likened them to software. First there is the design, which is laid down upon the matrix of time-space. Then there is the execution: "Let there be… light…a firmament…lights in the firmament." and so on.

Finally, there is the continuance of His creative power. It provides stability, a foundation upon which salvation is built. It is forever fixed; it cannot be moved, unless in some way He Himself alters it.

IT's A MIRACLE!

Given the reality that Jesus is the Word, the Designer of all that is, His ability to perform miracles is somewhat easier to comprehend. Not that we can really understand His actions, but neither are they beyond the realm of our imagination.

Before Jesus came to earth, the Jews taught that the Messiah would be recognized when He performed three different miracles. One of them would be the restoration of sight to a man born blind. As given in the ninth chapter of John, Jesus openly performed this particular miracle:

And as Jesus passed by, he saw a man which was blind from his birth. And his disciples asked him, saying, Master, who did sin, this man, or his parents, that he was born blind?

Jesus answered, Neither hath this man sinned, nor his parents: but that the works of God should be made manifest in him. I must work the works of him that sent me, while it is day: the night cometh, when no man can work. As long as I am in the world, I am the light of the world.

When he had thus spoken, he spat on the ground, and made clay of the spittle, and he anointed the eyes of the blind

man with the clay, And said unto him, Go, wash in the pool
of Siloam, (which is by interpretation, Sent.) He went his way
therefore, and washed, and came seeing. (John 9:1–7)

How did Jesus do this? A man born blind has never developed the
neurological capacity to see. The portion of the brain that interprets
color, light and shadow has never developed. His optic nerves and eyeballs are atrophied, shrunken, and useless.

In order to restore the man's sight, Jesus had to restore the entire
optical system—eyeballs, nerves, and brain. Billions of abnormal cells
were involved. Apparently, Jesus simply formed clay from the dust of
the ground, reminding us of the way in which Adam was made. This
clay might have been transformed into new eyeballs, but what about the
neural restoration? How was it accomplished?

Questions like this could go on forever, but if we really think about
it, Jesus is the designer and executor of the system we call "reality." All He
really had to do was rewrite the code that applied to the poor blind man's
visual system. And suddenly, from our point of view, there was a miracle!
From His perspective, there was simply a program modification.

And by the way, in our generation, this type of encoded design has
become known to man in the microbiological study of genetics, revealing the source code of all life. Recently, the Human Genome Project has
made remarkable progress in delineating the structure and function of
the human body. It has unlocked and translated the DNA code, which
is not only the basis of all life on earth, but the determining factor in
human design. The Lord wrote this code, and He can change it.

Without Christ's intervention for the blind man, his timeline would
have continued unaltered, and he would have remained blind. But when
Jesus acted to revise the timeline—the coding of creation—the man's
sight was restored.

Or, take another example, one on a grand scale. In the book of
Revelation, at the opening of the sixth seal, some amazing things begin
to happen. Are they simply metaphors, or do they really come about as
pictured?

And I beheld when he had opened the sixth seal, and, lo, there was a great earthquake; and the sun became black as sackcloth of hair, and the moon became as blood;

And the stars of heaven fell unto the earth, even as a fig tree casteth her untimely figs, when she is shaken of a mighty wind. And the heaven departed as a scroll when it is rolled together; and every mountain and island were moved out of their places. (Revelation 6:12–14)

Here, we might explain away the great earthquake, and even the darkening of the sun and moon. (Earthquakes are common and volcanic dust sometimes blots out the sun and moon.) But stars falling like figs and the heaven rolling up like a scroll are concepts that are difficult to believe. In particular, how can the heavens be rolled up?

But given the mind of the Great Designer, such a thing is easily imagined. The One who designed them can alter their design as He wills. Thus, this "miracle"—the negation of natural law—is actually a smaller accomplishment than the initiation of their design. If He could unroll the heavens in the beginning, He can certainly roll them up any time He wishes.

Which is easier: the initial creation of the heavens, or altering their design at a later date? The answer seems simple enough. Of course, in this life, we will never understand the Lord. But the attempt fills us with ever-growing levels of awe and respect for the Lord, our Creator.

HEAVEN: A PARALLEL UNIVERSE

Cosmologists are mathematical theoreticians who have followed in the wake of men like Albert Einstein. Their theories are devoted to understanding the shape of time, space, gravity, electromagnetism, and matter in the universe...the cosmos.

They are driven to discover the true relationship between matter and energy, ultimately to acquire the ability to create their own matter at the atomic level. They also desire to master the shape of time-space, to warp from one place to another in an instant, or to transmit force over long distances. They see our universe as multidimensional and as one of many parallel universes. They postulate other realities, now invisible to us. (As Christians, we know that there are, indeed, other dimensions that we can't see.)

The cosmologists' wildest dreams are devoted to control, first of our planet, then of our sun, and finally of the universe itself. Since their equations do not include a Creator God, they imagine that this position has been left open to a fickle, evolutionary creation governed by cold mathematics. Their hope lies in the thought that humanity is presently on the long road to godhood. Now, they are bent upon creating scientific shortcuts so that by some means, man's journey toward an upward evolutionary swing might be accelerated.

Seen in broad perspective, today's cosmology is structured upon the evolutionary hypothesis. The Bible plainly denies this hypothesis, instead laying out a multilevel Creation. Heaven, earth, and the various levels of the underworld are matters of the Christian faith.

Cosmologists see the world as the natural mathematical outgrowth of force and matter. Bigger and better atom smashers are bringing them closer and closer to peering through the dimensional veil of another reality, the spirit world. Because of this fact, the time draws ever nearer when the Lord will intercede in their plans.

EVOLUTIONARY HOPE

Imagine that the theory of evolution, as it is currently postulated, were really true. Then imagine that in an infinite universe, given an infinite amount of time, every possibility would necessarily evolve. This being the case, various forms of intelligent life would eventually evolve into a state of super-intelligence.

An astronomer in the old Soviet Union—Nikolai Kardashev—once postulated that such highly evolved life could be categorized as Type I, II, and III civilizations. Type I would have arrived at the technological level necessary to control the assets of an entire planet…weather, energy, water, and all.

A Type II society would control not only its own planet, but also those of its own sun, directly tapping its resources. This civilization would begin to explore nearby star systems.

A Type III society would control the power of its entire galaxy, making use of the power generated by over a billion stellar systems. It is widely theorized that a civilization at this level would have developed the power to control the variables of time-space, warping from one place (or time) to another in the twinkling of an eye.

On such a scale, contemporary earthlings would be classified at the humbling level of Type 0 (zero). In other words, we have barely tapped the resources of our planet, but we do not yet control them.

Observing the present state of humanity, secular scientists usually place it at the earliest stages of development. They are then forced to consider that the universe has probably witnessed the development of many other sentient beings and societies, some of which have reached levels of realization that place them far above present humanity. In our eyes, they would be as gods; to them, we would be as dumb animals.

Thus, in the eyes of evolutionists, time and chance would have literally "created God." In other words, they see any potential god as an evolved being, whose ancestors were once as primitive as the apes.

This thinking allows men to smile to themselves and imagine that humanity itself is on the way to that same godhood. In this view, self-awareness is simply a matter of mathematics. Given enough variables, anything, including intelligence, can and will happen.

We must quickly add that this is not the Christian characterization of reality. We can also thank our Creator God that this is not His view of things. Judeo-Christian belief strongly affirms that after creating everything that exists, God created a superior being—man—whom He named Adam. Humanity has not evolved upward from Adam. Rather, his actions created a physical and spiritual degeneration, which has continued to this day. Man is not evolving; he is devolving.

The biblical philosophy of human history asserts that given enough time, humanity would degenerate to the point of utter corruption. That is, if it weren't for the coming of the Second Adam, humanity would collapse into nonexistence.

PURPOSE AND LOVE

By way of contrast, our "owner's manual" for this universe—the Bible—is built around two central ideas.

First, everything that is created was purposefully created by God: "In the beginning God created the heaven and the earth" (Genesis 1:1).

Here, in the Bible's first verse, the "heaven" is translated from the Hebrew *shemayim* (שמים), which is plural, as in "the heavens." This idea will become more important as our discussion unfolds. The New Testament restates Creation with even greater emphasis upon its deliberate unfolding:

> In the beginning was the Word, and the Word was with God, and the Word was God. The same was in the beginning with God. All things were made by him; and without him was not any thing made that was made. In him was life; and the life was the light of men. (John 1:1–4)

Here, we have the simple statement that there was a beginning to everything. Was this the famous "big bang" that so intrigues modern science? The Bible actually suggests a much more controlled creative act. The "Word" is an intellect, engendering all the attributes of building, from design to completion.

Furthermore, at that beginning, the Word (God the Creator) was already present. He made everything from nothing. More than that, He is the essence of all life. In other words, life is not merely the electrochemical result of a fortunate confluence of organic chemicals (evolution). It emanates from what the Bible calls "the light of life" (John 8:12). Life did not evolve, it was designed. This thought totally derails the secular theory mentioned above. The universe did not happen out of blind chance. Nor is civilization evolving. It is participating in God's carefully formulated plan.

Second, God is love. There is no mathematical formula for love. It is intelligent nurture that includes mathematical formulas, but is not controlled by them.

God's *agape* love, only dimly understood by humanity, is the organizing principle of all that we can see or conceive. His love takes the purpose of creation to the level of the heart…and the mind of a Creator who nurtures His creation to a point that is far beyond human comprehension: "For God so loved the world, that he gave his only begotten Son, that whosoever believeth in him should not perish, but have everlasting life" (John 3:16).

This verse is often used to introduce the gospel to someone who has never heard about God's saving grace. Yet it is also a continuous reminder to believers that He proceeds in a selfless way, promising the faithful that He will finish the work He has begun in us.

Seen through a giant telescope, the universe seems a cold and remote place, punctuated by occasional explosions and collisions. Without the love of God, it would be a positively frightening spectacle. After all, we humans are less than dust motes in comparison with the span and scope of our own galaxy. We are faced with a myriad of fears that include earthquakes, tidal catastrophes, volcanic holocausts, or solar instabilities that could freeze us or burn us in a millisecond.

Counterbalancing the stark vision of light-years of frigid nothingness in the cold and far-flung expanses of space, there is the intimate relationship with God through His Holy Spirit: "And we have known and believed the love that God hath to us. God is love; and he that dwelleth in love dwelleth in God, and God in him" (1 John 4:16).

The great mystery of the indwelling Christ and His body of believers is filled with comfort, hope, purpose, and ultimate eternal existence. It also promises a restored universe.

> Herein is our love made perfect, that we may have boldness in
> the day of judgment: because as he is, so are we in this world.
> There is no fear in love; but perfect love casteth out fear:
> because fear hath torment. He that feareth is not made perfect
> in love. We love him, because he first loved us.
> (1 John 4:17–19)

Contrast this with the evolutionary scheme of thinking, where plan and purpose are relegated to virtual nonexistence. There is no love in the random combination of elements. Neither is there purpose…or hope.

If randomness could produce superior beings, one would think of a Type III civilization with inner qualms exploding into stark terror: What if they view us in the same way we inspect prime beef…as food?!

For the Christian, such thoughts are immediately cancelled by the solid assurance that we have been adopted into the immediate family of the Creator. This thought excludes the fear of the unknown or the thought of an alien attack that might reduce humanity to slavery. In case you hadn't noticed, this is often the central theme of modern science fiction. Somehow, superior civilizations are always hostile and bent upon conquering the universe. The gods of evolution are the super-beings of science fiction. In their worlds, love (either theoretical or spiritual) is practically nonexistent.

PHYSICS AND THE PARALLEL UNIVERSE

Nevertheless, secular thought controls the course of academia. Contemporary intellectuals consider the biblical offer of eternal life to be the height of fantasy. But only the Lord's offer of salvation transcends our physical universe, offering perfection in the presence of the Creator.

The secular mind would rather follow the evolving mathematical schemes that pretend to unravel the secrets of the universe. At the turn of the twentieth century, Einstein and those of his ilk started a literal gold rush to harness the secrets of creation. That was (and is) their chief motive. Along the way, relativity and atomic theory spawned nuclear fission and fusion.

Einstein was followed by the legions of "quantum physicists," whose highly persuasive mathematical formulas state that the universe is defined by forces contained in minuscule packets of energy. These packets, called *quanta,* are said to define everything about matter, energy, and chemistry.

Scientists theorize that the tiny particles they observe flying from the targets of atom smashers interact with various forces to create matter. They say that if it were not for the perfect quantum balance of forces, the electrons that orbit the nuclei of atoms would instantly collapse into nothingness.

Christians believe that "[Jesus is]...upholding all things by the word of his power" (Hebrews 1:3). But physicists are still confronted with their ongoing failure to understand and resolve seemingly irresolvable forces. For example, electromagnetism and gravity have never been mathematically reconciled. For the last century or so, formulaic speculations have crashed again and again, like so many ships upon so many rocks. Albert Einstein attempted to create a "Unified Field" theory of the universe, but died before he could succeed.

His followers have tried to complete his "formula that explains everything"—the Grand Unified Theory. So far it remains just a dream. In fact, Einstein argued to his dying day that his theory of relativity held the answer for explaining the universe. He saw quantum theory as a momentary diversion that would soon pass by the wayside.

Instead, quantum theory has grown in influence. It is now the major authority in theoretical physics. Furthermore, it has had a major influence upon the current conception of physical reality. It dictates the natural man's notions about God's creation. He would love nothing more than to rise to a level that would allow him to control it.

Stephen Hawking, one of the world's leading mathematicians and discoverer of the phenomenon known as the "black hole," has led the charge to unlock the secrets of the universe. In his book, *Hyperspace,* Dr. Michio Kaku writes the following about this brilliant thinker:

> Hawking is one of the founders of a new scientific
> discipline, called *quantum cosmology.* At first, this seems like
> a contradiction in terms. The word *quantum* applies to the
> infinitesimally small world of quarks and neutrinos, while
> *cosmology* signifies the almost limitless expanse of outer space.
> However, Hawking and others now believe that the ultimate
> questions of cosmology can be answered only by quantum
> theory. Hawking takes quantum cosmology to its ultimate
> quantum conclusion, allowing the existence of infinite numbers
> of parallel universes.[62]

And as if an infinite array of universes weren't enough, Dr. Kaku explains that advanced mathematical theory seems to work better when extra dimensions are added to our own universe. Currently, theorists say that our universe has eleven dimensions and that it is like a bubble floating in hyperspace. Hyperspace, he defines as, "the space beyond three dimensions of space and one dimension of time."[63]

If you find his statements confusing, you're not alone. Even though the math behind cosmology may be far beyond us, we take the mathematicians' own words that they are in conflict with each other. Their speculations simply cannot be visualized, as we would visualize a pasture, house, or car.

Instead, we are presented with a bizarre view of reality. Its features are a bewildering, infinite hodgepodge of universes, each suspended freely in nothingness. One suspects that the most fantastic science fiction couldn't make sense of this mélange of multidimensional "multiverses." Mathematicians go so far as to say that they are quite unable to visualize the scenarios conjured up by their own equations.

Nor are they agreed upon the many structural schemes dreamed up in their hypotheses. To name just a couple, one is called "F-Theory," and another is called "M-Theory." Respectively, the two initials stand for "father" and "mother." As is often the case in scientific endeavor, the names given to proposed theories reflect a whimsical kind of wishful thinking. Here, one gets the impression that cold science is being dressed up in the glow of a loving household.

It seems strange that the cold reckoning of cosmology is warmed up with terms usually reserved for family. When all is said and done, there seems to be no substitute for relationship.

A Progressive Unfolding

On this note, we come to the Bible. Its central story is God's relationship with man and His love for the humanity He created.

But it also reveals more about "cosmology" than all the theoreticians and all their computers put together. Instead of confusion and conflict, it presents time-space as a believable environment, peopled with comprehensible beings who have clear-cut motives. It promises that out of the confusion and conflict of this universe will come a divine order…the restoration of all that we presently deem to be broken and beyond repair.

The preceding explanation of quantum cosmology is but a cursory description of a theoretical reality. Pulled deeper and deeper into the unknown by numerical conjecture, present-day science is wandering in a kind of enchanted land, blinded in a dizzying swirl of light and form, force, and darkness. Actually, this science hasn't the slightest notion of what really lies outside our physical universe.

Amazingly, any of the Old Testament prophets or New Testament apostles has a much greater grasp of life in other dimensions than does the most brilliant mathematician. When they brought the "word of the Lord" to the people, they spoke the very words of heaven. When they authoritatively intoned "thus saith the Lord," their words carried the weight of heavenly proclamations that came directly from the spirit world, in its many dimensions.

In the Old Testament scheme of things, heaven was rarely spoken of, as such. Certainly, there was the thought that God dwelt in the spirit world, but there was only the remotest inference of the world we call "heaven."

A good example of this is seen in the relationship between God and Moses. When the Lord spoke to him, it was in the context of visible flame—the burning bush, or Mount Sinai, covered in the fire of the Lord. In other words, He came to Moses and the children of Israel, and met them on their own terms.

SHEOL, EARTH, AND HEAVEN

But the Lord's message bore the stamp of heaven. Time and again, He carefully instructed Moses to follow the plan of the Tabernacle and all its accompanying features, including the altars, tables, menorah, and ark: "And let them make me a sanctuary; that I may dwell among them. According to all that I show thee, after the pattern of the tabernacle, and the pattern of all the instruments thereof, even so shall ye make it" (Exodus 25:8, 9).

This pattern was not of earthly origin. Rather, it reflected a design that had already been executed in heaven. Astonishing as it may seem, there was an original Tabernacle in heaven. The Mosaic Tabernacle was a copy of the real thing. The book of Hebrews gives us a great deal of insight into the matter:

> For if he were on earth, he should not be a priest, seeing that there are priests that offer gifts according to the law: Who serve unto the example and shadow of heavenly things, as Moses was admonished of God when he was about to make the tabernacle: for, See, saith he, that thou make all things according to the pattern showed to thee in the mount. (Hebrews 8:4, 5)

Nor is there any doubt that the pattern came from heaven. The ninth chapter of Hebrews, speaking of the blood atonement, mentions that the risen Christ, acting as our High Priest, entered into the original, heavenly Tabernacle:

> And almost all things are by the law purged with blood; and without shedding of blood is no remission. It was therefore necessary that the patterns of things in the heavens should be purified with these; but the heavenly things themselves with better sacrifices than these.
> For Christ is not entered into the holy places made with hands, which are the figures of the true; but into heaven itself, now to appear in the presence of God for us. (Hebrews 9:22–24)

Indeed, the whole book of Hebrews centers upon the idea that the sacrifices made in the Tabernacle (later, the Temple) are superseded by Christ's atoning blood in the heavenly Tabernacle:

Now of the things which we have spoken this is the sum:
We have such an high priest, who is set on the right hand of
the throne of the Majesty in the heavens; A minister of the
sanctuary, and of the true tabernacle, which the Lord pitched,
and not man. (Hebrews 8:1, 2)

The writer to the Hebrews draws a sharp distinction between the
earthly and heavenly Tabernacles. But we must recall that when the Lord
met Moses at the door of the Tabernacle, He was in the form of a column
of smoke: "And it came to pass, as Moses entered into the tabernacle, the
cloudy pillar descended, and stood at the door of the tabernacle, and the
LORD talked with Moses" (Exodus 33:9). It is perhaps not too much to
say that this "pillar of fire" was a connection between heaven and earth.

In the earthly system, the priesthood offered continual sacrifices on the
basis of an annual festival calendar. These rituals and sacrifices were specifically geared to the life of the spiritual man on planet earth. Neither was their
hope in the heavens. By faith, they followed their father Abraham, who
was promised the Holy Land from the river of Egypt to the Euphrates.

Furthermore, when Abraham died, he entered into a place of waiting, which came to be called "Abraham's bosom." This expression implies
close, familial relationship within the household of faith.

But there is something else. The twelve tribes were closely linked
to the earth. Their system of sacrifices promised not a heavenly kingdom, but an earthly one. Their king, David, and their Messiah were both
linked to the idea of a physical throne in Jerusalem, which would extend
divine reign over the entire world.

THE DIMENSION OF THE LOST

Dimensionally speaking, their spiritual hope was also earthly, since
Abraham's bosom was lodged deep under the earth, in a place called
sheol. It is the underworld, presenting us with the incongruous picture of
a paradise beneath the earth.

The King James Old Testament always renders *sheol* by translating it as "hell." Apparently, the underworld's deepest and gloomiest parts are reserved for the unrighteous:

> For if God spared not the angels that sinned, but cast them
> down to hell, and delivered them into chains of darkness, to be
> reserved unto judgment. (2 Peter 2:4)

> And the angels which kept not their first estate, but left their
> own habitation, he hath reserved in everlasting chains under
> darkness unto the judgment of the great day. (Jude 6)

The "darkness" mentioned by both Peter and Jude is the deepest, gloomiest, and most secure part of the underworld. Apparently, it has levels, ranging from pleasant to punishing.

The doomed of the Old Testament who go there are referred to as "the dead": "For in death there is no remembrance of thee: in the grave who shall give thee thanks?" (Psalm 6:5).

In this psalm, "the grave" is translated from *sheol.* It refers to the dead who are deemed to be unrighteous. They are also mentioned in Psalm 88:

> Wilt thou show wonders to the dead? shall the dead arise and
> praise thee? Selah. Shall thy lovingkindness be declared in the
> grave? or thy faithfulness in destruction? Shall thy wonders
> be known in the dark? and thy righteousness in the land of
> forgetfulness? (Psalm 88:10–12)

However, David and other Old Testament writers consider *sheol* as a place where existence continues; it is not a place of annihilation. The righteous who once resided there were graced by the presence of God: "If I ascend up into heaven, thou art there: if I make my bed in hell, behold, thou art there" (Psalm 139:8).

Here, the translators have rendered *sheol* as "hell." This has led theologians to believe that *sheol* is the residence of both the righteous and unrighteous dead. Prior to the resurrection of Christ, they were both there, but separated from each other in some way that is difficult to understand.

The classic depiction of this situation was given by Jesus Himself, as witnessed in the sixteenth chapter of Luke. As previously noted, the Lord gives a true account of two very real people. One of them, a rich man, went to his death in a state of unrighteousness. The other, a beggar, was judged to be righteous and went to be with father Abraham.

In this classic narrative, the rich man and Lazarus were both in *sheol* (called *hades* in the New Testament). But they were separated. One thing is made clear. The righteous of the Old Testament did not go to a place of death, darkness, and torment. Rather, they were comforted by Abraham, the father of the faithful (see chapter ten and "Hades—Subterranean or Subdimensional?").

Theologians hold that the righteous were taken to heaven by Christ at His resurrection. The following verses state this clearly, in the context of His ascension, when He not only took the Old Testament righteous to heaven, He also replaced the system of prophets with "gifts" of a new form:

Wherefore he saith, When he ascended up on high, he led captivity captive, and gave gifts unto men. (Now that he ascended, what is it but that he also descended first into the lower parts of the earth? He that descended is the same also that ascended up far above all heavens, that he might fill all things). (Ephesians 4:8–10)

These "gifts" (as we discover in verse 11) were the leaders of a new body of righteous believers. They were the, "apostles…prophets…evangelists…pastors and teachers." At Christ's Ascension, a new system—the church—was set in place.

HEAVEN, ANOTHER UNIVERSE?

Unlike the old system, it related directly to heaven. The former system was (and to the present moment, still is) entirely linked to the earth. Its hope was the earthly kingdom. Its righteous waited beneath the surface of the earth.

Now, the righteous have a clear promise:

> Therefore we are always confident, knowing that, whilst we are at home in the body, we are absent from the Lord: (For we walk by faith, not by sight:) We are confident, I say, and willing rather to be absent from the body, and to be present with the Lord. (2 Corinthians 5:7, 8)

The ancient world of Israel and the prophets was inexorably linked to the physical earth. Its Messiah was the promised descendant of David through the tribe of Judah. Its land was Israel. Its capital was Jerusalem. Zion was its future hope. Its God was Jehovah. But when the promised Messiah came, He presented heaven as a reality. John the Baptist, His representative and the last of the Old Testament prophets, came preaching an entirely new message, centered upon the promise of heaven: "In those days came John the Baptist, preaching in the wilderness of Judaea, "And saying, Repent ye: for the kingdom of heaven is at hand" (Matthew 3:1, 2).

In the end, national Israel refused the offer of this Kingdom. They were entirely convinced that Jesus' offer didn't agree with their view of Scripture. In fact, it didn't. While Israel remained linked to earth, He was connected to heaven. They firmly held to the coming of an earthly king who would be their strong political leader. They wanted a strong man of God who would defeat the Romans and establish Jerusalem as the head of all earthly capitals.

When John baptized Jesus, the evidence of His connection with heaven was more than apparent. Though it was an earthly event, its heavenly import was unmistakable:

> And Jesus, when he was baptized, went up straightway out of the water: and, lo, the heavens were opened unto him, and he saw the Spirit of God descending like a dove, and lighting upon

him: And lo a voice from heaven, saying, This is my beloved
Son, in whom I am well pleased. (Matthew 3:16, 17)

Note that at this signal moment, the Father, Son, and Holy Spirit
were all present.

HEAVEN: A PARALLEL UNIVERSE

When Jesus came, He did more than change history. He actually
changed the relationship between heaven and earth. His Crucifixion and
Ascension shifted the focus of spiritual activity away from the physical earth and one of its dimensions—sheol. In so doing, He pointed to
another universe: heaven.

Jesus made no secret of His mission: "From that time Jesus began
to preach, and to say, Repent: for the kingdom of heaven is at hand"
(Matthew 4:17).

When He taught the people how to pray, He turned their thoughts
toward the universe of the Father in heaven: "After this manner therefore
pray ye: Our Father which art in heaven, Hallowed be thy name. "Thy
kingdom come. Thy will be done in earth, as it is in heaven" (Matthew
6:9, 10).

The place called heaven is mentioned well over 250 times in the
New Testament. Is it a parallel universe? In fact, it does fit that description. It is the eternal world of God and the angels. By definition, the
physical world of time-space is different from eternity. Heaven is a place
where events seem to operate on a different scale than it does here, in
our universe.

On the other hand, sheol and hades, the Old and New Testament
names for a dimension "below," are tied to this universe by the very
terminology of their location...the underworld. This world, in other
words, has an "underworld." Perhaps it is one of the multiple dimensions believed by cosmologists to comprise our universe.

Heaven seems distinct from earth in many ways, a universe unto itself. Just before Stephen was martyred, he was somehow enabled to peer into that universe. It was as though a door opened and he saw the Lord. Those nearby heard him declare what he saw. Then moved by rage at what they interpreted as blasphemy, they killed him.

> But he, being full of the Holy Ghost, looked up steadfastly into heaven, and saw the glory of God, and Jesus standing on the right hand of God, And said, Behold, I see the heavens opened, and the Son of man standing on the right hand of God. (Acts 7:55, 56)

Stephen saw the throne of God and was given the supreme privilege of announcing to a synagogue of Hellenistic Jews that Jesus now stood at the right hand of God. To admit that this was true, they would have had to acknowledge that the man they had just crucified was their own long-awaited Messiah.

Some years later, another man, exiled to the Island of Patmos, was visited by the risen Christ, who declared to him the mystery of the seven churches. Then, a dimensional door was opened to John. It must have looked much the same as the one through which Stephen had peered:

> After this I looked, and, behold, a door was opened in heaven: and the first voice which I heard was as it were of a trumpet talking with me; which said, Come up hither, and I will show thee things which must be hereafter. And immediately I was in the spirit; and, behold, a throne was set in heaven, and one sat on the throne. (Revelation 4:1, 2)

And so John was also given a vision of God's throne. But somehow, he was lifted up, and his experience expanded into a trip through space...and time. Instantly, he was in the future—in fact, in a time still future to us as this is written. But somehow, his visit was more than just a trip to the future.

It was a trip to a vantage point that allowed key events to be viewed either serially, or as vignettes. Taken together, the scenes that John recorded offer the Bible's most complete view of the place called heaven. It is the destination of the faithful, and much more.

It would be difficult to find a better definition of the parallel universe we call heaven than that written by W. E. Vine. In *An Expository Dictionary of New Testament Words,* he describes heaven as "the eternal dwelling place of God." Then, he writes the following beautiful summation. Filled with abbreviations and references, it puts that universe into a paragraph:

> From thence the Son of God descended to become Incarnate, John 3:13, 31; 6:38, 42. He "ascended far above all the heavens," Eph. 4:10, and was "made higher than the heavens," Heb. 7:26; He "sat down on the right hand of the throne of the Majesty in the heavens," Heb. 8:1; He is "on the right hand of God," having gone into Heaven, 1 Pet. 3:22. Since His ascension, it is the scene of His present life and activity, e.g., Rom. 8:34; Heb. 9:24. From thence the Holy Spirit descended at Pentecost, 1 Pet. 1:12. It is the abode of the angels, e.g., Matt. 18:10; 22:30; cp. Rev. 3:5. Thither Paul was "caught up," whether in the body of out of the body, he knew not, 2 Cor. 12:2. It is to be the eternal dwelling-place of the saints in resurrection glory, 2 Cor. 5:1 From thence Christ will descend to the air to receive His saints at the Rapture, 1 Thess. 4:16; Phil. 3:20, 21, and will subsequently come with His saints and with His holy angels at His Second Advent, Matt. 24:30; 2 Thess. 1:7. In the present life heaven is the region of the spiritual citizenship of believers Phil. 3:20. The present heavens, with the earth, are to pass away, 2 Pet. 3:10, "being on fire," ver. 12 (see ver.7); Rev. 20:11, and new heavens and earth are to be created, 2 Pet. 3:13; Rev. 21:1, with Is. 65:17, e.g.[64]

Vine's words offer only a tiny hint of the glory that awaits the believer! The Bible begins with the creation of our visible universe. It ends with the restoration of that universe. The entire operation has been overseen by a loving God who has lavished grace and kindness upon a wayward and fallen humanity. His countless careful nuances have gently nudged man toward his glorious future.

Along the way, sin corrupted that universe as Lucifer aspired to godhood. The motives of the evil one remind us of secular cosmologists who try to unlock the secrets of this universe. (Lucifer tried to do the same thing in the universe of God).

Lucifer, (the Dragon, the Serpent, Satan) is somehow attached to this world and this universe. Once he superintended this region, apparently with access to the parallel universe of eternity…heaven. His fall from heaven to earth, then to the pit, traces the path of human misery. In the end, his fate involves yet another dimension, namely, the lake of fire.

The single element that draws together all the variables of time-space is the Cross of Christ:

> For it pleased the Father that in him should all fulness dwell;
> And, having made peace through the blood of his cross, by him
> to reconcile all things unto himself; by him, I say, whether they
> be things in earth, or things in heaven.
>
> And you, that were sometime alienated and enemies in
> your mind by wicked works, yet now hath he reconciled.
> (Colossians 1:19–21)

To reconcile means to alter so completely that the broken relationships of the ages would once again function in accordance with God's original design. Note that Christ's completed work reconciled *all* things, in earth and in heaven.

The Cross is the mediation point between two universes. In a way, the cosmologists are right. Multiple dimensions and parallel universes are not only possible; they are the norm.

But scientists miss the point. In their frenzied attempts to describe the environment, they leave out the myriad beings who populate it. The real drama transcends the mere mechanics of its construction. A description of the house is insignificant, compared with the minds, hearts, and love of its occupants.

In the parallel universe called heaven, our Lord has built a magnificent house. One day it will transport itself to this universe. Dimensionally and esthetically incomparable, it will be only a simple reflection of the Creator.

> And I saw a new heaven and a new earth: for the first heaven
> and the first earth were passed away; and there was no more
> sea. And I John saw the holy city, new Jerusalem, coming down
> from God out of heaven, prepared as a bride adorned for her
> husband.
>
> And I heard a great voice out of heaven saying, Behold, the
> tabernacle of God is with men, and he will dwell with them,
> and they shall be his people, and God himself shall be with
> them, and be their God. (Revelation 21:1–3)

Our eternal home, the New Jerusalem, seems capable realizing the fondest dream of science. It is capable of travel between universes! The Lamb is its light. It is a literal gem, imbued with the power to transcend time-space. Let the cosmologists look toward it with envy.

18

JERUSALEM:
A CITY ON THE EDGE OF ETERNITY

There are two Jerusalems. On earth, the city in Israel is the center of international dispute. In heaven, there is the home of the saints, a shining jewel that will one day be revealed above planet earth. But both cities embody a single idea: the restoration of this sin-wracked planet and the final, visible presence of God's glory. The two cities are knit together in a wealth of meaning and insight. Spiritually, they are one. Let us see how past and future come together, how the struggles of Zion become the glory of the Holy City.

At the end of the preceding chapter, we briefly mentioned New Jerusalem, the incomparable house that will be home to the faithful throughout eternity. In heaven, the universe that parallels our own, the Lord has built this house on the basis of His direct promise to His disciples.

He told them:

> In my Father's house are many mansions: if it were not so, I
> would have told you. I go to prepare a place for you. And if I
> go and prepare a place for you, I will come again, and receive
> you unto myself; that where I am, there ye may be also.
> (John 14:2, 3)

Presumably, this place has already been prepared in heaven. But it has not yet been visibly presented to the people here. It is a long-awaited dream that the faithful hold as a tangible hope. They view it as their ultimate home…a magnificent reflection of the Creator Himself. It will be everything that He is. As discussed earlier, in chapter thirteen, it is a living statement of mathematical perfection.

John's testimony shows us that it is a mobile city, capable of navigating time-space in the dimensions between heaven and earth. Perhaps, in this age of science fiction, we can think of it as a kind of spaceship, beyond technology as we know it: "And I John saw the holy city, new Jerusalem, coming down from God out of heaven, prepared as a bride adorned for her husband" (Revelation 21:2).

Imagine a huge ship, larger than the average asteroid. It is capable of traveling from one place to another! Moreover, its travels are not limited to this universe alone. The above verse tells us that it is quite capable of moving from the dimension of heaven to the dimension of earth. Its arrival here is the fulfillment a long chain of biblical prophecy. Without a doubt, its appearing will be the most spectacular astronomical event in the history of this planet. Later, we'll look at the full implications of its coming.

But first, imagine its enormous presence. The Bible describes the New Jerusalem as "foursquare." Though we can't be certain of its shape, we can get some idea of its size: "And the city lieth foursquare, and the length is as large as the breadth: and he measured the city with the reed, twelve thousand furlongs. The length and the breadth and the height of it are equal" (Revelation 21:16).

This verse tells us that its length and width are about 1,377 miles. This length is based upon the distance marked off by the Greek *stadion,* the unit of measurement from which "furlong" is translated, which equals 606 modern feet. Twelve thousand times this number equals 7,272,000 feet, which, divided by 5,280 (the number of feet in a mile), gives us the 1,377-mile figure.

Though we can't be absolutely certain about the configuration of the New Jerusalem, we can arrive at an approximation of its volume. If, as some believe, it is structured as a cube, the length of its diagonal axis

---

would be about 2,385 miles! But imagine its volume, which must be about 2,611,000,000 cubic miles—that's two billion, six hundred and eleven million cubic miles! That's a lot of living room—and many dwelling places!

Though we can only guess at its structural and esthetic perfection, it's safe to say that it will literally be the wonder of the universe...a place that projects perfection in every aspect. But above all, it is the focus of spiritual truth and perfection, illuminated by the Father and the Son with the primeval light of Creation.

THE LONG, LONG JOURNEY

In the matter of the Holy City, the Bible takes us on a long and circuitous journey from archetype to fulfillment. As we follow that long road from past to future, we discover that there is much truth to be discovered.

Abraham, the father of the faithful, was told to go to a place far away from his homeland. Following a route laid out by God, he came to Canaan. Doubtless, it was a difficult trek across dusty, gritty, and lawless badlands. Traveling with a large company, he was probably consumed with the details of the trip.

His obedience to God's command carried with it a promise...a distant promise. He and his household became the first Hebrews. In Genesis 14:13, where Abraham is first called a "Hebrew," it is in the context of his battle against the four kings who represent the empires of the Gentiles: "And there came one that had escaped, and told Abram the Hebrew; for he dwelt in the plain of Mamre the Amorite, brother of Eshcol, and brother of Aner: and these were confederate with Abram."

Abram, a son of nobles, now renounced his native territory and its idolatries forever in favor of obedience to the true God. With his commitment came the responsibility for defending it against the enemies of his great faith. Bear in mind that at this point, it was still in the infancy of its founding.

Still ahead lay the LORD's promise to him, the ratification of the perpetual covenant, and the offering of Isaac. Though his eyes were pre-occupied with myriad earthly difficulties, the vision of Abraham—the spiritual man—was steadfastly locked upon the far future, and a city of divine origin…New Jerusalem: "For he looked for a city which hath foundations, whose builder and maker is God" (Hebrews 11:10).

Following Abraham's lead, the faithful now look toward the same place. They have never seen it but know it exists. Since it was promised by God, its existence is unquestioned. But the journey toward this city began long ago, when young Abram and his retinue crossed over the river Jordan into Canaan. The very word "Hebrew" is said to have originated from the Semitic term that refers to one who has "crossed over" from the other side. The word is *eber* (עבר), meaning "to pass," "to cross," or "to go beyond."

In crossing the river, he symbolically stepped into the future. It was as though he leaped from one state of existence into another. This is, in fact, the essence of faith. Abram, a noble of Chaldea, gave up his earthly citizenship in favor of a new world. He had not yet seen it (nor would he ever see it during the long years of his earthly life). But it was never hidden from his spiritual vision.

He was the first to regard it as real. But since then, those who have caught his vision also operate on the basis that their true destiny is that of spiritual citizenship: "But now they desire a better country, that is, an heavenly: wherefore God is not ashamed to be called their God: for he hath prepared for them a city" (Hebrews 11:16).

This idea is often expressed in the New Testament. In the most literal terms, Paul states that the Christian's concept of national identity should be that of Abraham. We are now literally citizens of heaven: "For our conversation is in heaven; from whence also we look for the Saviour, the Lord Jesus Christ" (Philippians 3:20).

In this verse, the word "conversation" comes from the Greek *politeuo*, which literally means "national identity" or "citizenship." Of course, it is the root word for our modern English "politics" or "political." In other words, the Christian identifies himself with heavenly interests. Thus, he sees beyond the earthly power which will ultimately be concentrated in the evil leadership of an international consortium, headed by the "man of sin" (2 Thessalonians 2:3).

Much as in the days of Abraham, the Gentile world powers are arrayed against the household of faith, not in favor of it. The four Gentile kings he battled foreshadow the last great battle: Armageddon. The apostle Peter, speaking of the faithful, uses much the same terminology to identify the household of faith with their heavenly association:

> But ye are a chosen generation, a royal priesthood, an holy
> nation, a peculiar people; that ye should show forth the praises
> of him who hath called you out of darkness into his marvelous
> light: Which in time past were not a people, but are now the
> people of God: which had not obtained mercy, but now have
> obtained mercy. (1 Peter 2: 9, 10)

Here, the spiritual status of believers ("priesthood") is interwoven with their national status. In the passage above, "nation" is a translation of the Greek *ethnos,* meaning "a nation or people." It implies national status. Peter is quite clear in his identification of Christians as a spiritual nation whose home is in heaven. Perhaps it is more accurate to say that they will be residents of the Holy City, New Jerusalem.

For believers, the implications of this citizenship are truly awe inspiring. And they begin with the journey of Abraham toward the city built by God. His first contact with the Holy City came in conjunction with a war.

SALEM

Genesis 14 relates the episode of the invasion of Canaan by Amraphel (of Babylon), Arioch (representing the future Greece), Chedoerlaomer (the territory that would become Persia), and Tidal (symbol of the fourth empire: Rome). Their invasion of the territory of Sodom in southern Canaan resulted in the kidnapping of Lot:

And when Abram heard that his brother was taken captive, he armed his trained servants, born in his own house, three hundred and eighteen, and pursued them unto Dan.

And he divided himself against them, he and his servants, by night, and smote them, and pursued them unto Hobah, which is on the left hand of Damascus. And he brought back all the goods, and also brought again his brother Lot, and his goods, and the women also, and the people.

And the king of Sodom went out to meet him after his return from the slaughter of Chedorlaomer, and of the kings that were with him, at the valley of Shaveh, which is the king's dale. And Melchizedek king of Salem brought forth bread and wine: and he was the priest of the most high God. And he blessed him, and said, Blessed be Abram of the most high God, possessor of heaven and earth: And blessed be the most high God, which hath delivered thine enemies into thy hand. And he gave him tithes of all. (Genesis 14:14–20)

It also resulted in a transaction at the Holy City. Here, we find that a victorious Abram, after vanquishing the four kings, returned to a specific place called "the valley of Shaveh." The location of this place is key to the understanding of prophecy. It lay a few hundred yards west of what later became the city of David and the Temple Mount.

Its king-priest, the mysterious Melchizedek, presided over the surroundings. Even at this early date (perhaps 1900 BC), the Lord had placed His unction upon the Holy City. Here, it was known as "Salem." Its name means, simply, "peace." Later, as "Jerusalem," it becomes identified as "the city of God's peace." As New Jerusalem, it is simply God's city.

Melchizedek is, in fact, one of the greatest types of Christ in the entirety of Scripture. He is made the representative priest of the "most high God." This title reflects God in the totality of His power and sovereignty. *El Elyon* (אֵל עֶלְיוֹן), the "God Most High," is thought to be one of the Deity's most ancient titles:

For this Melchisedek, king of Salem, priest of the most high
God, who met Abraham returning from the slaughter of the
kings, and blessed him;

To whom also Abraham gave a tenth part of all; first being
by interpretation King of righteousness, and after that also King
of Salem, which is, King of peace; Without father, without
mother, without descent, having neither beginning of days, nor
end of life; but made like unto the Son of God; abideth a priest
continually. (Hebrews 7:1–3)

Later, when the "Most High God" directly addresses Abraham, it is
as "Lord." This, of course, is the English translation of *Jehovah* (יהוה).
This title is used when God addresses the faithful. One is formal, the
other is personal. Yet, when the two titles are compared, they obviously
describe the same Divine Person.

When God spoke to Moses from the burning bush, He used the
same title, Jehovah:

And when the LORD saw that he turned aside to see, God called
unto him out of the midst of the bush, and said, Moses, Moses.
And he said, Here am I.

And he said, Draw not nigh hither: put off thy shoes from
off thy feet, for the place whereon thou standest is holy ground.

Moreover he said, I am the God of thy father, the God of
Abraham, the God of Isaac, and the God of Jacob. And Moses
hid his face; for he was afraid to look upon God. (Exodus 3:4–6)

Notice that when Jehovah addresses Moses, He makes reference to
Abraham, father of the faithful. Throughout the Bible, faith is always exem-
plified by Abraham. God's promise to him reaches out across the ages:

And God said moreover unto Moses, Thus shalt thou say unto
the children of Israel, The LORD God of your fathers, the God

of Abraham, the God of Isaac, and the God of Jacob, hath sent me unto you: this is my name for ever, and this is my memorial unto all generations.

Go, and gather the elders of Israel together, and say unto them, The LORD God of your fathers, the God of Abraham, of Isaac, and of Jacob, appeared unto me, saying, I have surely visited you, and seen that which is done to you in Egypt. (Exodus 3:15, 16)

In the two verses above, the Lord God makes sure that Moses remembers Abraham. Even Moses, the deliverer of his people and the bringer of the Law, is enjoined to remember Abraham.

Abraham's faith is particularly denoted by his interaction with Melchizedek in Salem. His meeting with the priest-king marks the first mention of Jerusalem, the spiritual capital of the world. It gives to believers an opportunity to observe the origin of the earthly city that is a counterpart of the Holy City mentioned in Revelation 21.

It later became the home of the Davidic throne and Solomon's Temple. Wracked by sinful leaders and numerous invaders, including Assyria, Egypt, Babylon, Greece, and Rome, Jerusalem was sacked again and again. But its true destiny, as the home of the Davidic throne and the Temples of the Lord, was never lost. Salem not only became Jerusalem. It also acquired the title "Zion." As seen in Psalm 76:1 and 2, its earliest name is closely associated with this title of its political and spiritual destiny: "To the chief Musician on Neginoth, A Psalm or Song of Asaph. In Judah is God known: his name is great in Israel. In Salem also is his tabernacle, and his dwelling place in Zion."

THE ASSAULT UPON ZION

Zion seems to be the name the Lord Himself placed upon the hallowed ground of the Temple Mount. Its meaning comes from a cluster of ancient roots. *Zion* (צִיּוֹן) means "structure" or "to protect." In later usage, it can mean "sign" or "landmark." Certainly, all of the above meanings apply to the site of the Holy Temple, centerpiece of Jerusalem.

Psalm 87 shows the incredible value that the Lord places upon this real estate, the forerunner of the final, heavenly city. It is depicted as the foundation of His work and the object of His love. It is a place destined for glory.

More importantly, it is associated with spiritual birth. To be "born in Zion" seems to be a metaphor for spiritual birth. Zion then becomes emblematic of the heavenly lineage of the saved, and of their spiritual struggle. However, it also carries future implications. Zion is a heavenly hope.

> A Psalm or Song for the sons of Korah. His foundation is in the holy mountains. The LORD loveth the gates of Zion more than all the dwellings of Jacob. Glorious things are spoken of thee, O city of God. Selah.
>
> I will make mention of Rahab and Babylon to them that know me: behold Philistia, and Tyre, with Ethiopia; this man was born there. And of Zion it shall be said, This and that man was born in her: and the highest himself shall establish her. The LORD shall count, when he writeth up the people, that this man was born there. Selah. (Psalm 87:1–6)

The Bible's first mention of Zion comes during the history of a significant battle. It recounts David's challenge to his men, who stormed the mountain, securing the holiest spot on the face of the earth for the kingdom of David:

> Nevertheless David took the strong hold of Zion: the same is the city of David. And David said on that day, Whosoever getteth up to the gutter, and smiteth the Jebusites, and the lame and the blind, that are hated of David's soul, he shall be chief

and captain. Wherefore they said, The blind and the lame shall not come into the house.

So David dwelt in the fort, and called it the city of David. And David built round about from Millo and inward. (2 Samuel 5:7–9)

David's men bravely ascended a crevice in the cliff ("the gutter"). The Jebusites had insulted them as lame and blind, but they won the day against seemingly overwhelming opposition.

But David did more than take the mountaintop by force. He also bought the ground that would later become the location of the first Temple. He paid its owner, Ornan the Jebusite, fifty shekels of silver. But that was only the beginning.

Additionally, he bought the ground that would become site of the Holy of Holies, paying Ornan three hundred shekels of gold, saying, " I will verily buy it for the full price: for I will not take that which is thine for the Lord, nor offer burnt offerings without cost" (1 Chronicles 21:24).

Thus, from that day to this, the ownership of the holy ground has officially remained the property of the Davidic dynasty. It is important to remember that Mount Zion was literally bought and paid for by the king. No subsequent transaction has transferred ownership to any other individual or group.

Three thousand years have passed since then, and many conquerors since then have set themselves up as the owners of Zion. But they were only temporary custodians. They never really appreciated the value of this, God's beloved ground. They were only interested in founding a competing dynasty. Certainly, they had no idea of its timeless promise.

That goes especially for the present era, when the followers of Mohammed have invented a series of tales that supposedly give provenance of the mountain to the prophet of the Koran. Try as they may to destroy its divinely ordained history, they will never succeed. In fact, its true destiny is only now about to be unfolded.

The False and the True

Probably the most famous usurper of the Temple mount was Antiochus IV Epiphanes. In 167 BC, he erected an image of himself as the Olympian Zeus—in the very place David had purchased hundreds of years before.

This evil despot is commonly viewed as the forerunner and archetype of the Antichrist. In fact, the eleventh chapter of Daniel documents him in precisely this way. This key chapter chronicles the succession of Greek kings who followed the conquests of Alexander the Great. His four generals divided the empire: Cassander, Lysimachus, Ptolemy, and Seleucus ruled the four corners of Alexander's domain.

Daniel 11 is particularly devoted to following the lineage of Seleucus, who took the eastern portion of the territory, including Aramea (Syria) and the land of Israel. Many generations of his descendants ruled under the title "Antiochus," finally becoming absorbed into the legions of Roman nobles, some of whom achieved ruling statues in Rome.

Daniel 11:21 mentions Antiochus Epiphanes as the pretender who comes in as savior and rises to invoke the dark powers of demonology: "And in his estate shall stand up a vile person, to whom they shall not give the honour of the kingdom: but he shall come in peaceably, and obtain the kingdom by flatteries."

This is the way of the pretender to the throne. He appears benign, even blessed. But he conceals an inner lust to be worshipped as God.

> And arms shall stand on his part, and they shall pollute the
> sanctuary of strength, and shall take away the daily sacrifice,
> and they shall place the abomination that maketh desolate.
> And such as do wickedly against the covenant shall he corrupt
> by flatteries: but the people that do know their God shall be
> strong, and do exploits. (Daniel 11:31, 32)

Here, we have the evil act of Antiochus, as he profaned the Temple with an "abomination." This insult is coupled with the exploits of the heroic Jewish warriors who subsequently overcame him.

On a larger scale, it is important to remember that what we are seeing here is the first attempt by pagan Gentile forces to overthrow the Davidic throne, replacing it with the despotic rule of a Gentile world empire.

The phrase "abomination that maketh desolate" refers to the wicked act of Antiochus in the distant past. This interpretation is logical, because of the verses that follow it. They foretell the centuries of Jewish diaspora and martyrdom that were yet to come before the "time of the end" and the judgments of the Tribulation period.

> And they that understand among the people shall instruct many: yet they shall fall by the sword, and by flame, by captivity, and by spoil, many days.
>
> Now when they shall fall, they shall be holpen with a little help: but many shall cleave to them with flatteries. And some of them of understanding shall fall, to try them, and to purge, and to make them white, even to the time of the end: because it is yet for a time appointed. (Daniel 11:33–35)

The abomination mentioned in verse 31 is past. It describes a documented event in the history of Israel, meant to establish a precedent, and mark out a recognizable pattern for the future. In the same context, verse 36 follows the Seleucid lineage into the far future:

> And the king shall do according to his will; and he shall exalt himself, and magnify himself above every god, and shall speak marvellous things against the God of gods, and shall prosper till the indignation be accomplished: for that that is determined shall be done.

This verse has been called the "prophecy of the willful king." Clearly, it refers to the latter-day Antichrist. But both spiritually and genealogically, he is the offspring of Antiochus Epiphanes. Historically, the dynasty of the Seleucids intermarried with the families of Roman nobles, who became the kings, queens, dukes, and duchesses of the Holy Roman Empire. Their descendants are alive today, embedded in a variety of royal lineages. In particular, one of them will rise to power as the infamous "man of sin."

As has been retold again and again, Daniel prophesies that the people who destroyed Jerusalem and the Temple would be the ancestors of the "prince that shall come" (Daniel 9:26). Antichrist will be of Greco-Roman descent. He will come to finish the work left undone by his ancient ancestor Antiochus IV Epiphanes:

> And he shall confirm the covenant with many for one week:
> and in the midst of the week he shall cause the sacrifice and the
> oblation to cease, and for the overspreading of abominations he
> shall make it desolate, even until the consummation, and that
> determined shall be poured upon the desolate. (Daniel 9:27)

Zion in the New Testament

The progress from ancient Zion to its final realization has now taken some three thousand years. Since David bought it from Ornan, the ancient mountain has witnessed the coming and going of two Temples and two major dispersions of the Jews.

But several New Testament prophecies highlight the importance of Zion. The most obvious is Jesus' own quotation of Daniel 9:27. In the famous conversation with the disciples, He explains the timing and context of Daniel's prophecy: "When ye therefore shall see the abomination of desolation, spoken of by Daniel the prophet, stand in the holy place, (whoso readeth, let him understand:) Then let them which be in Judaea flee into the mountains" (Matthew 24:15, 16).

Here, sitting at the feet of Jesus, we learn that He took Daniel's prophecy quite literally. He told His disciples (and by extension, the twelve tribes of Israel) that the future would bring a horrible event to Israel. He mentions Judea by name. Traditionally, this is the territory south of a line from Joppa, east to the Jordan River. It would include today's Tel Aviv, Jerusalem, Hebron, Beersheba, and other desert areas in the south.

To "flee into the mountains" probably indicates an escape route to the east, into the mountains of ancient Ammon, Moab, and Edom. Jews (not Christians) are explicitly told to watch for the horror that would appear in the "holy place." There is not the slightest doubt about its location. It is the same piece of real estate once conquered, then purchased, by David for three thousand shekels of gold. The abstract for the purchase is Holy Scripture. If it is recorded there, it is a permanent, eternal transaction.

The legacy of David, Jerusalem, and Zion is summed up in Acts 15, where James recalls the prophecy of Amos: "After this I will return, and will build again the tabernacle of David, which is fallen down; and I will build again the ruins thereof, and I will set it up" (Acts 15:16).

In this prophecy, Amos links the first and second arrivals of the Tabernacle of David on the Temple Mount. This ceremonial arrival is recalled in 1 Chronicles 16 and Psalm 105, when the Ark was brought up to the mountain and placed there, within the Tabernacle that David had built for it.

Whether the Tabernacle will be the desecrated holy place mentioned by Jesus or whether it will be a temporary temple is unknown. But one thing is known for sure. The holy place will once again be located, dedicated, and consecrated. We know this because of another New Testament prophecy written by Paul:

> Let no man deceive you by any means: for that day shall not come, except there come a falling away first, and that man of sin be revealed, the son of perdition;
> Who opposeth and exalteth himself above all that is called God, or that is worshipped; so that he as God sitteth in the temple of God, showing himself that he is God.
> (2 Thessalonians 2:3, 4)

Here, Paul plainly states that the Day of the Lord will be timed to follow the general revelation of the "son of perdition," the Antichrist. This passage clarifies Daniel's statement about the desecration of the Temple, later quoted by Jesus as the "abomination of desolation."

As Paul describes this consummate act of blasphemy, he refers to the Antichrist's act as taking place in the "temple of God." The Greek word translated as "temple" is *naos,* a specific term used only in reference to the Holy of Holies—the spot reserved for the placement of the Ark of the Covenant. Once again, we are brought back to ground purchased by David for an altar of sacrifice.

Thus, the Antichrist stands in the place usually reserved for the High Priest, and then only once a year, on the Day of Atonement. Even worse, he presents himself as God! This assault upon Zion is an ultimate act of sacrilege.

All this suggests that in the near future, the location of the holy place must be rediscovered, marked, and agreed upon by Israeli religious authorities. Currently, there are active steps being pursued by both the Jerusalem Temple Institute and the newly reestablished Sanhedrin.

In Revelation, we see what appears to be a survey of the Temple Mount, no doubt centered on the idea of precisely locating the Holy Place. It appears that this will be done in preparation for the Temple worship that is later usurped by the Antichrist.

> And there was given me a reed like unto a rod: and the angel stood, saying, Rise, and measure the temple of God, and the altar, and them that worship therein.
> But the court which is without the temple leave out, and measure it not; for it is given unto the Gentiles: and the holy city shall they tread under foot forty and two months. (Revelation 11:1, 2)

This "court of the Gentiles" seems to be an artifact of the Tribulation Temple. We shall see that both Ezekiel and Revelation refer to it.

Just as the ancient Antiochus IV Epiphanes, garbed as the Olympian

Zeus, placed an image of himself there, the coming Antichrist will revisit the evil act: "And he had power to give life unto the image of the beast, that the image of the beast should both speak, and cause that as many as would not worship the image of the beast should be killed" (Revelation 13:15).

THE THIRD TEMPLE

The Antichrist—representative of the final Gentile world empire—will worship in some kind of Temple, to be sure. But apparently, it is only temporary. It could be the ancient tent fashioned by David, or it could be a temporary building.

But the real and lasting Third Temple will be built by Messiah Himself. This lengthy and detailed development is described by Ezekiel chapters 40 through 48. Among the significant aspects of the process is the confirmation of the Holy Place: "So he measured the length thereof, twenty cubits; and the breadth, twenty cubits, before the temple: and he said unto me, This is the most holy place" (Ezekiel 41:4).

After this, there is an interesting detail that reminds one of Revelation 11. Ezekiel speaks of the return of the *Shechina* glory. But he also refers to a "profane place" that is apparently provided for Gentile use.

> He measured it by the four sides: it had a wall round about, five hundred reeds long, and five hundred broad, to make a separation between the sanctuary and the profane place.
> Afterward he brought me to the gate, even the gate that looketh toward the east: And, behold, the glory of the God of Israel came from the way of the east: and his voice was like a noise of many waters: and the earth shined with his glory. (Ezekiel 42:20–43:2)

This reminds us of Revelation 11, where a court for the Gentiles is specifically laid out.

Jerusalem Rebuilt

The Kingdom Temple described by Ezekiel in great detail is often referred to as the Third Temple. It will be the greatest and most detailed municipal plan ever undertaken. "Jerusalem, the Golden" will be its rightful name. It will be the seat of the Davidic throne. Perhaps Ornan's ancient threshing floor will be somehow preserved and displayed as the site of the Holy Place.

A thousand years of Messianic rule will bless the earth. During that time, everyone on earth will pay homage and tribute to the reigning house of David. Satan will have been bound, and the earth restored.

But at the end of the Millennium, Satan will be released, and there will come a new rebellion and judgment. Following the divine retribution of the Great White Throne and the renewing of heaven and earth, Jerusalem will finally realize its destiny.

It will suddenly appear above earth (perhaps in stationary orbit above the site of the old Jerusalem?) as a gleaming gem. Its very structure is laden with meaning, with twelve foundations for the apostles and twelve gates for the tribes of Israel.

Its streets of transparent gold are beyond the imagination. But most amazing of all, it is illuminated by God:

> And I saw no temple therein: for the Lord God Almighty and the Lamb are the temple of it. And the city had no need of the sun, neither of the moon, to shine in it: for the glory of God did lighten it, and the Lamb is the light thereof.
>
> And the nations of them which are saved shall walk in the light of it: and the kings of the earth do bring their glory and honour into it. (Revelation 21:22–24)

Notice that New Jerusalem has no temple. The body of the redeemed, the Lord God, and the Lamb become one. They are literally the new Temple, as given in Revelation 3:12:

Him that overcometh will I make a pillar in the temple of my God, and he shall go no more out: and I will write upon him the name of my God, and the name of the city of my God, which is new Jerusalem, which cometh down out of heaven from my God: and I will write upon him my new name.

Abraham and all the faithful will have eternal, complete, and irrefutable identity with the living God. Like the Jews, let us remember the heart's cry of our destiny: Next year in Jerusalem!

19

TRANSDIMENSIONAL RAIDERS, THE DEMONS

In Christian thought, the dark world of the Devil and his demons is always just below the surface. Sometimes, in dark, occultic tales or chance encounters with demonic phenomena, it emerges full-blown into a wave of fear that must be put into the perspective of God's love. The nonspiritual usually snicker at the very idea of a world of demons, relegating them to the level of myth or fantasy.

However, in our continuing discussion of biblical time-space, we must frankly address the pursuits and ultimate destiny of the demons. Jesus and the apostles made it perfectly clear that we must not be naïve about the world of darkness.

There is a war going on. It is staged between this dimension and the one just beyond our sight. In the regions of earth, wars are accompanied by soldiers, spies, traitors, money, politics, and all manner of treachery. And so it is in the spirit world.

As the Bible describes the great conflict, the legions of hell are bent upon covertly undermining and overtly raiding the dimension that we know as our daily reality. They are best described as transdimensional raiders. Because our world is populated with fallen creatures, these raiders regard us as fair game. Without the coverage of the Lord's Holy Spirit, human beings are quite vulnerable to their ploys.

Demons aren't stupid. They have many methods, schemes, and tricks. Their *modus operandi* is to discern a point of weakness and enter there. Having gained access, they advance the cause of their lord, Satan.

As delineated in chapter four, they are organized under his leadership through a descending chain of command, ranked as *archons* (principalities), *exousions* (authorities), *kosmokrators* (rulers), and *pneumatikons* (spiritual underlings).

Their hierarchy (perhaps it would be more appropriate to call it a "lowerarchy") is entirely devoted to thwarting the Lord's redemptive plan. Their unseen dimension seems concentrated around planet earth, although it may extend to the distant reaches of the solar system. Their leader operates on the assumption that Satan is lord of the planet. God seems to have granted him that mandate. Satan's dealings with Job provide ample testimony that he has been granted an earthly domain. The Lord allows him to torment Job, just short of taking his life: "And the LORD said unto Satan, Behold, all that he hath is in thy power; only upon himself put not forth thine hand. So Satan went forth from the presence of the LORD" (Job 1:12).

Satan operates as a spiritual overlord. But the dark spirits who are his lackeys and underlings appear to function as a bureaucracy. Like most earthly bureaucracies, efficiency is sacrificed to slavish obedience. One gets the strong sense that the fallen of this world are not in any way happy or blessed. Rather, they function as automatons, going through the motions of obedience, at the same time, desperately seeking some resolution of their own miserable condition.

One of the most well-known books by Christian apologist C. S. Lewis deals with this very subject. *The Screwtape Letters* depicts hell's daily drudgery in an amusing but sharply critical way. Author Lewis claims to have somehow come into possession of letters from Screwtape to his nephew Wormwood.

His letters are preoccupied with instructing his underling nephew in the ways of demoralizing and destabilizing his human "patients." With diabolical patience and cunning, he shows Wormwood how to lure them away from any hope of redemption.

The uncle seems to operate at a mid to upper level of management in the bureaucracy of hell. He could be a "ruler," or perhaps an "authority." The nephew does the dirty work at street level. He deals in subtle propaganda and allure. His ploys seem part of the competitive corporate hum. He functions as a cog in a multilevel competitive enterprise that is bent on harvesting human souls for its own use.[65]

If demons have a motive, it is to save themselves from some dark fate that has haunted them since the days of Satan's fall. They operate under eternal guilt; they know they are wrong and that they will be judged. They must, therefore, suffer an extraordinary, constant fear that they will be caught and punished by the Great Judge.

In the New Testament, we have an excellent example of their situation. There, we find an account that brings demons face-to-face with Jesus. In the process, we discover the way in which He views the problem of their existence:

> And when he was come to the other side into the country
> of the Gergesenes, there met him two possessed with devils,
> coming out of the tombs, exceeding fierce, so that no man
> might pass by that way.
>
> And, behold, they cried out, saying, What have we to do
> with thee, Jesus, thou Son of God? art thou come hither to
> torment us before the time?
>
> And there was a good way off from them an herd of many
> swine feeding.
>
> So the devils besought him, saying, If thou cast us out,
> suffer us to go away into the herd of swine.
>
> And he said unto them, Go. And when they were come
> out, they went into the herd of swine: and, behold, the whole
> herd of swine ran violently down a steep place into the sea, and
> perished in the waters.

And they that kept them fled, and went their ways into the city, and told every thing, and what was befallen to the possessed of the devils.

And, behold, the whole city came out to meet Jesus: and when they saw him, they besought him that he would depart out of their coasts. (Matthew 8:28–32)

THE DEMONS KNOW THE TIME

This incident, recorded here by Matthew, and also by Mark and Luke, affords us a remarkable view of the relationship between the Lord of the universe and the hordes of corrupt evil spirits who haunt the world of men.

In all three accounts of the incident, it comes immediately after Jesus had preached in Galilee. He and His disciples entered a boat with the intention of crossing the Sea of Galilee. A storm arose and threatened to swamp their little craft, but Jesus stilled the winds. The sea calmed and they sailed to the east coast of the sea.

Arriving at a little seaside village called Gergesa (still there today as the town of Kursi), they encountered two demon-possessed men. These men are described as "exceedingly fierce," from the Greek word *chalepos*. It means "difficult to handle, or ragingly insane." They are possessed with demons, spirits whose normal state is disembodiment, but who seek to inhabit the physical bodies of living creatures. In an episode we will later examine, Jesus describes them as wandering in a desert in search of a home.

We cannot know the exact nature of this "desert," but one thing is certain. It is not a pleasant place. But as intolerable as it must be, it is still better than their ultimate destination in the lake of fire. The story of the men's encounter with Jesus makes this abundantly clear.

The first and most amazing thing that we discover in the narrative is that the demons recognize Jesus. The people of Gergesa and Gadara certainly did not. Gadara, mentioned as a capital of the local people in

Mark's and Luke's account of this episode, is about six miles east of the sea. This region, to the east of the sea and the Jordan River, was called "The Decapolis." Its Aramean population was composed of a multitudinous jumble of pagans who were the hapless inheritors of generations of Seleucid rule.

Demonic power always rises to its greatest extent in such a culture. And in this simple encounter, we learn that in the dimension of the dark spirits there is common knowledge of the spiritual battle that rages just beyond the visual range of ordinary human beings.

Think of it…the demons not only knew the real identity of Jesus, but they acknowledged him as Lord, calling Him "Son of God." Not even His closest disciples had come to realize that He was the God incarnate. Though they had some dim recognition of His status, at this time, they were still thinking of him as the political "Messiah ben David" who had come to restore David's throne and defeat their Gentile oppressors.

Neither the Jews nor the Gentiles of the day had come to realize His true identity. In the entire Old Testament, the term is used only once, in the book of Daniel, where the three Hebrew men were bound and thrown into Nebuchadnezzar's fiery furnace. There appeared with them a fourth man, whom Nebuchadnezzar himself described as having the form of the "Son of God."

In the New Testament, this title is first used in the fourth chapter of Matthew, where Jesus is tempted by the devil. Twice, the old Serpent calls Him the "Son of God." These incidents tell us that from the top down, the demonic world knew the truth about Jesus. They knew that He had come to earth on a mission as the Son of God, to redeem this sin-wracked place. And they knew that if He succeeded on this mission, they were doomed.

As the angel Gabriel told Mary, this title would accompany His incarnation: "And the angel answered and said unto her, The Holy Ghost shall come upon thee, and the power of the Highest shall overshadow thee: therefore also that holy thing which shall be born of thee shall be called the Son of God" (Luke 1:35).

The demons were obviously well informed about the implications of this event. In retrospect, it seems that they were remarkably well informed about both His identity and His power. For example, in the fifth chapter of John, we find a statement whose implications are often overlooked. Humanity has to ponder the extent of its meanings. The demons know it as a living, moment-by-moment reality:

> For the Father judgeth no man, but hath committed all judgment unto the Son: That all men should honour the Son, even as they honour the Father. He that honoureth not the Son honoureth not the Father which hath sent him.
>
> Verily, verily, I say unto you, He that heareth my word, and believeth on him that sent me, hath everlasting life, and shall not come into condemnation; but is passed from death unto life.
>
> Verily, verily, I say unto you, The hour is coming, and now is, when the dead shall hear the voice of the Son of God: and they that hear shall live.
>
> For as the Father hath life in himself; so hath he given to the Son to have life in himself; And hath given him authority to execute judgment also, because he is the Son of man.
>
> Marvel not at this: for the hour is coming, in the which all that are in the graves shall hear his voice, And shall come forth; they that have done good, unto the resurrection of life; and they that have done evil, unto the resurrection of damnation. (John 5:22–29)

This remarkable passage boldly proclaims the equality of the Son with the Father. But it begins with a statement that the demons know all too well. Namely, that the Father has placed all judgment under the jurisdiction of the Son. James, in his epistle, leaves no doubt that demons understand that the Righteous Judge will one day surely mete out the penalty they deserve: "Thou believest that there is one God; thou doest well: the devils also believe, and tremble" (James 2:19).

And what, precisely, do those demons believe? From their outcry on the eastern shore of the sea, it is obvious that they know of God the Father and His Son. This means that they must also know that He is the Creator, and the Jehovah of the Old Testament. They knew of His incarnation, and must have wondered about all its ramifications. They probably didn't know that He would allow Himself to be crucified on Passover as "the Lamb of God, which taketh away the sin of the world" (John 1:29).

But they certainly knew that this world would never be the same, now that He had arrived.

BEFORE WHAT TIME?

The demons' question to Jesus ("Art thou come hither to torment us before the time?") reveals that they knew He would punish them at an established, future time. Actually, the word "time" here is translated from the Greek *kairos*. This word is used to describe a due season, or a time period when an event or series of events is scheduled to come due. It speaks of something long awaited and sure to happen. It does not speak of duration, but of expectation.

It is more than obvious that the demons expect to be judged at a certain future time. That is, they knew that His first coming was not in judgment. They expressed shock and surprise that Jesus had appeared in face-to-face opposition to men they had possessed.

Of just what "time" were they speaking? In other words, when will the Son of God advance in judgment? Obviously, it is the Day of the Lord, referred to by Jesus as the Great Tribulation, called "the hour of his judgment" in Revelation 14:7.

Among the spirit beings of heaven, this "time" has been well-known for ages past. And on earth, from the dawn of the human race, it has been prophesied as the coming of the Lord. We call it "the Second Coming." Since His First Coming, we have a pretty good idea of how the events of the judgment will proceed. Most probably, the dark spirits did not know the details of His incarnation and Resurrection. Nor did they know about the subsequent formation of His called-out body of believers, the church.

But they knew He was coming. And so did the earliest members of Adam's family:

> And Enoch also, the seventh from Adam, prophesied of these, saying, Behold, the Lord cometh with ten thousands of his saints,
>
> To execute judgment upon all, and to convince all that are ungodly among them of all their ungodly deeds which they have ungodly committed, and of all their hard speeches which ungodly sinners have spoken against him. (Jude 14, 15)

The demons obviously know about this future time. And the demons who met Jesus that day were deeply fearful, begging Him not to cast them into a place from which they would not be able to return. Apparently, Jesus could have sent them to dark chambers of imprisonment and torment.

But they implored Him that when they were cast out, they would be allowed to possess a nearby herd of swine. This He did, and when the demons inhabited those pigs, they stampeded madly down an embankment and into the sea. Apparently, they had committed suicide.

DRY PLACES

Why? Because no matter how uncomfortable their present situation as wandering spirits, it was still preferable to imprisonment...or worse. Actually, we don't really know what Jesus had planned to do to them.

But much of His public ministry was devoted to casting out demons. In fact, the sages of ancient Israel had always taught that Messiah could be recognized by His ability to cast out the dumb demon. This dark spirit has the power to completely captivate a person so that he is unable to speak. Jesus accomplished this feat, as recorded in Matthew 12:22: "Then was brought unto him one possessed with a devil, blind, and dumb: and he healed him, insomuch that the blind and dumb both spake and saw."

The crowd watching this amazing event immediately demanded that Jesus be recognized as Messiah. The Pharisees, on the other hand, accused Jesus of calling upon Beelzebub to cast out the demons.

In the dialogue that followed, Jesus rebuked the Pharisees who demanded that He perform a sign to validate His Messianic claim. In His criticism, He described the phenomenon of demon possession. He likened Israel to a man who had been cleansed of a demon, only to have it return to take up residence again. Being comfortable, this demon then invites his best friends to come and share his attractive abode!

The Israel of Jesus' day had once again fallen into apostasy and idolatry. This rendered the nation vulnerable to demonic assault. In the past, there had been revivals, but the demons of satanic worship returned... first one, then many:

> When the unclean spirit is gone out of a man, he walketh
> through dry places, seeking rest, and findeth none. Then he
> saith, I will return into my house from whence I came out; and
> when he is come, he findeth it empty, swept, and garnished.
> Then goeth he, and taketh with himself seven other spirits
> more wicked than himself, and they enter in and dwell there:
> and the last state of that man is worse than the first. Even so
> shall it be also unto this wicked generation.
> (Matthew 12:43–45)

Demons seem to regard human habitation as a house, perhaps a home. Jesus refers to their natural place of habitation as "dry places." One thinks of trackless deserts, where no comfort can be found. There is only stark discomfort, without amenities of any kind. Food, water, lodging, and any sense of belonging are totally absent. Demons wander in a hostile land, the land of hell, or hades.

We are immediately reminded of the rich man in hades (Luke 16:19ff.) who was in torment, desiring even a drop of water to cool his tongue. Like the demons, the rich man was consigned to a place of homeless torment, awaiting the final judgment.

What is Hell?

As we have often noted, the underworld is a very real place. In the Old Testament, it is a place of waiting. Sheol is both the place of Abraham's abode and the habitat of imprisoned spirits. It seems to be a parallel dimension that is very close to the one we call reality. Between us and the region of the spirits, the veil is quite thin.

We have an excellent illustration of this in the life of Israel's ancient King Saul. Because of his failure to execute the Lord's command to destroy Amalek, he had been banished from the throne to be replaced by David. From then on, he was obsessed by the consequences of his own failure and Israel's subsequent calamities. The prophet Samuel, upon whom Saul had deeply depended for advice and spiritual counsel, had recently died. Saul was inconsolable. Somehow, he knew he had to speak with Samuel.

In desperation, he visited a woman at Endor who had a "familiar spirit." In modern terms, we would call her a spirit medium. She was practicing the iniquitous art called "necromancy"—calling up the spirits of the departed. With the help of an intruding demon, she was able to communicate with the underworld. Saul, who had recently banned all necromancers from the land of Israel, knew very well that he was breaking God's Law. Nevertheless, he instructed her to bring back the spirit of the departed Samuel:

Then said the woman, Whom shall I bring up unto thee? And he said, Bring me up Samuel. And when the woman saw Samuel, she cried with a loud voice: and the woman spake to Saul, saying, Why hast thou deceived me? for thou art Saul.

And the king said unto her, Be not afraid: for what sawest thou? And the woman said unto Saul, I saw gods ascending out of the earth. And he said unto her, What form is he of? And she said, An old man cometh up; and he is covered with a mantle. And Saul perceived that it was Samuel, and he stooped with his face to the ground, and bowed himself.

And Samuel said to Saul, Why hast thou disquieted me, to bring me up? And Saul answered, I am sore distressed; for the Philistines make war against me, and God is departed from me, and answereth me no more, neither by prophets, nor by dreams: therefore I have called thee, that thou mayest make known unto me what I shall do. (1 Samuel 28:12–15)

The brazen and willful Saul had spawned a wicked act. Samuel had been rousted from his place of rest in sheol…Abraham's bosom. This was not supposed to happen. Through his prophets, God had made it plain that the underworld was to remain inviolable.

But this remarkable incident shows us that if one chooses to break God's law, it is a simple thing to violate the barrier that stands between us and the world of the spirits. Saul, in disguise, had tricked the medium into calling up Samuel. When he arrived—to the shocked surprise of the woman—the chicanery was exposed, and an angered Samuel delivered the ex-king a horrible decree: "Moreover the LORD will also deliver Israel with thee into the hand of the Philistines: and to morrow shalt thou and thy sons be with me: the LORD also shall deliver the host of Israel into the hand of the Philistines" (1 Samuel 28:19).

The deposed Saul had received a death sentence. In his arrogant selfishness, he had gone too far. Even after death, Samuel spoke the prophetic word that Saul and his sons would die. And that they did—in ignominious defeat at the hands of the Philistines. Deprived even of the death of a warrior hero, the wounded Saul fell upon his own sword.

The medium of Endor had opened a forbidden door to the spirit world. In a split second, the spirits instantly enabled her to discern Saul's true identity. Having done so, she cried out in fright, because the monarch had lately banned all necromancers from the land. But he assured her that he was only interested in obtaining an audience with the dead prophet. He asked her what she saw, and she told him she "saw gods ascending out of the earth."

In Hebrew, she used the term for "gods" or "celestial beings" coming up from beneath the earth (that is, from sheol). She seems actually to have been shocked when Samuel arose, wearing his prophet's mantel, the *miel* (מְעִיל) that had been a badge of his earthly office.

She had prophesied by the *ob* (בָאוֹב), a familiar spirit who would do her bidding, but Samuel appeared in a powerful way that exercised authority over her accustomed spirit guide. Of course, Saul knew all too well that the Law of Moses strictly forbade his illicit activities:

> There shall not be found among you any one that maketh his son or his daughter to pass through the fire, or that useth divination, or an observer of times, or an enchanter, or a witch, Or a charmer, or a consulter with familiar spirits, or a wizard, or a necromancer.
>
> For all that do these things are an abomination unto the LORD: and because of these abominations the LORD thy God doth drive them out from before thee.
> (Deuteronomy 18:10–12)

Obtaining access to forbidden powers can be accomplished through a variety of occult practices. The black arts run the gamut from infant sacrifice through astrology, drug-induced trances, dark invocations, mediumship, and sorcery. The Lord has forbidden them all.

The reason seems obvious. Sinful man desires power, and believes that he can manipulate the forces and beings of the other world to his own advantage. Actually, he is playing the fool. He is the one being manipulated...by beings with wicked experience that extends back into the distant past. It is for man's own good that he is warned away from contact with the dark spirits.

But why hasn't the Lord simply made the veil so strong that it can't be penetrated? The Bible's answer is that Satan has some prescriptive right to this planet. He was allowed into the Garden of Eden to tempt the first couple. His fallen angels were allowed to enter this dimension and corrupt the human genome. They coupled with earth's women, producing a strain of monsters whose souls were beyond redemption.

After the Flood of Noah, he allowed the same spirits to influence the worship of the Babylonians, Medo-Persians, Greeks, and Romans. In fact, the native residents of all of the world's continents had systems of worship based upon the dragon, the serpent, and the demons. In China, the dragon is still exalted. If you doubt it, visit the nearest Chinese restaurant. In the ancient Americas, the feathered serpent was honored as the source of all power.

Sorcerers and shamans have long practiced the art of penetrating the forbidden veil. Rather than closing it, the Lord gives His redeemed the choice of avoiding it...or not. In His grace, He extends to man the honor of making the proper choice. Then, through His Spirit, He has given man the power to uphold that choice.

The spirit leaders of hades apparently have the power to wage war, but the focal point of their assault is the body of the redeemed. Jesus once plainly told His disciples that these powers (He called them "gates") would be a constant threat, but in the end, would be vanquished: "And I say also unto thee, That thou art Peter, and upon this rock I will build my church; and the gates of hell shall not prevail against it" (Matthew 16:18).

In the rules of warfare, He has forbidden any form of communication between this world and the underworld...hades.

THE WAITING PLACE EMPTIED

Since the Resurrection of Christ, the abode of Abraham and the departed faithful has been transferred to another region, leaving only the damned in hades. When He arose, the veil of Herod's Temple was torn in two. There was an earthquake, and "many bodies of the saints which slept arose, And came out of the graves after his resurrection, and went into the holy city, and appeared unto many" (Matthew 27:52, 53).

There is a common belief that in the process of fulfilling all the aspects of His Resurrection, Christ took the Old Testament saints from the abode of Abraham in their underworld paradise to the Kingdom of Heaven.

The redeemed of the Old Testament were taken up to await the general resurrection. From that time forward, the redeemed who pass from this world are immediately ushered into the presence of the Lord in heaven. The spiritual fulfillments of Christ's sacrifice have made this possible.

As Paul puts it, Christ escorted "captivity" (the Old Testament saints) into their heavenly home, after first descending into the underworld to gather them. Even the fathers of the early church expressed the belief that Jesus had taken these saints to the throne of God:

> Wherefore he saith, When he ascended up on high, he led
> captivity captive, and gave gifts unto men. (Now that he
> ascended, what is it but that he also descended first into the
> lower parts of the earth? He that descended is the same also that
> ascended up far above all heavens, that he might fill all things.)
> (Ephesians 4:8–10)

During that descent into hades, Jesus defeated the *archons* and their delegated authorities. Perhaps the dark spirits had believed that some day, even Abraham and the redeemed might fall into their hands. But when Jesus entered their domain, He took from them any hope of possessing the saints. He "spoiled" them…taking from them any hope of gain or treasure: "And having spoiled principalities and powers, he made a show of them openly, triumphing over them in it" (Colossians 2:15).

In a triumphal parade, He led paradise into the realms of heaven. Left in the ruined remains of the underworld, the spirits now languish, derelict in the midst of wreckage. They must be a depressed lot, since Jesus also chose the time of His momentous victory to announce His

GARY STEARMAN

triumph. From that point forward, there could be no possible doubt among the damned that their ultimate judgment was now a certainty:

> For Christ also hath once suffered for sins, the just for the unjust, that he might bring us to God, being put to death in the flesh, but quickened by the Spirit:
>
> By which also he went and preached unto the spirits in prison; Which sometime were disobedient, when once the longsuffering of God waited in the days of Noah, while the ark was a preparing, wherein few, that is, eight souls were saved by water. (1 Peter 3:18–20)

When Jesus descended into hades, it was as a conquering hero. He proclaimed that His sacrifice upon the Cross had sealed the rift caused by sin, both in heaven and upon earth.

We must wait to find out what He actually told them. Most probably, He explained to them that His sacrifice had pleased the Father in heaven. Beyond that, He must certainly have informed them that His right to the throne of planet earth was now secured. Satan, their leader, had been deposed by this action. All that remained was a "clean-up" period among the men on the surface of the earth.

Within the context of these verses, we also learn that the ringleaders of the underworld are imprisoned there because they tampered with the human race in the ancient antediluvian world. We have often recounted their crimes among the men of Noah's day.

Their sentence is ruin, imprisonment, and death. Their legacy is spiritual and physical degeneracy. The residue of their crimes rains down on earth like nuclear fallout. Storm clouds of swarming demonic spirits swirl overhead, raging with winds, and lightning. Among men waves of fog envelop the unsuspecting and the reprobate, who are quietly spirited away into the realms of death. Hades is around every street corner.

But the body of Christ is empowered to walk through fog and storm, secure in the knowledge that He has already won the victory. This "hell on earth" is manifested in the daily barrage of self-styled, arrogant, immoral frauds, and criminals that parade through the daily news:

> This know also, that in the last days perilous times shall come. For men shall be lovers of their own selves, covetous, boasters, proud, blasphemers, disobedient to parents, unthankful, unholy, Without natural affection, trucebreakers, false accusers, incontinent, fierce, despisers of those that are good, Traitors, heady, highminded, lovers of pleasures more than lovers of God; Having a form of godliness, but denying the power thereof: from such turn away. (2 Timothy 3:1)

Paul's prophetic pronouncement to Timothy and the faithful who live today has a curious connection with the demonic world. Earlier, we looked at Jesus' encounter with the demon-possessed men on the eastern shore of the Sea of Galilee. As noted, they are described as "exceedingly fierce," from the Greek word *chalepos.*

This Greek term is used only twice in the entire New Testament. The other place is here, in Paul's letter to Timothy. When he uses the term "perilous" to describe the prophesied season of psycho-social chaos, it is translated from that same term, *chalepos.*

In other words, the raging insanity of the demoniacs beside the sea will become the environmental norm for latter-day society. The demonic will become openly visible. The stark realization of where this will soon take us might cause our blood to run cold, if it weren't for one fact: Jesus is as powerful and authoritative today as He was in that ancient seaside encounter. He does triumph.

THE DEATH OF HADES

Hades is still in operation today, but not for long. Its days are numbered. Once, Jesus warned His listeners that whoever would offend one of the little children (a metaphor for those who come to God through Christ as little children) would be thrown into the fire of hell.

He told them that if one's hand, foot, or eye were to be an offense, it would be better to remove them than enter hell with the body intact. Of course, He was speaking metaphorically. The hand can represent either an act of charity or of theft. The foot can either carry the gospel of peace or the fire of war. The eye can oversee either love or hate, charity or covetousness.

But the fact remains, Jesus warned about hell: "And if thy hand offend thee, cut it off: it is better for thee to enter into life maimed, than having two hands to go into hell, into the fire that never shall be quenched: Where their worm dieth not, and the fire is not quenched" (Mark 9:43, 44).

Three times, Jesus repeats the warning about going into hell. Three times, He describes it with the powerful imagery of the immortal worm and the unquenchable fire. In fact, He is quoting from the Old Testament, and the final words of the prophet Isaiah: "And they shall go forth, and look upon the carcasses of the men that have transgressed against me: for their worm shall not die, neither shall their fire be quenched; and they shall be an abhorring unto all flesh" (Isaiah 66:24).

This is the last verse of Isaiah's prophecy. It tells about the final disposition of the spirit world, the new heavens and earth, and the eternal state of the wicked.

When Jesus quotes Isaiah, He too invokes the vision of the far future. In the passage recorded by Mark, Jesus uses the word "hell" three times. All three times, He uses the word "Gehenna." He is not speaking of hades, but of the final disposition of hades. Gehenna, once the burning garbage pit outside Jerusalem's walls, becomes the symbol of the eternal lake of fire.

At the final judgment, even hades will be destroyed there. At the Great White Throne, hades (mentioned in the following verses as "hell") will, itself, be thrown into the ever-burning refuse pit called "the lake of fire":

And the sea gave up the dead which were in it; and death and hell delivered up the dead which were in them: and they were judged every man according to their works. And death and hell were cast into the lake of fire. This is the second death. And whosoever was not found written in the book of life was cast into the lake of fire. (Revelation 20:13–15)

And so, just as paradise was taken to heaven, hades will be taken to the Lake of Fire. It appears that an entire *dimension* will be forever taken out of the way. The base from which the transdimensional raiders we call "demons" stage their invasions will be no more.

When Jesus spoke of hell, He already knew of the final judgment, for He was already the final Judge. Let us be more and more aware of this as hades edges more and more deeply into our daily lives.

20

FROM PATMOS TO PERSIA:
BACK FROM THE FUTURE

The more we examine the Lord's time-space creation, the more obvious it becomes that He constructed time and the physical universe for at least one purpose—namely, the stage upon which the redemption of humankind would be played out. He foreknew that the sin and chaos of this system would ultimately bring forth a new heaven and earth, and a new people who would glorify His Name.

As the Word, the Lord created time as a kind of matrix upon which would be built His creation, both in ancient days and in the world to come. To Him, they are universally accessible. He is omnipresent because He has access to the entire timeline. He is omniscient because all its information is readily available to Him.

A bit later, we will observe two specific instances in which the Lord traveled through time in order to visit two different men, each of whom was given the responsibility of writing a prophecy. Taken together, these two prophecies are like bookends that link the Old and New Testaments in a very special way.

Before we look at these two men, let us recall His act of Creation, as related in John chapter 1:

In the beginning was the Word, and the Word was with God, and the Word was God. The same was in the beginning with God.

All things were made by him; and without him was not any thing made that was made. In him was life; and the life was the light of men. And the light shineth in darkness; and the darkness comprehended it not.

There was a man sent from God, whose name was John. The same came for a witness, to bear witness of the Light, that all men through him might believe. (John 1:1–7)

In these verses, we are given the plain and marvelous truth about creation. Jewish sages had taught all along that the Word of Creation spoke the universe into existence with the twenty-two letters of the Hebrew alphabet. John opens his Gospel with a concise and unmistakable statement to this effect. Any Jew familiar with the Talmudic and rabbinic traditions taught in the centuries after Christ's Ascension would understand this concept.

These verses speak of the origin of all that is—brought into existence from absolutely nothing. Something being created from nothing is completely outside human experience.

Not only that, but the Word made everything exclusively. That is, nothing exists that He didn't make. Here, we are also told that the Word is the originator of life. From the human perspective, life is indefinable. More than just an electrochemical process, it is the inexpressible spark that empowers all living, breathing things. No one has ever really defined the nature of life, but anyone can recognize it. Whether a thing is alive or dead is instantly obvious to even the most unthinking of observers. Life is blatantly and immediately obvious.

He is life, and transmitted something of Himself into this universe. But in this world of sin and disarray, life is also time-limited. This, in fact, is the key to understanding God's prophetic plan, which is like a repeated pattern: "The days of our years are threescore years and ten; and if by reason of strength they be fourscore years, yet is their strength labour and sorrow; for it is soon cut off, and we fly away" (Psalm 90:10).

He created all matter and energy and the space to contain them. Then He gave life to the living. Originally, it was life eternal, but when sin entered the world, it was limited to a brief period. These things are well known and often discussed.

But it is not commonly taught that these verses also speak of the creation of *time*. Verse one speaks of a "beginning." What does this word mean? It is translated from the Greek, *arche* (αρχη), meaning "first" or "beginning." It literally refers to the beginning of time-space, or as we think of it, the timeline. It might be said that an accurate translation of this phrase is, "In the beginning of time."

A moment's reflection reveals that the Lord, functioning as the Word, created what we call "time." In the first chapter of Genesis, He is called *God*. Again, His actions commence *in the beginning*. Here, the Hebrew word is *rehshit* (ראשית), meaning "beginning," "chief," or "first." But like its Greek equivalent, this word also indicates the "first phase, step, or element in a course of events." Just as in John 1:1, the Bible's first words describe the creation of the timeline:

> In the beginning God created the heaven and the earth. And the earth was without form, and void; and darkness was upon the face of the deep. And the Spirit of God moved upon the face of the waters.
>
> And God said, Let there be light: and there was light. And God saw the light, that it was good: and God divided the light from the darkness. And God called the light Day, and the darkness he called Night. And the evening and the morning were the first day. (Genesis 1:1–5)

The Lord's Days

The timeline is measured in days, this being the first. These scriptural days are not the same as the mundane, routine passage of the sun and moon that mark the days of human events. They are, in fact, the elements of a creation, which began at a finite point in history, rolling inexorably forward to reveal the unfolding of God's sovereign plan.

The seven days of Creation are, in fact, a pattern upon which is built God's redemptive plan for mankind. He sees them as complete and resolved—a view that is only possible when one stands outside the timeline.

Wherever we look in the Bible, time is used as a sort of device that brings closure within a series of inevitable steps that mark the approach of the Lord's final judgment. The twelfth chapter of Revelation is one of Scripture's most obvious statements of this principle: "Therefore rejoice, ye heavens, and ye that dwell in them. Woe to the inhabiters of the earth and of the sea! for the devil is come down unto you, having great wrath, because he knoweth that he hath but a short time" (Revelation 12:12).

The devil began in the eternal state, an anointed cherub at the throne of God. There, he failed the test of temptation, imagining himself as an equal with God. His horrendous offense had eternal consequences, disrupting the heavenly order. But the results of that sin extended even to the physical universe of time-space, and to the human realm.

Acting judicially, God brought the eternal sin of the old Serpent down to the world of finite time-space. The once-glorious cherub was brought into a time-limited environment, where his end is ignominious prosecution and incarceration: "Yet thou shalt be brought down to hell, to the sides of the pit. They that see thee shall narrowly look upon thee, and consider thee, saying, Is this the man that made the earth to tremble, that did shake kingdoms" (Isaiah 14:15, 16).

The beautiful being of eternal glory, now distorted by evil, is thus prosecuted and sentenced in time-space before being cast into the eternity of hell and an inescapable pit.

Time is no accident; it has purpose and meaning. Whatever happens in time-space will forever stand as an exhibit of Satan's folly versus God's intelligence and glory.

GARY STEARMAN

Two Men and Two Times

Now, back to the two men mentioned earlier. They are the prophet Daniel and the apostle John. These men stand as excellent examples of the biblical view of time…namely, that it is a barrier only to those confined to the physical world. From the Lord's perspective, time is tantamount to a series of names, places, addresses, and locations that He can visit at will.

As recorded in the tenth chapter of Daniel, the Lord traveled in time to visit Daniel. The prophet earnestly prayed concerning his people, and three weeks later, the Lord came to him. The date was about 536 BC, under the reign of Cyrus, king of the Persians. About two years before, a vanguard of Jewish exiles had, with the permission of Cyrus, returned to Israel to rebuild Jerusalem and the Temple. They faced enormous obstacles.

Doubtless, Daniel had heard about the miserable conditions they encountered back in his homeland. Enemies of the Hebrew people were rampant there. The Temple had been ransacked and lay in ruin. The work of rebuilding proceeded at a snail's pace amidst fighting and political chaos.

Now, at the time of Passover, Daniel lamented what had once been a time of celebration, during the first of the year's three pilgrimage festivals. He was probably in some state of deep sorrow at the realization that the few who had returned were faced with almost insurmountable obstacles. Though the altar of burnt offering had been rebuilt, the old men who had seen the Temple in its glory wept and mourned that it would never again be the same.

Under these mournful conditions, Daniel fasted and prayed to the Lord. Most probably, he inquired about Israel's future, imploring the Lord to restore the nation's lost blessing:

> In the third year of Cyrus king of Persia a thing was revealed unto Daniel, whose name was called Belteshazzar; and the thing was true, but the time appointed was long: and he

understood the thing, and had understanding of the vision. In those days I Daniel was mourning three full weeks. I ate no pleasant bread, neither came flesh nor wine in my mouth, neither did I anoint myself at all, till three whole weeks were fulfilled.

And in the four and twentieth day of the first month, as I was by the side of the great river, which is Hiddekel; Then I lifted up mine eyes, and looked, and behold a certain man clothed in linen, whose loins were girded with fine gold of Uphaz:

His body also was like the beryl, and his face as the appearance of lightning, and his eyes as lamps of fire, and his arms and his feet like in colour to polished brass, and the voice of his words like the voice of a multitude.

And I Daniel alone saw the vision: for the men that were with me saw not the vision; but a great quaking fell upon them, so that they fled to hide themselves.

Therefore I was left alone, and saw this great vision, and there remained no strength in me: for my comeliness was turned in me into corruption, and I retained no strength.

Yet heard I the voice of his words: and when I heard the voice of his words, then was I in a deep sleep on my face, and my face toward the ground. (Daniel 10:1–9)

Beginning in the first month—Nisan—Daniel had begun his fast. The first fourteen days took him to Passover, and he grieved that he could not be in Jerusalem at the time of the paschal sacrifice. His fast did not conclude there, but continued on through Passover week, including Unleavened Bread and Firstfruits, the day that later marked our Lord's Resurrection.

Then, on the twenty-first day, he looked up and saw a man whose glorious appearance sent his mind reeling. From our current perspective, the man appeared markedly similar to other manifestations...of the Lord Himself. This man clothed in linen is, in fact, a familiar figure.

Many have likened his vision to that seen by Ezekiel. Decades before Daniel's experience, he had stood by the river Chebar in Babylon when a celestial vehicle swept across the plain and came to rest nearby. Its description includes a view of the Lord's throne:

> And above the firmament that was over their heads was the likeness of a throne, as the appearance of a sapphire stone: and upon the likeness of the throne was the likeness as the appearance of a man above upon it.
>
> And I saw as the colour of amber, as the appearance of fire round about within it, from the appearance of his loins even upward, and from the appearance of his loins even downward, I saw as it were the appearance of fire, and it had brightness round about.
>
> As the appearance of the bow that is in the cloud in the day of rain, so was the appearance of the brightness round about. This was the appearance of the likeness of the glory of the LORD. And when I saw it, I fell upon my face, and I heard a voice of one that spake. (Ezekiel 1:26–28)

Here, Ezekiel encounters someone who looks like a "man." Seated on a sapphire throne beneath a crystal canopy, He has the appearance of fire. Surrounded by a rainbow of glory, He is unmistakably the Lord God. But is He the Jehovah of the Old Testament or the resurrected Christ of the New Testament? Few have bothered to ask this question, but it is quite important. And we would ask the same question about the man in Daniel's vision.

Did Daniel and Ezekiel experience the same person in their visions?

DANIEL'S THEOPHANY

It is vital to understand the man who came to Daniel in the daunting time of the Temple's rebuilding. As the representative of his people,

Daniel was about to receive a specific timeline, and the encouragement that he and his people needed to persevere. The prophecy he received was sweeping in the grandeur of its timeline ("the time appointed was long") and magnificent in its complexity.

Its scope takes the viewer through the reigns of the Persians, Greeks, and Romans through the reign of the Antichrist and the end of the Tribulation. As Daniel stood by the River Hiddekel (Tigris), he was visited by a man clothed in linen, whose body was like a precious stone and whose face was like fire and lightning. His arms and feet resembled polished bronze. So powerful was his appearance that Daniel fell to his face as a dead man.

Many have stated that this visitor must have been an archangel, but it seems more likely that Daniel was personally visited by the Lord. This is the view of C. F. Keil and F. Delitzsch in their *Commentary on the Old Testament*. Speaking of Daniel's vision, they write:

> This heavenly form has thus, it is true, the shining white *talar* [white linen garment] common to the angel, Ezekiel 9:2, but all the other features, as here described—the shining of his body, the brightness of his countenance, his eyes like a lamp of fire, arms and feet like glistering brass, the sound of his speaking— all these point to the revelation of the כבוד יהוה [*kvod Yahweh*, the glory of the Lord], the glorious appearance of the Lord [Ezekiel 1], and teach us that the איש [*ish,* or "man"] seen by Daniel was no common angel-prince, but a manifestation of Jehovah, *i.e.* the Logos [or Word].[66]

There is no doubt that Keil and Delitzsch have done their research well, even to the point of calling this man a manifestation of Jehovah and the Logos, or Word, whom John declares as the Creator of all things.

In a dream, Daniel had already seen the One known to Ezekiel as the "Son of Man." He had beheld him in the *future* context of the final judgment, at the opening of the books of life and death: "I saw in the night visions, and, behold, one like the Son of man came with the clouds of heaven, and came to the Ancient of days, and they brought him near before him" (Daniel 7:13).

Now, in a *theophany,* or appearance of God, the Son of Man had actually come to visit Daniel in person. Keil and Delitzsch emphasize this by stating that what Daniel saw was exactly like the person described in the book of Revelation: "This is placed beyond a doubt by a comparison with Revelation 1:13–15, where the form of the Son of Man whom John saw walking in the midst of the seven golden candlesticks is described like this glorious appearance seen by Ezekiel and Daniel."[67]

In other words Ezekiel, Daniel, and John all saw the Lord God, Creator of heaven and earth, and Ruler of the universe! But in what form did they see Him? The simplest and most direct explanation is that they all saw Him as a real and present *physical* being who had entered into this dimension from eternity—an eternity that encompasses the past, present, and future of our limited, physical dimension.

It is common for Christians to speak of Jehovah, the Lord of the Old Testament, as the "preincarnate" Christ—that is, the Jehovah who deals directly with His covenant people, Israel, came to them in flesh as a tiny baby, born in the physical lineage of the House of David. In so doing, he became the Son of Man, or as Paul calls him, "the second Adam."

As astonishing as it is to think of it, God, the Word, became human. His fleshly appearance was the hope of mankind:

> Let this mind be in you, which was also in Christ Jesus: Who, being in the form of God, thought it not robbery to be equal with God: But made himself of no reputation, and took upon him the form of a servant, and was made in the likeness of men: And being found in fashion as a man, he humbled himself, and became obedient unto death, even the death of the cross.
>
> Wherefore God also hath highly exalted him, and given him a name which is above every name: That at the name of Jesus every knee should bow, of things in heaven, and things in earth, and things under the earth; And that every tongue

should confess that Jesus Christ is Lord, to the glory of God the Father. (Philippians 2:5–11)

In this well-known passage of Scripture, Paul describes the incarnation as a humbling experience…perhaps one of the greatest understatements of all history. Then, after His death upon the Cross, God exalted Him. But now He had a new name, "Jesus," before which the entire created universe must bow in reverent respect.

He descended into flesh as the Word, but He arose as the glorified Christ. Before, He was eternal God; now He is the God-Man, still eternal, but forever human in the sense that humanity was originally intended to be. He is the first of a new race, and is calling out a people to be known by His Name.

When, then, did the Lord become a human being? From the perspective of our timeline, not until His incarnation. Then, and only then, He became a man.

THE SON OF MAN

As earlier mentioned, there is a remarkable similarity between the Lord's visit to Daniel and a similar visit paid to John on the Lord's Day. The parallels between His two appearances are both physical and spiritual. In the Old Testament, we know Him as the Lord who speaks forth creation. In Revelation, He is the Alpha and Omega, another way of expressing the Word:

> I was in the Spirit on the Lord's day, and heard behind me a great voice, as of a trumpet, Saying, I am Alpha and Omega, the first and the last: and, What thou seest, write in a book, and send it unto the seven churches which are in Asia; unto Ephesus, and unto Smyrna, and unto Pergamos, and unto Thyatira, and unto Sardis, and unto Philadelphia, and unto Laodicea.

And I turned to see the voice that spake with me. And being turned, I saw seven golden candlesticks; And in the midst of the seven candlesticks one like unto the Son of man, clothed with a garment down to the foot, and girt about the paps with a golden girdle. His head and his hairs were white like wool, as white as snow; and his eyes were as a flame of fire; And his feet like unto fine brass, as if they burned in a furnace; and his voice as the sound of many waters.

And he had in his right hand seven stars: and out of his mouth went a sharp twoedged sword: and his countenance was as the sun shineth in his strength.

And when I saw him, I fell at his feet as dead. And he laid his right hand upon me, saying unto me, Fear not; I am the first and the last: I am he that liveth, and was dead; and, behold, I am alive for evermore, Amen; and have the keys of hell and of death. (Revelation 1:10–18)

Was John's experience simply a vision, or was it what we would call a physical visit, made by a physical being? Verse 17, above, causes us to opt for the latter, since, when John fell prostrate at His feet, the Lord laid His right hand on him in a consoling gesture.

This event is remarkably similar to that experienced by Daniel. He and his friends were standing by the River Tigris when the Lord came to Daniel. They fled in a panic, and he fell upon his face in a dead faint, just as John did. But as with John, a consoling hand touched him, giving him comfort and strength:

And, behold, an hand touched me, which set me upon my knees and upon the palms of my hands.

And he said unto me, O Daniel, a man greatly beloved, understand the words that I speak unto thee, and stand upright: for unto thee am I now sent. And when he had spoken this word unto me, I stood trembling.

Then said he unto me, Fear not, Daniel: for from the

first day that thou didst set thine heart to understand, and to chasten thyself before thy God, thy words were heard, and I am come for thy words.

But the prince of the kingdom of Persia withstood me one and twenty days: but, lo, Michael, one of the chief princes, came to help me; and I remained there with the kings of Persia. Now I am come to make thee understand what shall befall thy people in the latter days: for yet the vision is for many days. And when he had spoken such words unto me, I set my face toward the ground, and I became dumb. (Daniel 10:10–15)

Upon comparison, Daniel and John both had physical encounters with the same person. Here, Daniel is told that he is about to receive a very special prophetic message pertaining to his people. The vision is long-range, and has to do with the rise and fall of world systems.

Daniel, an Israelite exiled in Persia, is informed of the existence of the "prince," or guardian spirit who watched over the country of his imprisonment. We can speculate that the function of this evil one was to stand with the rulers of Persia, acting to influence them against Israel. It seems likely that the Lord came to remove this evil power from his place of influence.

The Lord was aided by the archangel Michael, whose name in Hebrew means "who is as God." Michael is constantly seen in Scripture as the one who possesses a mighty power very much like that of God. It goes without saying that the glorified Christ didn't need Michael's strength, or even his authority. Why, then, was Michael brought into play?

Most probably, it was a matter of heavenly protocol. Michael was acting as Christ's emissary in the world of angelic powers. This, of course, would be the dimension closest to this earth, where Satan reigns. We know that the devil, his angels, and demons presently have full access to the world order. Here, they circulate freely, undermining morally upright institutions and governments. And here, they are opposed by our Lord's angelic force, apparently headed by Michael. He seems to be the Lord's representative in matters of enforcement and discipline.

Daniel's prayer thus had two consequences. First, through the power of the Lord (enacted by Michael), the dark spiritual power over the then-dominant Persia was displaced. Secondly, the Lord revealed to Daniel a very special view of Israel's destiny in a prophecy that would be sealed until the "time of the end" (Daniel 12:4).

Only in the last few years—since the birth of modern Israel—has it begun to be truly understood. Daniel's prophecy encompasses the millennia from the Babylonian captivity, through the coming of Messiah. It details the Grecian dynasties of the Ptolemies and particularly the Seleucids, out of whom will come the Antichrist. Daniel chronicles parts of his life and rule, bringing his prophecy to a close at the end of the Tribulation period. The scope and detail of his text make it the definitive outline for understanding the outcome of events destined for national Israel.

A Remarkable Parallel

Like Daniel, John was visited by a man in white linen, with a face and eyes of flaming fire. John also witnessed the Lord's feet like burnished bronze. The voice of the risen Christ is likened to the sound of rushing water. This description is quite similar to Daniel's testimonial about hearing the "voice of a multitude." To Daniel, He brought a message critically important to his people, Israel.

To John, He detailed the seven churches. Taken together they represent the cyclical development of all the churches that would exist from Pentecost to the catching away of the church. Of course John was also given the most detailed view we have of the Tribulation period.

John's vision also reveals the true meaning of the ancient menorah. Christ, the Servant Lamp, stands at the center of the seven lamps. He thus displayed Himself as the spiritual center—the Head—of the body of believers, which would be brought together until the moment of their completion at the catching away of the church. The seven lamps are the seven churches.

"And he had in his right hand seven stars." John was told that these represented the seven angels superintending the development of the seven archetypal churches. John saw war, famine, catastrophe, and the Lord's divine judgment in the march toward New Jerusalem, eternal home of the church. Together, Daniel and John bring us a chronicle of the ages—a prophetic panorama that assures believers their faith is not in vain. There will be resolution and glory to the Lord.

BACK FROM THE FUTURE

Two very special men were visited in very similar ways by the Lord of glory. As we have already seen, His appearance as a "man" was identical to both of them. And as we have already suggested, it was a *physical* appearance, as opposed to a *spiritual manifestation* or *vision*.

As commonly envisioned, a spiritual manifestation would be something like a projection or holographic image focused before the eyes of the beholder. Certainly, one good example of this sort of experience is given to us in 1 Samuel 28. Summoned up from the grave by the spirit medium of Endor, the deceased Samuel appeared in this way in the presence of King Saul. This unfortunate incident shows both the reality and the danger of illicit contact with the spirit world.

On the other hand, a vision is a phenomenon of the mind, when a spiritual impression is given with such detail that is appears "real." Not that it isn't real, but it is a different sort of reality. It is a reality of the percipient's spirit and soul. It impresses the mind with such force that it is exactly the same as having a direct experience.

Why insist that the Lord's presence before Daniel and John is physical? Very simply, because it places great emphasis upon the truth of His resurrection. In his first epistle, John places great stress upon this truth. And he does so in the context of an explanation of the Antichrist's belief system:

> Beloved, believe not every spirit, but try the spirits whether they are of God: because many false prophets are gone out into the world.

Hereby know ye the Spirit of God: Every spirit that
confesseth that Jesus Christ is come in the flesh is of God: And
every spirit that confesseth not that Jesus Christ is come in the
flesh is not of God: and this is that spirit of antichrist, whereof
ye have heard that it should come; and even now already is it in
the world.

Ye are of God, little children, and have overcome them:
because greater is he that is in you, than he that is in the world.
(1 John 4:1–4)

John wrote these words sometime around AD 95–96, or perhaps a
little earlier. There is no real date marking their first appearance, but most
expositors place his epistles at or near the end of the reign of Domitian
(AD 81–96). Thus, it is virtually impossible to determine whether or not
they were written before or after John's Revelation experience.

However, it seems quite likely that they were written after his return to
Ephesus following his Patmos exile. He served as bishop of the Ephesian
church until his death. In his *Church History*, Eusebius writes:

> But after Domitian had reigned fifteen years, and Nerva
> succeeded to the government, the Roman senate decreed that
> the honor of Domitian should be revoked, and that those who
> had been unjustly expelled should return to their homes, and
> have their goods restored. This is the statement of the historians
> of the day. It was then also, that the Apostle John returned from
> his banishment in Patmos, and took up his abode at Ephesus,
> according to an ancient tradition of the church.[68]

This historical scenario makes a great deal of sense, particularly when
one reads John's first epistle, where the word "antichrist" is used four
times. This is the only place in the entire Bible that this term can be
found. Bear in mind that in his trip to the future apocalypse, John had
actually seen the beast whose mystery number is "666." With his own
eyes, he had seen the Antichrist's rise to power. If it is, in fact, true that

he wrote his epistles upon his return to Ephesus from Patmos, the reality of the Antichrist would have been firmly implanted in his thinking.

Note in the above Scripture that John stresses the physical nature of the risen Christ, saying that the core belief of the Antichrist system is that Jesus came in "spirit" rather than physical form. During John's lifetime, elitist gnostic theologians had already begun to teach that Jesus was only a spirit being who gave the illusion of a physical body. Even today, we hear that some modern "messiahs" are possessed of the "Christ spirit," making them equal with Jesus. John says this will be the medium of their deceit. The failure to profess Christ's physical reality lies at the very center of all apostasy.

Both before and after Jesus' Resurrection, the Beloved Apostle had touched and been touched by Him. And as we have already seen, the glorified Christ of Revelation had reached down and laid His right hand upon John. Nothing is as reassuring as loving, physical contact.

PRESENT AND FUTURE

When the glorified Christ appeared to John on Patmos, it had been more than sixty years since His Ascension. His appearance is best understood as substantial and corporeal. That is, He simply stepped bodily through the dimensional barrier into John's time-space, *in the present,* where He spoke of the mysteries of the church, the Tribulation, and the world to come. As we have written elsewhere, Jesus then took John into the future…into *our* future, where he personally witnessed many things to come.

He assured John that He was alive, in the human and physical sense of the term: "I am he that liveth, and was dead; and, behold, I am alive for evermore, Amen; and have the keys of hell and of death" (Revelation 1:18).

The One who had begun as Jehovah God had now added to Himself the heritage of Adam. Forevermore, He will carry the stamp of his human experience. Through the apostle John, He assures all believers that they will undergo a like transformation in the Rapture and resurrection.

Christ's bodily appearances to John and Daniel were separated by a span of about 631 years, yet, as we have seen, they were made by one and the same divine Person. Is it really possible that the risen and glorified Christ had traveled back from the future to visit Daniel in physical form? Absolutely!

As we have repeatedly seen, Jesus is the master of time-space. He created it and He supports it "by the word of His power" (Hebrews 1:3).

The distance from Persia to Patmos is perhaps fifteen hundred miles. For the Lord—master of time-space—the trip is no distance at all. And the 631 years between them is no time at all.

As He was to Daniel and John, so is He to us.

21

THE BOOK OF TIME

The Bible is structurally unlike any other book that has ever been written. This is true on many levels. Examining one aspect alone, it is astonishing that the Bible is literally a Book of Time. No other text can make this claim.

The biblical *past* is founded in the Bible's first sentence, Genesis 1:1: "In the beginning God created the heaven and the earth."

Here, we are allowed to observe that God declared a "beginning." By all our understanding of time-space, this tells us that He existed before the "beginning." (If He created the beginning, He had to exist prior to it.) Physicists tell us that our universe is probably something like a bubble that floats in another medium, which they call "another dimension." The Bible simply calls that medium "eternity." Science views our universe as a lesser dimension, floating around inside a greater one.

This verse grounds us with respect to eternity. We cannot refer to it as "eternity past" since it exists always and everywhere. From that perspective, we are told that a clock started ticking "in the beginning." This, we define as "time," organized and presented in Scripture as the canvas upon which the universe is painted. More importantly, it is human history. God created the universe and He created man. To do this, He created *time.*

Now look at the biblical *present.* If the past is at the beginning of the book, then the present should be at its middle. And it is, in the middle chapter of the Bible—Psalm 117: "O praise the LORD, all ye nations: praise him, all ye people. For his merciful kindness is great toward us: and the truth of the LORD endureth for ever. Praise ye the LORD."

Here, at the very center of the Bible, are two brief verses that give the status and perspective of the *present.* What is the present? It is that infinitesimally small moment, poised between past and future...the "moving now" that never stops. Its very essence is *action.* Relative to God, it is motion...either toward Him or away from Him. It is our very existence, and He created it.

Look carefully at the two verses above. They begin and end with praise to the Lord. They urge all nations and peoples to give Him due honor. They invoke the two attributes of His character that appeal to all—merciful kindness and truth. The latter is said to endure forever. The constant progress of the *now* is linked with the stately stability of the *eternal.*

The brevity of this Psalm in no way detracts from its importance, for it presents the theme of the entire Bible.

Only eight verses away from Psalm 117, we find the middle verse of the Bible: "It is better to trust in the LORD than to put confidence in man" (Psalm 118:8).

Note that this verse picks up the theme of Psalm 117 and amplifies it in one simple statement. These words present one with a basic, moment-by-moment choice. You can trust man or the Lord. You can choose, but the better choice is to trust the Lord. His mercy and truth are worthy of trust.

Here, at the center point of the Book of Time, we find the balance point. It is poised upon the central concepts of faith, namely, praise and trust. These are vital realities that form the biblical *present.*

The clock ticks off the seconds of "today." Human history passes at the present moment. From the beginning until right now, the Lord is nurturing his Creation with loving kindness, mercy, and truth. But past and present are not presented as lone and isolated quantities. In the Bible, they are intertwined inseparably with the future.

What of the future? How is it defined, and more importantly, how are we related to it? Remarkably, but predictably, the Bible asserts that the future is already accomplished.

All believers have looked ahead to the end of the Book of Time. There, they have seen the unfathomable beauty of a New Jerusalem, set like a jewel in a renewed cosmos, described simply as "a new heaven and a new earth." What became of the old order? Ravaged by sin and entropy—the depletion of energy—it was cast aside as a worn-out garment.

The future displays an entirely new order of things:

> And there shall be no more curse: but the throne of God and
> of the Lamb shall be in it; and his servants shall serve him: And
> they shall see his face; and his name shall be in their foreheads.
> And there shall be no night there; and they need no candle,
> neither light of the sun; for the Lord God giveth them light:
> and they shall reign for ever and ever. (Revelation 22:3–5)

The Book of Time views past, present, and future as a single entity, set in the immense backdrop of eternity. It never separates the context of the past from the future, nor the present from the past. Cause and effect are mentioned in the same breath...the breath of God.

The Master of Time

It is as when Jesus stood up to read Scripture in His local congregation. His precise understanding of past, present, and future is dazzlingly displayed in the following account:

> And he came to Nazareth, where he had been brought up: and,
> as his custom was, he went into the synagogue on the sabbath
> day, and stood up for to read. And there was delivered unto
> him the book of the prophet Esaias. And when he had opened
> the book, he found the place where it was written,

The Spirit of the Lord is upon me, because he hath anointed me to preach the gospel to the poor; he hath sent me to heal the brokenhearted, to preach deliverance to the captives, and recovering of sight to the blind, to set at liberty them that are bruised, To preach the acceptable year of the Lord.

And he closed the book, and he gave it again to the minister, and sat down. And the eyes of all them that were in the synagogue were fastened on him.

And he began to say unto them, This day is this scripture fulfilled in your ears. (Luke 4:16–21)

Elsewhere, we have referred to Jesus as "the Master of Time." He created it and understands its every nuance. Here Jesus literally stopped short in the middle of a sentence in Isaiah. Had He continued, He knew that He would have violated the timeline.

He announced to His audience that a prophecy of the future had been literally fulfilled in their day. The Spirit of the Lord had brought the gospel to Israel. This, He announced, was the year they had all waited for. Past prophecy had become present reality.

Reading from Isaiah, He had quoted chapter 61, verse 1, and the first phrase of Isaiah 61:2. They read as follows, complete with the phrase that Jesus omitted:

The Spirit of the Lord GOD is upon me; because the LORD hath anointed me to preach good tidings unto the meek; he hath sent me to bind up the brokenhearted, to proclaim liberty to the captives, and the opening of the prison to them that are bound; To proclaim the acceptable year of the LORD, and the day of vengeance of our God; to comfort all that mourn.

Jesus knew that the final phrase of verse 2 and the verses that follow specifically speak of the Day of the Lord and beyond. From our current perspective, the comma in the middle of verse 2 represents a time span of nearly two millennia!

Of course, Jesus knew this. When He rolled up the scroll, He tacitly announced that His Word was a precise indicator of time, if only one had the power to decipher it correctly. As the Word made flesh, who dwelt for a time among us, He holds the key to understanding its timing.

Certainly, the biblical timeline is quite precise. But we are guilty of a certain error in perception if we regard it as simply linear. Indeed, it is that, but it is much, much more. In actuality, it is more like a pattern than a line. It views time as a symmetrical balance between past and future. Furthermore, it portrays the future from the same perspective as the past. They are proportionate, and they are one and the same—two parts of the same singularity.

The Menorah and the Dispensations

It is often taught, even from the days of the apostles and before, that the world of man is divided into seven historical days, each a thousand years in length. The seven millennia of human history correspond to the seven days of creation given in the first chapter of Genesis. And just as the seventh day is a day in which the Lord rested, so the seventh millennium will be the day of man's rest in the earthly Kingdom Age. The pattern of the seven dominates all of human history, particularly from the viewpoint of spiritual truth.

We have often observed that the biblical number seven represents a fundamental symmetry. Rather than being a serial continuum from one through seven (the common human way of looking at things), it is two sets of three each, balanced around a center point.

The ancient presence of the menorah in the Tabernacle called attention to this pattern. In a dramatic way, it demonstrated that the power of God enters at the central focus of earthly life, and radiates in both directions.

There, in the Holy Place, it represented God's Holy Spirit, the active principle in man's redemption. Its lamps were carefully tended in a prescribed manner that emphasized the center lamp, called the *shamash*

(שמש), or "servant." Set higher than the others, it was used to rekindle them during cleaning and refueling. It depicted an infusion of power from on high.

But in a larger sense, it also represents time-space and human history. The promised Messiah fulfilled its pattern, coming as He did at the midpoint of the sweeping panorama of the millennia.

Upon His arrival, roughly four thousand years had elapsed since the creation of Adam. He came as Abraham's promised "seed," offering salvation to all who would receive Him by faith. Those four millennia had seen the great crises of sin in the Garden of Eden, the Flood, the Tower of Babel, and Egyptian bondage.

He came as a lowly servant, but nevertheless, as a light that will eventually enlighten the whole world. In this latter sense, He is the "Sun of righteousness" mentioned in Malachi 4:2. The Hebrew word for "sun" is *shemesh* (שמש), spelled the same way as "servant," but pronounced differently. He is both Servant and Sun.

As mentioned in chapter eleven, Flavius Josephus held an idea common with first century Jews. He saw the menorah as the symbol of God's power entering into our solar system. His spirit merges into our physical universe, linking time and eternity—the dimension of heaven with the dimension of earth.

On the basis of this grand perspective, we will examine the Lord's relationship in time, with the oft-mentioned seven dispensations, which depict past, present, and future human history. The seven lamps present a pattern that opens a vista of time-space from man's point of view. They are the seven dispensations of human history—Innocence, Conscience, Human Government, Promise, Law, Grace, and Kingdom—that constitute a sort of parenthesis in the continuum that we call "eternity." And they are keyed to the passing millennia, beginning with creation and ending with the Kingdom. Before Christ was born, four thousand years had passed.

He is the Servant Lamp, and by definition, He stands at the center of time. If this is the case—two thousand years having already elapsed since

His birth—then we still have another two thousand years of history to account for in Scripture.

How then, can we divide the historic periods into meaningful segments?

WHAT IS A DISPENSATION?

In the New Testament, we find the word "dispensation" used in four different verses, each time suggesting a kind of metaphysical truth that cries out for an extended explanation. The term is translated from a Greek term, *oikonomia,* most often used to describe the operation of a household and its internal affairs. The word is compounded from *oikos,* "house," and *nomos,* "law."

Many think of "dispensation" as a term applying primarily to the church (the House of God) and its management. However, as can be seen from the following passage of Scripture, time and the dispensations actually apply to the Lord's entire redemptive program in all its implications and inferences:

In whom we have redemption through his blood, the
forgiveness of sins, according to the riches of his grace; Wherein
he hath abounded toward us in all wisdom and prudence;
Having made known unto us the mystery of his will, according
to his good pleasure which he hath purposed in himself:
That in the **dispensation of the fulness of times** he might
gather together in one all things in Christ, both which are
in heaven, and which are on earth; even in him: In whom
also we have obtained an inheritance, being predestinated
according to the purpose of him who worketh all things after
the counsel of his own will: That we should be to the praise
of his glory, who first trusted in Christ. (Ephesians 1:7–12,
emphasis added)

Note that here Paul uses the term "dispensation" in conjunction with the plural "times," which is here the Greek *kairos,* implying a definite, set period…a season. The plural use of the word here implies more than one of these periods. Taken as a whole, they present a composite picture of the Lord's work. These times will come to fullness. That is, God's grace and truth will ultimately become the one and only standard in this universe.

It is especially important in the light of our current study to observe that these times are pulled together into a progressive completion, affecting developments both on earth and in heaven. Thus two different dimensions—time and eternity—are pulled together into one, unified in Christ. How shall we understand these "times?"

Let's take a brief look at dispensational thinking as it rose to prominence and came to full recognition in the last couple of centuries. Christians who interpret the Bible literally and prophetically tend to take the dispensational interpretation of history for granted.

We forget that many scholars and teachers struggled long and hard to standardize this way of understanding God's plan. Some succeeded; others became so involved in a myriad of detail that they all but lost their way.

In the early years of the nineteenth century, there was an amazing spiritual awakening. Centuries had elapsed since the Reformation, but in terms of understanding the times and seasons, the church continued in slumber. In Europe, the great faiths were still ensconced in granite and marble halls beneath gothic arches. Their priesthoods were bound to king and state.

In the new United States of America, breakaway congregations were struggling to establish themselves in a free and democratic society, but their focus was on evangelism and individual piety. The great missionary movements of the late nineteenth century were still in the future. Furthermore, Israel was still in the depths of the Diaspora. Most Christian denominations still taught the eschatology of Augustine of Hippo (AD 354–430). His fifth-century writings taught that Israel had been set aside and would never again return to the Holy Land, much less grow to become a world power. Following his theological dominance, the concepts of Rapture, Tribulation, and the Second Coming of Christ to establish a Kingdom on the throne of David were either unknown or relegated to the dark status of unwelcome speculation. Centuries passed, and the Dark Ages came and went.

DARBY, BULLINGER, AND SCOFIELD

Things began to change on the spiritual front when a brilliant student by the name of John Nelson Darby entered Dublin's Trinity College in 1815. It was an Anglican instutition and he graduated with highest academic honors. In 1826, he was ordained as an Anglican priest at Christ Church Cathedral in Dublin. But as he later wrote, he was not yet a believer at that time.

His priestly duties continued until the year 1828, when he fell from his horse and suffered a serious fracture of the leg. His convalescence lasted for a full three months, during which time he had an opportunity to read the Bible with complete concentration. He discovered something new.

The biography *John Nelson Darby* by Max S. Weremchuk presents a letter written shortly after Darby's recovery. In part, it says:

> Isaiah 32 it was that taught me about the new dispensation.
> I saw there would be a David[ic] reign, and did not know
> whether the Church might not be removed before 40 years
> time. At that time I was ill with my knee. It gave me peace to
> see what the Church was....
>
> Isaiah 32 brought me to the earthly consequences of the
> same truth, though other passages might seem perhaps more
> striking to me now; but I saw an evident change of dispensation
> in that chapter, when the Spirit would be poured out on the
> Jewish nation, and a king reign in righteousness.[69]

Slowly, Darby came to another foundational truth. Weremchuk writes, "Darby believed that soon after the death of the apostles, believers began wrongly to take Old Testament prophecies and promises and apply them to themselves."[70]

Thus Darby slowly began to think in terms of the church as one order of things, as opposed to the Davidic Kingdom as another—and entirely different—order. He and his followers, "The Brethren," became the leaders of a new Bible study movement dedicated to recovering and teaching the doctrine of the apostles. He firmly believed in the catching-away of the church, to be followed by a new order of events (a dispensation) surrounding the reestablishment of the Davidic Kingdom.

For all this, he never fully propounded a complete picture of the dispensations. The full picture of dispensationalism from Adam to Christ to the present and future awaited the work of other men. Even at the turn of the twentieth century, men like E. W. Bullinger, although professing themselves to be dispensational in outlook, were unable to assemble historical periods into a composite that fit with the two categories of church and Kingdom.

In *The Foundations of Dispensational Truth,* Bullinger saw the dispensations as six in number, roughly as follows:

- Adam to Moses
- Moses to Christ's baptism
- Christ's baptism to His burial
- Acts and the general epistles
- Christ's announcement of the Holy Spirit to the prison epistles
- "His servant John"...Revelation[71]

Bullinger tried very hard to develop a meaningful historical analysis of the Bible. But brilliant as he was, he completely omitted the obvious divisions between Adam, the pre- and post-Flood civilizations, and God's promise to Abraham. Further, he divided the church into three periods, while failing to mention that Revelation's first three chapters are also devoted to the age of the church.

Still, he attempted to divide the times into significant segments. But as can be easily seen, he was preoccupied with fine distinctions rather than natural divisions. In other words, he had not yet fully defined the parameters that distinguish where one dispensation ends and another begins.

Perhaps the most revolutionary dispensational Bible-study document in modern church history was published in 1909 by C. I. Scofield. It was not a book, as such, but was an annotated Bible: *The Scofield Reference Bible.* It laid out Scofield's notes alongside the biblical text. He carefully arranged these annotations to explain the redemptive pattern of God in the now-well-known pattern of seven dispensations.

When it was first published, the Bible study movement—long before begun by Darby and the Brethren—had grown, and was now part of an international missionary movement.

The day in Genesis 1:28, when God instructed Adam and Eve to begin their stewardship (dispensation) of the earth, Scofield called "The First Dispensation." This, he defined in a footnote: "A dispensation is a period of time during which man is tested in respect of obedience to some *specific* revelation of the will of God. Seven such dispensations are distinguished in Scripture."[72]

In each of these, Scofield emphasized God's testing and man's failure to obey His clearly stated will. This resulted in a series of crises, each of which brought the collapse of the faithful, and a new test.

The First Dispensation—Innocence—thus ended with Adam's failure to obey God with respect to the tree in the midst of the garden of Eden and the command to avoid its fruit.

The Second Dispensation—Conscience—ended in the judgment of the Flood.

The Third Dispensation—Human Government—began after Noah and his three sons were charged with setting up a new civilization in which mankind would be ruled by man himself.

The Fourth Dispensation—Promise—came after man fell to idolatry and brutality at the end of the preceding dispensation. Abram was called to go forth to the new land that would become Israel.

The Fifth Dispensation—Law—was instituted by Moses, as the chosen people were delivered from the bondage of Egypt and brought into the Promised Land.

The Sixth Dispensation—Grace—originated with the blood sacrifice of Christ, His Resurrection, and the coming of His Holy Spirit. This dispensation will end with the apostasy of the church and the removal of the faithful remnant before the Tribulation.

The Seventh Dispensation—Kingdom—will be instituted by Jesus' Second Coming to be received as King. This dispensation will also end in a crisis, as followers of Satan arise in rebellion.[73]

Note that the Fourth Dispensation—Promise—occupies the center position among the dispensations. It was God's promise to Abraham that the promised seed (Christ) would come. By faith, Abraham claimed this promise, and all the faithful since are said to have come to Christ in precisely the same way he did.

Again, we see the balance of time. The dispensations are symmetrically arranged around the promise that God made to Abraham. Before his time, we see the periods of Innocence, Conscience, and Civil Government. Afterward come the intervals of Law, Grace, and Kingdom.

THE TEST OF TIME

The operant principle in all seven dispensations is testing, obedience, and discipline. In every case, God gives His people a clear mandate for action, then monitors their daily observance of His command. Time and time again, they fail to keep even His simplest instructions. And time and time again, He sends His prophetic Word through appointed representatives. The prophet's call seems never welcome…and is often met with severe reprisals, even death.

Still, the Lord's love is such that the prophets never give a warning without an accompanying assurance.

In this respect, the prophets also view history as a balance between past and future. For example, Isaiah's sixty-six chapters mirror the sixty-six books of the Bible. Like the books of the Old Testament, the first thirty-nine chapters speak of man's failures and the accumulated judgments that would come because of them. Judah, Israel, Jerusalem, and the nations surrounding them are thoroughly condemned.

But Isaiah's concluding twenty-seven books, corresponding with the layout of the New Testament, are filled with blessings and encouragement. They open with the famous words of Isaiah 40:1, which says, "Comfort ye, comfort ye my people, saith your God."

Once again, we see the familiar pattern in which the future and the past are joined in a single purpose. Time is a fluid whole, in which past foretells future. That purpose is to redeem and establish God's people forever.

The book of Jeremiah also foretells destruction. His sermons condemn Judah's apostasy and idolatry, and the failures of her kings. It rails against Egypt, Philistia, Moab, Ammon, Edom, Damascus, Kedar and Hazor, Elam, and Babylon. It closes with the fall of Jerusalem.

But Jeremiah's prophecy is girded up at its midpoint by the assurance of future restoration. Judah and Israel are mentioned in the context of a reconfirmed covenant:

> And they shall teach no more every man his neighbour, and
> every man his brother, saying, Know the LORD: for they shall
> all know me, from the least of them unto the greatest of them,
> saith the LORD; for I will forgive their iniquity, and I will
> remember their sin no more. (Jeremiah 31:34)

As in all the prophets, the evils of the past are never separated from the blessings of the future. Again, in Ezekiel, it is well known that the prophet begins with the judgment of Judah, in which he describes the departure of God's glory from the Temple. At the same time, he also pronounces judgment upon the Gentiles.

Ezekiel ends with the uplifting picture of Israel's return to the Land

and the supernatural defeat of a great combined Gentile army from the north. Finally, we are treated to his vision of the new Millennial Temple. In his prophecy, the First Temple falls and an even more glorious Third Temple arises. There is no thought of past defeat without future glory.

Daniel's prophecy begins in the terrible wake of the Israel's final destruction by the Babylonians, then reaches out into the far future. His incisive and profound delineations of the four great Gentile world empires is virtually the key to understanding the "times of the Gentiles," the phrase used by Jesus in Luke 21:24.

From the perspective of Daniel's generation, Israel was on the verge of being crushed into nonexistence. His prophecy lays out the solid hope that though the four Gentile empires will grow strong—even to trampling down the Lord's beloved Jerusalem—a final blessing will come. In the end, says Daniel, the archangel Michael will fight for his people during a great "time of trouble" (12:1) that will end in a blessing: "Blessed is he that waiteth, and cometh to the thousand three hundred and five and thirty days" (Daniel 12:12).

Once again, the anguish of Israel's past is never disconnected from her future glory. Among the Minor Prophets, this familiar scenario is seen again and again. Hosea decries Israel's spiritual adultery, but prophesies that the Lord will come again to the House of David…on the third day.

Amos preaches that Israel's coming judgment in the Assyrian captivity is well deserved but ends with five promises that Israel will be restored.

Micah's proclamations condemn Samaria and Jerusalem; Judah is judged. But Micah also brings one of the most encouraging prophecies in the entire Bible. Two hundred and fifty years in advance of the actual event, he forecast the release of the Jews from Babylonian captivity! He saw the king of Israel coming out of Bethlehem.

The point is this: Every transgression of God's people is, in reality, a test that refines a new and divinely ordained remnant of the faithful.

The New Menorah

Earlier, we mentioned the seven lamps of the ancient Tabernacle menorah as the pattern for seven thousand years of human history, each labeled as a day. But actually, if one counts the "New Heavens and New Earth" period in the historical picture, there are eight days.

Interestingly, as we have elsewhere written, the menorah of seven lamps grew into a menorah of eight lamps.

There is another menorah—the lampstand of Hanukkah. Its nine branches commemorate an event that occurred in 165 BC, as a famous man became a type of the Antichrist. His name was Antiochus IV Ephiphanes. He was determined to destroy the Jewish religion by forbidding them to practice the rituals of the Law of Moses.

His actions sparked the Maccabean revolt, in which his armies were finally defeated by heroic Jewish forces. On the 24th day of Kislev of 165 BC—three years to the day after its desecration—the Temple was cleansed and dedicated.

Miraculously, one day's supply of consecrated oil lasted for eight days…until a new supply of oil could be provided. A prophecy in the fourth chapter of Zechariah completes the picture of the miraculous eight. He shows two extra branches at the ends of the seven-branched menorah:

> Then answered I, and said unto him, What are these two olive trees upon the right side of the candlestick and upon the left side thereof?
>
> And I answered again, and said unto him, What be these two olive branches which through the two golden pipes empty the golden oil out of themselves?
>
> And he answered me and said, Knowest thou not what these be? And I said, No, my lord. Then said he, These are the two anointed ones, that stand by the LORD of the whole earth. (Zechariah 4:11–14)

The two olive branches in Zechariah's vision supply the menorah by way of two golden pipes. These may be seen as two arms—one on each side—creating a new menorah of nine branches. This menorah is associated with Hanukkah, and celebrates grace, not the Law of Moses.

This new menorah of grace has a center lamp (*shamash* [שמש]), with four lamps at each side. Remarkably, this results in a pattern of eight elements balanced around a center point, which, of course, represents the coming of Christ.

The four days to the left of the center represent four thousand years, from Adam to Christ. The four days to the left of the center are four thousand years from Christ to the New Heavens and Earth. They would include the two thousand years of the Church Age, the thousand-year Kingdom, and the New Earth, which is a new day of at least a thousand years, but actually of unknown duration.

The Cross stands at the center of these eight days, as a light and witness over all that happens, past, present, and future. Here, we should revisit the phrase that we discussed earlier, "the dispensation of the fullness of times." These times, or seasons, represent the entire timeline, from eternity to eternity: "For it pleased the Father that in him should all fulness dwell; And, having made peace through the blood of his cross, by him to reconcile all things unto himself; by him, I say, whether they be things in earth, or things in heaven" (Colossians 1:19, 20).

In verse 20, the word "reconcile" is a translation of the Greek *apokatallasso,* a word that means "to change radically; to change one thing into another."

Could it be that Christ's final work will radically alter this time-limited universe so that it merges seamlessly with the vaults of eternity? The words of Paul to the Colossians seem to suggest that this is the case. He tells us that the Cross bridged the gap between heaven and earth... between eternity and time.

Is it any wonder then, that the Book of Time—the Bible—presents our entire timeline as a single entity? Thumbing back and forth through the Bible is much like journeying back and forth through time.

Paul was made a steward of this great mystery. The search for the true meaning of a dispensation began with his observation that time and eternity had been reconciled. He revealed a great mystery:

> Whereof I am made a minister, according to the dispensation of God which is given to me for you, to fulfil the word of God; Even the mystery which hath been hid from ages and from generations, but now is made manifest to his saints: To whom God would make known what is the riches of the glory of this mystery among the Gentiles; which is Christ in you, the hope of glory. (Colossians 1:25–27)

Ages and generations have passed, each perceiving itself as unique and self-directed. But the truth of the matter has only now been revealed to the saints. The Cross suffuses our timeline with God's glory, making it part of eternity.

22

TIME IS PLIABLE!
JOSHUA'S GREAT LEAP IN TIME

As strange as it may sound, many scientists and scientific organizations are now doing serious experimentation in time travel. Advanced mathematical theory suggests that time-space can be manipulated in various ways. It should be no surprise that the Bible offers the greatest illustration of this fact. As we shall later see, it came in a command issued by Joshua. But in these last days, when science scrupulously avoids the evidence offered by a biblical figure like Joshua, methods are being proposed that allow serious research into actual time displacement.

In short, the last few decades have brought mankind to the realization that the natural world is a mathematical construct. It is a delicate balance of energy fields and forces—attractions and repulsions. Copernicus saw the planets revolving around the sun. Sir Isaac Newton's laws of motion gave the universe a clocklike regularity. For him, time was an unchanging universal constant.

Internationally acclaimed theoretical physicist Paul Davies has written a book with the unassuming title *How to Build a Time Machine*. He quotes Newton's view of time as "absolute, true and mathematical time, flowing equably without relation to anything external."

Davies writes:

Everyone assumed without question that, whatever one's preferred definition, time is the same everywhere and for everybody. In other words, it is absolute and universal. True, we might *feel* time passing differently according to our moods, but time itself is simply time. The purpose of a clock is to circumvent mental distortions and record, objectively, *the* time.[74]

He goes on to outline what everybody knows, that time is past, present, and future. The present is *now,* and *now* is the same for everybody. Like all modern physicists, he strongly disagrees with this most common perception. He labels it, "wrong—deeply and seriously wrong."

In 1905, Albert Einstein published his revolutionary Special Theory of Relativity. In it, he predicted what has come to be called "time dilation," allowing mankind its first peek around the corner into the strange world of light-speed and dimensionality.

He noted that if the speed of light remains constant regardless of the motion of those traveling through it (and experiments have proven that it does), then something else must "give." That something is *time.* The math behind this truth is enormously complex for the average person. But it is extremely important to note that the truth of this postulate has been repeatedly demonstrated in clear-cut experiments.

In his book, *Time Travel in Einstein's Universe,* J. Richard Gott describes the first such experiment:

In 1971, physicists Joe Hafele and Richard Keating demonstrated Einstein's slowing of time in moving objects by taking very accurate atomic clocks on an airplane trip east around the world, a journey in which the plane's velocity adds to that of Earth's rotation. The physicists observed that the clocks were slightly slow—by 59 nanoseconds—relative to clocks on the ground when they returned, an observation in exact agreement with Einstein's predictions. (Because of Earth's rotation, the ground is also moving, but not as fast. Clocks on the ground are slowed less than those on the plane.)[75]

In other words, the faster the speed of a clock in a plane (or a rocket) relative to the speed of a similar clock on earth, the slower that clock seems to run. The clock in a rocket will show that *less time has passed* than its duplicate on earth will show.

By extension, two human beings—one on earth and the other in a rocket traveling near the speed of light—will have different body clock rates. In the classic illustration, they are twin brothers. One of them goes into space at hyperspeed. He will have a slower heartbeat and metabolic rate than his earthbound brother. After the astronaut completes a round trip to a nearby star, he will return to see not his twin, but an old man waiting to greet him.

Again, we must say that a bizarre illustration such as this is not mere imagination. Astronauts who have spent years orbiting the earth in the NASA International Space Station are aging at a slightly slower rate than those of us on earth below. Because of their greater rate of speed, they experience what to us is a slower rate of time.

However, they are experiencing the passage of time as *normal.* In their immediate vicinity, clocks and physical processes are proceeding at *what appears to them* to be the same rate as if they were on earth.

There are two important ideas at work here. One is that there is no universally definable "now." The present, which we call "now," is a local phenomenon, governed by one's rate of speed in the local universe.

The other is that astronauts who leave earth and travel at increasing rates of speed, perhaps approaching the speed of light, are moving into the *future!* As we have already seen, they return to earth with their own physical and bodily clocks having advanced less that the ones they left behind. On their return from a trip such as the one described above, they could easily come back twenty to thirty years in earth's future!

Many physicists hold this idea to be not only absolutely true, but quite achievable, given the ability to travel at extreme rates of speed. But as Dr. Davies points out, "High-speed travel and gravitational time dilation can be used only to go forward in time. But just as the future is surely out there, so is the past, it's there for the visiting. The trick is to figure out a way to reach it."[76]

Davies then refers to a method—albeit seemingly impossible—to visit the past. All one has to do, he says, is discover a place where gravitational fields are strongly arranged in such a way that they act as a slingshot to catapult the time traveler at a speed faster than light. That being accomplished, his ship then enters a "time loop" that curves back into the past. Speed manipulation, then, can be theoretically used to take one anywhere (and "anywhen") he wishes to go.

We recall an old *Star Trek* episode in which the starship *Enterprise* is aimed close to the sun in order to sling itself into a faster-than-light orbit that takes the intrepid crew back to the twentieth century in order to save the (then-extinct) whales. Having obtained a couple of twentieth-century whales, Captain James T. Kirk executes a similar maneuver (presumably, this one is slightly below light speed) that loops them back to the future. There, the whales are returned to the ocean, where they sing a song that placates an angry intergalactic probe. Such fictional forays (and there are many) emphasize the deep desire in mankind to step outside the ordinary progress of events to save the world from a million imagined disasters. Somewhere, deep in his own soul, man realizes that time-space can be manipulated.

Great velocity below the speed of light can be used for a leap "forward in time." On the other hand, travel faster than light produces a trek "backward in time." One thing may be gained from this thought, namely, that time is not constant. An individual's observation point has everything to do with the perceived flow of events.

THE UNIVERSAL CONSTANT

Like many others who implicitly believe the Bible, we hold that the six days of Creation were literal twenty-four hour days. This is a prime article of faith. But as we have just seen, time may be considerably dilated. Some have said they might actually have been longer than twenty-four hours, referring to Psalm 90, which refers to God's perception of time:

"For a thousand years in thy sight are but as yesterday when it is past, and as a watch in the night."

Are we to take this statement as literal? It doesn't seem so, even though the distance from "yesterday" to today is twenty-four hours. And, how long is "a watch in the night?" Depending upon the time of the year and one's latitude, it might be from six to twenty hours. The idea being expressed in this Mosaic psalm is that time from God's perspective is somehow shorter than it is from ours. That is, He doesn't *experience* time in the same way that mortal man does. As we have already seen, the physics of today regards light as constant, and time as malleable. We remember that "God is light, and in him is no darkness at all" (1 John 1:5). If He is light, He is constant. Interestingly, the speed of light is mathematically designated as "c," for "constant." It is familiar to most of us in Einstein's famous formula, $E=mc^2$.

The Bible asserts that the Lord existed before He created our time-line. He is in complete control of it. From within its confines or from outside, in the realm of eternity, He is quite able to see what we call "time" as fast, slow, or stationary.

He shows His prophets clear views of the timeline, whether to remind people of their past misdeeds, their present sin, or their future judgment. Their writings reveal the eons past, as in the fall of Satan, depicted as Lucifer in Isaiah 14, or the "king of Tyrus" in Ezekiel 28. They reveal the hidden things of the present, as when the Minor Prophets expose the sins of the northern and southern kingdoms. And they make known the future "Day of the Lord" prophecies, and beyond, into the Kingdom Age.

Obviously, mankind lives within the scheme of twenty-four-hour days, months, years, and centuries. He has been deliberately placed into this environment for his instruction and testing.

Returning for a moment to Psalm 90, we see that its seventeen verses are arranged in a way that hearkens back to the seven days of Creation. Written by Moses, it links these early days to the life of a human being. It begins with the creation of the earth. Then it speaks of the waters upon the earth. After that, it recalls the creation of vegetation, the sun, stars and planets, the animal creation, and finally, man himself. It concludes with the thought that his highest calling is to acquire the wisdom of the Lord.

In this psalm of Moses, the days of Creation are reinterpreted as an instruction to the righteous man who desires to pursue the wisdom of God.

Moses' purpose is to place man in the Genesis account of the six days of Creation, where originally he was not even a factor; he wasn't present at all. Psalm 90 places him in the context of those six days, which he must strive to understand: "So teach us to number our days, that we may apply our hearts unto wisdom" (Psalm 90:12).

Not until the sixth day was he breathed into life, and then at the very end of a sequence of events in which God harnessed time-space and created this universe.

A Stretch in Time, and Imagination

Are the days of Creation literal twenty-four-hour days? According to Dr. Gerald R. Schroeder, author of *The Science of God*, they are. But Schroeder goes farther—much farther—expressing the viewpoint of the cosmologist attempting to reconcile a Creation that appears to be almost 15 billion years old.

He says, "Deep within Psalm 90, there is the truth of a physical reality: the six days of Genesis actually did contain the billions of years of the cosmos even while the days remained twenty-four-hour days."[77]

Schroeder is described as "an applied theologian with undergraduate and doctoral degrees from the Massachusetts Institute of Technology." In brief, he is a brilliant mathematician who believes both the biblical account of Creation and the theoretical assessment of contemporary physics. He declares that he believes in a Creation that is both seven, twenty-four-hour days and 15 billion years in length. How is this possible?

Using calculations far too complex to be mentioned here, Dr. Schroeder first postulates the following idea:

We know three facts *with complete certainty* about the description of time in the Bible:

1. The biblical calendar is divided into two sections: the first six days of Genesis and all the time thereafter. Those six days are not, and never have been included in the calendar of the years which follow Adam.

2. Time in the biblical calendar after Adam *must have been* Earth-based. Archaeology proves this. The radioactive dates of archaeological discoveries related to the post-Adam period, such as the early Bronze Age, the beginning of writing, the battle of Jericho, closely match the dates derived from the biblical calendar for those same events. That radioactive decay occurred here on Earth in Earth time. Since the dates are a good match, the corresponding dates of the Bible must also use an earth-based calendar. There are no effects of biblical relativistic time dilation after Adam.

3. Most important of all, we know that there is no possible way for those first six days to have had an Earth-based perspective simply because for the first two of those six days there was no Earth. As Genesis 1:2 states, "And the earth was unformed."[78]

Like all modern physicists, Dr. Schroeder postulates that the universe originated as a tiny ball of hot plasma. It rapidly expanded into the reality that we see as galaxies, stars, and open space. As it cooled and rapidly expanded, it "clumped" into local gravitational anomalies which moved at different speeds. He says that these different local conditions (again, because light-speed is a constant) flowed at different rates of time.

He writes:

This immense stretching of space since the big bang has strong implications for our cosmic clock. Waves of radiation that have propagated in space since the early universe have been stretched, expanded, by the same proportion that the universe has expanded. For example, as the universe doubled in size, the distance between wave crests (and hence the time between ticks of its clock) also doubled as the wave was stretched by the expanding space. For that clock, time would be passing at half its original rate.[79]

Thus, the stretching of the early universe would result in a reduction of time measured by an earth clock. Schroeder emphasizes that in measuring the age of the universe, we are really looking backward in time, from the perspective of an earth clock running at a rate set by conditions since Adam. This, he calls the "local view."

On the other hand, the clock before Adam had a different perspective: "The Bible's clock before Adam is not a clock tied to any one location. It is a clock that looks *forward* in time from the creation, encompassing the entire universe, a universal clock tuned to the cosmic radiation at the moment when matter formed."

Then comes Schroeder's main point: "This cosmic clock records the passage of one minute while we on Earth experience a million million minutes." Then he adds, "The dinosaurs ruled the Earth for 120 million years, *as measured by our perception of time....* At this million-million-to-one ratio those 120 million Earth years lasted a mere hour."[80]

More to the point, using what he calls "peer-reviewed physics," he brings the days of Creation down to a time span that is quite familiar to any reader of the Bible: "In terms of days and years and millennia, this stretching of the cosmic perception of time by a factor of a million million, the division of fifteen billion years by a million million reduces those fifteen billion years to six days!"

"Genesis and science," he says, "are *both* correct. When one asks if six days or fifteen billion years passed before the appearance of humankind, the correct answer is 'yes.'"[81]

Schroeder's lengthy scientific explanation of this fact must be carefully studied by the layman. Whether he is right or wrong, he does make a point. Before the creation of Adam, all time was seen through the eyes of God, looking forward from Creation. From His point of view, **Day One** was twenty-four hours, or "evening and morning." From the present earth perspective, looking backward, Schroeder's calculation show that same day as 8 billion years in length. From God's point of view, each of the six days was an "evening and morning," or twenty-four hours.

From man's perspective, the days were billions of years long, each day growing shorter as the expansion of the universe slowed. **Day Two** was 4 billion years. **Day Three**, 2 billion years. **Day Four**, 1 billion years. **Day Five**, half a billion years. **Day Six**, a fourth of a billion years. Taken together, the six days total 15.75 billion years.

But as God sees them from *His objective position,* they are six twenty-four-hour days. As is commonly understood, God created Adam on the sixth day. From then on, time on earth was reckoned according to Adam's perception. We, his progeny, have since calculated time in accordance with the local perspective of sun, moon, planets, and stars. And God rested on the seventh day.

Hearkening back to the words of Psalm 90, those thousand years that God experiences in the same way that we experience a single day are probably not to be taken as a literal and exact thousand years, We know that God operates exclusive of time—that He has access to the total timeline of this Creation. Therefore, it might be more accurate to paraphrase Psalm 90:4 in the following way: "In Your eyes, a thousand years are like yesterday when it passes and like a watch in the night." Both yesterday and a night watch are indeterminate periods of time. Therefore, this verse does not operate as a mathematical formula, into which finite values may be calculated.

Rather, the intention is that a very, very long time in man's sight is practically no time at all to God. Peter picks up and expands upon this very same idea. But in his case, he uses the metaphor of a thousand-year day to point to the millennial-day theory, that the seven days of Creation will be reflected in seven millennia of human history. They provide a model for man's ages-long history.

> But, beloved, be not ignorant of this one thing, that one day is with the Lord as a thousand years, and a thousand years as one day.
>
> The Lord is not slack concerning his promise, as some men count slackness; but is longsuffering to us-ward, not willing that any should perish, but that all should come to repentance. But the day of the Lord will come as a thief in the night; in the which the heavens shall pass away with a great noise, and the elements shall melt with fervent heat, the earth also and the works that are therein shall be burned up. (2 Peter 3:8–10)

Here, Peter prophetically looks forward to the "day of the Lord." This day will be a thousand years long, initiated by the Tribulation period and brought to completion with the release of Satan to go forth and delude the men who populate the earth at the end of the Millennium.

The millennial day is not the way God experiences time. Rather, it is a pattern of development based upon the pattern He used in the original creation of our universe. Certainly, Peter is not saying that there is a fixed ratio (in this case, 365,242 to 1) between God's experience of time and ours. But again, it is a certainty that God views and experiences time in quite a different way than we do.

From our perspective, it operates at a fixed rate. From His, it is no doubt infinitely flexible.

JOSHUA'S LONG DAY

An excellent illustration of this in found in the book of Joshua. There, we find an account that strains credulity to the maximum. Holy Scripture requires us to believe that the sun actually stood still in the sky, allowing Joshua's troops the extra time to defeat their enemies! In the context of our present line of thought, it seems very likely that the Lord somehow influenced time itself in order to aid the army of Joshua.

Various writers have attempted to explain this miracle in scientific terms.

Current naturalistic explanations for it have focused upon planetary interactions that slowed down the earth's rotation for a brief time. We shall look at these explanations, then present the possibility that time itself was stretched as mentioned above to produce the effect described in the Bible. The account of this prodigious phenomenon is given in Joshua 10:11–14, where Joshua's troops defeat the armies of five kings at Gibeon:

> And it came to pass, as they fled from before Israel, and were in the going down to Beth-horon, that the LORD cast down great stones from heaven upon them unto Azekah, and they died: they were more which died with hailstones than they whom the children of Israel slew with the sword.
>
> Then spake Joshua to the LORD in the day when the LORD delivered up the Amorites before the children of Israel, and he said in the sight of Israel, Sun, stand thou still upon Gibeon; and thou, Moon, in the valley of Ajalon.
>
> And the sun stood still, and the moon stayed, until the people had avenged themselves upon their enemies. Is not this written in the book of Jasher? So the sun stood still in the midst of heaven, and hasted not to go down about a whole day. And there was no day like that before it or after it, that the LORD hearkened unto the voice of a man: for the LORD fought for Israel.

How can we believe this account? For the sun to stand still "a whole day" requires that the earth completely stop its rotation for perhaps eight to ten hours. This means that the laws of motion and inertia had to be suspended all over the earth. If the planet suddenly stopped its rotation, everything on its surface would continue forward at a thousand miles per hour! All life would be catastrophically snuffed out. Obviously, this didn't happen.

Instead, Joshua and his troops used the extra time to rout the enemy completely. Certainly, the Lord can (and did) perform this miracle. But how? Many men have sought an explanation in the realm of the natural.

In his 1950 book, *Worlds in Collision,* Immanuel Velikovsky looked back at various historical accounts and concluded that the ancient orbits of Mars and Venus brought them so close to the earth that on several occasions, earth's rotation was slowed—or in the case of Joshua—virtually stopped altogether!

He mentioned that the experience of Joshua was most likely attributable to a large comet, which collided with Mars, knocking it out of orbit. This resulted in its close approach to earth, with consequential terrestrial catastrophes. In particular, he said that the strange experience of Joshua's army could only be explained by an extremely close approach of Mars to earth.

He writes:

> According to the knowledge of our age—not of the age when the Book of Joshua or of Jasher was written—this could have happened if the earth had ceased for a time to roll along its prescribed path. Is such a disturbance conceivable? No record of the slightest confusion is registered in the present annals of the earth. Each year consists of 365 days, 5 hours, and 49 minutes.
>
> A departure of the Earth from its regular rotation is thinkable, but only in the very improbable event that our planet should meet another heavenly body of sufficient mass to disrupt the eternal path of our world.[82]

Both Velikovsky and the Bible, in Joshua and 2 Samuel, mention a "book of Jasher." The account given in this apocryphal book adds some detail to the narrative. We quote it as follows:

And the Lord confounded them before the children at Israel, who smote them with a terrible slaughter in Gibeon, and pursued them along the way that goes up to Beth Horon unto Makkedah, and they fled from before the children of Israel.

And whilst they were fleeing, the Lord sent upon them hailstones from heaven, and more of them died by the hailstones, than by the slaughter of the children of Israel.

And the children of Israel pursued them, and they still smote them in the road, going on and smiting them.

And when they were smiting, the day was declining toward evening, and Joshua said in the sight of all the people, Sun, stand thou still upon Gibeon, and thou moon in the valley of Ajalon, until the nation shall have revenged itself upon its enemies.

And the Lord hearkened to the voice of Joshua, and the sun stood still in the midst of the heavens, and it stood still six and thirty moments, and the moon also stood still and hastened not to go down a whole day.

And there was no day like that, before it or after it, that the Lord hearkened to the voice of a man, for the Lord fought for Israel. (Jasher 88:60–65)[83]

If the thirty-six "moments" were fifteen minutes each, we have a time period of nine hours. Today, no one knows for sure what they represent.

Velikovsky made much of the large hailstones, saying that they were an artifact of the atmospheric disturbance stirred up by Mars' close approach.[84]

Another writer, Donald Wesley Patten, in the 1988 book, *Catastrophism and the Old Testament,* believed that the Mars-earth encounters happened on a regular basis. He writes:

This catastrophe was also caused by a close flyby of Mars, perhaps between 25,000 and 30,000 miles distant. It was a sunward side flyby, during the morning (Jerusalem time). It occurred during the morning of October 24th, 1404 BC. It was on the 1080th anniversary of the Flood of Noah. It also occurred on the 540th anniversary of the Tower of Babel Discharge.

During this particularly close flyby, the Earth behaved like a gyroscope experiencing precession. A gyroscope is a rotating sphere. A precession is a wobble. Mars in its close flyby was putting a gravitational torque on the earth's spin axis.… In addition to spin axis precessions and torques, there was also to a significant extent some crustal skidding.[85]

Patten postulates interplanetary torque and the skidding of earth's crust at the same rate as the setting sun, making it appear to stand still. If this happened, it is perhaps a greater miracle than the Lord's simple declaration that earth cease its rotation.

The first-century historian Josephus had his own view of the matter, which he apparently regarded as almost unbelievable, since he referenced then-extant histories to prove that it actually happened:

The place is Beth-horon; where he also understood that God assisted him, which he declared by thunder and thunderbolts, as also by the falling of hail larger than usual. Moreover, it happened that the day was lengthened, that the night might not come on too soon, and be an obstruction to the zeal of the Hebrews in pursuing their enemies; insomuch, that Joshua took the kings, who were hidden in a certain cave at Makkedah, and put them to death. Now, that the day was lengthened at this time, and was longer than ordinary, is expressed in the books laid up in the temple. (*Antiquities*, V. I. 17)[86]

Obviously, he believed the explanation given in those "books" that were stored in the Temple. He felt that they were sufficient authority to give the story credibility. We, too, believe.

More than that, it is our belief that the Lord God, as Creator, is the veritable Author of time. He functions as its Lord.

TIME IN AND TIME OUT

Therefore, no stretch of the imagination is required to believe that the event at Beth-horon is quite simply an occurrence of time dilation. If the Lord merely isolated the timeline of ancient Israel from the solar system timeline, He could have caused the event described in the Bible. No planetary interactions would have been required at all.

Here's how it might have happened. As Joshua pursued the armies of the five kings, evening drew near. If night fell, the remnant enemy forces might escape to regroup on the next day…perhaps to launch a successful assault on Joshua's troops.

That it was late in the day is clearly seen in the fact that the moon had already risen in the east, appearing over the Valley of Ajalon. With the late afternoon sun in the west and the moon in the east, it would be easy for Joshua and his men to gauge any angular change, as one rose and the other fell.

Then the Lord spoke to him. Joshua's response is a quotation that by almost universal agreement is taken from the Book of Jasher. He openly commanded the sun to stand still. He believed the Lord, who had told him, "Fear them not: for I have delivered them into thine hand" (10:8).

Then a strange thing happened. Suddenly, Joshua had all the time he needed to complete his victory. Heavenly time, on the other hand, had stopped. It must have been an awe-inspiring sight to see the hours roll by, with no change in the heavens. Though the great hailstorm had decimated the enemy, Joshua's troops were required to complete the bloody business at hand.

For Joshua and the Canaanite enemy, time flowed as normal. Had the wristwatch existed in that era, Joshua's would have recorded the minutes and hours moving by as usual. Somehow, his time zone had been isolated from the time zone of the solar system, which had come to a complete halt. Joshua (and perhaps all earth's citizens alive at that time) had gone forward several hours into the future, while the solar system remained stationary. It seems that at will, the Lord can isolate any locale in the universe and control the flow of time.

Is this an outlandish idea? Not according to modern physics, which has the mathematics to prove that the perception of time is keyed to one's immediate surroundings. As witnessed earlier in this article, contemporary physics regards time as completely arbitrary.

In effect, the Israelites "gained time" by going forward while the solar system stopped. What then, happened to the accrued time that this miracle had created?

THE SUNDIAL OF AHAZ

Remember that the event that enabled Joshua's victory happened in the fifteenth century BC. For centuries after that, as far as we know, the children of Israel lived out their days as normal, even though they had gone into the future by several hours. Without knowing it, they carried a "time surplus" forward through the years.

But they probably weren't aware of it, as such. There is no record of anyone standing up and lamenting the fact that Israel had experienced a time displacement. There is, however, a record of a subsequent "time loss."

It happened in the days of King Hezekiah, late in the eighth century BC. Almost 750 years had passed since Joshua's victory on that extra-long day. Now, in about 710 BC, Isaiah informed Hezekiah that he would soon die. Not only that, but the Assyrians threatened the kingdom.

Hezekiah prayed, and soon afterward, Isaiah came to inform him that the Lord had heard his prayer:

> Then came the word of the LORD to Isaiah, saying, Go, and say
> to Hezekiah, Thus saith the LORD, the God of David thy father,
> I have heard thy prayer, I have seen thy tears: behold, I will add
> unto thy days fifteen years.

And I will deliver thee and this city out of the hand of the
king of Assyria: and I will defend this city. And this shall be a
sign unto thee from the Lord, that the Lord will do this thing
that he hath spoken;

Behold, I will bring again the shadow of the degrees, which
is gone down in the sun dial of Ahaz, ten degrees backward.
So the sun returned ten degrees, by which degrees it was gone
down. (Isaiah 38:4–8)

Not only would Hezekiah's prayer be answered, but it would be
accompanied by a great sign. It is thought that the great sundial of Ahaz
was a tall obelisk (gnomon) that cast its shadow down upon a series of
rising steps to its east and to its west. Each of these steps represented an
increment of time. Perhaps these increments were half an hour each,
maybe more, but no one knows for sure.

When the shadow of the great gnomon retreated by ten degrees
("steps" in the Hebrew), it "turned back" Israel's clock by approximately
five to eight hours, or more. May we hazard a guess, as have others, that
here, Israel's clock was corrected backward by **exactly the same time** that
it had gone forward in Joshua's day? This would certainly make sense.

We have a clue to this effect in a parallel account of Hezekiah's great
sign, as given in 2 Kings. There, Isaiah asks the king to name the direction time will be changed. His answer suggests that he was aware of
Joshua's experience:

And Isaiah said, This sign shalt thou have of the LORD, that the
LORD will do the thing that he hath spoken: shall the shadow
go forth ten degrees, or go back ten degrees?

And Hezekiah answered, It is a light thing for the shadow
to go down ten degrees: nay, but let the shadow return
backward ten degrees.

And Isaiah the prophet cried unto the LORD: and he
brought the shadow ten degrees backward, by which it had
gone down in the dial of Ahaz. (2 Kings 20:9–11)

Why did Hezekiah have such a firm opinion about the movement of time? Might he have studied the annals of Israel? (Remember the books that Josephus said were stored in the Temple?[87]) If Hezekiah had read them, he would have known that in the time of Joshua, Israel gained time. Remembering that episode, it would be natural for him to think that what God had done for Joshua—moving time forward—was easy.

In effect, he said, "Well, I know that the Lord can run time forward. Let's see if the He can run time backward." And indeed, the Lord proved that He could.

He is the Creator and the Light. He is the one constant factor in the universe. Time for Him is flexible, pliable...malleable. He created it and chose to be incarnated within its limits. It is His to use as He will.

23

A WINDOW IN TIME:
TIME-SPACE AND THE TRANSFIGURATION

It was a unique moment when time met eternity. Past, present, and future merged into a single affirming moment. It was as though the Lord placed His stamp and seal upon the comprehensive plan that we humans see as biblical history.

The biblical account of the Transfiguration was more than a vision… more than a mere meeting of Jewish historical figures. It was a voyage into the future, and a preview of the Kingdom of God.

There, on the mountaintop, Jesus the King met with Moses the lawgiver and Elijah, representative of the prophets. At that moment, Peter, James, and John became witnesses to something phenomenally miraculous. Time was speeded up, revealing the far future. Or, perhaps it moved at a speed beyond light into a place where time as we know it ceased to exist. Whatever the case, this world was forever stamped and sealed with the promise of the Kingdom.

From that moment on, there could be no question about whether or not God's plan would be consummated. More to the point, the Transfiguration proved that His plan has *already* been brought to completion.

Matthew's description of this momentous occasion is terse, factual, and a masterpiece of dramatic focus:

And after six days Jesus taketh Peter, James, and John his brother, and bringeth them up into an high mountain apart, And was transfigured before them: and his face did shine as the sun, and his raiment was white as the light. And, behold, there appeared unto them Moses and Elias talking with him.

Then answered Peter, and said unto Jesus, Lord, it is good for us to be here: if thou wilt, let us make here three tabernacles; one for thee, and one for Moses, and one for Elias.

While he yet spake, behold, a bright cloud overshadowed them: and behold a voice out of the cloud, which said, This is my beloved Son, in whom I am well pleased; hear ye him.

And when the disciples heard it, they fell on their face, and were sore afraid. And Jesus came and touched them, and said, Arise, and be not afraid.

And when they had lifted up their eyes, they saw no man, save Jesus only. And as they came down from the mountain, Jesus charged them, saying, Tell the vision to no man, until the Son of man be risen again from the dead. (Matthew 17:1–9)

Three Gospels— Matthew, Mark, and Luke—carry this account. With minor variations, they all tell the same story. In general, they present the hope of humanity as resurrection into a glorified body. In this event, Jesus is featured from the perspective of His humanity. John, the Gospel that emphasizes His deity, omits the Transfiguration narrative.

To His closest disciples, Jesus revealed a truth about His Kingdom that had never before been expounded. Humanity was promised a resurrection into the realm of God's glory. Moses, Elijah, and Jesus had all been born into human bodies, but were now seen in glorified bodies, clearly displaying the future hope of glory for all redeemed human beings.

In the narrative above, the word "transfigured" is translated from the Greek *metamorphoo* (μεταμορφοω), meaning "to change into another form." An example from ordinary life is the butterfly that changes from a worm to a colorful creature endowed with the ability to fly. Paul's marvelous words about the Rapture and resurrection of the redeemed are grounded in the Transfiguration experience:

> And as we have borne the image of the earthy, we shall also bear the image of the heavenly. Now this I say, brethren, that flesh and blood cannot inherit the kingdom of God; neither doth corruption inherit incorruption.
>
> Behold, I shew you a mystery; We shall not all sleep, but we shall all be changed, In a moment, in the twinkling of an eye, at the last trump: for the trumpet shall sound, and the dead shall be raised incorruptible, and we shall be changed.
>
> For this corruptible must put on incorruption, and this mortal must put on immortality. So when this corruptible shall have put on incorruption, and this mortal shall have put on immortality, then shall be brought to pass the saying that is written, Death is swallowed up in victory. O death, where is thy sting? O grave, where is thy victory? (1 Corinthians 15:49–5)

Here, the word "changed" refers to being transformed into something entirely different. Of course, before Paul wrote these words, He had personally witnessed the risen and glorified Christ. But no doubt, he had also heard of the disciples' testimony concerning the Transfiguration experience. They had testified of the change that would take place.

THE PRIMEVAL LIGHT

Even more than the promise of physical resurrection and glorification, the Tansfiguration is a powerful testimony of an ancient teaching about the glory of God. Among the Jews, there is a long tradition that God's glorious light is invisible to the present sinful human population.

They believe that His spiritual light is thousands of times brighter than the sun. And they ask a question: If it is so bright, why then, can it not be seen? Rabbi Michael Munk, writing in *The Wisdom in the Hebrew Alphabet*, briefly synopsizes Jewish history regarding this phenomenon:

> *Rabbi Dov Ber of Mezritch*, successor to the *Baal Shem Tov*, explains that the great Primeval Light of Creation had been available to all, but when God saw that few people could be worthy of enjoying it, He concealed it. Where did He hide it? In the Torah. Therefore, through a diligent and unremitting pursuit of an understanding of the Torah, one can attain a measure of God's wisdom—revealed from between its lines and letters. That is the Primeval Light! As *Zohar* puts it: the words of the Torah are likened to a nut which has an outer shell while its kernel is securely preserved inside *(Midrash HaNeelam, Ruth).*[88]

To Gentile ears, this might at first sound like a strange and superstitious folk tale. But the inner light of the Bible functions in exactly this way. Munk mentions a book called *Zohar.*[89] Its title, meaning "radiance," is dedicated to Jewish conjectures about the nature of God's revelation. It regards His light as being hidden to the ordinary man. And though we might not agree with all its premises, the Bible does in fact, reflect its central notion.

In Hebrew, the Primeval Light is called *ohr haganuz* (אור הגנוז), meaning "hidden or stored light." It is the Light that is concealed in the Word.

When Jesus came, He revealed this light to His followers…but *only* to His followers. Jewish religious authorities scoffed when, once, He told them explicitly that He was the source of the light: "Then spake Jesus again unto them, saying, I am the light of the world: he that followeth me shall not walk in darkness, but shall have the light of life" (John 8:12).

And of course, John's Gospel opens with a well-known metaphysical treatise that provides the key to the ancient doctrine of the hidden light.

It states a truth that is unparalleled in its clarity. To the ancient teachers of Israel, the Word was nothing more or less than the Creation, itself:

> In the beginning was the Word, and the Word was with God, and the Word was God. The same was in the beginning with God.
>
> All things were made by him; and without him was not any thing made that was made. In him was life; and the life was the light of men. And the light shineth in darkness; and the darkness comprehended it not. There was a man sent from God, whose name was John.
>
> The same came for a witness, to bear witness of the Light, that all men through him might believe. He was not that Light, but was sent to bear witness of that Light. That was the true Light, which lighteth every man that cometh into the world. He was in the world, and the world was made by him, and the world knew him not. He came unto his own, and his own received him not. (John 1:1–11)

When Jesus came to Israel, it was as the Word. Jewish teaching states that God created the universe and everything in it by uttering the Word of Creation, spelled out by the twenty-two letters of the Hebrew alphabet. These letters are considered to be the virtual raw material of all Creation. This is what John writes about Jesus.

He is that Light that shines in the darkness of this world. But though the Light was here during His lifetime and later, through the ministry of his Holy Spirit, the world can't perceive it. To the high and mighty men of the first century (and today), Jesus was an ordinary man who made a false claim. They couldn't (and can't) see His hidden Light.

John's Gospel also mentions John the Baptist, sent as a witness of the Light. It is to be noted that a clear distinction is made between the True Light and any human agency or personality that might bear witness of the Light.

Here, John the Baptist witnesses to the Light, but he is not the Light.

Later, in a conversation with His disciples, Jesus spoke of John as Elijah, called "Elias" in the New Testament. Their interchange took place after John had been beheaded, and immediately following the experience of the Transfiguration.

What they had just seen on the mountaintop resonated in their thoughts. They remembered—no doubt from the prophecy of Malachi—that Elijah would come prior to the Day of the Lord. With this in mind as they descend from that mountaintop experience, they ask Jesus a question:

> And his disciples asked him, saying, Why then say the scribes that Elias must first come?
> And Jesus answered and said unto them, Elias truly shall first come, and restore all things. But I say unto you, That Elias is come already, and they knew him not, but have done unto him whatsoever they listed. Likewise shall also the Son of man suffer of them.
> Then the disciples understood that he spake unto them of John the Baptist. (Matthew 17:10–13)

In retrospect, we can see something that the disciples probably never really understood. John the Baptist—witness of the Light—had borne the spirit of Elijah. After his death, Elijah was seen in the glorified state. At the Transfiguration, Elijah witnessed to the truth of the Resurrection and the Kingdom Age. He, of course, was accompanied by Moses. The two of them are witnesses to Christ's glory.

It is rarely mentioned that Malachi's prophecy—the last of the Old Testament—also features Moses and Elijah:

> Remember ye the law of Moses my servant, which I commanded unto him in Horeb for all Israel, with the statutes and judgments.
> Behold, I will send you Elijah the prophet before the coming of the great and dreadful day of the LORD:

And he shall turn the heart of the fathers to the children,
and the heart of the children to their fathers, lest I come and
smite the earth with a curse. (Malachi 4:4–6)

Here are two men bearing witness to the reality of the Day of the
Lord. Moses and Elijah…the Law and the Prophets, testify through
Malachi that there will indeed be a Judgment Day. Out of that judgment
will come a new Israel, distinguished by spiritual revival and renewal.

PAST, PRESENT, AND FUTURE

Malachi ends with an exhortation to Israel. They are urged to remember
Moses and Elijah. Thus, Moses begins and ends the Old Testament. He
and Elijah constitute a witness to the certainty of the coming Kingdom.

From our present perspective, the Old Testament is past, but its
prophecies speak of the distant future. In the meantime, Moses and
Elijah at the Transfiguration provide a reminder to Christ's followers that
we will be glorified in the general resurrection.

In the future, these two men will witness in person. They will come
to Israel at the time when the Tribulation Temple is erected. They are the
two witnesses who will bolster Israel's efforts when everything is turning
against the brave nation. Eventually, even they will be eliminated by the
Antichrist:

And there was given me a reed like unto a rod: and the angel
stood, saying, Rise, and measure the temple of God, and the
altar, and them that worship therein.

But the court which is without the temple leave out, and
measure it not; for it is given unto the Gentiles: and the holy
city shall they tread under foot forty and two months.

And I will give power unto my two witnesses, and they
shall prophesy a thousand two hundred and threescore days,
clothed in sackcloth. These are the two olive trees, and the two

candlesticks standing before the God of the earth. And if any
man will hurt them, fire proceedeth out of their mouth, and
devoureth their enemies: and if any man will hurt them, he
must in this manner be killed.

These have power to shut heaven, that it rain not in the
days of their prophecy: and have power over waters to turn
them to blood, and to smite the earth with all plagues, as often
as they will.

And when they shall have finished their testimony, the
beast that ascendeth out of the bottomless pit shall make war
against them, and shall overcome them, and kill them.
And their dead bodies shall lie in the street of the great city,
which spiritually is called Sodom and Egypt, where also our
Lord was crucified. (Revelation 11:1–8)

Who are these two witnesses? A number of candidates have been for-
warded. But in fact, they are the same two who appear at the conclusion
of the Old Testament and in the experience of the Transfiguration. Note
that they prophesy during the period when the Temple is erected…the
first 1,260 days of the Tribulation. Elsewhere in the New Testament, we
read that this "Tribulation Temple" will become the central feature in the
Antichrist's false religion.

Daniel 9:27 says:

And he shall confirm the covenant with many for one week:
and in the midst of the week he shall cause the sacrifice and the
oblation to cease, and for the overspreading of abominations he
shall make it desolate, even until the consummation, and that
determined shall be poured upon the desolate.

The Antichrist's covenant begins the seven-year Tribulation. For
"sacrifice and oblation," a Temple must be present. At the midpoint of
the seven years, the Antichrist halts Temple worship and declares himself

to be God, just as predicted in Daniel 11:36, where we read: "And he shall exalt himself, and magnify himself above every god."

In the New Testament (Matthew 24:15), Jesus refers to this event as, "the ABOMINATION OF DESOLATION." Paul expands upon the event in 2 Thessalonians 2:4, where he describes the activities of the "son of perdition" (his term for the Antichrist): "Who opposeth and exalteth himself above all that is called God, or that is worshipped; so that he as God sitteth in the temple of God, shewing himself that he is God."

During his rise to power, the two witnesses are described in the Revelation passage above as having the ability to invoke the plagues brought against ancient Egypt at the time of the Exodus, and to stop rainfall. Since these are the works originally attributed to Moses and Elijah, how can they be anyone else?

A TRIP TO THE FUTURE

Picturing Moses and Elijah as it does, the Transfiguration experience links the past with the future. The significant feature of that future is the Day of the Lord, resulting in the punishment of the wicked and the reward of the righteous. Just before taking Peter, James, and John to the mountaintop, Jesus made a remarkable statement:

> For the Son of man shall come in the glory of his Father with
> his angels; and then he shall reward every man according to
> his works. Verily I say unto you, There be some standing here,
> which shall not taste of death, till they see the Son of man
> coming in his kingdom. (Matthew 16:27, 28)

Shortly after He said this, the four experienced a vision of the future. But was it just a vision? Apparently, the disciples didn't think so. To them, the future had become the present. Peter suggested that they build three booths. Such booths are routinely built every year at the Feast of Tabernacles. They are small, temporary structures decorated with fruit, flowers, and treasured objects symbolizing the blessed life in the future Kingdom of David. There, every man will own his own home and property, living in peace and eating the fruit of his own fields. Booths symbolize the Kingdom Age.

During the Transfiguration encounter, Peter took Jesus literally. From his perspective, he was *already* in the Kingdom Age. Moses and Elijah, who had been killed by the Antichrist and had risen from the dead, now occupied glorified bodies. This is in the future tense—even to us, today! But during the Transfiguration, it was not the future to Peter, James, and John. They were there. For them, the future had become the present!

So often, the Bible presents our time-space as a quantity that can be easily manipulated by God. But to live, as He does, in the "eternal now," the framework of time already exists in all its tenses. The Transfiguration beautifully illustrates this fact.

24

THE DIMENSION OF GOD:
KNOWING "UP" FROM "DOWN"

Everyone wants to go to heaven. Even if it's only the heaven of their imagination, they are drawn to some paradise of their own imagining. Secular man wants a heaven on earth. That which has always been thought of as "up," he would bring "down" to earth. As we shall see, they are not thinking of direction, but dimension.

Science continues to probe the state of creation. Driven by an inner fury to discover and decode the state of the universe, mathematicians and physicists spend billions as they labor to lay open the universe like a ripened fruit to be devoured by their lust to achieve the power of God Himself.

In one sense, they are constantly improving our basic state of existence, as their inventions, electronics, pharmaceuticals, synthetics, and genetics bring man closer to a sort of physical "paradise." They strive for utopia.

But in another sense, they are pursuing the knowledge forbidden to man after his great downfall.

And the LORD God took the man, and put him into the garden of Eden to dress it and to keep it. And the LORD God commanded the man, saying, Of every tree of the garden thou mayest freely eat: But of the tree of the knowledge of good and evil, thou shalt not eat of it: for in the day that thou eatest thereof thou shalt surely die. (Genesis 2:15–17)

What is this knowledge? Why is it so stringently forbidden to man on planet earth? It must certainly be a type of knowledge quite accessible in the Kingdom of Heaven, but utterly banned here where we live, on the physical plane. In our created universe, a human being with a deep knowledge of the methods of its creation could well become a reigning despot-genius—the darkest kind of villain—a veritable Satan, with the power of legend come to life. The world's literature abounds with such characters.

From out of the historical mists, a picture of the mad scientist emerges. Shall we call him a wizard, shaman, necromancer, astrologer, soothsayer, alchemist, mystic, parapsychologist, or simply a worker of signs and wonders? Today, he is called a cosmologist—one who diligently disentangles the mathematical cobwebs that block the door to the "other side." The delicate web cannot be torn; it must be penetrated by profound manipulations of subatomic truth that is stranger than fiction.

His research may begin in innocence, but as it approaches the vaults of power, corrupting influences assert themselves. The transition from scientist to mad scientist is so subtle that he may cross to the dark side without even knowing it.

There, in a world of protons, electrons, pions, mesons, quarks, and astronomical forces, there are secret energy states that offer the keys to the universe. More valuable than all the gold of creation, they are delicately balanced in a stability that only the Creator can maintain, "upholding all things by the word of his power" (Hebrews 1:3).

But having lost direct access to God in the sinful collapse of the great Fall, man seeks to replace that lost sense of power and control in a diligent pursuit of the secret knowledge of creation.

This is the story of man's beginning. In the simple account of the

Serpent and the woman, the Devil proffers the secret knowledge that has ever since been the center of an assiduous search for supremacy and control. He convinces her that godhood comes through the opening of the mind. This, he tells her, can be achieved simply by partaking of the fruit that promises the knowledge: "For God doth know that in the day ye eat thereof, then your eyes shall be opened, and ye shall be as gods, knowing good and evil" (Genesis 3:5).

In the pre-Flood years, the sons of God entered the physical world and conspired with mankind to create their own autonomous kingdom. The major drive of the culture they created was the pursuit of that forbidden knowledge. God doused their plans in the great Flood.

But the ravages of that Flood didn't dampen men's desires to storm the vaults of heaven. The infamous Tower of Babel incorporated some now-lost methodology of metaphysics. Through it, men would have penetrated heaven itself.

As strange as this seems, it is the clear biblical record. God recognized the potential outcome of their efforts and took measures to stop the project:

> And the LORD came down to see the city and the tower, which the children of men builded.
>
> And the LORD said, Behold, the people is one, and they have all one language; and this they begin to do: and now nothing will be restrained from them, which they have imagined to do.
>
> Go to, let us go down, and there confound their language, that they may not understand one another's speech.
> (Genesis 11:5–7)

Note that the Lord came "down" to view the illicit work. As we shall see, His movement indicates travel along a forbidden pathway that men wish to travel, but cannot. Yet they try, and their experiments turn reality into a muddle of apparent contradictions.

LIFE, DEATH, AND QUANTUM ENTANGLEMENT

There is a lower state of existence and a higher state. Even scientists speak of dimensional levels or "universes." In our universe, certain rules hold forth. Here, there is "life" and "death." It is fascinating that the esoteric postulates of physics play at understanding that which ordinary men leave to the Almighty.

At the subatomic level, as one approaches more and more closely to the finer threads in the fabric of the universe, the accepted rules of daily reality begin to change. Odd and inexplicable things begin to be noticed. Then, as the picture is magnified, they loom into view; they become the rule. Objective reality, taken for granted in the macrocosm of our daily life, disappears in the microcosm of quantum mechanics.

In the inconceivably tiny world of the quantum state, nothing can be directly observed. Common sense becomes nonsense. The stuff of life and creation looks less and less like balls bouncing off each other on a pool table...more and more like an energetic glow. In this glow there must be form, but no one knows what it is. The following account clearly illustrates the problem faced by physicists.

In his book, *Beyond Einstein,* the eminent physicist Dr. Michio Kaku writes the following:

> The notions introduced by quantum mechanics are so novel that Erwin Schrödinger devised a clever "thought experiment" in 1935 that captured its apparent absurdity.
>
> Imagine a bottle of poison gas and a cat trapped in a box, which we are not allowed to open. Obviously, although we cannot peer into the box, we can say that the cat is either dead or alive. Now imagine that the bottle of poison gas is connected to a Geiger counter, which can detect radiation from a piece of uranium ore. If a single uranium nucleus disintegrates, it releases radiation, which sets off the Geiger counter, which in turn breaks the bottle and kills the cat.

According to quantum mechanics, we cannot predict with certainty when a single uranium nucleus will disintegrate. We only can calculate the probability of billions upon billions of nuclei disintegrating. Therefore, to describe a single uranium nucleus, quantum mechanics assumes that it is a mixture of two states—one where the uranium nucleus is inert, the other where it has decayed. The cat is both dead and alive. In other words, we must assume statistically that the cat is a mixture of two states.[90]

Remember, just as it is impossible to observe quantum particles, it is impossible to peek at the cat without ruining the experiment. In the delicate world of quantum mechanics, the act of measuring or observing determines the energy state. Opening the box would determine whether the cat is dead or alive. The observer cannot separate his own actions from the reality of the tiny world he is observing.

It is as though something exists only when we don't look directly at it. When we look away, it's there; when we glance at it, it's gone. We catch it only out of the "corner of our eye." But physicists are driven to observe and identify these spooky forces, because they promise power to the one who can manipulate them.

Einstein, among others, objected to quantum calculations as a violation of what we understand as objective reality. And yet, there is a quantum underpinning…a force that pervades this universe. No one can define it, yet science observes its effects.

Strangely, these effects intersect with the behavior of man and all living things. There seems to be a point at which life and the material creation become one and the same thing. Mystic religions have operated on this premise for centuries, but they have never come to a knowledge of the truth.

PARAPSYCHOLOGY AND SUBSPACE

In the decade of the 1960s, esoteric ideas began to penetrate Western science. One example of this came when Dr. J. B. Rhine of Duke

University pioneered the study of what came to be termed "parapsychology." Formerly, this branch of study was called "psychical research." It was preoccupied with telepathy, clairvoyance, and the survival of life after death.

In a series of famous experiments, laboratory subjects tried to discern—through mental imagery—the symbols on a set of cards being turned by a partner. Dr. Rhine began to postulate that there was some kind of underlying channel of communication. Thus, clairvoyance became institutionalized in a hypothesis that suggested a mental connection with the outside world. His work popularized the phenomenon known as extrasensory perception (ESP). Such experiments continue on a massive level.

Today, researchers have expanded into a practice called "remote viewing," in which clairvoyance is raised to the level of technology. It is said that some governments have trained "observers" to view enemy secrets at a distance, by envisioning a scene at a distance. The psychic and the physical met on the field of battle.

Another famous event took place on February 2, 1966, when polygraph (lie detector) expert Cleve Backster decided to use his instruments to measure plants in his office. He wanted to see if they showed any response to external stimulus. So he attached probes to their leaves. As it turned out, they reacted wildly, displaying a galvanic response that measured huge changes in electrical conductivity.

When "threatened" with being pruned or burned by the flame of a match, the meter on the polygraph would spike. When the threat was removed, they would return to normal. Amazingly, Backster discovered that when an adjoining plant was threatened, the first plant—the one attached to the meter—reacted just as strongly! It was as though, on some level, they were communicating.

He automated these experiments, allowing mechanical threats to take place when no human was present. The plants responded in exactly the same way. He separated them by longer and longer distances. The plants responded as before. But on what level were they able to communicate? Plants have no brains or nervous systems. They have only life, but who can define that? Backster speculated that perhaps there is a "force" or connection at some level, unknown to science.[91]

Theoretically, there is no limit to the distance over which plants… and indeed, all living things…can communicate. Imagination has become reality. We recall the intrepid adventurers of *Star Trek*. Just as Kirk, Spock, and Scotty communicated instantly over what they called "subspace radio," today's scientists routinely speak of effects that are coupled over incredible distances. Something is operating at a level below the threshold of visibility.

Backster's experiments have grown into funded research. Science is now convinced that something happens at such a subtle level that renders direct observation impossible. Thus, parapsychologists are faced with the same difficulty as quantum physicists. Researchers in both fields can "see" something happening only indirectly. They cannot peek inside the box.

THE CAT HAS MANY LIVES

And now comes a new discovery, recently publicized by the National Institute of Science and Technology (NIST). In a news release dated November 30, 2005, they announced that "NIST Physicists Coax Six Atoms into Quantum 'Cat' State." The cat they mention in this release is none other than Schrödinger's Cat!

> Boulder, Colo.—Scientists at the Commerce Department's National Institute of Standards and Technology (NIST) have coaxed six atoms into spinning together in two opposite directions at the same time, a so-called Schrödinger "cat" state that obeys the unusual laws of quantum physics. The ambitious choreography could be useful in applications such as quantum computing and cryptography, as well as ultra-sensitive measurement techniques, all of which rely on exquisite control of nature's smallest particles.[92]

Note in the above news release that six atoms are spinning in unison in two opposite directions at the same time! In our humdrum world of daily existence, this is flatly impossible. But what follows moves into the world of the bizarre:

> NIST scientists entangled six beryllium ions (charged atoms) so that their nuclei were collectively spinning clockwise and counterclockwise at the same time. Entanglement, which Albert Einstein called "spooky action at a distance," occurs when the quantum properties of two or more particles are correlated.[93]

In the experiment, one of the six atoms is targeted by an ultraviolet laser beam, causing it to change its spin to a known direction. The others, "entangled" with it, change their directions, too. NIST physicist Dietrich Leibfried said, "During this process, the ions all 'talk' to each other at the same time, like in a conference call."[94]

This effect was first demonstrated at the University of Paris in 1982, when physicist Alain Aspect performed a quantum experiment that prompted the observation that communication is possible over any distance. Science now says that past, present, and future all exist at the same time, and that every point in three-dimensional space is equally distant from every other point. Time-space is an interwoven whole.

Here's the bottom line: Theoretically, there is no limit to the distance over which separated, "cat-state" atoms can communicate. Atoms entangled at the quantum level could be on opposite sides of the galaxy, and still react to each other at the same instant.

Thus, at a very deep level, there exists a universal connection between all things. The secret knowledge sought by science is virtually indistinguishable from metaphysics—the investigation of knowing, being, cause, identity, substance, time, and space.

This, then, is the secret knowledge that the Serpent promised Eve. He told her that she and Adam could be like gods, knowing not just the glories of God in Heaven, but the "dark side" as well—good and evil.

THE BIBLE AND ULTIMATE REALITY

At this point, lest we fall into the whirlpool of secular confusion, we must return to the certainty and confidence of biblical truth. How does the Bible view the subject of objective reality versus the apparent knowledge that all we see is simply illusion?

First, it draws a clear distinction between time and eternity. We live "trapped" in time, always faced with the fact of our own ignorance. In terms of position, we are limited to the barriers of time-space. Inquiring about God necessarily results in a series of paradoxes.

We ask how God can be every place at the same time (omnipresent). We might just as well ask how He can be every time at the same place (omniscient). Again, we might ask how He can alter the conditions of time-space (omnipotent). His every action demonstrates His dominion. He created our universe and maintains it.

He is that indefinable force...the One who gives sense to all that is.

We walk in a world of paradoxes, where the deeper spiritual truths often defy intuition. We are puzzled and perplexed by apparent ambiguities and seeming contradictions. But that is only because of our position...far inferior to God's. We are down; He is up: "For my thoughts are not your thoughts, neither are your ways my ways, saith the LORD. For as the heavens are higher than the earth, so are my ways higher than your ways, and my thoughts than your thoughts" (Isaiah 55:8–9).

It is a given that God's attributes are higher than man's—infinitely higher. His thoughts and His ways are higher. In other words, both His intellect and His situation are higher. His place is superior.

In what way are man's thoughts inferior to God's? Of course, we don't possess His intellect. Nor do we operate from a position of power, with access to any location. But most importantly, we are restricted to a lower dimension. This can be easily seen in a simple exercise of the imagination.

We often use the phrase "the heavens above." But when we do, we are not referring to direction, as in "up the hill" or "down in the valley." Rather, we are speaking of an upward move in status, position, or dimension. Eternity is everywhere, no matter which direction we point. It is the eternal "here and now."

If "the heavens above" were directional, a man in the United States might point it out to a friend while pointing in the general direction of Polaris, the North Star. A man in Australia talking to his friend about heaven might gesture toward the Southern Cross. Of course, they would be pointing in opposite directions. One with a simplistic understanding of the meaning of "up" would dismiss the whole idea that a heaven really exists. After all, even Christians in two different hemispheres can't agree on its location. Its very existence must, therefore, be in question.

Upon hearing about this seeming contradiction, the cynic would smile knowingly and scoff at the whole naïve notion of heaven and the ignorance of those who believe in it.

But with the proper understanding of dimensionality, we understand that both the American and the Australian are correct when they point upward. Heaven *is* up…in a higher dimension, where God's "thoughts" and "ways" both lie above the parameters of our universe.

His "ways" come from a translation of the Hebrew word *derek,* meaning "pathway, road or walk." In other words, the state in which God walks is *above* the state in which we walk. In fact, in our present physical state, we cannot walk there, because we are, by definition, a lower creation.

TRANSCENDENCE, TRANSLATION, TRANSFORMATION

This condition is beautifully illustrated in the Bible's brief narrative about the life of Enoch. This righteous man presents us with an amazing exception to the usual rule of the human walk:

And Jared lived an hundred sixty and two years, and he begat
Enoch: And Jared lived after he begat Enoch eight hundred
years, and begat sons and daughters: And all the days of Jared

were nine hundred sixty and two years: and he died. And
Enoch lived sixty and five years, and begat Methuselah: And
Enoch walked with God after he begat Methuselah three
hundred years, and begat sons and daughters: And all the days
of Enoch were three hundred sixty and five years: And Enoch
walked with God: and he was not; for God took him.
(Genesis 5:18–24)

Enoch, the son of Jared, was in the godly line of Seth. The name
"Enoch" comes from a Hebrew word root that means "trained or edu-
cated." It is universally taught that he was directly translated to heaven
without dying.

At the age of sixty-five, Enoch fathered Methuselah, then he lived
another three hundred years, at which time he walked right off the pages
of Scripture and into the dimension of God. It was as if he went through
a door into heaven. At the moment of his disappearance, he was raised
to the higher dimension of God.

Had we been standing close to him at the time, he would probably
have just "winked out." In mid-stride, he would have simply disappeared.
He had risen to God's level...gone "up" to the place where God walks.
Nor was it his own volition that took him up to that level.

God must have recognized in him a finely tuned fellowship, and so
"took him."

Historical explanations of Enoch's experience usually state that he
was transformed—changed in some way that made him compatible with
the higher dimension we call heaven.

But was this in fact the case? Might he not have been simply allowed
access to the dimension of eternity without undergoing a transformation?
There is good reason to ask this question, since we seem to find other
scriptural evidence that suggests the possibility that a normal human
being can enter heaven.

Since the Resurrection of Jesus in a transformed and glorified body,
the faithful have longed to undergo the experience of glorification. Enoch
simply walked with God. The body of Christ will experience a sudden

transformation. The promise of Christ does not teach the faithful to expect the same sort of change that came to Enoch, who was unique. But his example is given to us as a way of explaining dimensionality.

That is, from his day to our own, the faithful have lived with the promise that they will ascend into the place where God eternally dwells. The only prerequisite is to be sufficiently righteous in God's eyes.

THE CHARIOT AND THE CLOUD

But there seems to be another biblical cause for one to be taken into heaven. Elijah, for example, was commissioned for a special work. He was destined to be more than a prophet in the era of his birth. He was also to be a beacon of God's design during the era of Christ. Not only that, his work will continue into our future!

His calling came during the reign of the wicked King Ahab. That calling stretched across the ages to the Transfiguration, where he and Moses appeared on the mountaintop before Jesus, Peter, James, and John.

It will reach into the future as Elijah becomes one of the two witnesses who stand against the Antichrist, as he once did before Ahab and Jezebel. The prophet Elijah became a prophecy remembered by the Jews at every Passover seder when they set a place at the table, expecting him to come.

Like Enoch, Elijah was lifted into heaven—but in his case, we are given some detail about the translation. A fiery chariot took him. This was no mere physical chariot. It was a celestial vehicle, capable of inter-dimensional travel. When it disappeared, it was seen no more:

> And it came to pass, as they still went on, and talked, that, behold, there appeared a chariot of fire, and horses of fire, and parted them both asunder; and Elijah went up by a whirlwind into heaven.
>
> And Elisha saw it, and he cried, My father, my father, the chariot of Israel, and the horsemen thereof. And he saw him no

more: and he took hold of his own clothes, and rent them in
two pieces. (2 Kings 2:11, 12)

One second, Elijah was visible to Elisha. The next second, he was not.
Though he went to heaven, his real work as a prophet of God was yet to
be done. One day, he will return to his people as a physical being.

There is no indication that he was transformed at the time he was taken
aboard the chariot. As Elisha witnessed his departure, the powerful vehicle
took Elijah into heaven. There is no record that he was changed in any way.

In fact, at the Transfiguration, Jesus changed before the disciples' eyes,
glorified into a being of light. But Moses and Elijah simply appeared.
There is no record of their glorification: "And, behold, there appeared
unto them Moses and Elias talking with him" (Matthew 17:3).

Elijah seems to have been taken into heaven bodily, while remaining
human. The prophecy that he will return to Israel in the latter days does
not suggest that he will be born into a new body at that time. Perhaps he
will simply be dropped off near Jerusalem in the same way he was picked
up so many years ago.

The point is this: In Christ, the subtleties of interdimensional existence have form and purpose and identity. They have personalities and
names. Heaven is a reality that makes sense, not an ambivalent state of
apparent contradictions.

OUR LORD ASCENDS

After His Resurrection, Jesus revealed Himself to His followers and
many others. In every record we have, He was seen as a normal, physical
human being during the forty-day period following His Resurrection.

But then He went back to heaven. Interestingly, He went in some
sort of celestial vehicle:

And when he had spoken these things, while they beheld, he
was taken up; and a cloud received him out of their sight. And

while they looked stedfastly toward heaven as he went up,
behold, two men stood by them in white apparel;

Which also said, Ye men of Galilee, why stand ye gazing up
into heaven? this same Jesus, which is taken up from you into
heaven, shall so come in like manner as ye have seen him go
into heaven. (Acts 1:9–11)

Why did Jesus enter a cloud for His return to heaven? He might have
simply thought Himself there, and would instantly have arrived. More
than likely, He wanted to make His return to heaven "official." Many
watched him enter the cloud (which, by the way, was no ordinary cloud).
After that, probably for hours, the saints gazed upward to see if He would
reappear. Two angels came to the scene to redirect their attention to normal daily life. They told His followers to go on with the pursuits of daily
living, keeping in mind that He will return, just as He left.

BODILY ASCENT TO HEAVEN

The apostle Paul relates his own experience in dimensional travel, and
his description of the event underscores the difficulty of determining the
exact nature of the phenomenon. As far as he was concerned, he went
there bodily. But twice, he asserts that though the situation involved him
personally, he couldn't be sure whether he was experiencing his travel in
his physical body, or in the spirit:

It is not expedient for me doubtless to glory. I will come to
visions and revelations of the Lord. I knew a man in Christ
above fourteen years ago, (whether in the body, I cannot tell; or
whether out of the body, I cannot tell: God knoweth;) such an
one caught up to the third heaven.

And I knew such a man, (whether in the body, or out of
the body, I cannot tell: God knoweth;) How that he was caught
up into paradise, and heard unspeakable words, which it is not

lawful for a man to utter. Of such an one will I glory: yet of myself I will not glory, but in mine infirmities.
(2 Corinthians 12:1–5)

However, based upon a comparison with the incidents in the lives of Enoch, Elijah, and Jesus, travel in the body seems perfectly reasonable. But note that Paul says that he was "caught up." He uses the same term used to describe what has come to be called "the Rapture." Both here and in his Rapture passages, Paul's term suggests a rapid upward movement. But this is only a suggestion, since, as we have already established, "up" is not a directional term, but a dimensional one.

In heaven, Paul learned many things that he was forbidden to repeat when back on earth. No doubt, much of what he heard is the knowledge that the Serpent used to deceive the woman. In his present state, sinful man is simply not allowed to know the secrets of this universe, much less those of heaven!

"Come Up Hither"

And then, there is the experience of John, who entered heaven through a "door." But this was not his normal experience of walking through a door. This one took him upward:

After this I looked, and, behold, a door was opened in heaven: and the first voice which I heard was as it were of a trumpet talking with me; which said, Come up hither, and I will shew thee things which must be hereafter. And immediately I was in the spirit: and, behold, a throne was set in heaven, and one sat on the throne. (Revelation 4:1, 2)

In this instance of travel to heaven, we have John's observation that "immediately" he was "in the spirit." We must remain ignorant of the precise meaning of this expression. Does it mean that John didn't go in his body, or does it mean that his body was somehow modified for a temporary stay in heaven? There is no way to know.

Probably, if we could have put this question to John, he would have said, "Whether in the body, or out of the body, I cannot tell."

But if the narratives of Enoch and Elijah can be generalized, John went in his body. Furthermore, he went into the future. As we have written elsewhere, his perspective was that of a man already in the future, observing things that were happening to him *right now*. To him, the events of the apocalypse were current and powerful present realities.

BEFORE EARTH'S FOUNDATION

When Jesus walked in this world, He brought the vastness of time-space into the life of a single human being. Furthermore, He reduced the complexities of creation into a single word: love. Love is, in fact, the true secret of creation…the strong force that befuddles science. They cannot know it unless they know Him.

Love was manifested eons ago, before there was ever a human race. Even then, God saw humanity and the Son of Man, who would come to live among those He created. More than a descriptive term, love is the central action through which the eternal God manifests Himself in this dimension. It was love that Jesus recalled in His prayer in the garden:

> I in them, and thou in me, that they may be made perfect in one; and that the world may know that thou hast sent me, and hast loved them, as thou hast loved me.
>
> Father, I will that they also, whom thou hast given me, be with me where I am; that they may behold my glory, which thou hast given me: for thou lovedst me before the foundation of the world. (John 17:23, 24)

Jesus' prayer invokes the love of the Father as He speaks of the perfect fellowship of the saints. This process began before this earth's foundation was laid, then was brought to its conclusion in Adam, and will be perfected in Christ, the "second Adam."

Many have written about the complexities and paradoxical contradictions of predestination. Yet we are now becoming able to perceive, however dimly, that God dwells in the eternal present. He allows man to make choices, yet can foresee those choices. For Him this is normal; for us, it is paradoxical:

Blessed be the God and Father of our Lord Jesus Christ, who hath blessed us with all spiritual blessings in heavenly places in Christ: According as he hath chosen us in him before the foundation of the world, that we should be holy and without blame before him in love: Having predestinated us unto the adoption of children by Jesus Christ to himself, according to the good pleasure of his will, To the praise of the glory of his grace, wherein he hath made us accepted in the beloved. (Ephesians 1:3–6)

He chose us, yet we chose Him. At some crucial point in the life of everyone who is redeemed, a decision was made. The saved stand upon the threshold of heaven, where the eternal present abolishes all our preconceptions about cause and effect.

God's plan for redemption was completed before there was ever an Adam and an Eve, or sin in the Garden of Eden.

Forasmuch as ye know that ye were not redeemed with corruptible things, as silver and gold, from your vain conversation received by tradition from your fathers; But with the precious blood of Christ, as of a lamb without blemish and without spot: Who verily was foreordained before the foundation of the world, but was manifest in these last times for you, Who by him do believe in God, that raised him up from the dead, and gave him glory; that your faith and hope might be in God. (1 Peter 1:18–21)

How could God have foreseen this need for human redemption? Because His love—the creative force of our universe—demanded that He give the cleansing blood of His only begotten Son. He was ordained to this cause before the creation of the world.

Only faith and a biblical understanding of the delicate pathways between heaven and earth can give us the peaceful acceptance of what is otherwise inexplicable. The bizarre paradoxes of creation are peacefully reconciled in the person of Jesus Christ. He is the underlying force who can only be perceived in the act of faith. He is the Word of Creation. He *is* love.

25

LIFE IN THE COSMOS

Thousands of years ago, the Lord's work of salvation began when the Serpent brought downfall to Adam and Eve, and by extension, to all humanity. With the Fall came God's promise of a Man—an offspring of Eve—who would bruise the Serpent's head.

This event marked the strange beginning of man's long journey to eternity. From the human perspective, the trek is marked off by the events of history—the twists and turns of an evil past, told in the characters and events of biblical history. But within the evils and intrigues of the narrative, one finds good. More than that, one discovers holiness.

For though man would travail through the millennia, his salvation was already an accomplished fact. There are two views of salvation. One regards it as already achieved; the other sees it as precariously balanced on the knife-edge of destruction, poised to be lost in a moment of time.

But the Bible consistently views the Christian's salvation as something *already accomplished.* Though we will not reach glorification until some future date, the Bible presents our salvation as already attained *in the present,* and as having been assured in the distant past. In other words, believers now possess eternal life. John's first epistle is built around this assurance: "And this is the record, that God hath given to us eternal life, and this life is in his Son. He that hath the Son hath life; and he that hath not the Son of God hath not life" (1 John 5:11, 12).

We might leave it at that, except for an observation peculiar to eternal life as we now think of it. By definition, eternity envelops all of the past, present, and future. This means that if we now possess it, it is as though we always possessed it. Certainly, it is a primary article of our faith that, having believed in the Lord, we now stand before the Father in a state of complete exoneration from the penalty of sin. As Paul put it: "There is therefore now no condemnation to them which are in Christ Jesus, who walk not after the flesh, but after the Spirit" (Romans 8:1).

The word "now" implies the present, or our present status. But this status was obtained through the finished work of Christ. From our perspective, the process of redemption actually began in ages past. Perhaps it would be more accurate to say that it was totally accomplished in ages past.

An Irony of Time-Space

As physical creatures who live on a finite timeline, we may have decided to follow Jesus only weeks, months, or years ago. Yet, our common salvation is presented as having been secured in the ancient days before time was kept. In His intercessory prayer before His Father, Jesus identifies Himself with the redeemed, asking the Father that they (we) might be brought into the same loving relationship that He enjoyed. That relationship, of course, existed prior to His incarnation, even prior to the existence of the "world:"

> I in them, and thou in me, that they may be made perfect in one; and that the **world** may know that thou hast sent me, and hast loved them, as thou hast loved me.
>
> Father, I will that they also, whom thou hast given me, be with me where I am; that they may behold my glory, which thou hast given me: for thou lovedst me **before the foundation of the world.** (John 17:23, 24, emphasis added)

Here, Jesus prays that believers might experience the Father's love in the same way that He knew it in ages past. In the opening exposition of his letter to the Ephesians, Paul states the same idea. However, this time, another theme is presented. He informs us that the saints were chosen before the "world" was established: "According as he hath chosen us in him **before the foundation of the world**, that we should be holy and without blame before him in love" (Ephesians 1:4, emphasis added).

Among Christians, this statement has provoked much discussion. Some, taking the extreme position, have concluded that it means believers were predestined to salvation before they ever had a choice in the matter. The inference—and subject of a thousand books—is that an individual really has nothing to do with his own salvation, except to accept and enjoy it. Freedom of choice is ruled out, because the decision was made before he was ever born.

But there is an irony of time-space here. Before there was ever a "world," our salvation was complete, as good as finished. This seems impossible unless we see the eternal as simultaneous with the "now." Or, in other words, why would the Lord create the "world" and put us in it, if He controlled our choices in advance?

Unless we ourselves were truly allowed to make choices for or against Christ, such choices would be utterly meaningless.

This discussion begs another question: From Christ's perspective, when was the "world" created? The answer is obvious: He created it in the "eternal now." As He said, "Before Abraham was, I am" (John 8:58). But the full answer is much more complex than this.

Nor have we properly identified what, exactly, is meant by the "world." This, we shall attempt to do a bit later. But first, look at Peter's first epistle.

He uses the same expression in speaking of Christ's completed work when, in the ageless past, He was ordained to do His work of redemption. Here, the context is not the salvation of the individual, as such, but the ordination of Christ in a past era.

It is important to remember that from our perspective, His work began before a certain point in time, namely, the foundation of the world system:

> Forasmuch as ye know that ye were not redeemed with corruptible things, as silver and gold, from your vain conversation received by tradition from your fathers; But with the precious blood of Christ, as of a lamb without blemish and without spot: Who verily was foreordained **before the foundation of the world**, but was manifest in these last times for you. (1 Peter 1:18–20, emphasis added)

In all the above instances, the word "foundation" is translated from the Greek, *katabole,* meaning "a casting-down" or "laying a foundation." It is common knowledge that structures have foundations. They represent the initiation of a project…in this case, the "world," or the world system.

THE TEMPORAL WORLD

In the quotations above, the "world" comes from the Greek word *kosmos.* It is used more than 180 times in the New Testament. From this point forward, we shall use this word as a technical term. It speaks of the existing temporal design and situation of the earth, and by extension, the solar system and even the universe. It has often been called the "world order" or the "world system."

Romans 1:20 illustrates this use of the word: "For the invisible things of him from the creation of the **world** are clearly seen, being understood by the things that are made, even his eternal power and Godhead; so that they are without excuse" (emphasis added).

Here, Paul uses the Greek term *kosmos* (again, translated as "world") to describe all that may be seen of God's creation. It is a grand display of His design and order. Specifically, it is the sum total of the temporal order. It is never to be confused with the eternal, sinless harmony of the heavens above.

Specifically, the *kosmos* refers to the fallen and sinful creation that is locked in time. More specifically, it is a timeline that has a date with destiny. The *kosmos* has been likened to a stage upon which the human drama is played out to its dramatic conclusion. It is much as depicted in one of William Shakespeare's most famous quotes, from *As You Like It*:[95]

All the world's a stage,
And all the men and women merely players.
They have their exits and their entrances,
And one man in his time plays many parts,
His acts being seven ages.

Those ages—infant, whining schoolboy, young lover, soldier, judge, emaciated elder, and final death—are the very image of sin and dissipation.

The *kosmos* is an evil place. Its race is fallen; its systems are in disarray, with storms, winds, grime, decay, earthquakes, volcanoes, and the roaring of restless seas of water, gases, and ice. Even the solar system is pockmarked and cratered, fragmented and swept by deadly cosmic winds.

FIRST CORINTHIANS

From the biblical perspective, the collective wisdom of the cosmos is a sad recitation of failure and colossal ignorance. One book in the Bible seems devoted to proving this distressing reality. It is delivered by Paul as a letter to the most worldly and decadent of ancient Greek cities. Corinth boasted the latest in Greek philosophy and fashionable trade goods. Its arts and cuisine were the pinnacle of Graeco-Roman culture. Its morals and manners were debauched. In every sense, it was "modern."

In Paul's letter, it provides the perfect exhibit of the failed *kosmos*. The following paragraph is a collection of verses from 1 Corinthians. At the end of each sentence the appropriate verse is indicated, because some verses are skipped. In every case where the word "world" appears (in boldface), it is a translation of *kosmos:*

> Where is the wise? where is the scribe? where is the disputer of this **world**? hath not God made foolish the wisdom of this **world**? (1:20). For after that in the wisdom of God the **world** by wisdom knew not God, it pleased God by the foolishness of preaching to save them that believe (1:21). But God hath chosen the foolish things of the **world** to confound the wise; and God hath chosen the weak things of the **world** to confound the things which are mighty (1:27); And base things of the **world**, and things which are despised, hath God chosen, yea, and things which are not, to bring to nought things that are" (1:28).

Note that those things regarded by the "world" *(kosmos)* as wisdom are in reality base, foolish, and weak. In the following paragraph, another compilation of verses from 1 Corinthians contrasts the eternal wisdom of God with the vain and ignorant knowledge of this cosmos.

> But we speak the wisdom of God in a mystery, even the hidden wisdom, which God ordained before the world unto our glory (2:7). Which none of the princes of this world knew: for had they known it, they would not have crucified the Lord of glory (2:8).
> But as it is written, Eye hath not seen, nor ear heard, neither have entered into the heart of man, the things which God hath prepared for them that love him (2:9). But God hath revealed them unto us by his Spirit: for the Spirit searcheth all things, yea, the deep things of God (2:10). For what man knoweth the things of a man, save the spirit of man which is in him? even so the things of God knoweth no man, but the Spirit of God (2:11). Now we have received, not the spirit of the world, but the spirit which is of God; that we might know

the things that are freely given to us of God (2:12). For the wisdom of this world is foolishness with God. For it is written, He taketh the wise in their own craftiness (3:19).

THE COSMOS DEFINED

The foregoing verses from 1 Corinthians represent only a small selection from Paul's emphatic condemnation of the "world." He makes it more than clear that the "world"—the *kosmos*—is a place of corruption and misery. Except for Christ it would be utterly without remedy, hopeless, yet deluding itself in the belief that it had some hope after all. It is a place of foolishness and vanity.

The biblical Greek *kosmos* translates directly into English as "cosmos." It denotes the visible universe. As the late Carl Sagan often said, "The cosmos is all that there is…or ever will be." As a mathematician and physicist, he entered the field of study called "cosmology," devoting himself to theorizing about the origin and development of the universe.

Like others of his persuasion, he wrote about astronomy and particle physics. He speculated that the "big bang" created the universe and all that it contains. His "wisdom" excluded God and Creation. And yet modern science holds cosmology high as the key to all understanding the universe.

To the eyes of a human being, the cosmos may appear limitless, when in fact it really serves to limit the range of humanity. We are trapped on the surface of the earth. Given a few more decades, we may venture as far as Mars. But still, humanity is limited to a place ruled by the passionate lust for power. As long as we are imprisoned here, other dimensions are safe. But humanity's jailer is a cruel overlord whose history and personality are well known.

Planet earth may well be likened to the infamous "Devil's Island," a prison off the coast of French Guiana. It is a tiny place…about thirty-five acres in extent. From 1852 until 1946, it was used by the French as a place of extreme isolation, from which escape was impossible. Political prisoners, thieves, and murderers sent there often disappeared, never to be heard from again. Brutal and vicious treatment was the norm. Disease and torture were routine. Its cruel guardians made the place a living hell. Ruling over this place, they truly played the role of devils.

SATAN AND THE COSMOS

The cosmos has a ruling hierarchy, with Satan at the top of the order. Those who serve him are often referred to as princes. We recall the "prince of Persia," a dark angel who hindered the heavenly messenger sent to Daniel.

In the following passage, these princes are mentioned twice. First, they are presented as those who will eventually fall from power. Second, though powerful, Scripture always shows them to be completely blind to God's plan of redemption:

> Howbeit we speak wisdom among them that are perfect: yet not the wisdom of this **world**, nor of the princes of this **world**, that come to nought:
> But we speak the wisdom of God in a mystery, even the hidden wisdom, which God ordained before the **world** unto our glory:
> Which none of the princes of this **world** knew: for had they known it, they would not have crucified the Lord of glory. (1 Corinthians 2:6–8, emphasis added)

These are not human princes. They are the higher powers—the powers behind the throne—who translate the policy of the unseen spiritual world into the visible and violent acts of powerful men. As Paul writes in Ephesians 6:12, "For we wrestle not against flesh and blood, but against principalities, against powers, against the rulers of the darkness of this world, against spiritual wickedness in high places." These are the dark princes, their delegated authorities and the demonic hordes who do their bidding.

In 2 Corinthians 2:4, the leader of these princes is called "the god of this world" who has "blinded the minds of them which believe not."

This, of course, refers to Satan, whose active principle is that of debunking spiritual truth. In modern terms, one might say that he operates a continuous disinformation program, specifically aimed at making God's spiritual truth appear ridiculous. Among other things, he is constantly bent on making the fallen cosmos appear attractive.

This fundamental truth is that Satan is the chief of all the princes, and he is so named in Ephesians 2:2: "Wherein in time past ye walked according to the course of this world, according to the prince of the power of the air, the spirit that now worketh in the children of disobedience."

He sets the direction and focus of the cosmos, even in its latest earthly incarnation, the "New World Order." Here, Satan is identified as the leader of the spirit world. It is he who travels through the atmospheric heavens, superintending the territory that he regards as his and his alone.

SATAN AND JOB

In the biography of the righteous Job, Satan is revealed in a detailed portrait, as he interacts with Jehovah...the Lord. Though he is a lesser being than the Lord, Satan displays a surprising autonomy. He is quite free to interact with the Lord, even to the point of disagreement about the righteousness of an ordinary man called Job:

> Now there was a day when the sons of God came to present
> themselves before the LORD, and Satan came also among them.
> And the LORD said unto Satan, Whence comest thou? Then
> Satan answered the LORD, and said, From going to and fro in
> the earth, and from walking up and down in it. (Job 1:6, 7)

It will come as no surprise to anyone who has studied the Bible that Satan considers the world (the cosmos) his home territory. In fact, he freely travels throughout its entire extent. If the cosmos extends to cover the entire solar system, his range of authority is large, indeed. And it may, in fact, extend beyond that, since the cosmos seems to be a term that covers the whole creation, which Paul describes as follows: "For we know that the whole creation groaneth and travaileth in pain together until now" (Romans 8:22).

This "creation" would include the universe, and all that is in it. "Groaning" and "travailing" are certainly an accurate characterization of Job's plight. On this note, it is absolutely amazing that we are allowed a glimpse of the culture of heaven, but that is exactly what the book of Job gives us.

Having exchanged polite greetings with Satan, the Lord asks him a question about a righteous mortal, a man who lives on the earth below. In the brief conversation that follows, we learn something very interesting:

And the LORD said unto Satan, Hast thou considered my servant Job, that there is none like him in the earth, a perfect and an upright man, one that feareth God, and escheweth evil?
Then Satan answered the LORD, and said, Doth Job fear God for nought? Hast not thou made an hedge about him, and about his house, and about all that he hath on every side? thou hast blessed the work of his hands, and his substance is increased in the land.
But put forth thine hand now, and touch all that he hath, and he will curse thee to thy face. (Job 1:8–10)

Here, we learn that Job's compound—his lands, household, and live-stock—is under the Lord's protection and blessing. This emphatically establishes the *need* for such protection. As a citizen of the cosmos, Job required the covering of the Lord in order to prosper. In other words, he was living in an alien environment.

Satan scoffs at the Lord's suggestion that he is a righteous and upright man simply because it's the right thing to do. He challenges the Lord on this ground, saying that Job's faith is dependent upon what he manages to get from the Lord. He accuses Job of following the Lord for profit.

The Lord's reaction is to allow Satan to test Job. Why? Because the cosmos is precisely that—a test for humanity, or more precisely, a test bed upon which the drama of light and darkness is played out.

In Job's case, the Lord's protection is lifted, allowing the horrors of the cosmos to flood in upon Job's life. Through the agency of Job's enemies and even fire and wind from heaven, Job's fortunes are eradicated. Crops, livestock, homes, and families were all swept into oblivion.

Job passes the test. He blesses the Lord:

And said, Naked came I out of my mother's womb, and naked shall I return thither: the LORD gave, and the LORD hath taken away; blessed be the name of the LORD. In all this Job sinned not, nor charged God foolishly. (Job1:21, 22)

In an amazing display of faith, Job continues to trust the Lord. His simple statement displays an amazing understanding of God's love. It is one thing to trust the One who provides; it is quite another to continue in faith when blessing and protection are removed.

It is clear that the Lord trusted Job's steadfast belief. Why else would He have used this righteous man as a demonstration against Satan? In some way, Job knew that the Lord had this trust in him. Why else would he have held firm in the face of such disaster?

Undaunted, Satan challenged the Lord once again. Take note; this meeting on high reveals a scheduled meeting, or some sort of heavenly protocol:

Again there was a day when the sons of God came to present themselves before the LORD, and Satan came also among them to present himself before the LORD.

And the LORD said unto Satan, From whence comest thou? And Satan answered the LORD, and said, From going to and fro in the earth, and from walking up and down in it.

And the LORD said unto Satan, Hast thou considered my

servant Job, that there is none like him in the earth, a perfect and an upright man, one that feareth God, and escheweth evil? and still he holdeth fast his integrity, although thou movedst me against him, to destroy him without cause.

And Satan answered the LORD, and said, Skin for skin, yea, all that a man hath will he give for his life. But put forth thine hand now, and touch his bone and his flesh, and he will curse thee to thy face.

And the LORD said unto Satan, Behold, he is in thine hand; but save his life.

So went Satan forth from the presence of the LORD, and smote Job with sore boils from the sole of his foot unto his crown. (Job 2:1–7)

Thus begins the saga of Job. The rest of the story is devoted to a tortuous series of discussions from the human point of view. Job's deep deliberations with his peers are the Bible's most thorough investigation of God's motives. Their reasoning ranges from ridiculous to sublime. Still, they are unable to understand God's operations and intents.

Overall, they charge the Lord with being unfair to Job—punishing him for some imagined sin left unconfessed, or self-righteousness, or hypocrisy. None of their guesses are anywhere close to the mark. In the end, Job is adjudged righteous, but his friends are chastised for their faithlessness.

THE INVISIBLE COSMOS

By now, we have more than enough information to conclude that residents of the cosmos are ensnared in the time-space continuum, where they live in a condition of isolation from God. In their natural state, they live in the sphere of their own vain imagination.

It is generally the case that residents of the cosmos completely fail to understand the will and purpose of God. When Jesus came into the cosmos, its culture neither recognized nor understood Him. John's Gospel calls Him the Word:

> In the beginning was the Word, and the Word was with God, and the Word was God. The same was in the beginning with God.
>
> All things were made by him; and without him was not any thing made that was made. In him was life; and the life was the light of men. And the light shineth in darkness; and the darkness comprehended it not.
>
> There was a man sent from God, whose name was John. The same came for a witness, to bear witness of the Light, that all men through him might believe. He was not that Light, but was sent to bear witness of that Light.
>
> That was the true Light, which lighteth every man that cometh into the **world**. He was in the **world**, and the **world** was made by him, and the **world** knew him not. (John 1:1–10, emphasis added)

In verses 9 and 10 of the magnificent description above, the word *kosmos* is used four times, translated "world." Again, we see that the cosmos is utterly blind, not only to God's existence and presence, but to the fact that He created the very world in which they walk.

With today's scoffers condemning the teaching of "Intelligent Design" in the classroom, we see that nothing has changed. The state of mind in the cosmos is blissful ignorance, coupled with the confidence that all things are unchanged from the past to the present. To the cosmic mind, the heavens and the earth proceed in a uniform and predictable fashion, flowing along in accordance with scientific predictability.

Jesus Meets the Ruler of the Cosmos

Before His public ministry, Jesus went into the wilderness, where He was tested by the one known as the god of this world... Satan, "the prince of the power of the air." It is of particular interest that, here, the old Serpent appears as the "devil."

This term—translated from the Greek *diabolos*—identifies Satan in his role as the "slanderer." He systematically maligns and disparages Jesus, acknowledging His divinity, but probing the seriousness of His commitment. In the process, he discovers that Jesus' holiness and dedication are absolute.

Apparently, Satan realizes that Jesus is on earth to do some important work. Nevertheless, he tries to corrupt the Lord and nip His mission in the bud. The test involves a trip into a dimension from which it is apparently possible to view the world in its entirety...its geography, control centers, and political intrigues:

"Again, the devil taketh him up into an exceeding high mountain, and sheweth him all the kingdoms of the world, and the glory of them" (Matthew 4:8).

In Luke's account of the test, there is an additional note—the element of time: "And the devil, taking him up into an high mountain, shewed unto him all the kingdoms of the world in a moment of time" (Luke 4:5).

Looking closely at this statement is quite revealing. Satan took Christ to a place described as a "high mountain." But there is no mountain on the face of the earth that affords the kind of view suggested here. This mountain must be in another dimension. Still, it must also be part of the cosmos that Satan rules, since he demonstrated the ability to come and go from that place as he pleased. So it is logical to conclude that there are parts of the cosmos not visible to human eyes. Nevertheless, as Satan roams in that dimension, he is able to see the earth while remaining unseen by the peoples of this planet. And of course, this is just what the Bible says about him.

Under normal circumstances, a tour of all the world's kingdoms would involve a great deal of time. Did Satan physically take the Lord on a trip to all the world's capitals? The text doesn't say that. But perhaps their trip consumed a period of what would be called "time" in our dimension. It seems that in that place, a second or two of our time offers the opportunity to do what would take years as we reckon time.

In short, the devil is shown to have great power in the cosmos. He has the ability to conduct a world tour in a mere moment. Somehow, he has possession of the power and glory of the cosmos. He offered it to the Lord.

But his action also demonstrates something else. It shows that he is ignorant of Christ's plan for the cosmos. Just as the opening words of John's Gospel tell us, Satan is somehow unable to see the truth of the Lord's motives and actions. It is truly remarkable that with such power over the cosmos, he can't visualize the truth about it. To paraphrase John, Jesus was in the cosmos—the cosmos was made by Him, but it didn't know Him. More to the point, it didn't recognize His work and intentions.

WHEN THE COSMOS WAS FOUNDED

As suggested earlier, the term "foundation of the world" poses the "when" question. Namely, when was the cosmos founded? Science answers this question in the realm of astronomy and geology. It has arrived at a figure of about fifteen billion years ago, give or take a little.

The Bible puts the creation of "the heavens and the earth" in a framework of six literal days, making the visible universe and solar system only a few thousand years old. But as we have seen in the episode of Satan's temptation of Christ, the cosmos also includes an invisible dimension, where heaven meets earth.

Certainly, it existed before the physical earth was created, as did Satan, who was formerly an anointed cherub, or guardian, at the throne of God. His iniquitous fall from that position certainly predates the creation of Adam and Eve.

Logically, then, the corruption of the cosmos began with Satan's fall. Adam and Eve were the progenitors of a new race, created by God with a purpose, to redeem this fallen cosmos. Out of their lineage would come the Messiah.

Ironically, He created the cosmos, but remains unknown by those outside the sphere of His redeeming love. To them He is a mystery. The idea that the universe or cosmos is currently in a fallen state is, to them, ludicrous.

The real answer to the time of the world's foundation lies in the fact that it was created from the perspective of the Lord, whom John's Gospel calls the "Word." He spoke time and the physical realm we call space into existence. The physical cosmos is a kind of parenthesis. Still, things done here have eternal consequences. These actions have effects that reach into the distant past and stretch to the far future.

As is demonstrated in many ways, the wisdom of God's eternity does not reach into this fallen cosmos. Yes, He does send emissaries here on various occasions. They bring His wisdom into this place. But they are routinely rejected. As Jesus once told the experts in Mosaic Law:

Therefore also said the wisdom of God, I will send them prophets and apostles, and some of them they shall slay and persecute: That the blood of all the prophets, which was shed from **the foundation of the world**, may be required of this generation. (Luke 11:49–50, emphasis added)

Think of it: The cosmos was established on the basis that it would require the blood of the prophets (and the blood of the saints, for that matter). Central to the existence of the cosmos is the shedding of Christ's own blood.

The acts of the prophets and saints were assumed from the moment the cosmos was inaugurated. Observers who see the parade of human history through eternity's window are not restricted to the "now," as we are. They might well see the acts of Abraham, King David, and Jesus as all happening at the same "time." They might even see those same events as happening *before* the cosmos was created, or after it was destroyed.

Strange as this may sound, if time is time and eternity is eternity, there is no real temporal connection between them. They operate independently. Hypothetically, if an individual made a decision for Christ on July 4, 2000, someone in eternity could view this event as happening "right now," even though he was viewing it from ten thousand years ago! (Or, a hundred thousand years ago, for that matter.) Would he be viewing it as a "future" event? Probably not.

Or what of the eternal observer watching the same event from a hundred thousand years in the future? Would he see this Fourth of July salvation as a past event? Again, probably not. It would simply be called, "An event that happened in that other dimension called the cosmos." To the host of heaven, our future and our past are both present.

Thus, the foundation of the cosmos has much more to do with order and commitment than it does with time. Seen in this way, the statement in Psalm 90 takes on a whole new meaning: "For a thousand years in thy sight are but as yesterday when it is past, and as a watch in the night" (Psalm 90:4).

We often speak of seven thousand years of human history, from the creation of the first couple to the termination of the Kingdom Age. But we hardly ever think of this world—the cosmos—as a "bubble" outside the realm of eternity. Things that happen inside this bubble are timely and important to those who regard them as the beginning and end of everything. The princes of this world apparently do. Remember how Satan tempted Jesus.

Outside the bubble, the actualities of God's eternity have an entirely different view. Think of the world—the cosmos—in this way as seen in Jesus' intercessory prayer for the saints:

> For I have given unto them the words which thou gavest me;
> and they have received them, and have known surely that I came
> out from thee, and they have believed that thou didst send me.
> I pray for them: I pray not for the **world**, but for them
> which thou hast given me; for they are thine. And all mine are
> thine, and thine are mine; and I am glorified in them.
> And now I am no more in the **world**, but these are in the
> **world**, and I come to thee. Holy Father, keep through thine

own name those whom thou hast given me, that they may be one, as we are. (John 17:8–11, emphasis added)

There is the mistaken tendency to think of those things witnessed before the foundation of the cosmos as written in stone, or unalterably predestined. But think of another thing: Jesus' prayer in the garden of Gethsemane was given quite a different perspective by Luke: "And he was withdrawn from them about a stone's cast, and kneeled down, and prayed, Saying, Father, if thou be willing, remove this cup from me: nevertheless not my will, but thine, be done" (Luke 22:41, 42).

Jesus is called "the Lamb slain from the foundation of the world" (Revelation 13:8). That is, before the cosmos was originated, He was already considered as having been crucified, buried, and resurrected. Yet here, Luke records Jesus' appeal to the Father that He might be spared from having to go through the experience. In other words, right up until the end, Jesus considered His execution to be an option! Why else would He appeal in this way to the Father?

This apparent paradox arises only because we think of everything as enslaved to time. This is not the case. Even before the cosmos was founded, it could be seen that at the crux of human history, Jesus and the Father would agree upon the necessity for the Crucifixion, and that it would take place, just as foreseen.

In the cosmos—the universe of time-space—the Crucifixion was an option. The "cup" of Christ's Crucifixion might have been removed. However, in the realm of eternity, it was not an option. The Crucifixion was an accomplished certainty before the foundation of the cosmos. But that night in the garden, Jesus also chose to go through with it.

IN THE COSMOS, NOT OF THE COSMOS

When He prayed that night, Jesus' conversation with the Father revealed an absolute familiarity with the dimensional situation of the cosmos. In the brief excerpt of His prayer that follows, note how He uses the word "world." In all six cases below, it is a translation of *kosmos:*

> I have given them thy word; and the **world** hath hated them, because they are not of the **world**, even as I am not of the **world**. I pray not that thou shouldest take them out of the **world**, but that thou shouldest keep them from the evil. They are not of the **world**, even as I am not of the **world**. (John 17:14–16, emphasis added)

Six times, Jesus uses the term for the created time-space continuum. In the most authentic sense of the language, as Jesus uses it, believers are not part of the cosmos. We are, in fact, the very antithesis of it.

And this answers the question that we posed near the beginning of this chapter. How can our salvation be considered as having been accomplished in the distant past…"before the foundation of the world"? The answer is that we are neither creatures of time, nor of time-space, but creatures of eternity. We are freed from this timeline called the cosmos, and the moment we became free in Christ, our names were added to the Book of Life—before the cosmos was ever founded.

26

THE SPEED OF THOUGHT

Have you ever heard someone say, "One day, we'll be able to travel at the speed of thought!" Usually, such an idea pops up in a discussion about life in the Kingdom of Heaven. We envision a kind of unlimited freedom in the glories of heaven, where the mere desire to be in a location results in instant relocation to that point. But here on earth, we're trapped in the scaffolding of time-space, where things creep along at a predetermined rate. In this domain, one's progress is blocked by traffic, fences, walls, doors, and dimensional barriers. This is simply the normal physical experience, sometimes accompanied by frustration when we're late or blocked by some obstruction.

But in the theater of our minds, travel is unlimited. On a stage set with things dreamed, we can be instantly transported to another room, another city…or, for that matter, another galaxy. This can be amazingly entertaining, but only to a point. Alas, the trip is not real. Who has not lamented the fact that such marvelous journeys are only flights of the imagination? Wearing a lightweight space suit, you search the sandy wastes of Mars for seashells. What a price they would bring on the open market!

Confronted with the multiplication tables or the rules of grammar, every schoolboy has made many such trips. He has flown out through a classroom window, over fields and farms, to that special place where he can escape to some paradise. Or better yet, he is engaged in the important work of saving the universe from evil. Perhaps he is a knight (whether Arthurian or Jedi). The superhero of modern literature is born in a world such as this.

Villains, dragons, and demons populate this amphitheater of thought. Some of these figures even find permanent status in the pages of science fiction and fairy tales, as well as the popular drawings of the comics. Life is given to these modern equivalents of ancient Greek demigods. The best-known personalities of this genre are Superman and Wonder Woman, but there are many, many more. In one important respect, however, they are quite different from their ancient predecessors.

The old gods of the ancient world were capricious and immoral. Often, they were the focus and source of all evil. Zeus and his wife Hera were fickle despots. The adulterous Zeus fathered Apollo by Leto, giving rise to a host of evil repercussions. As just one of the many families of Greek demigods, Apollo and his sister Artemis are remembered for curses, debauchery, adultery, murder, and torture. In one episode, Apollo's son Asclepius was slain by one of Zeus' lightning bolts. Yet, in spite of their gods' personal failures, the Greeks and Romans believed that the proper worship of these supernatural beings would bring fertility to crops and cattle, and blessing to government and household. Now, that's imagination!

Modern superheroes, by contrast, are not evil. In fact, they are its very antithesis, as they battle for truth and justice (and something called "the American way"). Many of us remember the Green Hornet and Kato, Batman and Robin, Captain Marvel, the Flash, and a host of others. They were the imaginative incarnations of American idealism.

It has often been said that the model for all such heroes is none other than Jesus. He is truth; He is justice; He exposes evil. In the end, He will come and establish the perfect Kingdom, as He abolishes that ultimate fiend, rogue, and oppressor, Satan...as well as his earthly representative, the Antichrist. The modern superhero is, in fact, a Jesus substitute, based upon the well-known story of His incarnation.

This saga is engraved in the heart of every human being. It is the universal dream that, somewhere, a "superbeing" must come forth to save the world from the forces of darkness. If, for whatever reason, the authenticity of Jesus is refused, the next step is to create a false hope in the person of a fictional character. Hence, we find the heart of Messianic themes that run through virtually all the great works of literature. The hero who saves the world (or a small town, for that matter) is the world's most popular literary device. Of course, it is also the central theme of the Bible.

In the secular world, those early schoolhouse voyages into the field of dreams mature into utopian visions, political schemes, and cultural engineering. That which innocently begins in the mind can birth a myriad of bizarre cultural codes and traditions.

In this world, the trip that begins in the mind usually crashes upon the hard rocks of this reality. The imagination may succeed, but its result is always failure. When human thought is translated into earthly reality, the usual result is disaster. The awful presence of sin always creates only a caricature of God's original intent for this planet.

THE HUMAN MIND

The collected legends, tales, myths, sagas, and epics of human history are fraught with disaster, intrigue, betrayal, murder, and debauchery. Occasionally, we encounter an uplifting incident, but it is the exception, not the rule. Before the Great Flood of Noah, mankind was allowed to operate in the sphere of his own conscience. But the dictates of his morality lay in the realm of his warped imagination, as described in Genesis 6:5: "And GOD saw that the wickedness of man was great in the earth, and that every imagination of the thoughts of his heart was only evil continually."

Here, the form of man's imagination, dictated by his inner motivations, is immortalized as totally evil—so evil, in fact, that the Lord destroyed all but Noah and his family. However, the Flood didn't cure man's intrinsic wickedness. Rather, it created a longing to return to the antediluvian world where the dark forces of the fallen angels fed a twisted human imagination.

To achieve this, mankind began a project. In the episode of the Tower of Babel, the Lord looked down upon the evil venture and concluded that the thoughts of men would take them into the very heavens. He ruled that they should be diverted before that happened. Notice that is it man's *imagination* that comes into question: "And the LORD said, Behold, the people is one, and they have all one language; and this they begin to do: and now nothing will be restrained from them, which they have imagined to do" (Genesis 11:6).

Later, Moses, in prophesying that Israel would one day be scattered over the earth, gave one clear reason why this would happen. It would be the *imagination* of the Israelites that would lead them to destruction: "And it come to pass, when he heareth the words of this curse, that he bless himself in his heart, saying, I shall have peace, though I walk in the imagination of mine heart, to add drunkenness to thirst" (Deuteronomy 29:19).

The Israelites allowed their own thoughts and ideas to lead them, rather than the mind of God. Their long and tortured history leaves no doubt about that. Certainly, they are quite gifted as a people. In each of the world's cultures to which they have been driven, they have become the leading lights. They are the scientists, authors, musicians, artists, philosophers, and inventors. The Lord has spoken through them to the world. They have lived by their wits and imagination, rather than the wisdom of God.

In the New Testament, when Mary met Elizabeth, she prophesied that the long-awaited Messiah would bring a new reality to humankind. Even though He had not yet been born, she spoke as if He had already achieved His revolutionary work in the world: "He hath shewed strength with his arm; he hath scattered the proud in the imagination of their hearts" (Luke 1:51).

The Israelites attempted to live by their wits...their secular wisdom...rather than by the wisdom of the Lord. Once again, the words of the Bible point the finger of guilt at the collective imagination of mankind. It is the real enemy of His work.

COURTING THE DEMONIC

This brings up a salient point. Man's imagination doesn't function in a vacuum. In this world, it is constantly being stimulated by Satan and his hordes of demons. The real battle, illustrated by Satan's temptation of Christ, is spiritual. Demons appeal to human vanity, arrogance, and intellectual pride, causing them to develop and promote wicked schemes in the name of progress.

David's son Solomon was divinely gifted with wisdom. But in his personal life, he often disregarded God's leading. In the end, he saw the value of that for which he had prayed. He likens the world's attraction to that of the wayward woman who lures a man away from the path of righteousness into the dark alleys of the lost.

Solomon depicts foolishness as a harlot. He begs the young man to follow the wisdom of the Lord, who will "deliver thee from the strange woman, even from the stranger which flattereth with her words; Which forsaketh the guide of her youth, and forgetteth the covenant of her God. For her house inclineth unto death, and her paths unto the dead" (Proverbs 2:16–18).

On the other hand, Solomon illustrates the wisdom of the Lord as a righteous woman who points one toward the Lord:

Wisdom crieth without; she uttereth her voice in the streets:
She crieth in the chief place of concourse, in the openings of
the gates: in the city she uttereth her words, saying, How long,
ye simple ones, will ye love simplicity? and the scorners delight
in their scorning, and fools hate knowledge?
Turn you at my reproof: behold, I will pour out my spirit
unto you, I will make known my words unto you. Because I
have called, and ye refused; I have stretched out my hand, and
no man regarded. (Proverbs 1:20–24)

Clearly, Solomon's intent is to show that the battle for true wisdom is fought on the grounds of emotion and allure, versus common sense and responsibility. The imaginative flight of fancy too often presides over common sense.

In his own life, Solomon repeatedly listened to the wrong voices. After years of worldly experience—including wine, women, and song—his collected Proverbs stand as a witness that wisdom is always there for those who will listen.

A millennium later, in the first century AD, James encouraged the believers of the early church to follow the Lord in unity. His words, written from the viewpoint of early Messianic Judaism, show that internal strife in the newborn church was planted there by demonic intrusion. He makes the point that "devilish" (demonic) ideology is planted to thwart the wisdom of the Lord. It operates in the arena of the imagination:

Who is a wise man and endued with knowledge among you? let him shew out of a good conversation his works with meekness of wisdom.

But if ye have bitter envying and strife in your hearts, glory not, and lie not against the truth. This wisdom descendeth not from above, but is earthly, sensual, **devilish**. For where envying and strife is, there is confusion and every evil work.

But the wisdom that is from above is first pure, then peaceable, gentle, and easy to be intreated, full of mercy and good fruits, without partiality, and without hypocrisy. And the fruit of righteousness is sown in peace of them that make peace. (James 3:13–18, emphasis added)

Once again, we see that the Bible shows two contrasting methods of thinking. One is from below, demonic and destructive. The other is from above in the dimension of God. The first is a counterfeit of the second. Only the wisdom (thinking) of God is productive. The false wisdom of this world system has only the power to destroy.

The Power of Thought

Men earnestly desire to give life to their thoughts. In one sense, they are able to do this, in that their inventions and commerce change the flow of history. The convoluted course of historical wealth and power has traditionally followed the perfection of marketing and weaponry. This produces a system that imbues itself with godlike power.

In the purest sense, this world is a contest between the thoughts of man and the thoughts of God. Or, is it a contest between the thoughts of Satan and the thoughts of God? Whatever the source of man's imagination, it is only a vain and passing exercise in futility.

Only the thoughts of God are worthy and permanent. More than that, only His thoughts have reality. That is, they result in something tangible and permanent, as written by the prophet Isaiah:

> Seek ye the LORD while he may be found, call ye upon him while he is near: Let the wicked forsake his way, and the unrighteous man his **thoughts**: and let him return unto the LORD, and he will have mercy upon him; and to our God, for he will abundantly pardon.
>
> For my **thoughts** are not your **thoughts**, neither are your ways my ways, saith the LORD. For as the heavens are higher than the earth, so are my ways higher than your ways, and my **thoughts** than your **thoughts**. For as the rain cometh down, and the snow from heaven, and returneth not thither, but watereth the earth, and maketh it bring forth and bud, that it may give seed to the sower, and bread to the eater:
>
> So shall my word be that goeth forth out of my mouth: it shall not return unto me void, but it shall accomplish that which I please, and it shall prosper in the thing whereto I sent it. (Isaiah 55:6–11, emphasis added)

This Scripture puts man's imagination in its place. It begins with a call to the "unrighteous man." Actually, its original language exhorts man to forsake the vanity inherent in his old pattern of thinking.

In the original Hebrew, "thought" is an expression created by the word *machshavah* (מחשבה), meaning, "an invention, idea or thought." Truly, the inventions of faithless men have been the basis of a million transgressions and the source of corruption.

Here, God asserts that His thoughts operate on a different and higher plane than the thoughts of man. At first, this statement would seem so blatantly obvious that it hardly needs to be stated at all. It's easy to say that His thoughts are higher than ours.

But notice that the Lord likens His thoughts to rain and snow. These meteorological realities actually cause the earth to function, giving life to what would otherwise be a barren waste. In other words, God's thoughts constitute a physical reality. When His thoughts are spoken as a "word" that goes forth from His mouth, His thought and His word literally take on substance and shape. They affect the world in which we live.

This seems to be the intent of Revelation 1:16, where John described the glorified Christ. His words are described as so powerful—so effective—that they can literally be seen: "And he had in his right hand seven stars: and out of his mouth went a sharp twoedged sword: and his countenance was as the sun shineth in his strength."

These Scriptures are far more than a mere statement about the quality of God's thought. They show us that His thoughts are of an entirely different order than our thoughts. Man's thoughts can modify that which is already in existence, but God can literally think things into existence in the first place...something impossible for humans.

It is this simple fact that is the greatest testimony to His existence. In his current sinful state, man actually *suppresses* God's thoughts, covering them with his own ideas. In the process, he comes to believe in the validity of his own ideas. In the following verses—Romans 1:18–23–that is exactly the meaning of the word "hold:"

For the wrath of God is revealed from heaven against all ungodliness and unrighteousness of men, who **hold** the truth in unrighteousness; Because that which may be known of God is manifest in them; for God hath shewed it unto them.

For the invisible things of him from the creation of the world are clearly seen, being understood by the things that are made, even his eternal power and Godhead; so that they are without excuse:

Because that, when they knew God, they glorified him not as God, neither were thankful; but became vain in their imaginations, and their foolish heart was darkened. Professing themselves to be wise, they became fools, And changed the glory of the uncorruptible God into an image made like to corruptible man, and to birds, and fourfooted beasts, and creeping things. (emphasis added)

Notice, too, that the result of their activities is vain imagination, those vagrant thoughts that imagine a better world...without God. As mentioned earlier, this is the world of human thought, of imagined superheroes and utopian ideals. In the end, it rejects God as Creator and Redeemer.

Instead, it worships the created world, which is the end product of God's thought. Men in their vanity, imagine this physical universe to have created itself through some evolutionary process. In the following passage, the word "creature" is from the Greek *ktisis,* which refers both to the act of creation and to its end product...that which is created. In the present condition of sin, the entire creation is in a broken condition, awaiting the healing that will be brought by the One who spoke it into existence in the first place.

By substituting their human imagination for the thoughts of the Lord, mankind has substituted opinion for reality. The result has been increasing chaos, decay, and ultimate corruption:

For I reckon that the sufferings of this present time are not worthy to be compared with the glory which shall be revealed in us.

For the earnest expectation of the creature waiteth for the manifestation of the sons of God. For the **creature** was made subject to vanity, not willingly, but by reason of him who hath subjected the same in hope,

Because the **creature** itself also shall be delivered from the bondage of corruption into the glorious liberty of the children of God. For we know that the whole creation groaneth and travaileth in pain together until now. (Romans 8:18–22, emphasis added)

Again, the word "creature" should be read as "creation," meaning "the entire creation." This would include all that the eye can see…from atoms to galaxies. Everything is in a state of decay and dissolution. But here, Paul rejoices in the coming deliverance. The "sons of God" are the redeemed who will come as the armies of heaven, with the returning Messiah in the Second Coming. Certainly, the religion, politics, and economy of the world will come under His judgment. But more than that, the very environment will be changed, making the earth a paradise once again. The mind of God will rule the world.

IMAGINATION VERSUS REALITY

Remember that trip of the imagination mentioned earlier? Flights of fancy are the stuff of human thought. But they can only result in tangible blessings if they are ordained of God. Things that last can be made only by God, as Abraham, the father of the faithful, knew all too well:

By faith Abraham, when he was called to go out into a place which he should after receive for an inheritance, obeyed; and he went out, not knowing whither he went.

By faith he sojourned in the land of promise, as in a strange country, dwelling in tabernacles with Isaac and Jacob, the heirs with him of the same promise: For he looked for a city which hath foundations, whose builder and maker is God. (Hebrews 11:8–10)

Abraham knew that wealth and power could never build an empire. There is a new construction coming. It will be built by the Lord Himself, probably in the same way He constructed the heavens and the earth. His direct command will result in the most perfect city ever seen.

By contrast, earthly kingdoms—devices of the mind of man—will end up in dust. The four great world empires prophesied by Daniel— Babylon, Medo-Persia, Greece, and Rome—already lie in dust. One by one, the empires of gold, silver, brass, and iron fell into obscurity. They were, of course, memorialized in the figure of a huge image, with a head of gold.

That fourth beast still has life left in it, and will experience a rapid resurgence to power. Many volumes have been written about this so-called Revived Roman Empire. In the end, it will be crushed at the Lord's Second Coming. This is only another of many examples that show the reality of God's thought. Note in the following verses, that Daniel saw a stone (Christ) made without hands. It is not the work of human effort or human ideology:

Thou sawest till that a stone was cut out **without hands**, which smote the image upon his feet that were of iron and clay, and brake them to pieces. (Daniel 2:34)

Forasmuch as thou sawest that the stone was cut out of the mountain **without hands**, and that it brake in pieces the iron, the brass, the clay, the silver, and the gold; the great God hath made known to the king what shall come to pass hereafter: and the dream is certain, and the interpretation thereof sure. (Daniel 2:45)

THE FORM OF THOUGHT

With the foregoing in mind, let's look at a few examples that illustrate the biblical view of thought speed. First and foremost, when "God created the heaven and the earth," it was done by utterance. His thought, expressed as words, became reality…in an instant. In the first chapter of Genesis, there is an orderly progression from disorder to order:

First, He said, "Let there be light" (v. 3).

Next, He said, "Let there be a firmament in the midst of the waters, and let it divide the waters from the waters" (v. 6).

Then, He said, "Let the waters under the heaven be gathered together unto one place, and let the dry land appear" (v. 9).

After that, He said, "Let the earth bring forth…" (v. 11).

After the earth brought forth, He said, "Let there be lights in the firmament of the heaven to divide the day from the night" (v. 14).

Following that, He said, "Let the waters bring forth…" (v. 20).

Finally, He said, "Let the earth bring forth…" and "Let us make man in our image" (vv. 22, 26).

In all these utterances, there is not the slightest mention of technique, engineering, or craftsmanship. His thought, expressed in words, became what we call, "reality." It began with light, suggesting an energy field of some sort. It was a presence that became differentiated into substance and form. Then it was gone, replaced by the light of the sun and stars that had come into existence.

How long did it take for all this to happen? No time at all. Certainly, there was the time span of six days. But each of the events is narrated as the simple act of utterance…of thought. When we imagine something, it never really appears. Our thoughts may be fascinating, but by themselves, they are ineffective. But when God thinks, things happen.

God's thought is an utterance, and this is what is meant by "the Word": "In the beginning was the Word, and the Word was with God, and the Word was God. The same was in the beginning with God. All things were made by him; and without him was not any thing made that was made" (John 1:1–3).

Out of nothing, God declared something. In fact, He declared everything. Throughout the Bible, we find that the Lord is more than Creator. He is also instantly able to affect His creation. He parted the waters of the Red Sea, allowing Moses to lead the children of Israel to freedom. He suspended the water, so that it formed a wall to the left and right of the fleeing Israelites:

> And Moses stretched out his hand over the sea; and the LORD caused the sea to go back by a strong east wind all that night, and made the sea dry land, and the waters were divided.
>
> And the children of Israel went into the midst of the sea upon the dry ground: and the waters were a wall unto them on their right hand, and on their left. (Exodus 14:21, 22).

Many have attempted to explain away this miracle by saying that a strong wind created a channel across the sea. Certainly, an east wind blew. However, any wind strong enough to hold back heaps of water would be a literal hurricane. (An east wind of this velocity would halt the Israelites' eastward march across the dry floor of the sea.) A force held the waters apart. God created that force by a thought.

Men, women, children, oxen, carts, tents, food, clothing, and the Egyptian treasure marched across the sea bottom, apparently unhindered. No force known to man can make water behave in this way. But for the Lord, a thought will suffice, creating a force of such intensity that even water would stand up in a wall, without affecting the Israelites. So far as we know, this is simply impossible.

It is equally impossible to form complex objects in an instant, but our Lord easily accomplished this, as shown in a miraculous event known to everyone who has read the Bible. Jesus healed a man blind from birth, one of the signs he brought to Israel. It had long been taught that when the Messiah came, He would restore sight to the man born blind. Nor is this a simple task. In this anonymous recipient of Jesus' grace, eyeballs, optic nerves, and even the brain itself had never been conditioned to see.

Had Jesus simply healed the man's physical systems, the man would still have had to be taught to see. It is interesting that, just as in the creation of the world, the light is given prominence:

> As long as I am in the world, I am the light of the world. When
> he had thus spoken, he spat on the ground, and made clay of
> the spittle, and he anointed the eyes of the blind man with
> the clay, And said unto him, Go, wash in the pool of Siloam,
> (which is by interpretation, Sent.) He went his way therefore,
> and washed, and came seeing. (John 9:5–7)

It has been said that Jesus created new eyes with balls of freshly made clay. But only His thought could have produced the working systems of sight. Or, how did Jesus walk on the water of the Sea of Galilee? By taking thought.

Thought holds the universe together. One day, as foretold in 2 Peter 3:10, it will be completely restructured: "But the day of the Lord will come as a thief in the night; in the which the heavens shall pass away with a great noise, and the elements shall melt with fervent heat, the earth also and the works that are therein shall be burned up."

By taking thought the Lord will unleash the elements to achieve His desired goal. In Hebrews 1:3, He is said to be, "upholding all things by the word of his power." As we have already seen, this "word" is simply the utterance of His divine thought. In an instant, the things we regard as solid and unmovable will suddenly assume new shape, form and flow, all at the speed of thought.

THE SPEED OF THOUGHT

How fast is thought? Just as we have imagined in our own dreams, it is instantaneous. We think about being somewhere—say, the British Museum or the Great Pyramid—and our thoughts are there in no time at all. But on God's plane of existence, it is also very real, as the apostle

John discovered when he was transported to the Kingdom of Heaven and simultaneously, to the future:

> After this I looked, and, behold, a door was opened in heaven: and the first voice which I heard was as it were of a trumpet talking with me; which said, Come up hither, and I will shew thee things which must be hereafter.
>
> And immediately I was in the spirit: and, behold, a throne was set in heaven, and one sat on the throne. (Revelation 4:1, 2)

The instantaneous nature of John's transport is conveyed with absolute authenticity. John actually experienced what the rest of us only dream about. He was taken to the dimension of eternity, where he could view events that we think of as "future." He saw war and famine, economic chaos and pandemics, astronomical and geological upheavals, reporting on them as a credible eyewitness.

Occasionally, he even questioned his heavenly guides, asking for explanations of what he saw. At the speed of thought, he was actually taken to a number of vantage points, from which he was able to report on the events of the Lord's Day of Judgment. His view of Mystery Babylon's fall and the Second Coming of Christ are indelibly etched upon minds of the faithful. Upon his return, he was released from his Patmos exile, to return to Ephesus, where he spent the rest of his life as the apostle of love. After experiencing a thought trip of magnificent proportions, his constant exhortation was to "love one another," as the Lord loves us.

Of course, the apostle Paul was also taken on an instantaneous trip to another dimension. His thought trip is well known. It bears the distinct marks of an actual experience:

> It is not expedient for me doubtless to glory. I will come to visions and revelations of the Lord. I knew a man in Christ above fourteen years ago, (whether in the body, I cannot tell; or whether out of the body, I cannot tell: God knoweth;) such an one caught up to the third heaven.

And I knew such a man, (whether in the body, or out of
the body, I cannot tell: God knoweth;) How that he was caught
up into paradise, and heard unspeakable words, which it is not
lawful for a man to utter. (2 Corinthians 12:1–4)

First and foremost, Paul found himself instantly borne aloft on a
thought in the mind of God. The term "caught up," from the Greek
harpazo speaks of something or someone quickly seized and pulled up at
breathtaking speed. It is, in fact, the very term used to describe the catching-away of the church: "Then we…shall be caught up" (1 Thessalonians
4:17).

Paul was instantly transported to another dimension, just as we shall
be at the proper moment. We shall travel at the speed of thought, to a
place where one can be transported into the past, present, and future
with equal facility.

For the Lord himself shall descend from heaven with a shout,
with the voice of the archangel, and with the trump of God:
and the dead in Christ shall rise first:
    Then we which are alive and remain shall be caught up
together with them in the clouds, to meet the Lord in the air:
and so shall we ever be with the Lord. (1 Thessalonians 4:16, 17)

The vocal command of the Lord reminds us of so many other similar
commands recorded in Scripture. The creation of the world, the parting of the Red Sea, the healing commands of Jesus, the cataclysms of
Revelation—all are the result of the Lord's thought, expressed as Word.

And the beautiful part of the equation is this: As faithful believers,
we have access to His thoughts. As Paul puts it, "For who hath known
the mind of the Lord, that he may instruct him? But we have the mind
of Christ" (1 Corinthians 2:16).

This is an amazing truth, expressing the idea that our salvation
grants us present access to the Kingdom of Heaven. Through prayer,
we can instantly travel to that place where the speed of thought is an

actuality. Paul urges believers to realize this great truth: "Let this mind be in you, which was also in Christ Jesus" (Philippians 2:5). Though presently locked in this place of time and space, our thoughts soar into eternity…the eternal present.

> But as it is written, Eye hath not seen, nor ear heard, neither have entered into the heart of man, the things which God hath prepared for them that love him.
> But God hath revealed them unto us by his Spirit: for the Spirit searcheth all things, yea, the deep things of God.
> (1 Corinthians 2:9, 10)

We have been given the perception of things beyond this world. It has given us the ability to know about the speed of thought in the dimension of the Lord. We patiently await its full realization.

27

HEAVEN, EARTH, AND TIME

F rom the human point of view, translating the eternal will of God
into the timeline of mankind is fraught with difficulties. He views
the "eternal now." We see the "now" as it unfolds one second at a time.
The past—be it one second or ten thousand years ago—is set in stone.
The future is like a white cloud in a blue summer sky, changing shape
moment by moment as we lie in the grass and struggle to give some
meaning to its contours.

The Lord's view regards past, present, and future with perfect clarity. He has told us that certain things will happen. We know that the
prophetic winds are blowing, shaping the future panorama. We also
know that the Lord is not a mere observer, but is actively determining the events on planet earth. His Spirit covers the earth. As Jesus told
Nicodemus, "The wind bloweth where it listeth, and thou hearest the
sound thereof, but canst not tell whence it cometh, and whither it goeth:
so is every one that is born of the Spirit" (John 3:8).

The apostles wrote that socio-political conditions would rapidly
worsen in the days before His return, and that a day of great upheaval
lies just ahead. In the light of their writings, we struggle to make sense of
our times...of time itself.

Among Christians who believe that the Great Tribulation, Day of
the Lord, and Kingdom of David lie in the future, the pretribulation

The apostles wrote that socio-political conditions would rapidly
worsen in the days before His return, and that a day of great upheaval
lies just ahead. In the light of their writings, we struggle to make sense of
our times...of time itself.

Among Christians who believe that the Great Tribulation, Day of
the Lord, and Kingdom of David lie in the future, the pretribulation

493

Rapture of the church is widely taught. It is also taught that this Rapture, or catching-away of the church, is a signless event that could happen at any moment, without the slightest warning. It is imminent, and has been so regarded since the days of the apostles. We long for a sign, and are even told at one point, "And when these things begin to come to pass, then look up, and lift up your heads; for your redemption draweth nigh" (Luke 21:28).

This exhortation, given by Jesus Himself, is spoken concerning latter-day Israel and the changes that will accompany its rebirth. We watch Israel and the Middle East. And we do look up, in the knowledge that the Rapture will happen without any preceding sign or warning.

However, the doctrine of imminence remains among the most difficult in the Christian faith. The problem is simple: On one hand, believers are urged to be aware of various signs that suggest the end of the Church Age. To cite the example just given, the rebirth of national Israel and subsequent growing conflict in the Middle East are often seen as indications of the near approach of the Rapture.

But on the other hand, Christians are cautioned not to set dates on the basis of visible geopolitical developments. Some theologians have warned against what they call "newspaper exegesis." This is the tendency to view news developments in Russia, Persia, Israel, or the growing global government as signs that Christ's return for the church is less than say, a decade in the future…perhaps only a year or two away.

The faithful have a challenge. We sometimes feel like a living dichotomy—looking for signs, excited by developments on the world stage, but constantly reminding ourselves that the Rapture is a signless event. How are we to view prophetic timing, and still stay within the bounds of proper biblical interpretation?

THE TIME IS AT HAND

This riddle of how the eternal now translates into the material timeline is never more challenging than when one attempts to understand the phrase, "the time is at hand." Let's look at a few examples of how it's used. The first one we'll cite is obvious and easy to understand.

As the time drew near for His final trial and Crucifixion, Jesus instructed His disciples on how to secure a place in which they could observe the Passover *seder:*

> Now the first day of the feast of unleavened bread the disciples came to Jesus, saying unto him, Where wilt thou that we prepare for thee to eat the passover?
>
> And he said, Go into the city to such a man, and say unto him, The Master saith, My **time is at hand**; I will keep the passover at thy house with my disciples. (Matthew 26:17, 18, emphasis added)

That night, in that place, He sat with them as they ate that Last Supper. Then, they went across the Kidron Valley to Gethsemane, where Jesus prayed before being taken into custody.

Earlier in the day, Jesus had said, "My time is at hand." From the Greek of the New Testament, the nearest literal translation of this sentence would be, "My time is near." And indeed, it *was near.* In fact, it was within a few hours of fulfillment. Here, the phrase "at hand" turns out to mean "very near."

Here, the word "time" is a translation of the Greek *kairos,* which means a favorable season or an opportune moment. It is never used to indicate a space of time, or a duration or interval between two points along the timeline.

In this case, the meaning of Jesus' words is literal and understandable: The opportune moment or designated time had arrived. As we look at the time intervals connected with His final hours, the issue of proximity is clear-cut. When Jesus says the time is near, He means it.

On the other hand, the same phrase is used twice in the book of Revelation. The first occurrence of "time" comes at the beginning of the book. It urges the reader to remember that the prophecies of the Revelation are about to be fulfilled: "Blessed is he that readeth, and they that hear the words of this prophecy, and keep those things which are written therein: for the time is at hand" (Revelation 1:3).

Here, and in the example to follow, the word used to express "time" is the Greek *kairos,* which describes an opportune season. In other words, things are right for the fulfillment of the prophecy.

At the opening of the book, the season of the seven churches was "at hand," or quite near. That section of the Revelation was already under fulfillment. At the time of its writing, the seven churches were already functioning, though the full development of their prophetic outcome would (and still will) take some two thousand years. This, we can easily understand.

But at the end of the Revelation, we find another "at hand" that's not nearly so easy to understand. At this point in his experience, John has seen it all, from the Church Age through the coming of the New Jerusalem. He stands in the future, taking in the panorama of time from a vantage point of astounding proportions.

Then come the urgent words:

Behold, I come quickly: blessed is he that keepeth the sayings of the prophecy of this book.

And I John saw these things, and heard them. And when I had heard and seen, I fell down to worship before the feet of the angel which shewed me these things.

Then saith he unto me, See thou do it not: for I am thy fellowservant, and of thy brethren the prophets, and of them which keep the sayings of this book: worship God.

And he saith unto me, Seal not the sayings of the prophecy of this book: for **the time is at hand**. (Revelation 22:7–10, emphasis added)

Once again, we see the familiar phrase, "the time is at hand." Its wording is precisely the same as the two other similar phrases we have seen. In Greek it says, "The time is near," using the word that indicates an opportune moment.

By way of review:

In the first case, the Lord used the expression to indicate His readiness to take the last Passover.

In the second, it spoke of the things that would shortly come to pass. In particular, it seems to refer to the seven churches and their combined prophecy of the Church Age.

In this final instance, words written nearly two thousand years ago urgently remind us that the season of Revelation's fulfillment is near. How are we to take these words? In other words, what does the Bible mean when it says that something of consequence is "at hand," or "near"?

PAUL THOUGHT IT WAS NEAR

This is not a new problem. The patient wait for Christ's return began in the first century. For literally the last 1,950 years or so, clear Bible teaching has stated that Christ could return to this planet at any moment to claim His called-out body of believers.

The apostle Paul, in his first epistle to the Thessalonians, writes to Hellenistic Jews and Gentiles who are recognized for their steadfastness in faith and love in the Lord. Paul compliments them on their, "work of faith, and labour of love, and patience of hope in our Lord Jesus Christ" (1 Thessalonians 1:3).

Their patience in the context of hope is a direct reference to the central subject of the letter. In it, Paul gives explicit details of Christ's return for the church and the phenomenon of the Rapture. As we think of his amazing exposition of a reality that had never before been taught, we try to imagine how those early believers must have reacted to his words. Most of the Thessalonians were Gentiles who had lived under the fierce reign of the Caesars and its cultic belief that they were gods.

THE ART OF WAITING

Furthermore, the Greek culture revolved around such revolting pagan practices as the oracles of vestal virgins and the worship of Diana, the fertility goddess. Mystery cults and superstition ruled their daily lives.

Having seen the fruit of paganism, many Greeks had turned to the ethical and moral stability of Judaism, and the worship of the one God. But they had never heard about His Son, or been enlightened as to prophetic truth.

The date of this letter is about AD 51. Claudius was the Roman Caesar, and in his efforts to expand the empire, he began to persecute the Jews. Only a few years later, Nero came to power. He ruled from AD 54–68. During that time, Christians became public enemy number one. Considering them merely another sect of Judaism, Nero expanded programs of arrest, torture, and execution. Throughout his reign, the Jerusalem Temple continued to function and Judaism thrived, still continuing to teach that the Messiah would come to destroy the Roman overlords and establish the Kingdom.

Paul was teaching something entirely different…that the resurrected Jesus was the Messiah who had been rejected by His people. Furthermore, He would return for the living body of believers…and that it could happen at any moment!

It was on the basis of their acceptance of his teaching that he commended them so profusely. Several times, he expresses this sentiment: "For what is our hope, or joy, or crown of rejoicing? Are not even ye in the presence of our Lord Jesus Christ at his coming? For ye are our glory and joy" (1 Thessalonians 2:19, 20).

Here, Paul praises the Thessalonian believers as his literal "crown of rejoicing." He longs for their presence with Christ at His return. Later in the letter, of course, he details the coming and what we have come to call the "Rapture of the church." The most striking thing about the above statement is Paul's assurance that these believers, living in AD 51, could reasonably expect the Lord's return during their lifetimes. A few verses later, he repeats this assertion:

Now God himself and our Father, and our Lord Jesus Christ, direct our way unto you. And the Lord make you to increase and abound in love one toward another, and toward all men, even as we do toward you:

To the end he may stablish your hearts unblameable in holiness before God, even our Father, at the coming of our Lord Jesus Christ with all his saints. (1 Thessalonians 3:11–13)

Again, Paul suggests that these living Thessalonians could very well expect to meet the Lord at His coming, accompanied by saints who had gone on before. He speaks of the Lord's coming as a real event that could be realistically expected by believers then alive.

Of course, Paul's most striking assertion is his widely quoted statement consoling believers whose relatives had since passed on.

Paul answers a question that must have plagued the Thessalonians: "Will our believing friends and relatives who have died experience the joy of the Lord's coming?"

For this we say unto you by the word of the Lord, that we which are alive and remain unto the coming of the Lord shall not prevent them which are asleep.

For the Lord himself shall descend from heaven with a shout, with the voice of the archangel, and with the trump of God: and the dead in Christ shall rise first:

Then we which are alive and remain shall be caught up together with them in the clouds, to meet the Lord in the air: and so shall we ever be with the Lord.
(1 Thessalonians 4:15–17)

There can be no doubt that if you were among the believers of the early church, you would have received these words with joyous excitement and anticipation. Paul is assuring the living body of Christ that their deceased friends would not be relegated to second place at the time of the resurrection.

This disclosure must have had the effect of emphasizing the nearness of the Rapture. To the Thessalonians, it strongly asserted that their relatives would be resurrected with them. Doubtless, they took this to mean that the great event would come while they were still alive. This must have been the buzz of the community!

Surely, they must have endlessly digested and recounted the words of this letter, telling all their friends that they were the generation destined to meet the Lord in the air. In 1 Thessalonians 4:17, the word "air" is from the Greek *aer*, meaning "atmosphere." Thus, these believers were being told that the Lord would descend bodily into their physical realm, where He would appear in the sky. He was coming back…physically!

The immediacy and reality of this description must have had a very dramatic effect upon the readers of Paul's epistle. Surely they knew of the incident related by Luke at the beginning of Acts, where Jesus' departure was described in the same terms: "And when he had spoken these things, while they beheld, he was taken up; and a cloud received him out of their sight" (Acts 1:9).

When Paul told them that they would be "caught up together with them in the clouds," their first thought must have been that the Lord would return in the same way that He had departed. That is, by making a physical appearance in the region of the atmospheric heavens.

What a comfort it must have been for them to think that, at any moment, He would appear to take them home! Indeed, this was Paul's motive as he wrote to them. A few verses later, he tells them exactly why he has written them: "For God hath not appointed us to wrath, but to obtain salvation by our Lord Jesus Christ, Who died for us, that, whether we wake or sleep, we should live together with him. Wherefore **comfort** yourselves together, and edify one another, even as also ye do" (1 Thessalonians 5:9–11, emphasis added).

Here, the "salvation" mentioned by Paul is not the believer's initial redemptive experience, but the deliverance promised to all believers, prior to the Day of the Lord. We shall be "caught up," taken away from the scene of the Lord's judgment. Nothing could be more comforting to them (and to us) than the assurance that they would be taken from the earth before the prophesied convulsions of the Tribulation.

Apparently, after the receipt of this letter, they had questions about the timing and nature of the Day of the Lord. So, soon afterward, Paul wrote them another letter. This one emphasized that they were not about to go through the perils of the Day of the Lord. Here, it is referred to as the "day of Christ:"

> Now we beseech you, brethren, by the coming of our Lord Jesus Christ, and by our gathering together unto him, That ye be not soon shaken in mind, or be troubled, neither by spirit, nor by word, nor by letter as from us, as that the day of Christ is at hand.
>
> Let no man deceive you by any means: for that day shall not come, except there come a falling away first, and that man of sin be revealed, the son of perdition; Who opposeth and exalteth himself above all that is called God, or that is worshipped; so that he as God sitteth in the temple of God, shewing himself that he is God. (2 Thessalonians 2:1–4)

This second letter is also dated sometime in AD 51. As Paul writes it, the Jerusalem Temple is still in full daily operation. Christ's resurrection is over twenty years in the past.

In one sense, Judaism is at a high point in its history at this time. It is politically recognized within the Roman Empire and ensconced in the beautiful and wealthy environs of the Herodian complex of palaces and fortresses. In fact, the Temple complex is still under construction during Paul's second missionary journey, having been begun about seventy years earlier. It would not be considered complete until AD 69. Then, it will be completely destroyed a year later, in AD 70.

Since the letter prophesies the revelation of the "man of sin" who will be revealed in the Temple, they would be carefully cognizant of the latest news from Jerusalem. With the Temple in its full glory, this might happen at any time. They would be watching for signs that the evil man was on the verge of revealing himself.

What Is the "Last Time"?

For at least the last four decades, it has been common for pastors to proclaim from the pulpit that "Jesus is coming soon!" Without a doubt, Bible-believing audiences who hear these words receive them with the implied expectation that the Rapture will come very, very soon.

These words imply that Jesus' coming is only a few years away...a few decades, at the most. They are uttered on the basis that the prophetic arena is now set with the necessary backdrops and political prerequisites indicated in Scripture. Israel is a nation once again. Russia and Persia are a strengthening nuclear front. Islamic terrorism has increasingly destabilized the geopolitics of the Promised Land.

Like those earlier believers in Paul's time, we are excited about the probability that Jesus coming is, "at hand." In other words, it is near. In fact, it's fair to say that just as we watch for the first signs of the approaching Tribulation Temple, believers of the first century were watching for signs that the regime of the man of sin was near.

Sadly, their zeal and patient attentiveness did not carry forward to succeeding generations. The immediacy of Paul's epistles was replaced by a different theology that emphasized political power. We shall now take a quick trip through the age of the church to illustrate the rise and fall of watchfulness.

The Church Age: Fast Forward

What first-century believers did not—could not—know, was that the "nearness" of Christ's return was couched in eternal terminology. A brief history of the Church Age begins with their anticipation. They patiently waited, and they waited...and they waited.

After Paul's converts witnessed the passage of two decades, the Romans laid siege to Jerusalem. Jews who didn't leave town were slaughtered. The Temple was sacked. Jews and Christians alike were hunted down and killed.

A little over half a century later, under the false messiahship of Simeon Bar Kochba, the Jews lost everything in a crushing defeat. They retreated to every corner of the world. Jerusalem became Aelia Capitolina. Israel became Palestine.

Christians struggled to maintain the momentum of the first-century church. In the second and third centuries, Roman persecution cooled, and the early fathers of the faith gradually replaced the imminent expectation of Christ's return with various pragmatic theologies. These were designed to stimulate moral and ethical living. They were often laden with bizarre allegorical interpretations designed to add dramatic effect to existing Scripture.

During this time, heresies rose and fell in succession. Finally in AD 312, under the guidance of the Roman Emperor Constantine, church councils codified the New Testament canon of Scripture. At the same time, church and empire became one. The expectant waiting for Christ's return was a thing of the past. The centuries rolled by, and the state church grew stronger. Its standard for salvation became less spiritual and more political. Darkness veiled the Western world.

As AD 1000 drew near, there was a brief "millennial fever," producing fervent speculation about Christ's return. Then came AD 1001, and the church returned to its former ecclesiastical gloom.

As time approached our era, the Reformation and Missionary eras brought the church into dramatic ferment, with competing theologies and politics. Some of these came to intersect Israel in the nineteenth century, as men like John Nelson Darby and, later, William Heschler, began to teach that prophecy called for the reestablishment of latter-day national Israel.

One of Darby's letters, written around 1830, marks a revolutionary change, saying:

> The coming of the Lord was the other truth which was brought
> to my mind from the Word, as that which, if sitting in heavenly
> places *in* Christ, was alone to be waited for, that I might sit
> in heavenly places *with* Him. Isaiah 32 brought me to the

earthly consequences of the same truth, though other passages might seem perhaps more striking to me now; but I saw an evident change of dispensation in that chapter, when the Spirit would be poured out in the Jewish nation, and a king reign in righteousness.[96]

How amazing! Some 1,750 years after Paul had elucidated the truth of the dispensations, Israel's partial blindness, and the details of the Rapture, these truths began to see the light of day once again.

Heschler came into contact with the Jewish Zionist Theodore Herzl. From that time forward, the two struggled to bring the World Zionist Organization to birth. In 1897, the First Zionist Congress met in Basel, Switzerland. Its goal was to bring a Jewish state to reality. Simultaneously, the Bible study movement and the dispensational teaching of Scripture became the foundation of the American evangelical movement.

Fifty years later, in 1947, after two world wars, Hitler, and a Holocaust, the United Nations declared Israel's right to self-determination. It also published a Partition Plan that gave Israel a right to declare statehood. The next year, national Israel became a reality: May 14, 1948. But would Israel stand against an onslaught of practically global proportions? Several wars answered this question in the affirmative...particularly the Six-Day War of June 1967, when Israel won Jerusalem and the Temple Mount.

BACK TO THE FUTURE

The preceding brief history is marked by one salient point. The followers of the first century apostles were active prophecy-watchers. Their zeal died and did not come to life again until the twentieth century, when it began again to be taught that Jesus is coming soon.

This brings us back, full circle, to the teaching of the apostle Paul, who regarded the events of the Tribulation as direct and personal. Like the Thessalonians of the first century, we see that Paul's comforting words apply directly to our lives, as we look for the Savior's coming in the clouds.

So, in a strange way, first-century Christians are our closest brethren. For centuries, their excitement about the Lord's imminent return was an artifact of the past. Now, it has returned, more vigorous than ever. Looking back, we can sympathize with the frustration they must have felt as the Roman state became more and more anti-Christian, even as they patiently waited for the Lord.

Like them, we live in a state of tension, sensing that the times tell us that He will come in the next moment, but knowing that He may not come for some time. We are tempted to set a date. Some have. Some have been condemned when their enthusiasm got out of control. We remember that cults and heresies have formed out of such false hope. Still, we watch, as Scripture says we should.

Last Days or Last Times?

Are we really living in the "last days"? Certainly, if the Holy Spirit has caused all those pastors to cry out that "Jesus is coming soon," we are. But this term cannot be used to designate a particular time. A good example of its biblical use is found in Paul's second epistle to Timothy:

> This know also, that in the last days perilous times shall come. For men shall be lovers of their own selves, covetous, boasters, proud, blasphemers, disobedient to parents, unthankful, unholy,
> Without natural affection, trucebreakers, false accusers, incontinent, fierce, despisers of those that are good, Traitors, heady, highminded, lovers of pleasures more than lovers of God; Having a form of godliness, but denying the power thereof: from such turn away. (2 Timothy 3:1–5, emphasis added)

Paul carefully instructs Timothy that days of apostasy will cloud his future, and by extension, the future of the church. In one sense, we can say that Timothy himself was involved with the type of people mentioned here. Such people characterized the fierce days of the Roman Empire.

On the other hand, Paul seems to be warning about a future societal breakdown that will mark the conditions just prior to Christ's return for believers. Are we seeing such a breakdown today? Certainly, we are. Are these the "last days"? Yes, but the last days seem to encompass the entire Church Age.

Peter used the same term in his second epistle:

This second epistle, beloved, I now write unto you; in both which I stir up your pure minds by way of remembrance: That ye may be mindful of the words which were spoken before by the holy prophets, and of the commandment of us the apostles of the Lord and Saviour:

Knowing this first, that there shall come in the **last days** scoffers, walking after their own lusts, And saying, Where is the promise of his coming? for since the fathers fell asleep, all things continue as they were from the beginning of the creation. (2 Peter 3:1–4, emphasis added)

The apostle John—bishop of the Ephesian church—presents much the same view of the prophecy, as viewed in the Spirit of the Lord:

Little children, it is the **last time**: and as ye have heard that antichrist shall come, even now are there many antichrists; whereby we know that it is the last time.
They went out from us, but they were not of us; for if they had been of us, they would no doubt have continued with us: but they went out, that they might be made manifest that they were not all of us. (1 John 2:18, 19, emphasis added)

Peter uses the same term in his first letter, obviously referring to events of the first century, in speaking of Christ, "Who verily was foreordained before the foundation of the world, but was manifest in these **last times** for you" (1 Peter 1:20, emphasis added).

Clearly, both of these references are descriptive of the first century. But the context in which they are written brings them into our era. John speaks of the Antichrist, both as a spirit and as a person.

In his second epistle, Peter uses the term "last days" in the context of Christ's coming: "Knowing this first, that there shall come **in the last days** scoffers, walking after their own lusts And saying, Where is the promise of his coming? for since the fathers fell asleep, all things continue as they were from the beginning of the creation" (2 Peter 3:3, 4, emphasis added).

Writing some time later, Jude recalls Peter's words, as he uses the term as a warning to his contemporaries when he writes, "How that they told you there should be mockers in the **last time**, who should walk after their own ungodly lusts" (Jude 18).

Here, Peter is talking about those people who would be alive at the time of Christ's coming. They are *not* the people of Peter's own era, though there were scoffers at that time. Peter could hardly have guessed at how far into the future his words would reach. These scoffers are those who will be alive at the coming of the Day of the Lord, which Peter says will come "as a thief in the night" (2 Peter 3:10).

Clearly, "last times," or "last days" are used to indicate the events of the entire Church Age.

Defining a "Set Time"

Looking at days, times, eras, and epochs, we arrive at two great truths. The first is the biblical view of date setting. Our Lord spoke with great plainness to those who were about to carry the gospel abroad to the whole earth:

When they therefore were come together, they asked of him, saying, Lord, wilt thou at this time restore again the kingdom to Israel?

And he said unto them, **It is not for you to know the times or the seasons**, which the Father hath put in his own power.

But ye shall receive power, after that the Holy Ghost is come upon you: and ye shall be witnesses unto me both in Jerusalem, and in all Judaea, and in Samaria, and unto the uttermost part of the earth.

And when he had spoken these things, while they beheld, he was taken up; and a cloud received him out of their sight. (Acts 1:6–9, emphasis added)

Christ's words absolutely exclude the setting of a prophetic date. But as we have already noted, he also urged watchfulness to those who would be alive at the time of Israel's latter-day struggle: "And when these things begin to come to pass, then look up" (Luke 21:28).

This brings us to the second great truth. Biblical timing is given to Israel, not the church. The prophets of the Old Testament link dozens of truths, forming a concise chain of events that will be played out as Israel assumes headship in the earthly kingdom.

The church is without such a prophesied chain of events. The Great Commission is never illustrated by possession of geography or government. It is a spiritual body whose head is in heaven. Certainly, Jesus instructed His followers to carry the gospel to "Jerusalem, and in all Judaea, and in Samaria, and unto the uttermost part of the earth" (Acts 1:8). This has been done many times over.

Missionaries have carried the faith to virtually every square foot of the earth. And where they have not walked, they have witnessed by book, pamphlet, satellite television, radio, tape, CD, DVD, and movie. Most pointedly, the great missionary movements have not sought to possess territory; the Great Commission is to evangelize, not politicize.

Nor is there a verse in the Bible telling us that when every last soul has heard the gospel, the age of the church will end with the Rapture.

Instead, we find that when people "say, Peace and safety; then sudden destruction cometh upon them, as travail upon a woman with with child; and they shall not escape" (1 Thessalonians 5:3). In other words, the age of the church will end with a surprise. As Christians are taken home, global institutions will fall in an unprecedented series of cataclysms.

For Israel, there are definite times and seasons. Furthermore, they are interconnected in a delicate balance of history and geopolitics, as in Psalm 102:

> Thou shalt arise, and have mercy upon Zion: for the time to favour her, yea, the **set time**, is come. For thy servants take pleasure in her stones, and favour the dust thereof. So the heathen shall fear the name of the LORD, and all the kings of the earth thy glory. When the LORD shall build up Zion, he shall appear in his glory. (Psalm 102:13–16, emphasis added)

This statement is made concerning a beleaguered Israel, surrounded by enemies and almost devoid of all recourse. If there is a hotly contested spot on earth, it is Zion, the ancient City of David, and the Temple Mount.

The conditions of this prophecy mark the Lord's return at the "set time." A time is appointed, but we have no idea what it is. We never forget that while the Lord was on earth, He told His followers that only His Father knew it. Nevertheless, for Israel, there is a set time when the Lord will come to the rescue of Zion.

In Revelation, a curious reference to time is shown in conjunction with this very event. An angel makes a declaration concerning time and Israel:

> And the angel which I saw stand upon the sea and upon the earth lifted up his hand to heaven, And sware by him that liveth for ever and ever, who created heaven, and the things that therein are, and the earth, and the things that therein are, and the sea, and the things which are therein, that there should be **time no longer:**

But in the days of the voice of the seventh angel, when he
shall begin to sound, the mystery of God should be finished, as
he hath declared to his servants the prophets.
(Revelation 10:5–7, emphasis added)

This, then, is the excitement among the faithful. The Church Age is
an open-ended opportunity to serve, to follow the leading of His Spirit
and to spread the Word of the gospel, while the opportunity exists.

AND NOW, THE FIFTH KINGDOM

To the Lord, time is a necessary structure. Upon that structure, He is
building a Kingdom. What we view as an unfolding series of events, He
views as completed architecture. We see Abraham, Isaac, Jacob, Judah,
David, and the Kingdom; He sees Himself seated upon David's throne.
We view the process; He sees the completed project.

For Gentiles, there is the prophetic procession of four kingdoms.
Babylon, Medo-Persia, Greece, and Rome march by in a grotesque procession. The memory of their passing lingers like so many ghosts and
ramshackle mansions…a trail of broken bodies and shattered spirits.

In our era, the spirit of Rome thrives today in a burgeoning global-
ism that we see in the lengthening shadows of its growing edifices. It
is the fourth kingdom, prophesied to cover the earth with an unprecedented spiritual darkness.

The day is coming when the bright light of the Lord will expose its
evils. But this has nothing to do with the church, the body of Christ. Paul
makes that more than clear: "Ye are all the children of light, and the children of the day: we are not of the night, nor of darkness. Therefore let us
not sleep, as do others; but let us watch and be sober" (1 Thessalonians
5:5, 6).

And what is it we watch for? Quite simply, we are to look for the
hopeful rise of the fifth kingdom—Israel. As we have seen, that hope
lay dormant for centuries. Then, in the nineteenth century, the dawn

broke and the Lord regathered His people. Israel has been called "God's Timepiece." Nothing could be truer.

We of the church already live in eternal realms. We are neither time-limited nor time-connected. We live with men like Enoch, Elijah, Paul, and John. He has given us eternal life, "And hath raised us up together, and made us sit together in heavenly places in Christ Jesus" (Ephesians 2:6). We serve the Lord, the Master of time and eternity.

Israel will inherit the thousand-year Kingdom that includes a geographical and political destiny. At the same time, Christians will be living in a body of light. In a very real sense, the times and seasons have nothing to do with us. Nevertheless, we watch—but not for ourselves, and not for developments within the church.

Living in that blessed hope, we are watching Israel, the prophesied object of the Lord's reconciliation.

28

THE RIVER OF TIME

Today, we are obsessed with time. The atomic clock now sets the pace of business and science. Quartz oscillators by the millions grace the watches and cell phones that now number in the billions. Those oscillators change the digits on watches and spinning hands on clocks. Many of them regularly cross-check themselves by radio with the National Institute of Standards and Technology. Its atomic clock transmits virtually perfect time through global shortwave radio and satellite networks.

But the wonder of this technology is that it comes with a curse. When you live life by the second, you become its slave rather than its master. The common complaint that there are not enough hours in the day is an increasingly distressing phenomenon. It seems that the more time we keep, the less of it we have available. There is the common perception that time is moving faster and faster.

It wasn't always so. Years ago, the cities, villages, and districts across Europe and America each kept their own local time. For the most part, morning, noon, and night were as close to timekeeping as one really needed to get. As cities grew larger, they began to keep their own astronomical time. Shipping and navigation increasingly called for a closer approximation of solar, lunar, and sidereal time.

London and Paris competed as candidates for the prime meridian. London won the contest. The Greenwich Prime Meridian and the Astronomer Royal set the pace of global shipping. The race for better timekeeping was on. By the nineteenth century, accurate clocks were keeping records as steamships plied the seven seas.

In the New World, railroads began to cross the prairie, and soon their tight schedules and the telegraph demanded higher and higher standards. Once upon a time, if your pocketwatch was within fifteen minutes of when the sun was at the zenith, that was close enough. Not anymore.

Today, we even save daylight, an idea first seriously proposed by an Englishman, William Willett, in a 1907 tract called "Waste of Daylight."[97] He wrote, "Everyone appreciates the long, light evenings. Everyone laments their shortage as Autumn approaches; and everyone has given utterance to regret that the clear, bright light of an early morning during Spring and Summer months is so seldom seen or used."

His idea, first proposed by Ben Franklin in 1784, caught on…in a big way. The industrial revolution, mass production, and the twenty-four-hour, seven-day-a-week rat race are all now history. Technology has created a continual race against time. Time, in fact, has become a despotic dictator, calling for ever-greater efficiency, representing greater productivity.

Time, the fourth dimension after length, width, and height, is fundamental to our very existence. Some have likened it to a river upon which life flows at a leisurely pace, until the channel narrows, the declining riverbed steepens, and it becomes a stretch of rapids. All this seems good, since we will reach our destination sooner. Then we hear a distant roar and see rising mist. Could that be a waterfall?

Time is no longer just a provider. Now it has become a taskmaster. A basic fact of our very existence has begun to control us to become our oppressor. This is time in the secular sense…the annual race to pay taxes on time, or to give a birthday or Christmas present on time, or to get to work on time, or to the doctor on time, or to finish that project on time.

Time and Faith

However, there is another way to look at time. The Lord, the Author of time, has promised the faithful that time is on their side. What we view as a flowing stream, He views as a complete structure…both a foundation and a finished Temple.

Time is essential to faith, which anticipates the future fulfillment of key events, which themselves are the objects of one's faith. Moment by moment, time unfolds, as it has for as long as anyone can remember. We live in time. More than that, we live by time, which is the same as saying that we live by faith.

For now, the belief that the seconds will continue to click past in steady procession is the most basic fact of our existence. We plan and devise strategies on the basis of time. In one sense, man worships time as the great rewarder of personal diligence. In another sense, he resents time, as it holds out a vast promise, which in the end dwindles to nothing.

The past departs, cemented in place as an unmovable tableau. The present moves at what we perceive as a constant rate, like the sweep-second hand on a clock or the electronic march of seconds on a digital timepiece. Every click is an act of faith, the belief that the seconds will keep on coming. After all, the assumption is that these tiny parcels of time will continue what they have been doing for thousands—some say millions or billions—of years.

This belief in a uniform state of things is the mainstay of secularism. In the world of evolutionary theory, it is called "uniformitarianism." Simply put, it is the belief of evolutionists that we live in a stable universe, or at least a stable corner of the universe. It provides the foundational continuity upon which living things can thrive without interruption. In their eyes, it is simply a stable platform upon which natural processes play out the myriad interactions we call life.

Actually, evolutionists' faith is the faith that time and space, as currently observed, will not change. They assume that there is no force or constraint outside the visible universe, and that natural progressions will persist.

It can thus be seen that time is also the seed of the secularists' faith. The millions of years ahead are their hope and promise. They cling to the expectation that mankind will develop ways to achieve immortality and utopian peace. Their "god" is the steady march of time.

Setting an Alarm

On the other hand, Christian hope is not based upon time, but upon a discontinuity in time. More precisely, it rests upon several such discontinuities, each brought about by an era in which God spoke through His prophets. Moses, Elijah, Isaiah, Ezekiel, Daniel, John, and others each brought the future into the context of their present.

After all, they, and they alone, have given us the assurance that there is something outside the restrictive envelope of time. They have assured us that there is a Creator who lives outside its constraints.

Each time they spoke, it was as though a rift in time occurred, in which future events were laid out, offering hope to the Lord's chosen. Their prophecies knit together past, present, and future into a single entity, as solid as the Rock.

Their proclamations foretold the apostasies of Israel and Judah—and their subsequent captivities. They also spoke of the coming Messiah and his millennial Kingdom.

Imagine what the world would be like if there had never been prophets. The future would be a blank slate. Hope would be confined to a series of abstractions, based upon what could be gleaned from the present and the past. Given the past five thousand years of raw experience with human governments, the future would be bleak, indeed. In such a case, hope would wax and wane on practically a daily basis. Man would live under the black cloud of "scientific" uncertainty. The imagined future would change with each new theory about the universe.

In fact, this is exactly the state of the modern philosopher, whether he be existentialist, communist, social Darwinist, or nihilist, holding that nothing is verifiable. He does not believe the prophets. Rather, he believes in science, sociology, psychology, and economics. His faith depends upon human observation.

On the other hand, our faith is based upon God's revelation. When He spoke through His prophets, He gave us a future. In a sense, it is as though He set an alarm that would go off as His day drew near.

This observation brings out a cogent truth about time and faith. Faith is necessary only in the zone of time. In eternity, all will be known as it is now known. For Christians, time has already been linked to completed faith. In eternity...in the presence of the Lord...faith will no longer be necessary. Sight and experience will be the basis of our lives. Time and faith will become curiously distant.

Faith, then, has an object—the future fulfillment of prophecy. Time is laid out in a pattern of markers, each promised as a sure hope. Consider the following Scripture, and note that it speaks of time as "a little while":

> Cast not away therefore your confidence, which hath great recompence of reward. For ye have need of patience, that, after ye have done the will of God, ye might receive the promise.
>
> For yet **a little while**, and he that shall come will come, and will not tarry. Now the just shall live by faith: but if any man draw back, my soul shall have no pleasure in him. But we are not of them who draw back unto perdition; but of them that believe to the saving of the soul. (Hebrews 10:35–39, emphasis added)

These words were written about nineteen hundred years ago. Generations of the faithful have come and gone, each believing in the promise of God, that He would send His Son to judge the world and set things straight at last. From the biblical perspective, this will take only "a little while."

These are words of reassurance, given in the tones of God's love for His children. As you might tell a child during a stormy night, "Be patient, in a little while, the storm will pass, the clouds will clear and the sun will rise."

Time, then, is best measured by perspective. To the child, overnight is forever; to the parent, it is but a short time.

The key element in the passage above comes from the prophet Habakkuk, who mentally wrestles with the deep questions concerning God's will for Judah in the days just before the Babylonian invasion. First, the prophet asks how the Lord can continue to tolerate the wicked ways of Judah. God answers that he is raising up the Babylonians to judge them.

This leads Habakkuk to ask another question: How can the Lord judge Judah by using an even more wicked nation, whose sins are legendary? The Lord's answer to this knotty question begins as follows:

> And the LORD answered me, and said, Write the vision, and
> make it plain upon tables, that he may run that readeth it.
> For the vision is yet for an appointed time, but at the end
> it shall speak, and not lie: though it tarry, wait for it; because it
> will surely come, it will not tarry.
> Behold, his soul which is lifted up is not upright in him:
> but the just shall live by his faith. (Habakkuk 2:2–4)

As the writer to the Hebrews draws upon Habakkuk's prophecy, he makes at least two significant alterations. First, he changes "for an appointed time" to "for yet a little while." In so doing, he indicates that the time to fulfillment is much closer than when first prophesied.

Second, Hebrews changes "it will surely come" to "he that shall come will come." The "it" of Habakkuk's day has become the "He" of the New Testament era. He is the risen Christ.

Of course, the key phrase in both quotes refers to the "just" living by "faith," which is set in the context of the patient wait for that which will surely come. Time and faith are wedded in the concept of patience.

In his epistle to the Romans, Paul quoted Habakkuk in a similar context, namely, the Lord's coming judgment:

> For I am not ashamed of the gospel of Christ: for it is the
> power of God unto salvation to every one that believeth; to the

Jew first, and also to the Greek. For therein is the righteousness
of God revealed from faith to faith: as it is written, The just
shall live by faith. For the wrath of God is revealed from heaven
against all ungodliness and unrighteousness of men, who hold
the truth in unrighteousness. (Romans 1:16–18)

In time, things will be completed according to His long and complex
plan. The righteousness of God is yet to be revealed, and time is the
agency of its revelation. Again, we see that living in faith is of necessity,
living in time.

Here, God's judgment is seen as having been revealed from heaven,
against mankind, which is presented as suppressing the truth. For secular
man, time itself is the thing worshiped. Given enough of it, he says, any
variation is possible. Things can spontaneously combine in life-giving
ways. Over time, chemical and nuclear reactions can become godlike in
their manifestations.

For Christians, time is the motion toward His coming.

THINGS HOPED FOR

Directly following the Hebrews passage quoted above, we find the
summation of the matter. It is the eleventh chapter of the epistle.
This, the so-called "faith chapter," defines faith as time, for time necessarily means *delay*. By definition, those things promised have not yet
been realized. They are made evident by the substance (solidity) of
faith and its conviction that the timeline will take us to the prophesied
end:

Now faith is the substance of **things hoped for**, the evidence
of things not seen. For by it the elders obtained a good report.
Through faith we understand that the worlds were framed by
the word of God, so that things which are seen were not made
of things which do appear. (Hebrews 11:1–3, emphasis added)

Faith plus time equals hope, as substantial as though it has already been realized. Faith is here understood as temporary; that when one arrives at the anticipated time, faith will no longer be necessary. The key to hope is the recognition that from the Lord's point of view, faith is *now* complete.

Notice that the writer to the Hebrews illustrates faith by emphasizing that this universe was made by a Creator, who brought its material elements together out of nothing. As we have already seen, this universe is built around the concept of time—which, to the Lord, is simply another building block.

He uses time as we would use concrete. This is our faith. The secular mind worships time; we worship its creator. Since He constructed time, He speaks of it in a way that is often puzzling to those who live in it.

"I COME QUICKLY"

Many have pondered the Lord's three-word promise in the book of Revelation. Skeptics have mocked these words, saying that they were the result of the apostle John's wishful thinking. Nineteen hundred years later, they say, these words remain a hollow and empty promise. After all this time, He still hasn't come. They usually add that if the Lord spoke them at all, He was being quite deceitful.

The faithful, however, believe that not only did the Lord speak these words, but He meant exactly what He said. They are first voiced to His beloved Philadelphian church, as He promises that it will never experience the dramatic cataclysms of His judgment in the Day of the Lord: "Because thou hast kept the word of my patience, I also will keep thee from the hour of temptation, which shall come upon all the world, to try them that dwell upon the earth. Behold, I come quickly: hold that fast which thou hast, that no man take thy crown" (Revelation 3:10, 11).

As John penned these words in AD 96, he must have thought of the church in Asia toward which they were directed. He could not have known their full prophetic significance. From the perspective of time,

Christians now see this church as the model of evangelism and Bible study. In the seventeenth through the twentieth centuries, Philadelphia became the model of the open door, as missionaries traveled the earth and Bible teachers expounded the hidden truths of prophetic Scripture.

This church represents the love of God and the gifts of the Spirit. It is the recipient of a solid promise that it will be kept not "through," but "from," the "hour of temptation."

This great blessing is the Rapture of the church, which at a certain point will be removed from this earth so quickly that we cannot imagine it. John did not know when it would come, but he knew that it would be a sudden event. As the Lord said, it would happen "quickly."

This perspective is given great emphasis in Paul's first epistle to the Thessalonians:

> But of the times and the seasons, brethren, ye have no need that
> I write unto you. For yourselves know perfectly that the day
> of the Lord so cometh as a thief in the night. For when they
> shall say, Peace and safety; then **sudden** destruction cometh
> upon them, as travail upon a woman with child; and they shall
> not escape. But ye, brethren, are not in darkness, that that
> day should overtake you as a thief" (1 Thessalonians 5:1–4,
> emphasis added)

These words catch the quickness of the blessed event that is the hope of every Christian. The word "sudden" is from the Greek *aiphnidios,* meaning "suddenly and without warning." This latter aspect of its meaning is seen in Luke's gospel, in which the same Greek word is translated "unawares": "And take heed to yourselves, lest at any time your hearts be overcharged with surfeiting, and drunkenness, and cares of this life, and so that day come upon you unawares" (Luke 21:34).

When the Lord says, "Behold, I come quickly," He means it, but not in the worldly sense. Again, we see that time as we know it is relative to His plan. Skeptics may complain that Jesus misled His followers with an unfulfilled promise. But the faithful view the interim of time as necessary to His plan, which is doubtless far more complex than we can fully realize.

Also, we see that the future of this world is directly aimed at the Lord's Day. As if to emphasize this idea, the final chapter of Revelation repeats it three more times. The first time, as might be expected, reaffirms the importance of keeping the faith: "And he said unto me, These sayings are faithful and true: and the Lord God of the holy prophets sent his angel to shew unto his servants the things which must shortly be done. Behold, I come quickly: blessed is he that keepeth the sayings of the prophecy of this book" (Revelation 22:6, 7).

Faith, expressed as time, sees the Lord's work from His perspective. In a worldly sense, "shortly" means "in a brief time." In the heavenly sense, it means, "brought to completion when all the conditions have been fulfilled." John was privileged to see things from this heavenly perspective. He personally witnessed the completion of events that we still refer to as "future."

> And he saith unto me, Seal not the sayings of the prophecy of this book: for the time is at hand. He that is unjust, let him be unjust still: and he which is filthy, let him be filthy still: and he that is righteous, let him be righteous still: and he that is holy, let him be holy still. And, behold, I come quickly; and my reward is with me, to give every man according as his work shall be. (Revelation 22:10–12)

Notice here that time—addressed as "at hand"—is depicted as being laid out in advance. In the most literal Greek, Jesus says, "The time is near." In other words, the judgments of Revelation are imminent. Again, His perspective dictates the meaning of the phrase.

In the final use of the three-word phrase, the Lord then concludes with His personal assurance that the events of Revelation will come at a precise moment in time, and they will come with such speed that those alive at that time will be amazed.

"He which testifieth these things saith, Surely I come quickly. Amen. Even so, come, Lord Jesus" (Revelation 22:20).

Paul, Ahead of His Time

When Paul writes of his own apostleship, he is always amazed at the extent of the Lord's grace toward him. And rightly so, since he was devoutly opposed to the early church, persecuting it on behalf of his brethren, the Pharisees.

Toward the close of 1 Corinthians, he speaks of Christ's Resurrection and the order of events that followed it. Here, we have an important timeline with a twist. Since the Resurrection is the key element of all apostolic teaching, the element of timing is central to his statement. But Paul sees his own salvation as a curious deviation from the perceived timeline:

> For I delivered unto you first of all that which I also received,
> how that Christ died for our sins according to the scriptures;
> And that he was buried, and that he rose again the third day
> according to the scriptures: And that he was seen of Cephas,
> then of the twelve: After that, he was seen of above five
> hundred brethren at once; of whom the greater part remain
> unto this present, but some are fallen asleep.
>
> After that, he was seen of James; then of all the apostles.
> And last of all he was seen of me also, as of **one born out of due
> time.**
>
> For I am the least of the apostles, that am not meet to be
> called an apostle, because I persecuted the church of God.
> But by the grace of God I am what I am: and his grace which
> was bestowed upon me was not in vain; but I laboured more
> abundantly than they all: yet not I, but the grace of God which
> was with me. (1 Corinthians 15:3–10, emphasis added)

Here, Paul carefully recounts the order of those who met Christ after His Resurrection. When he comes to his own encounter, he refers to himself as "one born out of due time." In the literal Greek, he says, "Even as if to an untimely birth." What could he mean by this?

As one whose epistles repeatedly prophesy the events of the last days, Paul must have had an acute sense of the order of things. For him, time was not a monotonous flow of one day after the next, but an exquisite movement toward a momentous series of events.

His life was totally centered on Judaism and the Messianic hope of his people. Of the tribe of Benjamin and raised with the finest Hebrew education, his hope had always been inseparable from that of the twelve tribes. He was privileged to be a leader of his people, and later came to lament their blindness to the true identity of Jesus:

> For I could wish that myself were accursed from Christ for
> my brethren, my kinsmen according to the flesh: Who are
> Israelites; to whom pertaineth the adoption, and the glory,
> and the covenants, and the giving of the law, and the service of
> God, and the promises. (Romans 9:3, 4)

Here, in a burst of emotion, he wishes (knowing that it can't be so) that his new birth might be invalidated, if that would result in the salvation of Israel. He realizes that he has personally experienced the Messianic blessing that his people had always expected would come to the entire nation. For Paul, that was the "due time." In one sense, he was saddened to see himself raised up before the promised redemption of his Hebrew brethren at the inception of the Kingdom.

And *that* is the biblical view of time. It is more a matter of quality than quantity. For Paul, as for all the prophets and apostles, time is specifically linked to God's redemptive plan. It is never arbitrary.

"FULNESS"

The quality of time is known only to the heavenly Father. As Jesus said, "But of that day and hour knoweth no man, no, not the angels of heaven, but my Father only" (Matthew 24:36). Here, of course, Jesus refers to His Second Coming.

Its timing is apparently based upon the conjunction of time and conditions. The latter are referred to in Scripture as "fulness," as when Paul explained why his kinsmen had become spiritually blind:

> For I would not, brethren, that ye should be ignorant of this
> mystery, lest ye should be wise in your own conceits; that
> blindness in part is happened to Israel, until the **fulness** of the
> Gentiles be come in.
>
> And so all Israel shall be saved: as it is written, There
> shall come out of Sion the Deliverer, and shall turn away
> ungodliness from Jacob. (Romans 11:25, 26, emphasis added).

By the grace of the Lord, Paul had been saved far in advance of the promised salvation of "all Israel." This, of course, assumes all the elect of Israel, as Paul had previously stated: "Even so then at this present time also there is a remnant according to the election of grace" (Romans 11:5).

Time, then, includes the remnant of Israel as well as the remnant of the Gentiles. Time is not the enemy of the faithful; it is the friend, allowing those whom the Lord has chosen in ages past to come to their full potential. As He uses it, time is a quality, not a quantity. It is the essence of fulfillment:

> And when ye shall see Jerusalem compassed with armies, then
> know that the desolation thereof is nigh. Then let them which
> are in Judaea flee to the mountains; and let them which are
> in the midst of it depart out; and let not them that are in the
> countries enter thereinto.
>
> For these be the days of vengeance, that all things which
> are written may be fulfilled. But woe unto them that are with
> child, and to them that give suck, in those days! for there shall
> be great distress in the land, and wrath upon this people.
> And they shall fall by the edge of the sword, and shall be led
> away captive into all nations: and Jerusalem shall be trodden

down of the Gentiles, until the times of the Gentiles be
fulfilled.

And there shall be signs in the sun, and in the moon,
and in the stars; and upon the earth distress of nations, with
perplexity; the sea and the waves roaring. (Luke 21:20–25,
emphasis added)

Time, as the world sees it, is a race to produce something…anything.
It demands more product, more advertising, and more cash flow. Desire
becomes necessity, and necessity is touted as the highest attainment.
Time, as the Bible sees it, is simply an element in God's program.

"My Clock, Not Yours"

At the moment, it is quite clear that we are rocketing toward judgment.
A great war in the Middle East will soon change the standing rules
of international diplomacy. These days, everybody is talking about it.
Historians, novelists, and preachers are all casting a wary eye at Russia's
leader, who might just be the prophesied "Gog, the land of Magog, the
chief prince of Meshech and Tubal" (Ezekiel 38:2).

Many are familiar with this prophecy about how the Lord will bridle
Gog's jaws and lead him like a beast, dragging him into the vortex of
Middle Eastern conflict. From the perspective of time, the Lord's view of
this matter is quite interesting. According to Ezekiel's prophecy, as these
things begin to happen, a time marker will be triggered:

Thus saith the Lord GOD; It shall also come to pass, that **at
the same time** shall things come into thy mind, and thou shalt
think an evil thought:

And thou shalt say, I will go up to the land of unwalled
villages; I will go to them that are at rest, that dwell safely, all of
them dwelling without walls, and having neither bars nor gates.
(Ezekiel 38:10, 11, emphasis added)

Here, as the Lord draws Gog into the fray, an evil plan will come into his mind, apparently at the very beginning of the invasion. It appears that this is Gog's own idea, concocted on the fly as tensions mount in the theater of war.

But the matter of timing doesn't stop here; a few verses later, the Lord places another time marker that ties this signal event to Judgment Day:

> And it shall come to pass **at the same time** when Gog shall
> come against the land of Israel, saith the Lord God, that my
> fury shall come up in my face.
>
> For in my jealousy and in the fire of my wrath have I
> spoken, Surely in that day there shall be a great shaking in the
> land of Israel. (Ezekiel 38:18–19, emphasis added)

The movement of troops into the great latter-day battle is marked in time. For believers, this is a certainty. The days between now and then are few, and they are numbered. But that's not all. It is well known that the forces allied with Gog are dramatically defeated in such a way that the nations will know that Israel's victory is the Lord's doing.

And only a few short verses later, the Lord makes another mark in time: "Behold, it is come, and it is done, saith the Lord GOD; this is the day whereof I have spoken" (Ezekiel 39:8).

The Day of the Lord, so often mentioned by the prophets, is closely attached to the ticking clock—the time bomb—of the Middle East. "At the same time" that Israel is invaded and Gog's armies are defeated, the seven-year Tribulation will begin.

GOD'S TIMEPIECE

Israel is rightly called "God's timepiece." In Ezekiel's vision, it may be seen that tiny Israel is the focus of the greatest war in history. Its campaigns will begin with Gog and end with Armageddon. When Gog comes, it will be as though an invisible thumb pressed the button on an equally invisible stopwatch.

We have already seen the beginning. Israel has been born, not "out of due season" like Paul, but at the perfect time, and on a single day—May 14, 1948:

Who hath heard such a thing? who hath seen such things? Shall the earth be made to bring forth in one day? or shall a nation be born at once? for as soon as Zion travailed, she brought forth her children.

Shall I bring to the birth, and not cause to bring forth? saith the LORD: shall I cause to bring forth, and shut the womb? saith thy God. Rejoice ye with Jerusalem, and be glad with her, all ye that love her: rejoice for joy with her, all ye that mourn for her: That ye may suck, and be satisfied with the breasts of her consolations; that ye may milk out, and be delighted with the abundance of her glory.

For thus saith the LORD, Behold, I will extend peace to her like a river, and the glory of the Gentiles like a flowing stream: then shall ye suck, ye shall be borne upon her sides, and be dandled upon her knees. As one whom his mother comforteth, so will I comfort you; and ye shall be comforted in Jerusalem.

And when ye see this, your heart shall rejoice, and your bones shall flourish like an herb: and the hand of the LORD shall be known toward his servants, and his indignation toward his enemies.

For, behold, the LORD will come with fire, and with his chariots like a whirlwind, to render his anger with fury, and his rebuke with flames of fire.

For by fire and by his sword will the LORD plead with all flesh: and the slain of the LORD shall be many. (Isaiah 66:8–16)

The river of time has brought us close to "that day." The birth of Israel in a single day was marked and destined for a precise moment.

GARY STEARMAN

Today, Jerusalem is the focus of conflict. Isaiah sees it as the site of comfort. Israel, born in conflict, shall be the object of rejoicing.

Time as a river is not a mere metaphor. Time and faith flow forth from the Lord, bringing life and peace. Time brings the water of life to the faithful, but judgment to the lost. It should never be forgotten that in His Second Coming, He is accompanied by fire and the warrior host of heaven.

Though there is a great deal that we do not understand about time, we do know that it flows according to God's purpose. In the final chapter of the Bible, we are given the beautiful image of a river, flowing through our eternal residence, the New Jerusalem. It cannot be coincidental that is it shown in close connection with time and the seasons:

> And he shewed me a pure river of water of life, clear as crystal, proceeding out of the throne of God and of the Lamb.
>
> In the midst of the street of it, and on either side of the river, was there the tree of life, which bare twelve manner of fruits, and yielded her fruit every month: and the leaves of the tree were for the healing of the nations.
>
> And there shall be no more curse: but the throne of God and of the Lamb shall be in it; and his servants shall serve him. (Revelation 22:1–3)

Even there, time flows like a river. What wonders await us in its fullness!

About the Author

FLYING HOME

You could say that I was born to fly. I come from a flying family. During World War II, my relatives designed and produced the famous Stearman "Kaydet" Model 75, designated by the military as the PT-17. This biplane was used to train most of the beginning aviators who went to war. Almost eighty-five hundred of these wonderful planes were built. To this day, the Stearman is known as the biplane "built like a truck" that "flies like an angel." Nearly three thousand of them are still flying today.

My central observations about life were shaped in the drafting rooms, tool shops, manufacturing plants, and airports of my youth. I grew up in the exciting atmosphere of aircraft design and flying adventure. From then until now, I have taken to the air with joyous anticipation.

My father and uncle also designed and built private aircraft, which meant that as a child, I spent a lot of time at the local airport. Once, on a hot day, I watched as a plane landed and taxied to a stop nearby. The pilot walked away. Fascinated, I walked over to examine the beautiful machine. Running my hand over the rudder, I noticed that it was cool to the touch! It was nearly a hundred degrees on the ramp, but up there where that plane had been flying was a totally different world, somehow cooler than mine.

In my mind, I had touched another dimension. My excitement was sparked, as it is to this day when I think of another world "up there"— where one day, with the Lord's guidance, I'll experience that perfect, eternal climate that now, I can only dimly sense.

In a way, this book is simply an extension of my long-held interest in flying. A moment's thought reveals that flight through the air in three dimensions falls short of flight through time in four dimensions. But our ultimate flight as Christians rising to meet the Lord in the air will take us on that hoped-for journey into the fourth dimension.

During my college years, a change began to come into my life. I was studying at one of the best aeronautics schools in the country and working in aviation, but I began to find the pursuit of the family dream strangely unsatisfying. I discovered a love of languages and literature that soon eclipsed the math and science of the designer. I was introduced to philology and descriptive linguistics. Literary history and secular philosophy brought an exciting new consciousness of mankind's troubled march through the halls of heritage.

But the call of aviation was still strong. I felt that I could merge an engineering background with a writer's skills. I became employed as a writer in commercial publications at Beech Aircraft Corp. There, I developed the owners' manuals for several executive aircraft. Then later, at the Cessna Marketing Division, I held the dream job that combined flying with creative merchandising.

In an era when Cessna, alone, produced over twenty-five hundred aircraft each year, the pulse of aviation was robust and exhilarating. Being on the cutting edge of commercial aircraft production should have produced a satisfaction and contentment that brought peace.

But it didn't. I had been raised with only a smattering of formal "religion," but I never doubted the existence of God. I knew that somewhere in the vast reaches of the universe, He lived in supreme glory. Never in my wildest dreams, however, did I suspect that He could be reached, or that He could touch my life with His love.

Later, I had a wife, two small boys, and no real answers. Still, I searched. Then, while trout fishing on a family vacation in Colorado, I heard a well-known radio pastor on the car radio. It was J. Vernon McGee, explaining how Christ is depicted throughout the book of Leviticus.

Not only was I fascinated by his analytical method, I was spellbound by a sudden realization. Christ, the Messiah, had come at a certain time in history, in fulfillment of specific types, symbols, prophecies, and metaphors written by Moses a millennium and a half earlier! Driven by the desire to understand Scripture, I studied for days, and eagerly continued to listen to Dr. McGee. A short time later, I knelt alone in my study and prayed to receive Christ. By His Spirit, He graciously came to me, at last revealing the God whom I had always known was there, but never thought could care about me.

From that day to this (for the last forty years), I have studied the Word, filling my life with His wisdom and the shelves of my study with reference books. I delightfully discovered that the college time spent delving into languages and literature now gave me the tools I needed to discern the deeper meanings of Scripture.

I helped organize home Bible study groups that finally coalesced into a congregation. Since 1983, I have pastored the Bible Church known as Grace Fellowship in Oklahoma City. Like that first congregation so long ago, we expound upon the Apostles' doctrine, fellowship, communion, and prayer. Our goal: Maturing the saints.

Beginning in 1987, I worked with the late J. R. Church at the video and print ministry known as Prophecy in the News. We produce a monthly magazine, as well as weekly television broadcasts and daily webcasts, devoted to the exposition of Bible prophecy, applicable to these contemporary times, which we believe to be the latter days. In fact, we believe that the stage is set for the prophesied period known as the Great Tribulation. We teach the doctrine of the "blessed hope," commonly called the Rapture of the church, which we believe will take

Christians home to heaven before that horrific period of the Lord's coming judgment.

Early on, I was obsessed with the joys of physical flight. I love it to this day. But beside the spiritual flight that comes from pursuing the Word of God, it is nothing. Once, I thought I could find joy among the clouds of the earthly skies. Now, I look forward to that final flight among the clouds of heaven. Following His lead and His timing, I'm flying home.

NOTES

1 Stanislaw Lem, *The Star Diaries* (New York: Avon, 1976).

2 Stephen Hawking, *A Brief History of Time* (New York: Bantam, 1996).

3 Ibid.

4 Michio Kaku, *Hyperspace* (New York: Doubleday, 1994).

5 Flavius Josephus, *Antiquities: Josephus Complete Works,* trans. William Whiston (Grand Rapids, MI: Kregel, 1981).

6 Ibid.

7 Ibid.

8 Ibid.

9 R. H. Charles, trans., *The Book of Enoch (1 Enoch)* (London: Hollen Street Press, 1917).

10 John M. Cooper, ed., *Plato Complete Works* (Indianapolis, IN: Hackett, 1997), 1292 ff.

11 Ibid.

12 Ibid.

13 Josephus.

14 Gary Stearman, "Abraham Battles the Kings of Babylon, Medo-Persia, Greece and Rome," *Prophecy in the News,* June 1997.

15 Ibid.

16 Rabbi Meir Zlotowitz, *The Artscroll Tanach Series, Genesis (Bereishis),* Vol. 1(a) (Brooklyn, NY: Mesorah, 1988).

17 Cooper, 1224ff.

18 *Commentary of Hierocles on the Golden Verses of Pythagoras,* trans. from French by Andre Dacier (London: Kessinger, 2005).

19 Jacques Vallee, *Passport to Magonia* (Chicago, IL: Henry Regnery, 1969).

20 Ibid.

21 Robert Kirk, *The Secret Commonwealth of Elves, Fauns & Fairies* (New York: New York Review of Books, 2007). Note: This was written in 1691 but was not printed until the early nineteenth century.

22 Barney and Betty Hill and John G. Fuller, *The Interrupted Journey* (New York: Dial, 1965).

23 John E. Mack, *Abduction* (New York: Charles Scribner's Sons, Macmillan, 1994).

24 Brian Stross, "The ?IHK'ALS," *Flying Saucer Review,* May/June 1968, 12.

25 Gordon Creighton, "Middle American Creature Reports," *Flying Saucer Review,* May/June 1968, 12–15.

26 Edward Gibbon, *The Decline and Fall of the Roman Empire* (New York: Wise, 1943) 118.

27 Vendyl Jones, *Will the Real Jesus Please Stand?* (Arlington, TX: Priority Publications, 1983), 1-5.

28 Michio Kaku, *Beyond Einstein* (New York: Random House, 1995).

29 Louis Pauwels and Jacques Bergier, *The Morning of the Magicians* (New York: Stein & Day/Scarborough House, 1963), 185.

30 Ibid.

31 John C. Symmes, *To All the World* (St. Louis: April 10, 1818).

32 Michael Munk, *The Wisdom in the Hebrew Alphabet* (Brooklyn, NY: Mesorah, 1983).

33 Ibid.

34 Hyman E. Goldin, trans. and annot., *Pirke Abot Ethics of the Fathers* (from the Babylonian Talmud).

35 Munk.

36 C. I. Scofield, ed., *The First Scofield Reference Bible* (New York: Oxford, 1909).

37 Isaac E. Mozeson, *The Word* (Northvale, NJ: Jason Aronson, 1995).

38 Stewart Dingwall Fordyce Salmond, *The Christian Doctrine of Immortality* (Edinburgh: T&T Clark, 1901).

39 Raymond Bernard, *The Hollow Earth* (New York: Fieldcrest, 1964).

40 Ibid.

41 Ibid.

42 Bernard.

43 C. S. Lewis, *The Lion, the Witch and the Wardrobe* (New York: Macmillan, 1950).

44 C. I. Scofield, *The Scofield Study Bible* (New York: Oxford, 1945).

45 E. W. Bullinger, *Number in Scripture* (Grand Rapids, MI: Kregel, 1967).

46 Ibid.

47 J. R. Church and Gary Stearman, *The Mystery of the Menorah and the Hebrew Alphabet* (Oklahoma City, OK: Prophecy Publications, 1993).

48 Josephus.

49 C. F. Keil and F. Delitzsch, *Commentary on the Old Testament,* VII (Peabody, MA: Hendrickson, 1989), 18.

50 John E. Mack, *Abduction* (New York, Charles Scribner's Sons, Macmillan, 1994).

51 Petr Beckmann, *A History of* π *(pi)* (New York: St. Martin's).

52 Munk.

53 Ibid.

54 Ibid.

55 Philip Babcock Gove, ed., *Webster's New Third International Dictionary* (Springfield, MA: Merriam, 1971).

56 Kaku, *Hyperspace.*

57 Ibid.

58 W. E. Vine, *An Expository Dictionary of New Testament Words* (Old Tappan, NJ: Fleming H. Revell, 1940).

59 Munk.

60 Ibid.

61 Ibid, 18.

62 Kaku, *Hyperspace.*

63 Ibid.

64 Vine, 208, 209.

65 C. S. Lewis, *The Screwtape Letters* (New York: Macmillan, 1961).

66 Keil and Delitzsch.

67 Ibid.

68 Eusebius, *Church History: The Nicene and Post-Nicene Fathers of the Christian Church,* ed. Philip Schaff (Albany, OR: AGES Software, 1997).

69 Max S. Weremchuk, *John Nelson Darby* (Neptune, NJ: Loizeaux Brothers, 1992), 120.

70 Ibid., 121.

71 E. W. Bullinger, *The Foundations of Dispensational Truth* (London: Hollen Street Press, 1972).

72 C. I. Scofield, *The Scofield Reference Bible* (New York: Oxford, 1909).

73 Ibid.

74 Paul Davies, *How to Build a Time Machine* (New York: Penguin, 2001).

75 J. Richard Gott, *Time Travel in Einstein's Universe* (Boston: Houghton Mifflin, 2001).

76 Ibid.

77 Gerald L. Schroeder, *The Science of God* (New York: Broadway, Bantam, Doubleday Dell, 1997).

78 Ibid.

79 Ibid.

80 Ibid., emphasis original.

81 Ibid.

82 Immanuel Velikovsky, *Worlds in Collision* (Garden City, NY: Doubleday, 1950).

83 Unknown author, *Book of Jasher* (New York: M. M. Noah & A. S. Gould, 1840). The unidentified translator, in his "Translator's Preface," says Jasher is not a proper name in the Hebrew, and that

the correct title is "The Upright or Correct Record."

84 Velikovsky.

85 Donald Wesley Patten, *Catastrophism and the Old Testament* (Seattle, WA: Pacific Meridian, 1988).

86 Josephus, V, I, 17.

87 Ibid.

88 Munk.

89 Moses de Lion, *The Zohar an English Translation,* trans. Harry Sperling and Maurice Simon (Brooklyn, NY: Soncino Press, 1984).

90 Kaku, *Beyond Einstein.*

91 Cleve Backster, *Primary Perception: Biocommunication with Plants, Living Foods, and Human Cells* (White Rose Millennium Press, 2003).

92 U.S. Commerce Department's National Institute of Standards and Technology, "NIST Physicists Coax Six Atoms into Quantum "Cat" State," *NIST Physical Measurement Laboratory,* November 30, 2005, www.nist.gov/pml/div688/cat_states.cfm.

93 Ibid.

94 Ibid.

95 William Shakespeare, *As You Like It* (New York: Washington Square, 1997) Act 2, Scene 7.

96 Max S. Weremchuk, Darby letter 1830, *John Nelson Darby* (Neptune, NJ: Loizeaux Brothers), 120.

97 William Willett, *The Waste of Daylight* (UK, 1907, copyright 1914).